The Specter of Sex

The Specter of Sex

*Gendered Foundations of
Racial Formation in the United States*

SALLY L. KITCH

Published by State University of New York Press, Albany
© 2009 State University of New York

All rights reserved

Printed in the United States of America

No part of this book may be used or reproduced in any manner whatsoever without written permission. No part of this book may be stored in a retrieval system or transmitted in any form or by any means including electronic, electrostatic, magnetic tape, mechanical, photocopying, recording, or otherwise without the prior permission in writing of the publisher.

For information, contact State University of New York Press, Albany, NY
www.sunypress.edu

Production by Ryan Morris
Marketing by Anne M. Valentine

Library of Congress Cataloging-in-Publication Data

Kitch, Sally.
  The specter of sex : gendered foundations of racial formation in the United States / Sally L. Kitch.
      p. cm.
  Includes bibliographical references and index.
  ISBN 978-1-4384-2753-9 (hardcover : alk. paper)
  ISBN 978-1-4384-2754-6 (pbk. : alk. paper)
   1. Sex role—United States—History. 2. Gender identity—United States—History. 3. Blacks—Race identity. 4. Whites—Race identity. I. Title.

HQ1075.5.U6K58 2009
305.800973—dc22
                                                                            2008050663

10 9 8 7 6 5 4 3 2 1

For Tom

Contents

Acknowledgments ix
Introduction: The "Purloined Letter" of Gendered Race 1

PART I: Roots

Introduction: As the Twig is Bent 15

1. "Women are a Huge Natural Calamity": The Roots of Western Gender Ideology 17

2. The First Races in Society: Gendered Roots of Racial Formation 27

3. Gendered Racial Institutions: World Slavery and Nationhood 47

Conclusion: From Gender to Race 57

PART II: Bodies

Introduction: Whose Too, Too Solid Flesh? 61

4. The American "Body Shop": Gendered Racial Formation in the Colonies and New Republic 65

5. Enslaved Bodies and Gendered Race 77

6. Sexual Projection and Race: Science, Politics, and Lust 89

Conclusion: Embodying Race 105

PART III: Blood

Introduction: "Off Women Com Owre Manhed" — 109

7. Defining, Measuring, and Ranking Racial Blood: The Ungendered Surface — 113

8. Hardly Gender Neutral — 123

9. Gendered Anti-Miscegenation: Laws and Their Interpretation — 137

10. Preserving White Racial Blood: Rape Accusations and Motherhood — 147

Conclusion: Miscegenation as Racial Reconciliation? — 155

PART IV: Citizenship

Introduction: "My Folks Fought for This Country" — 159

11. What is Citizenship?: Gender and Race — 165

12. Engendering Citizenship: Dependency and Sex — 171

13. "No Can Do" Men and Their Others: Dependency and Inappropriate Gender — 181

14. Mixed Race, Suspect Gender: Both White and... Whatever — 201

Conclusion: Homosexual Citizenship — 219

PART V: Implications

Introduction: Patterns for a New Bridge — 225

15. Implications for Feminist Theories of Racial Difference and Antisubordination Politics — 233

16. Gender Implications for Theories of Racial Formation — 243

Conclusion: Interdependence — 251

Notes — 255

Index — 299

Acknowledgments

Any book that has taken eight years to research and write owes debts to many people. *The Specter of Sex* is no exception. Two categories of supporters need special mention. One is the group of research assistants from both Ohio State University and Arizona State University who have supplied me with prodigious amounts of research materials on everything from Latino legal history, to images of Chinese immigrants in the nineteenth century, to the journals and diaries of Europeans who explored (and exploited) Africa and the Americas during the Renaissance. I am grateful to the Department of Women's Studies at Ohio State for providing a slew of talented research assistants from the master's and PhD programs over many years, including Lu Zhang, Dong Li, Melanie Maltry, Rhonda Robb, and Kathryn Linder. I also thank those graduate students for being so bright, diligent, and supportive of this book project. Most recently, I am grateful to the College of Liberal Arts and Sciences and to Dean Deborah Losse at Arizona State for funding my research assistants, John-Michael Warner and Elena Frank, and for granting me a research leave at the beginning of my new job as founding director of the Institute for Humanities Research so that I could finish the book. Thanks also go to Carol Withers, assistant director of the Institute, who contributed greatly by making sure along the way that the manuscript was copied and delivered to the publisher to meet its various deadlines.

The second category of supporters consists of those who read and re-read chapters and proposals. I am particularly grateful to Paulette Pierce, Valerie Lee, and Mary Margaret Fonow, and to Tom Kitch for reading and commenting on the manuscript so often that he can now quote passages from memory. That is true devotion.

In addition, I want to acknowledge that this book is part of a larger conversation about the importance of racial differences to the very concept of gender that has taken place in different ways within the field of women and gender studies and in American society at large. I want to thank the many scholars, colleagues, and students throughout the years who have engaged me in that conversation and both contributed to and challenged my understanding of its central issues. This book represents my best effort to pay the intellectual debt that I owe to so many by delving deeply into the backstory of intersectionality and identifying the historical development of gender and racial interconnection in this diverse and contentious society.

Finally, I want to thank my editor, Larin McLaughlin, for her faith in the project.

Introduction

The "Purloined Letter" of Gendered Race

"Chinese men are effeminate." "Black men are studs." "White women are the fair sex." "Latinas are hot." Such stereotypes are commonplace in public discourse about race in contemporary American culture; so commonplace, in fact, that we may no longer hear what they say. Many people within earshot of such statements would see them as drawing distinctions among particular men and women on the basis of race: *that* "hot girl" must be Latina; *that* diminutive, un-muscular man must be Asian. But they can also be seen as constructing racial identities on the basis of gender: Asians are weak (like women); sexual excess is "natural" to Latinos and African Americans; female beauty is a white characteristic. *The Specter of Sex* analyzes the latter aspect of racial discourse as a *consistent historical analytic*; that is, in terms of the persistent use of gendered norms and judgments about appropriate or inappropriate gender standards to describe, classify, and stratify racial groups. By developing this historical analytic, the book exposes gendered patterns that repeated themselves as various groups were racialized in the U.S. over time.

The Specter of Sex has been inspired by decades of theorizing and debate among scholars, theorists, and students in the field of women and gender studies about what, exactly, constitutes the relationship between race and gender. This question is especially important for establishing a fair, accurate, and sensitive foundation for thinking about "women" as a collective while accounting for their vast differences. This book honors the diversity of opinion and continuous struggle entailed in that quest, but it also recognizes key areas of agreement, even among theorists and activists who may disagree about details.

Many theorists agree, for example, that both race and gender are socially, culturally, and discursively constructed in particular historical moments, though they may seem like self-evident and static categories.[1] As products of social processes, both categories are more rooted in ideas or ideologies than in biology, and are more analytic than "natural" categories, unless "Nature" itself is understood as "the object and product of human action."[2] At the same time, the two terms are not exact equivalents. *Gender* has been parsed into multiple components—sex, reproductive physiology, sexuality, sexual identity, gender identity—which help to frame its areas of constructedness. Through such parsing, it has become clear that even the shapes of bodies cannot be completely separated from culture and ideology.[3] No parallel glossary for *race* exists to probe its processes of social construction. As a result, *race* may seem an even more biological term than *gender*, even though it is farther from biological fact.[4]

Theorists also agree that the ideologies of race and gender are strongly, or even inextricably, interconnected, so that it is more helpful to think about *genderized race* or *racialized gender* than to think about the two terms separately.[5] Strong agreement on that proposition has replaced earlier feminist analyses of the additive "double whammy" experienced by women of color because of simultaneous racial and gender oppression. Concepts such as *intersectionality* and *relationality* have replaced that additive model and suggest the extent to which each identity characteristic defines and can only be understood in terms of the other. For everyone, including members of the dominant race, there is no way to extricate race from sex. We inhabit both categories 24/7.

Legal scholar and critical race theorist Kimberlé Crenshaw coined the term *intersectionality* in 1989, as she argued that women of color's experience "cannot be captured wholly by looking at the race or gender dimensions of those experiences separately."[6] Crenshaw argued that black women had been excluded from discrimination lawsuits because their experience of discrimination did not apply to all blacks or to all women (apparently, all the blacks were men and all the women were white). In addition to theorizing intersectionality, Crenshaw used it to argue discrimination law cases, with some success.

Versions of intersectionality theory followed throughout the 1990s and into the first decade of the twenty-first century, articulated by feminist scholars such as Bonnie Thornton Dill, Maxine Baca Zinn, Patricia Hill Collins, Jacquelyn Grant, and many others, including other critical race feminists.[7] In the late 1990s, theorists Leela Fernandes and Evelyn Nakano Glenn amplified *intersectionality* by defining respectively an *integrative framework* and *relationality*, in which race, class, and gender are understood as mutually constituted and inseparable.[8]

Introduction 3

As Glenn explained in 2002, the integration of race and gender is not just a matter of representation, since it segments the labor market and stratifies government benefits, among other material effects. At the same time, these effects interact with representations as well as with changing political movements and persistent social structures in which, as Foucault explained, power differentials are "both pervasive and dispersed, lodged in the taken-for-granted rather than enforced by coercion."[9]

Laura Gillman offered yet another variation on intersectionality in 2007, which she called a *double-voiced conjunctural approach*, designed not just to analyze but to redress power differentials between white women and women of color. Gillman concentrated on the different "racial scripts" different groups "speak from" because of their discrepant social positions. For women of color, she explained, racial discourse attempts to subvert terms that objectify and demonize darkness; for white women, racial discourse typically protects white supremacy, which is by definition invisible. The point of examining racial scripts is "to learn how power accrues and/or is contested within current cultural imaginaries, and to explore how those who oppress can learn to make sense of their exercise of white power in relation to those they have wounded with their oppressive acts."[10]

These theoretical approaches are crucial reference points for *The Specter of Sex*, but as significant as they have been for thinking about race and gender, they do not cover the territory that this book is intended to map. As such theories define the race-gender interconnection, they tend to take the intersections they witness as givens rather than to explain why they exist, what processes conspired to conjoin race and gender in the first place, and whether they were always inextricably fused. Even historically rooted theoretical analyses, such as Evelyn Glenn's and Eileen Boris's, do not typically consider those questions, although they recognize that the term "race" is full of assumptions about a human quality that does not really exist. This book argues that among those assumptions are many preconceptions about gender.

The Specter of Sex asks why a world already clearly bifurcated by *gender* was transformed into one also obsessed with ideas about *race* distinction starting in Europe and the English colonies in the late seventeenth century. In so doing, the book explores the role ancient gender ideology played in transforming *race* from a term denoting peoples or *gens*—as in "the French" or "Africans"—subject to changes in climate and "humors" into a permanent biological characteristic that measured human worth, shaped social institutions, and even united competitive Europeans under a single banner. In answering that question, *The Specter of Sex* provides a rare comparative study of racial formation that reveals its gendered patterns, which have repeated themselves with variations over time in the service of white racial dominance.

In reconstructing the historical "backstory" of race-gender intersectionality, *The Specter of Sex* argues that many assumptions about the ephemeral characteristic of race, particularly in the U.S., have been consistently associated with equally suspect biological claims and assumptions about gender—from behavior, to personality, to human value. These claims and assumptions constitute *gender ideology* and include prescriptions for heterosexual sex and reproduction, mandates for different male and female roles and personalities, judgments about men's superiority and dominance over women, and standards of sexual normalcy and deviance. The book reveals how gender has been racialized in the production of racial categories and hierarchies in the U.S. by providing evidence that gender prescriptions, stereotypes, and expectations haunted the process of racial formation like a ghost, as political, religious, scientific, and popular discourses shaped American *racial ideology*. This book's analysis suggests that the specter of sex has been so persistent that race as a concept and structural force in American society cannot be fully understood without a deep understanding of its gendered foundations in different cultural domains over time. By the same token, *racism* cannot be conquered until the *sexism* underlying it has also been defeated.

To say that gender ideology is foundational to racial ideology is not to claim that gender supersedes race as a justification for oppression. It is to say that deeply entrenched gender ideology was well established when various economic, political, scientific, and religious forces gradually and unevenly converged around the idea of race as a permanent, fixed, biological condition that determines human value. Gender provided organizing principles that fueled processes of racialization, including the concepts of gender binarism and the "natural" inferiority of women to men. Gender was a mechanism for conceptualizing and judging the diversity of human physiology and culture as the known world of Europeans expanded and colonialism flourished. It was especially helpful to English colonists as they tried to justify race-based chattel slavery in the New World.

In asking where intersectionality began—how we got to this place in American culture where "hot" Latinas, white "ladies," and slim Chinese men are emblematic of racial categories and hierarchical judgments—*The Specter of Sex* also explores what has been suppressed in the construction of racial difference and how the gendered history of race can inform contemporary debates. Exploring that suppressed history exposes structural relationships linking women of different races "in systematic ways," despite their varied experiences.[11] It also exposes structural linkages between women and men that further undermine the validity of racial and gender categories. Because the United States has played a crucial role in constructing racial categories across the globe, revealing those linkages could inspire new coalitions, even beyond American shores.

Book Structure and Methodology

The Specter of Sex argues that gender ideology helped to generate a "public epistemology" of race and to rationalize the racial devaluation of individuals and groups on the allegedly natural, biological grounds of gender difference, hierarchy, and normative standards. Gender may not constitute the full story of racial formation in the U.S., but it was (and is) a key strand in the web of naturalized racial ideology that functions to this day. The book probes a wide range of cultural narratives that together constitute racial ideology in order to identify and analyze its "gender strand."

In pursuing its goal, *The Specter of Sex* proceeds both chronologically and thematically from the roots of gender ideology in the ancient world and early modern Europe to twentieth century regulations of women's citizenship that defined racial difference and controlled the racial composition of the U.S. As a genealogy rather than a conventional history, *The Specter of Sex* focuses on dominant discourses that generated racial categories and hierarchies in gendered terms. Those discourses appear across religious, political, and scientific narratives, public policies and testimonies, laws, court cases, and newspaper articles that defined race in gendered terms. Sources for the discourses include primary documents as well as works of historical scholarship, specialized studies of racial groups, and texts from colonial and postcolonial studies, American studies, legal history, women's history, and feminist theory. Mining these sources for evidence of gendered discourses of race resembles an archeological dig, since the evidence lies within them like a purloined letter: there for all to see, but largely buried, overlooked, or unacknowledged.

This mining operation has also produced a temporally and culturally specific narrative history, organized into the themes and topics suggested by historical discourses and epistemologies of race. The specificity of the book's analysis grounds feminist theorizing about macro-structural topics and recurrent ideological patterns—the gendered foundations of racial ideology—without universalizing, essentializing, or obscuring differences among individuals and groups.[12]

Tracing a narrative history is not the same as chronicling lived experience, of course. Narratives do not equal actions or events. Written laws and court cases do not capture either their application or their contestation in real life, although laws and policies have frequently been inspired by events, as we shall see throughout the book. Yet, such narratives are invaluable for the mission of *The Specter of Sex* to identify and analyze the complex of ideas that evolved about race in gendered terms and formed the gendered racial ideology that still fuels intersectional identities and forms of oppression.

The Specter of Sex is also an origins story that contributes to scholarship about racial formation by focusing on what has been least addressed within it: the recurrent revision of racial ideology as the American body politic re-formed itself to absorb each new racialized group while retaining the infrastructure of dominance and subordination that was built with gendered blocks. Because racial formation is a recurrent as well as a sequential process that applies old standards to new situations, analyzing it requires both a longitudinal and a comparative study. Thus, *The Specter of Sex* traces the evolution of racial ideology over a two-hundred-year time period (seventeenth though mid-twentieth century) for five groups—American Indians, African Americans, European American whites (especially the English), Asian Americans (especially the Chinese), and Latinos (especially Mexican and Puerto Rican Americans). These origins stories are woven together within three core categories of American thought that governed racial formation from Colonial times to the mid-twentieth century: *bodies*, *blood*, and *citizenship*. These categories frame sequential as well as overlapping contexts for gendered racial formation. The book establishes that gendered narratives about the deficiencies or strengths of various so-called racial groups with regard to their bodies, blood, and capacities for citizenship, as well as about the superiority of the majority race over all others, were particularly effective in obscuring whites' self-serving economic and political motivations for stratifying races. Because racial formation is the book's major concern, analyses of each racial group and each core category do not extend across the book's two-hundred-year purview.

The three core categories of bodies, blood, and citizenship constitute the three main sections of *The Specter of Sex*. After an overview of the construction of gender ideology from ancient times to early modern European thought and practice (Part I, "Roots"), Parts II through IV trace the development of racial ideology in terms of the three core categories. Each part shifts the analytical lens to capture repeated, sequential, and overlapping patterns of gendered racial formation from different perspectives. Part V brings the book into the contemporary moment by evaluating and theorizing its historical revelations for the academy and for political activists. All parts include a thematic introduction, several chapters that advance the book's analysis and central arguments, and a conclusion.

The three chapters of Part I, "Roots," set the stage for understanding American gendered racial formation. Chapter 1 discusses gender ideology in Western culture, with "Western" understood as a political rather than a geographic location and as a term that connotes arrogance about cultural superiority that fueled the ideology of white supremacy. Chapter 2 investigates the earliest construction of racial difference by European explorers to Africa and the New World and by emerging anthropologists and naturalists from the fifteenth through the eighteenth century. The chapter divides discourses from those sources into three phases—*interpretation, classification,* and *ranking*—and reveals, among other things, how the two sexes were conceptualized as the first races. Chapter 3 analyzes two primary institutions that were crucial to the formulation of Euro-American racial categories and hierarchies—nationhood and slavery—both of which were gendered at their roots.

The three chapters of Part II, "Bodies," trace the convergence of gender ideology with visible characteristics of bodies in the construction of racial categories and hierarchies, starting in the American colonies and extending beyond the Civil War. Chapter 4 begins in the colonies, where geographic identities—African, English—first became racial categories through policies that arbitrarily distinguished between the laboring bodies of African and English women. Parallel policies "embodying" and thereby feminizing African and American Indian men also constructed race by assigning different prerogatives to men of different bodily forms. Chapter 5 reveals the gendered roots of body-based American chattel slavery. Chapter 6 analyzes the sexual desire and projection—often onto the bodies of men of color—entailed in the murder and lynching of African American, Mexican, and Chinese men before and after the turn of the twentieth century.

The four chapters of Part III, "Blood," explore the dilemma of race as an allegedly invisible human characteristic in the U.S. They emphasize post-Reconstruction and early twentieth-century gendered racial ideologies that promoted white racial dominance. The American fixation on racial blood led to the gendered policing of its composition and transmission. Indeed, blood regulation targeted black men and white women as the most threatening of all sexual and reproductive partners. Chapter 7 analyzes "blood" as a metaphor for race and discusses the processes of defining, measuring, and ranking racial blood that appear un-gendered or gender-inclusive on the surface but suggest their own gendered subtexts. Chapter 8 explains why racial blood itself is a gendered concept and reveals just how gendered those apparently neutral regulations of racial blood measurement, definition, and ranking really were. Chapter 9 exposes the gender biases built into anti-miscegenation laws targeting both blacks and "Mongols." Chapter 10 analyzes two key mechanisms whites used to promote racial fear and discrimination: specious rape accusations and the hyper-scrutiny of white motherhood. Both involved the cooperation and/or manipulation of white women.

The four chapters of Part IV, "Citizenship," discuss the gendered mechanisms of racial control that are both obvious and buried in American citizenship policies, starting in the colonies, and in the immigration policies and laws of the mid-nineteenth through the mid-twentieth century. The regulation of American citizenship focused on both gendered racial bodies and blood in defining racial difference and controlling the racial composition of the American polity. Chapter 11 explores definitions of citizenship as a gendered racial concept from colonial times to the twentieth century. Until surprisingly recently, manliness (or at least maleness) was the primary evidence of democratic capacity and the quintessential qualification for full rights as an American citizen. Chapter 12 details the evolution of American women's citizenship rights until the mid-twentieth century. That genealogy illustrates just how gendered citizenship was and how useful women's second-class citizenship status became for modeling the second-class citizenship of particular groups of non-white men. The chapter also chronicles free black men's greater access to voting rights as compared to women of any race, at least until women's second-class citizenship template took over in the early nineteenth century. Chapter 13 explores the use of this same gendered template to gradually identify free African American men, as well as Chinese and American Indian men, as innately dependent and inappropriately gendered and, therefore, unqualified for full American citizenship. Chapter 14 identifies racial mixture as a metaphor for suspect gender and explains how that metaphor functioned to limit Latinos' citizenship rights, specifically those promised to Mexicans and Puerto Ricans by negotiated treaties. Part IV concludes by analyzing how the U.S. government constructed homosexuals as members of a particularly undesirable gendered "race" whose threat to American society made them ineligible for naturalization or even admission to the country for over a century.

The two chapters of Part V, "Implications," conclude the book by assessing the implications of its gendered genealogy of racial formation in the U.S. for anti-racist feminist theories and politics, and for race-based theories of gender difference. These chapters are meant to generate new dialogue about a claim offered almost two decades ago by Susan Bordo that "the affirmation of difference" is *not* the only useful perspective for discussing gender and race.[13] Part V's introduction briefly explores the history of cross-racial and cross-gender coalitions in the fight for social justice in the U.S., which provides both guidance and reason for optimism that such alliances might be revived in the present. Chapter 15 addresses implications for feminist theory and feminist activists who struggle to formulate strategies for social justice in the context of continued racial misunderstanding. The chapter considers mechanisms for coalition building around structural connections that could link women in an *antisubordination* politics despite their differences. Chapter 16 addresses the book's implications for racial formation studies, as well as for race relations in American culture. It considers possibilities for hybrid racial as well as gender identities, particularly as a means for confronting the internal sexism still plaguing racial groups and social justice movements in the U.S.

Although much has been included in *The Specter of Sex*, much has necessarily been omitted. Many books could be written on the same topic, depending on scholars' disciplinary locations and methodologies, and I hope that more will come along to continue the conversation and refine the arguments. Other studies might focus on different narratives or different periods, or they might focus more directly on events or personalities. But years of work on this topic have convinced me that the book's basic argument is sound and critical. Race as a concept developed historically for many reasons, but justifications for its validity were often formulated along the familiar axes and assumptions that had long constituted gender ideology. The two concepts of race and gender now seem so completely fused that we cannot separate them. Understanding how they merged in our consciousness allows us to think more deeply about intersectionality, correct the lack of historical focus in much theorizing about gender and race, and even imagine collaborations across racial boundaries on new grounds.

Terms of Analysis

Gender, sex, and *race* are pivotal terms for this book's analysis, so I want to explain exactly what I mean by them. As already indicated, I consider all three to be cultural constructions, more rooted in ideology than in nature or biology. The use of *sex* in the book's title and *gender* in its subtitle is meant to express their shared cultural roots. The pervasive use of *gender* throughout reflects the book's inclusion of women and men as equally, if not always admittedly, sex-specific beings, as well as its recognition of *gendering* as a force that typically reduces a spectrum of sexual identities and proclivities into dichotomies of sexuality and sexual difference. By the same token, this book's use of *race* crosses a spectrum of racialized groups and processes of racialization and connotes the persistent tendency toward racial dichotomization reflected in the black-white racial paradigm that normalizes the concept of racial opposites. To honor the spectrum implicit in the term *race*, this book undertakes a comparative analysis over time for multiple groups. Because multiracial ethnicities, like Latino, have so often been considered races in the U.S., I include *ethnicity* as an implicit component of much racial ideology.

Most terms denoting racial categories in *The Specter of Sex* are common in contemporary discourse, but others reflect the time period being discussed. For example, *Negro* or *black* is more appropriate to the period of slavery than *African American*, which refers to more recent constructions of race and confirms the full citizenship of black Americans. I vary that usage depending on historical context. By the same token, *Native American* was not used politically until the late twentieth century, so the term *Indian* is more accurate for depicting the gendered racial narratives of previous centuries. That term has also been favored in the currently favored appellation "American Indian." *Mulatto* has gone out of favor completely, but there is no better way to represent the political and social significance of free persons of certain mixed-race heritages in the eighteenth and nineteenth centuries.

The Specter of Sex also distinguishes between the *British* who stayed at home and the *English* who came to the new world, by employing those different terms. Likewise, *Britons* denotes those who did not leave Europe. *Tejanos, Californios,* and *Mexicanos(as)* are Mexicans who were American citizens or were entitled to citizenship in annexed territories. *Anglos* are whites of European descent who occupied southwestern and western American territories and usually contested the assimilation of Mexicans into them.

I use *proto-racial* to denote ideas that developed before the term *race* was taken to mean permanent differences in the physiologies and human worth of particular groups of people. Likewise, *racialist* and *racialism* refer respectively to people and ideas that focused inordinately on physiological or cultural differences and hierarchies before the term *racism* was coined.

The only invented term in *The Specter of Sex* is *de-masculate* (and its cognate *de-masculation*), which I find preferable to *emasculate* (*emasculation*) because the latter suggests that male prerogatives are necessary to a man's sense of himself, and without them he is not a real man. *De-masculate* suggests instead that certain prerogatives have conventionally been associated with men and masculinity, and their denial is a political tool designed to make a man *feel* deprived, although in a just world he might not actually *be* deprived. In fact, he and everyone else might be better off.

PART I

Roots

Introduction

As the Twig is Bent

The history of gendered racial ideology in the U.S. begins in ancient and early modern European philosophical, religious, literary, scientific, and political discourses. Part I of *The Specter of Sex* explores such sources and analyzes the myriad ways in which ideas about women's inherent inferiority to men and various preconceptions about gender characteristics and relationships informed what would eventually become the concept of inherent and permanent biological race. The term *eventually* is important, because the concept of fixed, biological race evolved slowly over many centuries. Among other things, the idea of fixed racial differences had to overcome longstanding beliefs, starting with the Greeks, that changing climatic and geographical forces and influences formed mutable characters, appearances, and cultures of men. The term *men* is also important because it was the distinction between men from different regions and climates with different "complexions"—meaning more than skin color—that finally became the foundation of biological categories of race.

In charting the journey from gender ideology to racial ideology, Chapter 1 reviews the misogynistic heritage of Western thought that promoted Caucasian arrogance about racial value. Its exploration establishes both the chronology of gender and racial ideologies and their thematic and axiomatic interconnections. The chapter also identifies five principles of gender ideology that supported the development of racial ideology. Chapter 2 concentrates on racial ideology formation in Europe from the early modern period through the mid-nineteenth century. The chapter identifies the gendered precepts that informed European explorers' encounters with allegedly primitive peoples in the New World and Africa, including the idea that men and women actually constituted separate "races." The chapter organizes narratives from the period into overlapping but progressive stages of gendered racial ideology formation: *interpretation, classification,* and *ranking*. Chapter 2's discussion reveals the contrast between elite European men's reluctance to disparage other men on racial grounds—lest they undermine the concept of male superiority—and their enthusiasm for distinguishing themselves from women, even of their own "racial" group. Chapter 3 concludes Part I by discussing worldwide slavery and the nation-state as institutions and conceptual systems that promoted gendered racial ideology.

1

"Women are a Huge Natural Calamity"

The Roots of Western Gender Ideology

The Greek playwright Euripides satirized the essence of Western thinking about gender relations when he wrote in the fifth century B.C.E. that "women are a huge natural calamity,/against which men must take/strenuous measures."[1] Those words, however comically meant, not only capture the curmudgeonliest version of gender ideology in ancient times but also contain seeds of racial distinctions and hierarchies that would blossom in the works of Western philosophers, scientists, theologians, and politicians many centuries later. Among other links between gender and racial ideologies across the ages were repeated measurements of "others" against a particular male standard that Greek elites and their intellectual descendants mistook for the epitome of humanness and that later Europeans considered Caucasian as well as male. Characterizations of women as deviants from the dominant male standard provided a model for considering men's differences from that same standard as similarly deviant.

An obvious clue to gender's foundational role in Western conceptualizations of biological race can be found in the relative historical timing of gender and racial ideologies in European cultures. Claims about women's inherent biological and temperamental inferiority and permanent subordinate status to men appear in the earliest known texts and records.[2] The idea that differences among men were inherent, biological, permanent, and stratified, on the other hand, did not occupy Europeans' imaginations until the late seventeenth century and did not support fully blown racial taxonomies until the late eighteenth century. The physiologies and cultural practices that once marked geography, climate, or family lineages gradually became markers of men's fixed and biologically determined capacities. That biological interpretation came into full flower in the nineteenth century, and throughout the process, racial definitions and judgments were frequently couched in gendered terms. Beginning in earnest in the late eighteenth century, gender and racial ideologies evolved together, in terms of one another. In fact, the Gender Contract supporting patriarchal rule in Western cultures inspired the Racial Contract that promoted the global dominance of European males, especially over black Africans.

"Necessarily Inferior"

As feminist theorists and activists have long noted, much of what was thought or claimed about women before the mid-nineteenth century was thought and claimed by men. Male commentators typically considered themselves the human model and solipsistically regarded women as unfortunate imitations of, appendages to, or even curses upon the male norm. At various junctures, philosophers and scientists even identified women as a separate human species from men. The narratives that disseminated such attitudes, which linger in troublesome ways into the present time, reveal the gender themes and principles that both fomented the construction of racial distinctions and hierarchies and justified invidious racial comparisons, projections, and rankings. Such "racialist" or pre-racist thinking, in turn, further divided and stratified the sexes.

It is difficult to know just how ancient misogynist ideas about women really are, but when Euripides wrote that women were a natural calamity, he was echoing even earlier Greek references to women's inferiority and danger to men. Hesiod's *Theogony* (or "origins of the gods") was one such precursor. Dating from the last half of the eighth century to the first quarter of the seventh century B.C.E., the *Theogony* has important parallels to the biblical Book of Genesis, which dates from the fifteenth century B.C.E.[3] The *Theogony* makes clear that Zeus created woman only to torment and punish man in retaliation for a trick played on him by Prometheus. To accomplish that goal, Zeus made woman's external appearance so attractive that it would fool men into accepting "the wickedness that was inside her." The *Theogony* also defines woman's nature as inferior to man's and ranks her weak, larcenous, and deceitful mind closer to that of an animal than of a man, let alone of a god. The *Thegony* also likens women to "drones that contribute . . . to malicious deeds" by the men who swarm around them like bees, and claims that Zeus granted a sense of justice to man but denied that ultimate virtue to woman.[4]

Texts by Plato and Aristotle, which reflected and reinforced Hesiod's ideas about women, also preceded Euripides' dramas. Plato's fourth-century B.C.E. *Timaeus*, for example, defined the primordial human state as male and declared that women, who reside several steps below men from the gods, exist to punish men for their sensual desires. Although Plato is known for his proto-feminist views of extraordinary women (like those who serve as Guardians in Book V of the *Republic* alongside equally extraordinary men), his view of ordinary women in the *Timaeus* and the *Laws* was decidedly misogynistic. "Womanish" in such texts connotes a diminished intellect, as well as "obsessive appetites, and ungovernable emotions."[5]

Aristotle's views about women, honed in the same century, were influenced by both Hesiod and Plato, although Aristotle dismissed the Socratic idea that men and women who shared the same circumstances and education could achieve the same level of virtue.[6] Aristotle saw women's defects of character and behavior as intrinsic, resulting from their lack of heat. He claimed that women's coldness transformed male embryos into females, thereby thwarting their development into the pure human type. To Aristotle, women were essentially misbegotten males, cursed by nature with lamentable physical and emotional deficiencies, and useful only for reproduction (femaleness as a curse became a recurrent theme in gender ideology). Aristotle's infusion of conventional gender ideology into his scientific axioms also prefigures the complicity of scientific thought with cultural beliefs and preconceptions about gender—and, eventually, race—in virtually all subsequent eras, including our own.[7]

Ancient Greek ideas about maleness as the human norm and femaleness as a deviation from that norm parallel the influential "one-sex" view of Genesis 2 (2:18, 21–23): man came first, woman came from man's rib, and woman's differences were not an improvement on the original model. Genesis 1(1:26–27) offers a different version of creation—"male and female created he them"—in which man and woman are created separately, both in God's image. But few Christian sects have emphasized that version, although it was understandably favored by such nineteenth-century American feminists as Angelina Grimké and Elizabeth Cady Stanton as evidence of men's and women's equally divine origins and of God's plan for sexual equality. Fewer still have gone as far as Christian Science and Shakerism to consider Genesis 1 as evidence of both human equality and God's dual gender. Rather, most mainstream sects have emphasized the "rib" and "helpmeet" aspects of Genesis 2 to demonstrate woman's inferiority. In that interpretation, Eve's gendered inadequacies are exacerbated by her vulnerability to the serpent—which marks her as a danger to (hu)mankind—and are reinforced by God's curse that she give birth in pain and be ruled by her husband. That Adam was also cursed typically escapes those who embrace the biblical origins of woman's inferior nature and subordinate role.

These Judeo-Christian and Greek roots have exerted a powerful influence on the Western idea that women lack reason and are mired in passion. Starting in the first century C.E., Philo, the Jewish philosopher and Platonist, noted that woman's sensual nature situates her well below man, who represents the mind; and even below the animals, since God created them before her in the second creation story. To Philo, the order of creation proves that woman's inferiority, not her equality, was divinely ordained.[8]

By the Middle Ages, alchemists interwove Aristotelian gender principles and Genesis 2 to establish woman's inherent imperfection as an axiom of emerging sciences. Indeed, alchemy was dedicated to overcoming the female principle of cold through the superior male principle of heat by transforming cold female elements, such as lead, into warm male elements, such as gold. According to alchemists, even a hermaphrodite could be converted into a "powerful male nature" through the addition of warmth. Through such views, Aristotle's judgment of women as a "monstrous error of nature"—worthy of study only in unflattering comparison to a male standard—would be inscribed in the natural sciences for centuries.[9]

Medieval theologians and physicians used the same linkage to explain women's imperfections. Aquinas, for example, explained in the thirteenth century that the defects in women's active force were as important to their inferiority as their secondary role in creation. The female body was "not against the purpose of universal nature," he explained, just beyond the *immediate* "purpose of nature." The Greek physician Galen similarly invoked Aristotelian views in his pronouncement that female genitals were the inversion—which is to say the perversion—of the masculine form.[10] Woman's deficiencies of mind were evident in her original sin. Galen concluded from such evidence that females must be strictly controlled by superior males for the good of society. As we shall see, versions of that view endured throughout Europe and North America for centuries.

There were counter-narratives about gender, to be sure. Plucky women clearly existed in myth and history. The politically wily Lysistrata is legendary, although no more so than the vengeful murderess, Medea. And the Gnostic gospels brought women to the fore. Mary Magdalene, for example, registered an early complaint against

Peter by claiming that, unlike Jesus, he "hates our race," meaning women.[11] Her views were quickly suppressed: the dominance of misogyny was hard to overcome. Even as Protestant Reformationists in the sixteenth century tried to elevate woman's status in order to render them eligible for salvation, for example, they succumbed to the "one-sex" theory of Genesis 2. Martin Luther expressed a preference for Genesis 1, but he simultaneously emphasized woman's inferiority to man—as the moon is inferior to the sun—because she, not man, succumbed to the serpent's enticements. Likewise, John Calvin, who complimented women by promoting the value of marriage, still considered woman a lesser kind of man, worthy of male affection but still a "second degree" creation and, therefore, a second-rate image of God. Paracelsus (Theophrastus Bombastus von Hohenheim) declared in the early sixteenth century that woman was merely an image of an image of the universe, a "Littlest World," while men were a "Little World."[12] Throughout history, as women agitated for political and civil rights, detractors hauled out such adages and images and ridiculed the idea that women could be men's equals—serious and responsible about money, property, or politics. Even positive ideas about women's delicacy, sweetness, and nurturing qualities were typically turned against their efforts to achieve fully human status.

Five Principles of Gendered Racial Formation

The scientific and religious roots of misogynistic gender ideology established several principles in Western culture that would contribute both directly and indirectly to the construction of racial ideology, starting in the seventeenth century. The first principle is the use of a singular human standard to measure other groups, with predictably poor results. European men were confident that their gender aligned them with divine will and/or Nature's plan and guaranteed them a choice social role and high cultural value. They felt entitled to take their self-definitions as fact. That gender entitlement inspired similar ground rules for establishing Caucasian racial domination and superiority. In both cases, only the powerful had the right to establish the facts about human value and to interpret the heavenly or natural signs of their superiority. Anyone that dominant group deemed inferior to itself immediately became *ipso facto* evidence of the group's own superiority—a nasty syllogism if ever there was one.

A second principle carried forward from gender ideology into racial ideology is the interpretation of human difference as evidence of unequal value. Based on European men's historical interpretations of sex difference, it seems that the human mind—or, rather, the European male mind—has historically had difficulty holding within itself two categories or characteristics, let alone many, without ranking them. Derrida was right: binaries are rarely equivalents; one is typically more powerful than the other and defines that "other" in terms of its own plenitude and the other's lack.[13] Gender ideology helped to establish the axiom that difference entails inequality and to model the notion that even multiple differences devolve to two: dominant and subordinate.

A third principle inherent in Western gender ideology that promoted racial ideology is the idea that dependency proves inadequacy. Few philosophers or scientists before the fifteenth century questioned whether socially constructed gender stratification itself caused the economic and intellectual dependency men disparaged in women. Even then, the only thinkers and writers to observe the phenomenon were educated European women fighting for their own sex. Male social commentators, who were otherwise astute in the effects of social and political structures, typically considered women subordinate because of their inherent—not imposed—characters, behaviors, and qualities. Similarly, those benefiting from the subjugation of "inferior" races, including white women, seldom considered the effects of that same subjugation on the capacities or talents of their so-called inferiors. Their deficiencies, too, were deemed inherent.

A fourth principle established by traditional gender ideology that supported racial ideology is the connection between "scientific" theories about gender difference and capacities and cultural messages about gender. Although science has a reputation for objectivity, scientists typically observe only what they have been prepared to see both by normal science and by prevailing idea systems and cultural practices (especially observations that reinforce the scientists' own beliefs). This tendency stifles scientific innovation, according to sociobiologist David Barash: "Sensory evidence—seeing, smelling, hearing, touching—generally confirms our [existing] knowledge . . . remarkably often we only 'see' things when we are prepared to find them. . . . As frequent as this experience may be in daily life, it seems even more common among scientists."[14]

In addition, as contemporary sociobiology itself demonstrates, anthropomorphic gender differences and expectations constitute a primary metaphor in scientific investigations, even of the non-human and inanimate universe. Biologists in particular have often interpreted their findings in terms of stereotyped preconceptions about male and female desires, behaviors, capacities, and ostensible purposes in life. Because of that bias, female mammals' role in selecting their mates was hidden from scientific view for centuries, as was the "unmotherly" behavior of primates like female pandas, who typically abandon one cub from a set of twins. Thus, any scientific lens focused on gender difference risks becoming a mirror for observers' assumptions about "normal" behaviors and characteristics. Scientific inquiry into racial differences entails the same risk, in part because those differences so often involve gendered judgments.

A fifth principle linking gender ideology and racial ideology is the idea that a self-defined superior group is entitled to control both their alleged inferiors and society at large. Aristotle modeled that reasoning when he declared that "the male is by nature superior and the female inferior," and concluded that women should be confined to the domestic sphere (but controlled by men even there) and excluded from political and social life.[15] For good measure, he also proclaimed that slaves and females had equally deficient souls, which justified their equally abject status.[16] Although Greek slaves were of no particular "race," Aristotle's analogy helped to establish the gendered grounds on which white Europeans would later claim the right to exclude their racial "inferiors."

"The One Rules, and the Other is Ruled"

The fifth principle, which concerns political capacity, probably had the most devastating effect on all women and those men deemed racially inferior, so it is worth delving further into the transition in thought from gender to racial ideology in that regard. According to historical gender ideology, marriage is the proper mechanism for institutionalizing male control over women for the good of society. Aristotle and his legions of followers defined marriage as Nature's way to "civilize" women by containing their inherently promiscuous natures and channeling their naturally passionate attachments to their children.[17] The Roman statesman Cato reflected this view in the early second century B.C.E., when he reminded husbands that they had an obligation to control their wives' behavior in order to preserve the social order. Limiting woman to the domestic sphere through marriage and excluding her from public life also occupied Philo, St. Paul, and St. John Chrysostom, who concluded in the early centuries of the Common Era (C.E.) that woman's defective reasoning capacity (demonstrated by her susceptibility to the wily serpent), and her inferiority to man (evident in her "secondary" creation and God's curse), meant that she should stay at home.[18]

By the seventeenth century, European political philosophers naturalized women's exclusion from the public sphere on the grounds that Genesis 2 and the curse of Eden not only proved women's weakness and inferiority but also represented the natural social order. John Locke (1632–1704) claimed, for example, that woman's biblically mandated subordination to and dependency on man was Nature's plan, not a social convention. After all, women's suffering in childbirth was not a social artifact. Writing before the concept of biological race was widely accepted, Locke claimed that Nature had made all men independent and free, regardless of their many differences. But that same Nature had made women dependent and weak. Suggesting that women had a right to masculine freedom or to equal public roles with men was pure foolishness.[19] Men and women were simply not the same beast.[20]

By the eighteenth century, such views about women's political incapacity began seeping into European philosophers' developing views about race. Arguing that Eve's daughters posed a threat to men, for example, Jean Jacques Rousseau (1712–1778), insisted that young girls be trained to please rather than arouse men and to subordinate themselves to men in order to prevent familial—and, by extension, social—chaos. Adult women should also renounce the freedom that makes a person fully human (i.e., male), submit cheerfully to the will of others, and forfeit all desire for independence. "Never has a people perished from an excess of wine," Rousseau (erroneously) declared, but "all perish from the disorder of women." All of the evidence he needed for women's inherent untrustworthiness could be found in the female body's natural cycles.[21]

That same view of Nature's sexual hierarchy and female incapacities emerged in Rousseau's ideas about a natural racial hierarchy. Although he also romanticized non-white "natural savages," Rousseau regarded them as inherently uncivilized and disordered, like women.[22] His assertion that women could be trained to like their subordination and submit cheerfully to men presaged the myth that racial inferiors would enjoy serving their betters.

Immanuel Kant (1724–1804) also predicated woman's political subordination to man on Genesis 2 as a plan for the "natural" social order. Kant sweetened his mandate for gender inequality by suggesting that the sexes had equivalent and complementary rights: man had the "right" and duty to protect the "weaker sex," and woman had the "right" to man's protection. He granted woman control of the household, but he spared her the weighty judgments for which she was ill-equipped by declaring man in charge of the rest of the world. Like Rousseau, Kant believed that man had the right and duty to tell woman "what her will consists of."[23]

Kant's racial theory, which mirrored his gender ideology, did much to circulate the concept of race among Euro-American intellectuals.[24] Kant regarded race as a class distinction within species of animals, including humans, which was transmitted by inheritance. He projected onto "inferior" races, such as Africans and American Indians, the same deficient "unchanging and unchangeable inferior moral quality" that he postulated for women.[25] According to Kant, only white men had the intellectual and moral capacity for political and other leadership roles.

2

The First Races in Society

Gendered Roots of Racial Formation

It is unclear exactly when the word *race* or its linguistic cognates acquired modern connotations of permanent biological distinctions that justified stratifying human groups, but most historians agree that it did not occur before the eighteenth century and did not gain wide acceptance in Europe and the U.S. until the nineteenth century. This does not mean that medieval and early modern Europeans were blind to cultural and physical differences among themselves or between themselves and distant "others." Rather, as literary and cultural narratives from those periods reveal, there was a lively interest among Europeans in differences of religion, social organization, dress, and skin color, among other factors, primarily as they signified either threats to or opportunities for themselves. Even as they encountered and classified non-European groups, however, Europeans were often more concerned with the other nations on their continent, with whom they competed for cultural and economic dominance, than with the new peoples they met. They did not yet regard themselves as a biological or unified cultural entity; rather, they were Christians, and/or Britons or Spaniards, and they judged themselves against one another in terms of relative power and status. The idea of a Caucasian race that united Europeans and made them superior to Asians, Amerindians, or Africans evolved gradually and unevenly over centuries into a biological "fact."

Throughout that process, which occurred at different rates in different cultural domains, gender was a strong catalyst for interpreting and judging human differences. Indeed, as Ania Loomba observes, "women and men were perhaps the first 'races' in society," since "proto-racial difference" was routinely expressed in terms of gender and sexuality, and vice versa."[1] The gendered seeds of biological race germinated in religious, scientific, legal, political, and economic discourses, some of which we have already sampled. Added to them were commentaries by Renaissance European traders and explorers, Church proclamations like the sixteenth-century "blood laws" of the Spanish Inquisition, and theories of eighteenth-century naturalists and nineteenth-century phrenologists, physical anthropologists, and "scientific" racists.

Chapter 2 focuses on the gendered racial ideology formulated and propounded by (Christian) Europeans, particularly the British, as they contemplated the peculiarities of Moors, Jews, Asians, and North Africans already in their midst, encountered new human groups during their journeys to Africa and the New World, and tried to situate themselves within the diverse human family. Many of their gendered views of race served each nation's economic and political self-interest and desire to dominate Europe.

In order to organize multiple narratives and to theorize Europeans' often contradictory explanations for their own and others' cultural and, eventually, racial characteristics and value, I have identified three overlapping but progressive stages in the development of racial ideology: *interpretation*, *classification*, and *ranking*. Each of those phases depended in different ways on gendered precepts for racial definition, from the interpretation of differences, to the clustering and classification of those differences into distinct human categories, to the ranking of categories according to God's and Nature's apparent design for the human race. The next three sections of Chapter 2 explore each phase and its gendered foundations in turn.

Breasts and Civilization: Early Interpretations of "The Other"

The first phase, *interpretation*, had roots in classical and medieval texts but blossomed in the sixteenth and seventeenth centuries. Many interpretations of the "other" in the early modern period that would eventually become racial, had religion, specifically Christianity, at their core. Britons in particular regarded religion as a proto-racial marker, since they saw their form of Christianity as a kind of "humor" that shaped British national character and complexion, broadly understood. After 1707, the British state reinforced the "ideological connection between [Anglican] Protestantism, freedom, and prosperity" and used that link to challenge Protestant Dissenters, Catholics, Jews, Muslims, and heathens. The latter two groups were seen as especially deviant and, therefore, as perfect candidates for enslavement.[2] European anxieties over differences of culture, especially religious differences, undermined the general acceptance by Renaissance theologians and philosophers of St. Augustine's view that all human beings had developed from "one protoplast" and were descended from Adam. Evidence for such anxieties can be found in texts that portrayed non-Christians, including Asian "pagans" as well as Muslims and Jews, as the black offspring of Satan, and Africans as "Devils incarnate," because of their pagan religions and their skin color. Determined as they were to civilize the "heathen," some Europeans wondered if people whose beliefs were spawned by the devil could really purify themselves internally as well as externally through religious conversion.

Fueling that concern was the biblical admonition that neither the Moor nor the leopard can truly change his "coat" (Jeremiah 13:23). Was the skin a meaningless veneer, as many Europeans believed, or was dark skin a sign of deeper evil? The question echoed the ancient suspicion that women could be beguiling on the exterior but evil within. With such questions, concern about color and religion interacted with gender ideology from the Crusades onwards, as evident in racialized gendered conversion motifs, such as the fair-skinned Saracen woman accepting Christianity. Her conversion demonstrated not only the power of a superior patriarchal religion but also the significance of light skin as a sign of inner purity. Another motif featured the conversion of foreign black queens by powerful white kings (as Solomon had transformed the black-skinned Sheba). This motif signified the power of a European feudal monarch to contain "the danger of alien femininity."[3] Through such stories, religion in general was simultaneously gendered and colored as a proto-racial marker, and Christianity in particular was simultaneously masculinized and whitened.

For Britons during the Renaissance, religious anxieties were intertwined with the historical revisionism that followed the English Reformation, after Henry VIII broke with Rome. Britons rationalized Anglican Protestantism as a return to their true Teutonic roots, which signified Anglo Saxon superiority over Catholicized (feminized) Europeans. The claim that the Anglican Church could be traced to Joseph of Arimathea's visit to the British Isles, when he allegedly brought the Holy Grail, reinforced the British Teutonic heritage in which masculinity was associated with democratic institutions and respect for women, but did not recognize women's agency in their own freedom.[4]

In the midst of such anxieties, travel narratives and journals by European explorers and traders who voyaged to the Americas and southern Africa from the fifteenth through the seventeenth century, reinforced self-serving claims about cultural differences, but they did not yet track modern racial difference. When writers mentioned "complexion" in such narratives, they typically meant the circumstantial effects of climate and humors, which affected the skin and gave rise to varied personality and cultural types. For many, darker skin could accompany quite admirable traits.[5]

British notions about their (masculine) superiority in the sixteenth and seventeenth centuries had some associations with skin color. That is, many Britons credited England's felicitous climate and humors, which created their white and rosy complexions, for their booming economy. Invoking climate and humors as markers of superiority was not yet a racialist tendency, since both were considered incidental and not permanent biological attributes. Yet the function of such claims illustrates how racialism and racism work. Attributing success to their skin and geographical location allowed Britons to avoid acknowledging the role of the African slave trade in their national wealth and to delude themselves into believing that their interests "united mankind in the blessed chains of brotherly love, society, and mutual dependence."[6]

Literary and visual representations of skin color during the Renaissance suggest to some scholars a more judgmental undercurrent of black-skin racism in the early modern period. Kim Hall and Ania Loomba, for example, view the prevalent dark and light literary tropes and visual metaphors as proof of this view. Roxann Wheeler and Jennifer Morgan disagree, arguing that blackness was a complex, contradictory, and somewhat opaque symbol at the time. They claim that depictions of black people, especially in relation to whites, were more emblematic of religious and cultural differences than of racial valuation. Wheeler argues that visual artists used African figures to symbolize death and decay and to situate black men as foils for the whiteness and refinement of European women only in order to make a religious point. The skin contrast represented civilized, saved Christians versus uncivilized, damned heathens.[7]

Given the larger picture of "complexion" and religious anxiety during the Renaissance, the latter view seems more likely. In any case, both sides of the debate agree that skin color had gender connotations during the early modern period. Hall notes, for example, that "black" often connoted the polar opposite of beauty or "fairness," most frequently in reference to women's appearance or moral states. To be black, therefore, was to be "unwomanly," which translated into deviance from general European standards.[8] Moreover, skin color intermingled with ideas about women as a "race," a distinct group whose "physical difference corresponds to inner qualities." Emblematic of this theme was the ubiquitous mythical race of "mankind women," or Amazons, who represented a constant threat. Non-Europeans, non-Christians, and immigrants, like the Roma or Gypsies, were linked to a proto-racial idea. The Roma, for example, were seen as a dangerous mix of Moorish blackness, Catholicism, and Egyptian barbarity who threatened orderly hierarchical societies just as women allegedly did.[9]

Women's Bodies and Conquest

The importance of female physiognomy and sexual behavior to overall cultural classification was strikingly evident in Renaissance travel narratives, which commented in detail on women's bodes and sexuality.[10] Whether cloistered, as in Asia, or basically naked, as in parts of the New World, women's bodies became markers of cultural inferiority and/or savagery.[11] By the same token, lands to be explored or colonized were often described as unknown "female" territory and figured as bodies to be entered and conquered. To Christopher Columbus, " 'the earth was shaped like a breast, with the Indies composing the nipple.' " To Walter Raleigh, Guiana was a territory that "hath yet her Maidenhead."[12]

Amerigo Vespucci's narratives from his 1502 voyage to the New World clearly illustrate explorers' use of women's bodies to assess a new culture. Vespucci measured Amerindians' strangeness by their women's hyper-fertility and ability to "travayle in maner without payne," which contrasted with the reproductive patterns of their delicate European sisters. That such women were alleged to bite off the penises of their sexual partners constituted the " 'fylth' and shamelessness of all indigenous people." Vespucci also measured Amerindians' familiarity by their women; their un-"wimpeled" bodies and firm breasts linked their whole people to Europeans.[13] Italian explorer Gerlamo Benzoni also "sexualized indigenous women . . . as markers of difference." Because Venezuelan women were nude, painted their faces black, and wore earrings heavy enough to distend their earlobes, Benzoni declared the whole lot an "inhuman monstrosity."[14]

Journals and travel narratives also reveal that explorers and conquerors used the bodies of indigenous women as "the site of the strategic symbolic oscillation between [male] self and Other," in Stephen Greenblatt's words.[15] Christopher Columbus, for example, displayed Spanish civility and generosity by inviting a woman back to his ship, feeding her well, clothing her in "fayre apparel," and then releasing her back to her people. Unfortunately, the woman so used did not necessarily fare well. In the Latin American case, women seen as cooperating with invaders inspired the legend of La Malinche, or the Amerindian "Eve," whose alleged sexual betrayal with the conquering enemy, even through rape, has haunted Latinas ever since.

Because religion and clothing were such important measures of "otherness" in the early modern period, they intermingled both with each other and with gender and "complexion" as markers of an indigenous people's degree of civilization. Clothing represented "religious, class, national, and personal identity," according to Wheeler, and offered insight into character and quality of mind. But clothing also indicated a people's acceptance of "proper gender and political subordination," and native nudity, seen as monstrous by many Europeans, was a clear reminder of the importance of gender-appropriate clothing to civilization. (On the other side of the gaze, many indigenous people wondered why Europeans obscured their sex with garments. A few explorers even had to strip in order to prove they were men.)[16] Since nudity also marked a people as "heathen," clothing the natives was a way to convince them of their subordinate place in God's creation, just as European women had been convinced before them.

Breasts

Women's breasts were especially important indicators of civilization, and of Europeans' fluctuating assessments of Amerindians and Africans. Breasts were not an entirely new metaphor, since they had been prominently featured in depictions of mythical "alien or monstrous" peoples in ancient and medieval times.[17] But the flood of breast assessments as a key symbol of actual cultural observation was new in the early modern period, when European travel journals and narratives used them as barometers of imperial goals. For example, in his 1671 compilation of earlier texts, John Ogilby quotes British writers who praised the high perky breasts of the women of Hispaniola as signifiers of their defiance of Spanish rule. The women had aborted fetuses to deprive the Spanish of slaves. The same women's breasts began to sag in Briton's descriptions, as the visitors became warier of the natives, only to rise again in the late seventeenth century, when drooping breasts "all but disappeared" from explorers' accounts. When the political winds shifted again, Amerindian women's breasts sagged again, particularly in narratives about Granada, Guiana, and Chile. Among other things, sagging breasts associated South Amerindian peoples with Africans, whom Europeans increasingly disparaged.[18]

The profitable market in slaves, which by the late seventeenth century had an insatiable appetite for African bodies, was primarily responsible for making Africans "the parameters of the colonizing venture," according to Morgan. As a means of endorsing the lucrative slave trade, European exploration narratives and journals depicted both African men and women as sexually deviant. African men had unnaturally large "members," for example, which threatened to harm both women and fetuses. But it was the women's fecundity, sexual availability, monstrous bodies, proclivity for copulation with apes, and consistently pendulous breasts—especially their breasts—that primarily signified African deviance. What more evidence did Europeans need of African monstrousness than the sight of women's breasts so long that babies could suckle over their mothers' shoulders? Such anomalies symbolized the uncivilized nature of the entire continent.[19]

William Towrson was among the first Englishmen to use pendulous breasts as the primary symbol of African bestiality. Reporting on his journey in 1555, Towrson also claimed that elongated breasts were the only visible distinction between the sexes. His British audience would interpret that absence of gender differentiation as a further sign of African barbarism. For Towrson and his contemporary John Lok, among others, African women's bodies and behavior forever separated godless, uncivilized Africa from Christian, civilized Europe. Even when traders like Richard Jobson (writing in 1620–21), praised African women as beautiful, clean, and appropriately shameful (a mark of civilization), such virtues only reinforced the "precarious nature of African civility." African female virtues were just a thin veneer over an inferior culture.[20]

According to Felicity Nussbaum, the "inscrutable and sexually polymorphous" African woman, who contrasted starkly to the "chaste maternal" English woman, symbolized an entire continent "up for English consumption."[21] African women's sexual "behavior and physical characteristics [not only] degraded an entire race of people," but they also justified African subservience and slavery. The women's indifference to pain in childbirth was a further indication of Africans' proper contribution to the British international economy—hard physical labor plus perpetual childbearing.[22] Even in the eighteenth century, when classification turned to ranking, "the single most significant index of racial difference [was] to be found in the pendulous breasts of Hottentot and Negro women." Contrasts between African and European women's breasts and degree of suffering in childbirth "diminished Africa's access to certainty and civilization, thus allowing for the mass appropriation that was the transatlantic slave trade."[23]

Gender and Racial Difference

By the time the concept of biological race was established at the end of the 1770s and skin color became the primary symbol of racial categories and hierarchies, the significance of human differences had long been couched in gendered terms. Breasts, clothing, reproductive norms, gender dimorphism, and sexual anatomy and behavior were the most important proto-racial distinctions among various peoples from the fifteenth to the early eighteenth centuries. Europeans had long equated "civilization" with male dominance and gender dimorphism, or the opposition and stark distinction between the sexes. Peoples had long been judged by their women's sexual and reproductive characteristics. Indeed, such attention to female characteristics and assertions of male dominance actually retarded the development of full-blown racial ideology, since European men did not relish the prospect of undermining the rationale for their own gender superiority by declaring other men inherently and permanently inferior.

As we shall see in the next section, skin color moved from the ephemeral realm of humors into the indelible realm of biology in the classification schemes of the late eighteenth century. But it remained subordinate to gender distinctions for many theorists of race who regarded skin color as only one difference among many between people of different "complexions."[24] Gender characteristics, on the other hand, remained reliable markers of incommensurability between civilized Europeans and the "savages" who so needed European direction and rule.

Here's Who You Are: Gendered Racial Classification

The second stage, *classification*, began in the late 1600s but did not achieve the status of a science until the eighteenth century, when emerging naturalists and physical anthropologists began categorizing plants, animals, and human groups. The focus on gender characteristics continued in those texts, but the emphasis began to shift from sexual norms and deviance, especially women's, to "natural" justifications for male dominance.

European classifiers of the eighteenth century, like their Renaissance forebears, inevitably interpreted to their own advantage the varieties of human beings they categorized. The prevailing view of climate and humors remained strong, however, so most naturalists regarded all men as members of the same species, composed of the same raw material, and possessed of the same potential for moral and intellectual development, even if external influences had privileged some groups—such as the rosy cheeked English—over others.[25] Few saw biblical evidence that God had created biologically distinct varieties of men. Thus, the dominant view of men's differences was *monogenesis*, which defined variations within the human race understood as a single species. Women were another story. As Christians, scientists accepted women's subordination to men as divinely and naturally ordained, justified by Eve's "sin" and God's curse.[26] Following Genesis 2, some even saw women as a separate race from men.

Climatic influences leading to differences of complexion and civil society among humans included sun exposure, winds, elevation, proximity to water, fertility of the soil, and diet. Belief in the power of climate to affect human behavior and appearance can be traced to the Greeks, who thought their own medium complexions were most favored by climate. The Greeks also originated the theory of humors—blood, phlegm, black bile, and yellow bile. Greek humors related primarily to personalities, although they could also influence skin color, but "complexion" connoted more than skin. It also referred to the four humors and only acquired stable somatic meanings during the Renaissance.[27]

Well into the eighteenth century, most Europeans believed that changes in climate and humors could alter temperament and external appearance, depending on a person's age, sex, life conditions, and geographic location. If dark skin resulted from excessive excretions of black bile that seeped into the skin from the liver, then the skin itself could lighten with a change in that humor.[28] What constituted a humor also expanded, so that theorists identified educational, environmental, and cultural change as elements of the humoral mix, whose alteration could affect both appearance and behavior. British author Henry Fielding even identified commerce as a humor that could alter the complexion.[29]

Francois Bernier, who was the first European to use *race* in a physiological sense, was an exception. He did not accept the theory of climatic and humoral influences in the creation of human differences. Rather, in his "*Nouvelle division de la terre par les differents espèces ou races qui l'habitent*," published in 1684, Bernier identified four distinct human racial groups on the basis of physical appearance (including the women's attractiveness) instead of on the basis of geographic region or climate. On those new grounds, he linked Europeans with Maylasians, northern Indians, North Africans, and North Americans. Bernier did not immediately start a trend, however, possibly because of his counter-intuitive connections. Most naturalists, such as the Englishman Richard Bradley, stuck with region and climatic zones. In 1721 Bradley defined two black, two white, and one mulatto race on those grounds in his *A Physical Account of the Works of Nature*. Bernier's influence can be detected in Bradley's work, however, since he noted that skin color and hair texture also characterized those groups.[30]

Many other eighteenth-century theorists constructed racial and proto-racial taxonomies that reinforced the unifying single " 'chain of universal being,' " a Christianized version of the Greek Great Chain of Being, in which similarities among sentient beings outweighed their differences and "man" stood as a "middling creature" between inanimate things, the lowliest life forms, and intelligent animals, on the one hand; and ranks of heavenly creatures and God on the other.[31] Carl Linnaeus, for example, identified four groups (which he did not call races) within Nature's grand design in 1735, based on the four elements (air, earth, fire, and water) and the corresponding compass directions, the four humors, and the four known continents (America, Europe, Asia, and Africa).[32] Montesquieu defined three races in 1748 as equivalent and complementary contributors to the present world. Each race represented an historical stage or time period—political, feudal, and post-political and post–feudal—and each played an important role in human progress.[33]

Even Bernier's disciple, Johann Blumenbach (the "father of anthropology") accepted monogenesis as well as the theory of climate and humors to explain human differences. But Blumenbach's work marks a transitional moment in racial formation because he also ranked races. In 1775, he translated Linnaeus's four categories into five human *varietas*—Caucasian, Mongolian, Ethiopian, American, and Malay—and ranked each group's physical attractiveness, especially the women's. He selected Caucasians as the race most favored by climate and humors, and therefore the most beautiful, and proclaimed other races a degeneration of the original Georgian type. That choice implied the superiority of white skin, but it did not establish skin as the primary marker of racial value, since Blumenbach was equally interested in the shape of skulls and faces, and the texture of hair. In addition, his racial groupings were intentionally indistinct and overlapping, which undermined a strict racial hierarchy.[34]

The Male Racial Subject

While downplaying skin color, such theories departed from earlier depictions of "others" by accentuating the male role as primary racial subject. Scientific race was about men's differences from one another and women's relationship to men's desires and activities. Women existed in early scientific treatises only in terms of their sexual and reproductive attributes and their attractiveness to men. By the same token, climate and humors could not alter Nature's plan for the two sexes, which, not coincidentally, reinforced European custom. Males were always meant to be active, smart, and dominant, and females were always meant to be passive, attractive, and subordinate to men. Adherence to early patterns rendered some races civilized, like Europeans, and deviance from the patterns rendered other races savage, like Africans. Fixed notions of the sexes' "natural" differences from one another reinforced man's "objective" superiority over woman.

Bernier's selection of the male beard as a measure of racial distinction further illustrates the primacy of the male racial subject. Scanty beards linked Black Africans, Asians, and Lapps and marked their inferiority to Europeans and North Africans. Richard Bradley also used the beard to distinguish among five human types, although he did not consider beardlessness a sign of an inferior mind. Both American naturalist Richard McCausland and French theorist Montesquieu considered American Indians inferior because of their beardlessness or sparse beards. Indeed, the beard remained an important racial marker as late as 1848, when Charles Hamilton Smith pitted bearded Caucasians against beardless "Mongolics." Even when beards were not a theorist's focus, male racial primacy typically characterized his system of racial classification. Although Blumenbach, like de Rochefort, debunked the importance of the beard (on the grounds that Indians knew how to eliminate their beards by artifice—something akin to skin painting), he considered women's beauty a racial characteristic that served men's choice of reproductive partners.[35]

In assuming male racial primacy, such theories also reinforced the concept of male superiority. Beards, sweat, and semen had early associations with men's capacity to process heat; all were, therefore, signs of men's ability to resist the coldness of women. Men without facial hair (and, by extension, without semen and sweat) were not just racially inferior, they were also feminine, which further reduced their value in comparison to European men.[36]

Women did play a racially significant role for some environmentalists, like Blumenbach, who thought they could shape racial characteristics through their treatment or deliberate manipulation of babies. African mothers carried their babies against their backs, for example, so they had flat noses. German babies had big heads because mothers put them to sleep on their backs. Mothers might also manipulate babies' noses, lips, or heads to create specific characteristics, which some theorists thought could eventually be handed down through the generations.[37]

Overall, however, from Linnaeus forward, racial taxonomies typically omitted women except with regard to their sexual and reproductive characteristics. Little attention was paid to women's independent intelligence or behavior.[38] Linnaeus, for example, stayed fixated on African women's breasts, which gave abundant milk, and on "Hottentot" women's pelvises, which were narrow. Often "observations" of women's sexual and reproductive characteristics were directly correlated to some male characteristic, as when eighteenth-century naturalists concluded, on the still influential theory of humors, that women of the beardless races must lack a menstrual flow.[39] Given the focus on other anatomical features, breasts were subordinated in importance, but numerous classification systems still assigned racial value to differences between European women's spherical breasts and the elongated, sagging breasts of their primitive counterparts. When Blumenbach pointed out the inconsistency of breast size within races and the varied standards of beauty between races, he went largely unheard, since the prevailing tide was turning toward fixed notions of racialized sexual types.[40]

Cross-racial comparisons that highlighted female characteristics only focused on women's sexual allure to men or reproductive fitness—feminine beauty, the redness of lips, the length and style of hair, the size and shape of clitorises, the degree of sexual desire, and, most importantly, the size, shape, and position of pelvises, which allegedly determined a woman's suitability for childbearing. Of particular interest to European ethnographers in the realm of comparative female anatomy was the "Hottentot apron," the elongation of the labia minora, or inner vaginal lips, among that African tribe's women, first identified by John Ovington in 1689. On the basis of that anatomical detail, Ovington had concluded that Hottentot women were hermaphrodites. In the eighteenth century, Voltaire declared it a sign that Hottentots were a separate species of humans, thereby anticipating the rise of *polygenesis* in the next century.[41]

Gender Dimorphism, Male Dominance

No gender qualities were more important to judgments of stratified racial value among eighteenth-century racial classifiers than the concepts of radical sexual dimorphism, male dominance, and gender role complementarity in particular groups. Many physical anthropologists ultimately ranked Europeans highest among human groups because of the distinct differences between men's and women's anatomy, dress, and behavior. Using the same standard, they considered African women "masculinized," which further proved the bestiality of the Negro race.[42] As we shall see in Part II, Africans' alleged lack of radical sexual dimorphism became a tenet of race-based slavery in the U.S.

Botanists of the period also classified plants and animals according the same "fixed and inherent" European gender norms being used by budding anthropologists. Indeed, they considered reproduction Nature's key indicator of plant species design, even when that principle conflicted with observable traits. After botanists discovered in the seventeenth century that plants reproduce sexually and that sexual functioning differs across some plant species, the concept of radical sexual dimorphism became a primary principle for classifying the natural world. Sebastien Vaillant, Carl Linneaus, and Erasmus Darwin (Charles's father), all developed classification systems that emphasized plants' sexual organs and reproductive strategies. That Nature herself did not always require sexual dimorphism in plant reproduction did not deter them. Linnaeus in particular overlooked the fact that many plants were hermaphroditic in his *Systema Naturae*, published in 1735 and widely adopted through the first decades of the nineteenth century.[43] He called plants' reproductive parts husbands (*andria*) and wives (*gynia*) (from the Greek *aner* and *gyne*) and discussed plant reproductive behavior through marriage metaphors, such as bridal gowns and veils.[44]

Zoologists followed a similarly androcentric and sexually dimorphic path and produced similar paradoxes and contradictions. Most believed until the mid-eighteenth century, for example, that the ruling bee in every hive was a "king," even though that "king" gave birth. Early naturalists simply could not believe that male drones would work so hard for a female "queen"—another example of the triumph of human dimorphic social function over biological fact.[45]

The emerging fields of human medicine and anatomy extended the naturalists' and anthropologists' gender biases. Scholars in those fields were as focused on reproductive function as their colleagues in zoology and botany, but they went even further. They sought anatomical evidence of the "natural" division and stratification of the sexes in bones, organs, nerves, and hair as well as in reproductive physiology. The larger context, as Thomas Laqueur has argued, was the science of sexuality and sexual temperament, in which the "one sex" Aristotelian/Galenic/biblical model—with woman as an imperfect man—was being replaced by a "two sex" model "of radical biological divergence" that identified sexual difference as basic to the fabric of the human body. Like their fellows in other fields, anatomists also "found" those differences regardless of what was actually there and used them to justify gender inequality and the sexual division of labor and leadership as part of the "natural" social order.[46] The quest for distinct gender species would soon be reflected in the search for racially distinct species of humans.

Gender considerations also influenced medical theorists and practitioners to abandon environmentalism in the mid-eighteenth century. Physicians like Petrus Camper were particularly keen to refute environmentalism, especially women's role in shaping nature, in order to exclude women from science and medicine and, therefore, from any stake in the rising medical profession (an exclusion that would also be extended to men of "inferior races").[47]

A shift to bones as the focus of racial classification among anthropologists toward the end of the eighteenth century reinforced both the superiority of white skin and the primacy of the male racial subject. It was *men's* skulls, faces, and head bumps that would occupy phrenologists, from Johann Kaspar Lavater in the late eighteenth century to Dr. Charles Caldwell in the 1830s. It was *men's* cranial anatomy that determined human character and eventually provided "scientific evidence" of superior and inferior races.[48] (That skull size might, among other things, correlate with body size did not, apparently, resonate with these scientists.) Men of superior (larger, lighter-skinned) races had greater skull capacity—and thus greater intelligence—than their (smaller, darker-skinned) brothers. In effect, the mark of a man's inferiority was the similarity of his skull size to that of a woman. By the 1820s, many racial classifiers concluded that the lowest races were the most feminine of skull.[49]

Here's What You're Good For: Gendered Racial Ranking

The third phase, *ranking*, emerged gradually from the confluence of scientific, religious, economic, and political discourse in the late eighteenth and early nineteenth centuries. There were very early "rankers," such as John Ovington, who defined Hottentots in his *Voyage to Suratt in the Year 1689* as a "bestial. ... off-brand of Negro."[50] And mid-seventeenth-century scholar William Petty, founder of the British Royal Society, also linked physiological characteristics to the varied "qualities of [men's] minds."[51] But starting in about 1775, even monogenesist physical anthropologists began pointing toward stratified racial value by legitimizing "the idea that some variable formative force, moved by degenerative and regenerative processes of maturation and mixture, mutilation and milieus, accounted for observable [racial] differences" and produced better or worse races.[52] The American monogenesist, Princeton president Samuel Stanhope Smith, for example, explained in his 1787 *Essay on the Causes of the Variety of Complexion and Figure in the Human Species* that humans might be a single species, but environmentally-produced differences in physiques and mental capacities rendered white men superior to the darker races. Smith's essay dominated the discussion of race in the immediate post-Revolutionary period U.S.[53]

The first European text to identify systematic anatomical distinctions that "proved" Negro inferiority was also penned by a monogenesist, German anatomist Samuel Thomas von Soemmerring. Though he opposed slavery, Soemmerring argued his 1784 *Übber die körperliche Verschiedenheit des Mohren vom Europäer* (Concerning the physical difference between the Moor and the European) that Africans were a morally and intellectually inferior race. For good measure, he declared Africans' flat noses innate, rather than environmentally (or maternally) created.[54] Soemmerring's work remained the basic European text on African physique until the mid-nineteenth century.[55] That he quickly turned from studying racial anatomical differences to studying female anatomy, with the purpose of differentiating male and female physiques at the level of hair, bones, and sinew, further reinforces the underlying interconnection between theories of racial and gender species dimorphism.[56]

The serious ranking of races intensified when *monogenesis*, or the belief in variations among human groups within a single human family (created by God), was replaced by *polygenesis*, or the belief in multiple human species (possibly created in separate divine acts) with permanent, rankable differences, whose number was a matter of some dispute.[57] Polygenesis was not fully accepted, even in the U.S., until the 1850s, spurred by publication of *Types of Mankind* by George Glidden and Josiah Nott in 1854. Before that, physical anthropologist Samuel George Morton had popularized the idea that male cranial measurement was the key to racial difference. Morton delighted slaveholders by "proving" in his *Crania Americana* (1839) and *Crania Aegyptica* (1844) that large cranial capacity and white skin color were the gold standards of racial worth.[58] Slaveholders were even more delighted by Morton's claim in the latter work that large-skulled Egyptians were Caucasians who had enslaved cranially inferior black Africans.[59]

As we have seen, gender was a crucial element in the transition during the mid-nineteenth century from monogenesis to polygenesis, but polygenesis really shifted its focus. Measurements of female pelvises and breasts and evaluations of female sexual behavior took a further back seat to detecting degrees of gender dimorphism and male dominance in various races, as indicated primarily by the size of male skulls. Indeed, male cranial measurements became and "remained the central icon of racial difference until craniometry was replaced by intelligence testing in the late-nineteenth and early twentieth centuries," according to Londa Schiebinger.[60]

Skin color increasingly reinforced gender judgments in theories of polygenesis, thanks in large part to the slave trade that thrived on polygenetic rationales for the absolute superiority of white Europeans and the absolute inferiority of black Africans, which justified their captivity. Like European women, such inferior folks—male and female—required the supervision of Caucasian males.[61] As the white man's biological inferiors, Africans of both sexes and white women were incapable of public roles and unworthy of fully human status. They could only improve themselves by serving the white man's interests.

Religious Problems, Gendered Solutions

The transition to polygenesis was not entirely smooth, primarily because it required some fancy footwork by religious thinkers who had to reinterpret the Bible in order to justify species distinction between humans. They were aided in that task by a rare negative biblical association with dark skin that also had gender connotations.[62] Pamphlets and religious writings in the early nineteenth century chose Genesis 9:18–27—which recounts Noah's curse of Ham (really of Ham's son, Canaan) for having seen him naked and drunk—as proof that dark skin signifies racial inferiority.[63] Although the passages make no mention of either skin color or race, they provided determined believers with a post-creation story that explained both the existence of separate races and their stratification.

This conclusion was assisted by the tradition, going as far back as the medieval *Zohar*, of defining Ham as the darkener of the world and as the post-flood incarnation of Cain—the progenitor of demons and evil spirits. Ham's brother Shem was called the post-flood incarnation of Able—the father of peaceful and merciful descendants. "Darkener" and "black skin" are not synonyms, of course. In fact, the fourteenth century narrative, *The Travels of Sir John Mandeville,* identified Asians as the "dark" descendants of Ham.[64] But by the sixteenth century, the idea that black Africans were the sons of Ham (as well as Muslim infidels) was a staple of European religious, though not yet racial, thought. What was new in the nineteenth century was the idea, embraced by politicians and slave-owners, that Ham's curse constituted a permanent biological condition. American essayist J.J. Flournoy, for example, argued in 1835 that Negroes were descendants of Adam and Eve, but they became an inferior race when God revived the curse of Cain in Ham and his descendants. Thus, Africans were twice fallen.[65]

Such interpretations of Ham's fate were gendered because of the parallels interpreters could draw between the stories of Noah and the Garden of Eden. The *Zohar* made the connection explicit by linking the terms of Noah's curse with those used in Genesis to curse the serpent.[66] This link tied Ham's enslaved descendants to Eve's daughters and connected racial inferiority and slavery with both women's inferiority and their destiny to suffer and submit.

Embarrassing Implications

Even as many forces, including polygenesis, converged to condemn black Africans to racial inferiority on the basis of religious, cranial, cultural, and epidural arguments, some European men still saw a problem. If certain men's skulls were smaller and therefore inferior to other men's skulls, as phrenologists claimed, or if certain men's skin marked them as inferior, as advocates of slavery declared, then on what grounds could men's superiority to women be considered a universal fact of Nature? Swiss zoologist Carl Vogt (1817–1895) addressed this dilemma in his 1864 *Lectures on Man, His Place in Creation, and in the History of the Earth*. Vogt noted that male superiority, measured by cranial capacity, characterized advanced cultures, while the opposite was true in backwards cultures, like Africa. Male dominance, therefore, signified a culture's advancement. Vogt claimed that the whole black race was regressive because African men's and women's crania were similar in size. (Never mind that skull "measurements" were blatantly imprecise.) Through such machinations, the "production of blackness as sexual difference" paved the way for numerous subsequent scientific comparisons of black men and white women, according to Robyn Wiegman. Blackness was further feminized, and "Vogt advanced an understanding of race that pivoted on the paradigm of sexual difference." Now women were seen as the earliest stage of a race's development.[67]

Convoluted logic was also required to explain away another embarrassing comparative fact for polygenesists. Since many African women had bigger pelvises than European women, they could be seen as superior procreators. But so intent were race "scientists" to use gender data to prove Negro inferiority that they declared female pelvis size proof of Negroes' animality rather than of their childbearing capacity. Moritz Weber's 1830 *Theory of Fundamental and Racial Forms of the Skull and Pelvis in Humankind* went even further to proclaim the oblong African female pelvis a bestial characteristic that did not, in fact, promote ease in childbearing. It was women's primitive lifestyle not their anatomy that made childbirth painless. Moreover, Weber connected African women's oblong pelvis with their steatopygia (protruding buttocks), which he considered a natural adaptation meant to compensate for Negro racial deficiencies by mimicking the rounder pelvises of the "higher races."[68]

Gendered Racial Fitness

As ideas about racial species and hierarchies evolved in gendered terms throughout the nineteenth century, they were reinforced by the works of Herbert Spencer and Charles Darwin, published between 1842 and 1870. Spencer's followers found support for white supremacy in his argument that the quality of a society depends on the character of its members rather than on its design or industry. "The defective natures of citizens will show themselves in the bad acting of whatever social structure they are arranged into. There is no political alchemy by which you can get golden conduct out of leaden instincts," Spencer claimed.[69] The best societies, therefore, must control the racial quality of their citizens by monitoring the passage of racial blood, typically by controlling women's reproductive choices.[70]

Although Darwin argued that the ultimate potential of women and racial minorities could not really be determined because the conditions of their lives were so unlike those of white men, such disclaimers had little effect.[71] Darwinians also ignored the many similarities among the races described in *Descent of Man*, published in 1870, in favor of Darwin's claim that there was "no doubt that the various races, when carefully compared and measured, differ much from each other" in both physical and mental characteristics. That conclusion, plus his association of women's qualities with those of "lower races," undermined his egalitarian arguments and encouraged interpretations of his work as a mandate for social caution: control white women's reproduction to minimize the havoc that the lesser races might wreak on the social fabric.[72]

The "scientific racism" that emerged from Spencerian and Darwinian thought and was eventually supported by evolutionary biologists clearly demonstrates another role of gender in the construction of race. To racial rankers, the survival of higher cultures depended on preventing the dilution of "superior" blood by exposure to the inferior blood of minority races, especially that of Negroes (and the Chinese, who were sometimes classified as black). As the institution of slavery promoted white men's cross-racial reproduction, especially in the U.S., white women were increasingly held responsible for transmitting white racial blood and, therefore, for preserving white supremacy, as we shall see in more detail in Part III. That is why miscegenation between white women and black men ultimately became the most inflammatory issue in whites' opposition to the social assimilation of blacks. Ceilia Daileader traces this anxiety back to "Othellophilia."[73] Restricting white women's sexual and reproductive behavior became the lynchpin of white racial identity and alleged superiority.

3

Gendered Racial Institutions

World Slavery and Nationhood

Discourse and practice merged in two powerful social institutions that shaped racial ideology in gendered terms—the nation-state and slavery. Both had roots in ancient and medieval ideas and customs, but they evolved and ultimately converged just as Europeans were spreading their influence and asserting their will, often in competition with one another, across the known world. Chapter 3 discusses the gendered foundations of both institutions primarily in Europe, leaving a deeper discussion of their evolution in North America for Parts II and IV.

The Gendered Roots of Slavery

The African slave trade had obvious effects on the development of racial ideology—particularly on the construction of a black-white racial dichotomy—as we saw in Chapter 2. But long before slavery was equated with skin color in Europe and the New World, it had serious gender connotations that helped to construct racial hierarchies. Indeed, until the late fifteenth century, the concept of bondage had greater gender than racial connotations, since it had little to do with skin and much to do with feminizing certain men and hyper-sexualizing certain women. For much of its history, slavery had little to do with appearance at all because slaves were not born to their status. Rather, slavery was typically a status conferred upon rather than endemic to and perpetual for human beings and their progeny.

From Mesopotamia and Sumer (8000–2000 B.C.E.),[1] to Egypt (before 1700 B.C.E.), to Shang Dynasty China (between 1700 and 1100 B.C.E.), to Assyria and Babylonia (between 700 and 500 B.C.E.), to Greece (between 900 and 300 B.C.E.), to Rome (in the third century

B.C.E slave heyday), and even to the American colonies (until the late 1600s), most slaves were captives, often taken in war or on the high seas. (Some thought such captives lucky to be enslaved and alive rather than free and dead.) Slavery also befell certain criminals and hapless children whose parents sold them to settle debts. Under such circumstances, slavery was a matter of ill fortune, not an inherent or necessarily lifelong status. Nor was it necessarily an inheritable condition. Indeed, most slaves' offspring intermarried into and disappeared within the enslaving population.[2]

During the centuries when bondage was a temporary mark of human inferiority, however, sex was considered an inherent and permanent sign of human worth and status. Sex distinction, therefore, became a convenient model for master-slave relations. It was common for ancient slaveholders to justify their enslavement of men by equating them with women. Plato even argued that male slaves, like all women, had greater association with the body than did slave-masters and husbands, who allegedly transcended their bodies and signified the rational soul. Aristotle considered Greek women and slaves equally inferior to free Greek men.[3] His idea that natural slaves were "marked out for subjection.... from the hour of their birth" also invoked women's inherently inferior and subordinate "nature."[4] In both Greece and Rome, women and enslaved men achieved their allegedly true purpose in life through their oppression. The disparagement of slaves' humanity prefigured what we now call "racism," but it was initially closer to Greek gender ideology than to ideas about biological race.

Even before recorded history, slavery had a gendered identity. Historians now agree that the first slaves were probably women, as Gerda Lerner hypothesized decades ago, and that slaves' inferior status reflected women's inferior status in patriarchal societies. During the millennia when most slaves were captives taken in war, according to Lerner, women functioned as objects of exchange among men to promote economic and reproductive relationships. Thus, women were set up to become desirable spoils of war, especially when rape could produce offspring that would tie them psychologically to their captors' tribes or villages. "For long periods, perhaps centuries, while enemy males were being killed by their captors or severely mutilated or transported to isolated and distant areas, females and children were made captives and incorporated into the households and society of the captors."[5] Orlando Patterson also explains that hunting-and-gathering peoples typically killed male captives because they represented a threat, but women's reproductive capacity and agricultural skills qualified them for enslavement.[6] It wasn't until the second millennium B.C.E.

that a few advanced civilizations incorporated large numbers of male slaves into their social structures.[7]

Slavery's gendered roots also included sexual exploitation, starting in ancient times. Female slaves suffered most from that practice, but male slaves could also become pawns in their mistresses' sexual escapades. The Roman slave Aesop, for example, was seduced by (and eventually also seduced) his mistress, who lusted after a "young, handsome, athletic, good-looking blond slave" like himself. Muslim Arabs preferred female slaves in the seventh century, presumably for sexual and reproductive purposes, and castrated the men. (They later preferred male slaves, probably for labor capacity rather than sex.) Gender differences among slaves also determined the kind of work a slave could do, the potential growth of the slave population, and the safety of their captors. Gender stereotypes and entrenched gender norms also shaped the terms and enforcement of slavery, even when captors attempted to dehumanize and unsex enslaved populations.[8]

The feminization of enslaved men started early and continued for centuries. Male Sumerian slaves were required to lower their eyes, like women, to keep them from seeing the free female population.[9] Roman and Canon law feminized male slaves by declaring that their *peculium* or primary obligation belonged to their masters, which meant they must forego other responsibilities and obligations, such as those of marriage, that would undermine a master's authority.[10] That regulation de-masculated male slaves by denying them men's prerogative of dominion over a wife. It had less effect on female slaves, since women were obligated to obey a male master in any case, whether owner or husband.

Then Skin

Skin color became an important marker of slavery (though not yet of biological race) to Europeans sometime after 1470, when the Portuguese established a stable slave trade with African states.[11] At that point the trade increasingly involved African leaders who sold their own people, sometimes for gold and sometimes for European products. Enslavement, therefore, was no longer simply a matter of chance, conquest, captivity, or kidnapping, as it had been for centuries—a status conferred. Rather, the majority of slaves for export were a particular people, already enslaved, who happened to be black—a status inherent.[12] Thus, while many citizens of Lisbon and Seville in the 1450s regarded blackness as one skin color among many and assimilable to their population, by 1480 they were more likely to regard black skin as the mark of a pagan people destined for servitude.[13] Coupled with longstanding Arab prejudice against Africans, the Portuguese slave trade contributed to pejorative views of African peoples and cultures by the British from as early as the sixteenth century, although, as we have seen, they did not focus on blackness as a marker of inferiority until the 1680s, when they became solidly committed to the slave trade.[14] Even so, since black slavery predated wholesale black racism, many Africans imported to the young English colonies were temporary rather than permanent slaves.

All of this is not to say that physiological differences such as skin color and hair texture were completely ignored in the ancient and medieval worlds. Indeed, such distinctions were clearly observed as early as 1350 B.C.E., when they appeared in Egyptian tomb carvings of curly-haired Africans. Aristotle compared geographical groups and defined physiological distinctions among peoples from the cold north and the hot south, a view of "complexion" that only hinted at differences in skin color. He claimed, for example, that those living in a cold climate and in Europe were full of spirit but "wanting in intelligence and skill." Such judgments did not necessarily single out blackness, however. Indeed, even though biblical Hebrews as well as the Greeks and Romans were openly hostile toward many "others," including Egyptians, Canaanites, Persians, Phoenicians, Syrians and each other, and even though the Greeks and Romans definitely favored certain facial features, there seems to have been no distinct anti-black racism in antiquity.[15]

Rather, according to Scott Malcomson, for the peoples of the Mediterranean, "a rough equating of white and black, northern and southern, as naturally inferior populations continued . . . well into the fourteenth century." The Greeks, Spanish, and Portuguese extolled—no surprise—their own temperate middle-range complexions as the ideal human type. Muslim scholars considered Iraquis, who became the tenth-century standard human type in the Muslim world, the golden mean between the "undercooked" peoples of the cold north and the "burned" peoples of hot countries. Their pale brown color indicated "sound minds, commendable passions, balanced natures and high proficiency in every art." Such cultures deemed both extremes—whites and blacks—inferior and, therefore, good candidates for enslavement. That the word *slave* was derived from *Slav* reflects such a Mediterranean perspective.[16]

By the same token, Western slavery had a color scheme as early as the Middle Ages to the extent that buyers and sellers in the

Mediterranean might note the color of the merchandise: a Moor of intermediate hue, a black Saracen, a white Saracen, a white Tatar, etc. But at that point, the slave population was about 52 percent European, 20 percent Saracen, 18 percent *loro*, and 10 percent black. Moreover, slaves of all colors were seldom permanent slaves, as we have seen, and their descendents were usually free. Even the approximately four million sub-Saharan Africans transported to the Mediterranean markets between 700 and the mid-1400s typically intermingled with the native populations, thereby providing much of today's Mediterranean and European population with black African ancestors.[17]

Blackness crept into some medieval narratives about slaves and serfs because peasants' constant exposure to sun and dirt often darkened their skin. Paul Freedman argues that serfs and peasants in medieval Western Europe were "commonly depicted as subhuman and even 'black,'" although their pivotal role in food production helped to overcome their "bestiality" and filth. Contempt for such blackened peasants, when it existed, was more an expression of class consciousness than of racial discrimination.[18]

Then Both

Even as skin color came to dominate the institution of Western slavery, gender analogies remained important to its rationalization. That was partly because Christian slavery advocates had more luck finding biblical justifications for male dominance than for slavery. The Hebrew Bible even denounces slavery (at least for Hebrews, although Leviticus allows "heathens" to be enslaved), which inspired abolitionists to argue against brutally using and exploiting human beings created in God's image.[19] But New Testament passages that linked the master-slave relationship with the gender hierarchies God sanctions offered hope. A favorite passage was Ephesians (5:22–24; 6:5–9), where Paul simultaneously admonishes wives to defer to their husbands and slaves to obey their masters. Many Christians argued that the hierarchy among men constructed by slavery is analogous to the gender hierarchy and functional differences advocated in the Bible. Some even argued that those men who were fated to become slaves, like all women, lacked a genuine or fully-formed spirit or soul.[20]

Marriage offered another gendered biblical model for slavery advocates well into the nineteenth century. For Christians, marriage was a religious sacrament that institutionalized gender hierarchy on biblical (as well as Aristotelian) grounds: women's natural inferiority, deficiencies of soul, and uncontrolled passions. In marriage, the inferior, passionate female rightly depends on the rational, superior male for the good of society. Similarly, the inferior slave depends on the guidance of free men. The Bible also identifies some men (like all women) as "naturally" incapable of governing themselves and therefore in need of forceful restraint. That sentiment allegedly supports the violence inherent in both enslavement and marriage.[21] Reformationist Christians, especially the Puritans, "fretted endlessly over the 'masterless men' who once had a proper place in the social order" and regarded the strict control of slavery, as of marriage, a necessity for the common good.[22]

The Christian perception that good and evil are in inevitable and perpetual conflict in the world also justified slavery to Europeans, particularly the English Protestants who established race-based chattel slavery in the New World. That conflict was itself implicitly gendered since it was rooted in Eve's introduction of sin into the world and in womankind's subsequent threat to men. Thus, the "battle of the sexes" equaled the contest between God and Lucifer on Earth. As Protestants extended that gendered metaphor to slavery, they argued that enslavement would protect society from the inherent wantonness of those whom God had destined for bondage. Like the Greeks and Romans, they persuaded themselves that all women and slaves lacked the capacity for self-government and needed subjugation to better themselves.[23]

In the U.S., nineteenth-century Southern politicians played on such religious themes as they argued the wisdom of having a "class to do the menial duties" so there could also be a "class which leads progress, civilization, and refinement," in the words of Governor James Henry Hammond of South Carolina. Although Africans might not be a separate racial species, as Hammond argued in 1858, they were an inferior variation on the human standard, and they could do no better than work as slaves under superior masters.[24] Echoes of gender ideology reverberate throughout such race-based arguments.

The Gendered Foundations of Nation-as-Race

The gendered roots of the European nation-state, from the fifteenth to the nineteenth century, paralleled slavery in shaping the concept of race. Even the earliest European understanding of "nation" as the equivalent of "race" or *gens*—defined as common heritage, geographical location, bloodline, and (usually) religion—was implicitly gendered.[25]

Moreover, as developing nations faced incursions by other *gens*, gender norms and the principle of male dominance became standards for judging "others" and for asserting the primacy of "pure" national subjects, meaning males, as the proper recipients of power, resources, and opportunities.

That early modern understanding of nation-as-race (or *gens*) was gendered on many levels. For one thing, the very idea of a common heritage and bloodline implied patriliny. Indeed, the English word *race*, derived from the Anglo Saxon word *rice* and the Middle English word *ras* (used between the thirteenth and fifteenth centuries), connoted paternal lines of descent.[26] According to Holinshed's *Chronicles* of 1578, *race* meant a "house, familie, carrying of long time the same name, and the same profession," whose ancestors (either blood relations or spiritual ancestors in the Roman, Greek, or Christian political orders) had served their prince and country well.[27] Implicit in that definition is the paternal name as well as the father's profession and acts of public service. Thus, patriliny was the most important marker of a person's *gens* or race and determined his/her social role, status, and reputation.

The patriarchal view of nation-as-*gens* further implied male control of women, since the alleged female propensity for errant sexual behavior could easily disrupt lines of paternal descent.[28] As Rousseau argued, "a husband must be able to oversee his wife's conduct, because it is important to him that the children he is forced to recognize do not belong to anyone other than himself." Establishing individual paternity was the primary means of establishing the national genealogies that would eventually be biologized as race. As Nancy Tuana explains, "with both the institution of patrilineal inheritance and the belief that woman is subject to the dictates of her passions, particularly her sexual passions, the conclusion is inescapable": establishing the family, the bloodline, the nation, the race meant controlling women.[29]

The gendered foundations of nation-as-*gens* are also evident in the fact that men of different nations/races often felt more solidarity with one another than with the women of their own group. Indeed, before the concept of biological race, the cultural concept of race or *gens* sometimes created alliances among men that transcended nation. For example, Christian Crusaders who settled in Muslim lands found themselves assimilating easily with other Christians and converts, despite differences in languages, geographical origins, and cultures.[30] At other times, shared cultural values transcended religion. For example, Ivan Hannaford reminds us that, before the Inquisition, Jews "achieved a significant, honorable, and recognized place in Spain [at court and in the professions] for almost fifteen hundred years and the Moors for eight hundred years that was not determined by [religion or] 'race,' but in accordance with acknowledged political ideas, practices, and procedures." Even as the Spanish Inquisition got underway in 1480, arguments in defense of Jews and Moors were still being made on the grounds that they were descendents of different but noble lineages with a place in the history of Spain.[31] The Inquisition was designed to put an end to such assimilation by defining a "pure" Spanish Christian (paternal) bloodline and excluding deviants like Muslim Moors and "wandering" Jews.[32]

Early British explorers, such as Richard Jobson, also felt some kinship with their "primitive" male counterparts. Jobson found a lot to dislike among the Gambians, those descendants of Ham, including the men's large "members" and sexual appetites. But he admired Gambian women, as we have seen, as well as the men's curiosity and intellect, noting that they were as curious about physiological and cultural differences between themselves and Englishmen as the British were about the differences between themselves and Africans.[33] Such deference even to an inferior people reflects Jobson's appreciation of shared masculine prerogatives as well as his recognition of and respect for the patriarchal power of the princes and chiefs he likely met.[34]

Cultural camaraderie among men of different heritages, bloodlines, cultures, and/or religions was also rooted in the Greek and Roman concept of civic society, in which free, elite male citizens escaped the private or familial realm (the "community of wives and children") in order to participate in the public domain. Such men thereby distanced themselves from "idiots" (women and slaves) who were ruled by passions and "trapped in an endless, purposeless existence." Neither slaves nor free women had the opportunity to act publicly with reason, develop a good reputation, negotiate disputes, or reconcile differences peacefully. Thus, they were denied the possibility of virtue, if not by Zeus then by elite men who defined virtue as a product of distinguished service to the *polis*.[35]

Nation vs. Woman vs. Race

The gendered roots of emerging nations-as-*gens* or -races in the early modern period, including Spain, the Netherlands, France, Portugal, and England, can also be detected in nationalization processes that transferred aristocratic familial power to new central governments. The architects of those processes did not want female power included in that transference for fear of disrupting society with female passion, undermining the state's manly character, and diluting republican men's right to rule. Therefore, state formation itself "strengthened the household as an instrument of social control," as Joan Kelly explains, and reinforced patriarchy. "Laws concerning the poor and laws against vagrants, prostitutes, witches, and even religious orders in Protestant countries herded people into households for their livelihood and placed unpropertied males—and all women—under the governance of the household 'master.' Such social organizing weakened traditional supports for female authority and subjected women to patriarchal power in the family and the state."[36]

To assist in that effort, male officials resurrected and reinvigorated ancient and medieval diatribes against women, which demeaned their capacity for citizenship. Some elite women fought back with anti-misogynist tracts, known as *querelles des femmes*. Starting with Christin de Pisan's *The City of Women* in 1404, women of rank and education took issue with misogynist trends in classical texts, clerical defenses of women's confinement, and chivalric satires as the premise for women's domestic subordination in emerging states. Although the *querelles* did not stem the masculinist tide of nationalization, they did provide evidence of women's virtues as well as the causes of what Pisan called "so much slander and such blame of women and their condition." *Querelles* writers such as Pisan, Marie de Romieu (1591), Constantia Munda (1615), Anna Maria van Schuraman (1659), and Mary Astell (1703), produced multiple examples of learned and accomplished women, going back to classical Greece. They also identified men's attitudes as well as social institutions, such as marriage, as the source of women's weaknesses, thereby disputing the notion of women's inherent deficiencies.[37]

Britain's Queen Elizabeth I could have helped to reinforce women's right to political power, but instead she declined to reconcile female sexual practice with national/racial power by establishing herself as the Virgin Queen. Her celibacy even became a symbol of British imperial innocence, in contrast to the rapacity of enemy "bachelor" powers like the lustful Spaniards. Such imagery imparted moral authority to English colonial claims, including those against the Spanish for the un-possessed lands of Virginia, named for Elizabeth's chastity. Elizabethan rectitude also reinforced gender dimorphism as the foundation of English national authority, which inspired American colonists to establish Englishness abroad by recreating the patriarchal households and female domesticity that defined it at home, as we shall see in Part II.[38]

The masculine character of national/racial identities assumed in the sixteenth century would be reinforced by nationalist ideology from then on, as the control of women's behavior and rights was further institutionalized.[39] For example, British Common Law, which Anglo-Saxonophiles extolled as Teutonic in origin, promoted the concept of coverture and defined women as property—conjugal property—that was subject to governmental protection. Coverture empowered husbands, fathers, and even sons as governmental proxies to act as guardians and representatives of women's interests.[40] That same "natural" gender order was evident in the male *persona ficta* embedded in British Common law, according to which God and nature had decreed men heads of households and uniquely capable of social relations.[41]

By the nineteenth-century in Europe, "masculine and feminine, man and woman, [came] to 'embody' the logics of the 'national' in the shifting practices and ideas about norms of domesticity," according to Brackette Williams. Masculinity, defined not as brute force but as restrained energy, became the foundation of multiple nationalist ideologies, while women, or the feminine, represented the immutability underlying the dynamic, progressive (male) state. The best any woman could do was "contain her abnormality." Men of "lower races" were threats to the "national race" because of their "inappropriate gender," that is, their similarity to women and inability to control "their own" women. They were an enemy to civilization because they did not understand the so-called immutable and genuine forces of Nature, such as the fixed difference between the sexes. (Of course, Nature was opportunistically redefined as nationalist ideologies shifted.) As we shall see in more detail in Part IV, gender difference thus became the "vantage point from which the visibility of difference as race [in the nation-state] was sharply focused."[42]

Conclusion

From Gender to Race

Part I has considered Western gender ideology from its ancient religious and philosophical roots through mid-nineteenth century religious, philosophical, political, and "scientific" treatises, as that ideology supported and promoted the construction of racial categories and hierarchies. It has also considered the institutions of slavery and the nation-state, which nurtured those gendered roots into branches of racial ideology, particularly as the English colonies of the New World became the new republic of the United States.

From that discussion, we can see the principles of gender ideology that were repeatedly applied to the construction of racial differences, divisions, and hierarchies. Among them were ideas about racial "standards," "deviations," and "otherness" that had gendered roots. Also included were ideas about male entitlement, as defined by men, and numerous self-fulfilling prophecies about female and racial inferiority, as well as the wholesale manipulation of visual, physical, and cultural evidence in order to reach a predetermined end. Cultural, religious, and somatic differences were routinely interpreted in terms of gender differences. Racial value was a frequent metaphor for the unequal value of the sexes. But the ranking of peoples and races eventually hinged less on women's bodies and deviant behavior, which were, after all, merely sexual and reproductive, than on signifiers of male power, from male beards to cranial capacity, and on the appropriateness of male dominance.

The next three Parts of *The Specter of Sex* turn to the English colonies and the U.S., where narrative sources provide evidence for the gendered construction of race via three overlapping themes: *bodies*, *blood*, and *citizenship*. These categories capture the gendered framework that dominated racialist thinking from the seventeenth through the mid-twentieth centuries, as interpretations of gendered bodily differences; concerns about the preservation of patrilineage (gendered racial "blood"), and rationalizations of the unequal distribution of political rights and citizenship carried gender ideology into the construction of race. Obsession with gendered racial bodies, blood, and citizenship eventually fused the concepts of gender and race so completely that it is now difficult to imagine how race could have become such a dominant fault-line in American society without those naturalized gender associations.

PART II

Bodies

Introduction

Whose Too, Too Solid Flesh?

When Hamlet implored the heavens to "melt" his "too, too solid flesh ... and resolve [it] into a dew ... ," he was expressing the desire to transcend his physical being in order to fulfill his manly responsibility to his slain father. That desire has been a recurrent strain in Western thought, which celebrates man's reason, faculties, and powers of discernment but reviles his body as an encumbrance. The body reminds men of their links to the lower animals and, most threateningly, of their origins in the bodies of women. Powerful men may celebrate their bodies in the throes of competition or sexual conquest, but even when a powerful body signifies a powerful man, it never completely defines him. Male power in Western culture, even sexual power, transcends the limitations of the male body and prevails despite wilting muscles, bulging midriffs, balding pates, and sagging jowls. How else to explain the young wives of old men?

While rising above their own embodied state, however, powerful men have often written their stories on the bodies of others—smaller bodies, colored bodies, nubile bodies—linking *their* fates to bone and sinew, eyes, brows, skulls, skin, stature, and genitals. The "wrong" skin color, skull size, nose, jaw, and hair texture have historically signified inferiority for African American men, for example, despite claims about their imposing body (and genital) size. Slanted eyes, diminutive stature, and "peculiar" hairstyles have historically signified feminized inferiority for Asian men, despite their undisputed contribution to American industrial might. "Muddied" skin in Latino men has signaled suspect gender and insufficient manliness.

Women, regardless of size or color, have had particular difficulty transcending their bodies, which have historically defined their identities and destinies. For centuries, *woman* was virtually equated with *body* and simultaneously discounted as a collection of reproductive and sexual organs around which nature managed to build only an approximation of a person.

Interpretations and rankings of bodies have shaped power structures and social hierarchies as well as determined individual status. In the American context, such interpretations and rankings of "cultural bodies" make the presence of certain types of people seem "natural" to particular settings—women in kitchens and bedrooms, brown men in warehouses pushing brooms, and white men in boardrooms wearing suits. Other scenarios and combinations, such as female or brown male bodies in boardrooms, then become difficult to conceptualize let alone achieve.

Part I of *The Specter of Sex* established the significance of such gendered cultural bodies to racial formulations among early modern Europeans, including the British forebears of the American colonists. Part II analyzes the role of gendered cultural bodies in generating racial identities in the American context, from colonial times to the late nineteenth century. In pursing that analysis, this section relies on scholarship that theorizes human bodies as inscriptions and bearers of culture and history. Primary to that scholarship is the work of Michel Foucault, who defines bodies as the shifting "locus of subjective and social discipline." During the seventeenth century, for example, before the science of biology was invented, mechanical models of the body prevailed. They were replaced during the eighteenth century with a view of bodies as dynamic organisms whose functions could be redirected over time. By the nineteenth century, bodies were conceptualized as more malleable collections of developmental possibilities that responded to environmental stimuli, which could be manipulated to produce obedient bodies.[1]

Judith Butler takes Foucauldian analysis into the realm of gender. As she contests both the material and ontological existence of gender, Butler explains that bodies are primarily instruments of identity formation, which occurs through repeated performances of culturally expected gestures that are so familiar they seem natural extensions of the body's physiology. These gestures include props, such as clothing and hairstyles, which exaggerate gender difference and create the impression that gender distinction is integral to the functions, importance, and uses of human beings in social and familial systems. The very form of gendered bodies is manipulated over time through the cultural meanings attached to physical distinctions by evolving norms of femininity and masculinity, reproduction, and sexual power, as well as by the patriarchal entitlements attached to some bodies and not to others.[2]

In the process of racial formation in the New World, gendered cultural bodies were manipulated to suit economic, social, and sexual needs. As the concept of race evolved from a signifier of geographical origins (like England or Africa) to a signifier of human value, Robyn Wiegman explains, the encumbered embodiment of certain males (and all females) increasingly valorized "the white masculine as the disembodied norm against which a definitive body of difference could be... engaged."[3]

Given that evolution, this book understands race as "a product of history, not of nature, best understood in connection with other elements of ideology and not as a phenomenon *sui generis*," to quote historian Barbara Fields.[4] One key "other element" was the gender ideology discussed in Part I, which provided a vocabulary that shaped the idea of race in the New World, starting in the seventeenth century, to serve the cause of white English dominance and the slavery that supported it. Along with other vocabularies, gender ideology "attache[d] itself, unnoticed, to new things," giving those ideas "a boundless facility for usurping" human lives.[5]

In charting the development of race as a concept rooted in the placement, assigned functions, and supposed cultural significance of gendered bodies, Part II highlights the intersection of scientific and political narratives, opportunistic policies, and beliefs that naturalized gendered racial categories and hierarchies and made them seem natural and inevitable, at least until other forces came along to challenge and revise them. In addition, Part II chronicles the creation of the black-white racial paradigm that was eventually applied to many groups of varying hues and came to dominate racial formation in the U.S. Because that paradigm often distorted or ignored physical evidence, gender presuppositions could even pre-empt skin color in constructing racial categories.

Part II identifies overlapping themes in the gendered definitions of racialized bodies from colonial times through the nineteenth century: *competition, control, distinction, separation,* and *stratification*. That is, competition for the prerogatives of masculinity, including access to white women, motivated definitions of gendered racial difference and hierarchy through piecemeal measures that gradually circumscribed conditions for non-white bodies. Underlying that process of distinction, separation, control, and stratification was what Winthrop Jordan calls lust, the apparently inevitable titillation that arose from the physical and psychological containment and mortification of another human being.[6] Such lust was not always directly expressed, but its underlying presence further sexualized already-gendered racial formations and produced exploitative, even violent, sexual projection, typically *from* the hidden passions of "pure" white bodies *onto* the over-interpreted, "degenerate," hypersexualized bodies of racialized "others."

Chapter 4 traces the role of gendered cultural bodies in the construction of racial ideology by analyzing the containment of American Indians, the proto-racial distinctions imposed on English and African women's laboring and sexual bodies, and the "feminization" and de-masculation of African and Mexican men. Chapter 5 explores the gender ideology that helped to justify racialist interpretations of enslaved bodies and reinforced the feminizing "embodiment" of free and newly freed African American men. Chapter 6 analyzes the titillation implicit in degraded human bodies and the lust and sexual projection—both heterosexual and homosexual—that characterized race-based lynching as spectacle after the Civil War.

4

The American "Body Shop"

Gendered Racial Formation in the Colonies and New Republic

Though race-as-biology was only a nascent idea before the first English colonists arrived in the New World, various factors conspired to encourage their interest in that understanding of race. One such factor was the colonies' extensive racial and ethnic diversity. By 1732, when the British finished settling their thirteen colonies, the American "body shop" already contained more European groups in close proximity than had ever before been assembled. The New York colony included Dutch Christians, Danes, Norwegians; and Dutch Jews who had escaped from Brazil after the Portuguese takeover in 1652. Delaware was home to Swedes who had arrived before either the Dutch or the English. German, French, Scottish, and Irish immigrants, many of whom had come to the New World as indentured servants, were scattered throughout the colonies, as were numerous religious refugees, including French Huguenots, German Mennonites, English, Irish, and Welsh Quakers, German Protestants from the Palatinate, and Swiss Mennonites.[1] French and Spanish territories next door to the English colonies added their own ethnic and cultural mix to the continent.

Perhaps most significant was the intimate juxtaposition of three visibly distinct groups—Europeans, American Indians, and sub-Saharan Africans—in a relatively small geographical area for the first time in human history. With no geographic context to frame that variety, an important reality of human diversity was lost. Instead of seeing gradations of physical characteristics across a spectrum of human possibilities, many white Europeans interpreted the contrasting bodies as "ideal pure racial types."[2]

Based on their encounters with such distinct "others," the English colonists tended to assign greater significance to "complexion" than did the British back home. When the Crown proposed incorporating defeated Indian tribes and their territories into an extended British Empire, for example, thereby making Indians, the English colonists, and the Irish, equivalent British subjects, the colonists were offended by any suggestion that "red" men were their equals. They argued that Indians were a distinct *gens* of uncivilized not-quite humans and asked why *they* should qualify for British citizenship. Moreover, Indians' nomadic lifestyles and primitive rituals seemed to nullify their claims to the land they inhabited, which undermined their right to citizenship. The Declaration of Independence reveals the extent of that colonial conflict in its indictment of the Crown for inciting "domestic insurrections amongst us" and endeavoring "to bring on the inhabitants of our frontiers, the merciless Indian savages, whose known rule of warfare is an undistinguished destruction of all ages, sexes, and conditions."[3]

A related factor contributing to the English colonists' racialist thinking was a slightly stronger commitment to Anglo-Saxon proto-racial superiority than that of their brethren at home. Many colonial leaders saw their westward movement across the Atlantic as a continuation of the great Germanic migration that had wrested Anglo Saxon culture from the feminized Normans, according to Reginald Horsman. Their role was to undo the pollution of British religious and political values by the Norman Conquest. Even the American Revolution seemed to them less a rebellion than a way "to restore pristine Anglo-Saxon vigor." Such views made colonists quite "susceptible to racial explanations of the course of history."[4] Foucault describes this colonial contest as an implicit "race war" between early seventeenth-century Anglo Saxon Puritans and southern European Catholics.[5]

Emboldened by their racializing mission, the colonists also sparred with the British government over the treatment of free Africans. The Crown objected to various colonial policies and laws that curtailed the rights of free men on the basis of their skin color. The 1723 Virginia Assembly, for example, passed a series of laws that were deliberately designed to "keep free people of color in subordinate relationships" to Englishmen, according to Kathleen Brown. Some laws explicitly excluded free black, mulatto, and Indian men from the militia and sanctioned them if they appeared armed for muster. Others mandated that the free children of mulatto female servants be indentured for a period of thirty years, just like their racially mixed mothers. Most boldly, the Assembly denied the franchise to all free Negro, mulatto, or Indian men. In reviewing those laws shortly after their passage, the Lords Commissioners' legal counsel, Richard West, was aghast. He said he could understand containing slaves in order to ensure the security of their masters, but he could not "see why one *freeman* should be used worse than another merely upon account of his Complexion." He was particularly concerned about denying the franchise to property-owners for superficial reasons. He saw no legal grounds for excluding them from the "Rights of liberty" they had earned "by their industry."[6]

The Lords Commissioners initially failed to enforce West's ruling, which only encouraged the colonial governors to tighten somatic controls. Among other indignities, they further reduced the role of free male mulattoes, Negroes, and Indians to unarmed servile labor in the militia. When the Commissioners conducted another review of colonial laws twelve years later, they demanded an explanation for the continued exclusion of free black men from the privileges of white male citizenship, particularly the denial of voting rights, solely "on Account of their Complection." (Women's rights, regardless of complexion, were not mentioned by either side.) The then-governor, William Gooch, explained that he had to restrict free men of color in order to prevent conspiracies between enslaved blacks and free Negroes and mulattoes, even though he didn't have "legal Proof" to convict them. Gooch appealed to the Commissioners to trust him on the decision "to make the free Negroes sensible that a distinction ought to be made between their offspring and the Descendants of an Englishman, with whom they never were to be accounted Equal," because he knew the "Nature of Negroes, and the Pride of a manumitted slave" much better than they did. If a freeman of color had one white parent, Gooch argued, it was necessary to "mark" their cultural bodies, in case their skin did not sufficiently do so.[7]

The need for marking degraded cultural bodies both belies the racial source of English dominance and attests to the level of competition colonists perceived in the American body shop as they sought to control resources and opportunities in the colonies. As we have seen, English anxieties over that competition came primarily from two groups with alternative "complexions": Indians and Africans. Thus, the story of racial formation in the U.S. starts with the rationales and control mechanisms the colonists developed for differentiating the cultural bodies of those two groups from the cultural bodies of the English, sometimes in opposition to the British imperial government. As we shall see, it was a gendered story, and it continued through the first full century and more of the American republic.

Competition, Control, and Bodily Containment: Gendered Indian Racial Formation

The conflict between English settlers and American Indians, which spanned three centuries and nearly decimated the native population, is widely understood as a particularly egregious example of white imperialism. And so it was. Less evident, however, are the gender concepts that informed white Americans' ideas about power and entitlement and shaped their definition, treatment, and disposition of Indian bodies. Notions about masculinity—both manly bodies and male-identified weapons and prerogatives of self-rule—infused issues of territory and civilization. Whites disparaged Indian men's virility and demeaned them as a feminine inferior race that required long-term subjugation for its own good.

English-Indian relations did not, of course, begin as a battle. At least some Indians were initially welcoming and generous with the clueless Europeans who arrived on their shores in the early years of the seventeenth century, naively ill-prepared for the harsh conditions of an unknown continent. Many colonists were fascinated by Indians, as we shall see in more detail in Part III. Numerous influences remain from those halcyon days, from the material bounties of tobacco and corn still integral to the American agricultural economy, to the principles of democracy that whites from aristocratic Europe, including early feminists, witnessed in the citizen-participation practices of certain Northeastern tribes.[8] Cross-cultural harmony decreased, however, as the Indians discovered the Europeans' nefarious designs on the territory they occupied but did not really own, at least in the European sense.

As the Indians resisted those designs, the colonists responded with guns and repeated pronouncements of Indian inferiority. Even before the Virginia colonial governors argued with the Crown about Indians' eligibility for British citizenship, New England Protestant ministers, neo-Harringtonians, and Anglophilic common lawyers were promoting English entitlement to the New World's lands and resources on the strength of their physical and spiritual superiority.[9] Ministers praised the colonists as God's chosen people among all Englishmen (already superior to other Europeans), who were ordained to displace their "loathsome" inferiors. They even claimed that Indians' vulnerability to smallpox was a sign from God that the more robust bodies of Christian Englishmen were destined to replace native, "savage" bodies in a new political order.[10] Beneath those racializing judgments were gendered claims: Englishmen's special brand of masculine vigor would eclipse the feminized, simple, innocent Indians, whom the "manly" English must civilize and Christianize.[11]

From the Indian perspective, Englishmen's pride in their own masculine vigor was badly misplaced. They knew, for example, that the Indian foodstores and agricultural bounty the colonists had depended on in the early days were the products of women's work and social roles. Thus, the colonists' survival was less about masculine prowess than about their own feminized dependence. The English sense of sexual prowess was also a laugh, since Indian women's offers of sexual hospitality were *not* invitations to bond indirectly with tribal men, as the English assumed, but rather ploys to deplete English military potency.[12] In addition, according to Brown, Indian warriors found English soldiers "pale, hairy, and awkward compared to Indian men," despite the fearsome guns that made them feel powerful. And because Indian men valued above all things a warrior's stoicism in the face of death, they had contempt for the white soldiers who died screaming and whimpering.[13]

Indians' contempt for English men's false masculine pride did not prevent occasional imitations by their leaders of the English form of masculinity, as they calculated how to impress and defeat the white enemy. For example, Powhatan, the Algonquian "werowance," adopted the patriarchal forms of control he saw among the English in order to convince whites of his power. Powhatan understood that he could demonstrate his political power by flaunting his control of women's bodies. Such a mechanism violated the Algonquian culture's non-patriarchal structure, in which women had charge of agriculture and made the principal decisions about crops, households were matriarchal, and gender roles were distinct only during a man's prime warrior years (and even then only for the wealthiest of young warriors). Nevertheless, Powhatan decided to marry the most beautiful young women in his chiefdom, and to father one child with each of them. Then he sent all but the most favored back to their villages in order to establish his presence in the far corners of his domain. Powhatan's strategy did little to stop the English in the long run, but it did transform Algonquian culture according to the English model. Algonquin warriors gained status, and men established control over the cultivation of corn.[14] Women in similar tribes, including the Iroquois, learned from such experiences that full assimilation into English society, would disadvantage them.[15]

As conflicts continued with the Indians, the English took little notice of concessions or imitations. Rather, they interpreted every tribe's defeat as proof of feminine weakness. Indians who survived superior English military power required the same "protection" or coverture as English women had under British common law. Coverture mandated a husband's complete control over his wife's body and property during marriage and the subsumption of any woman's public and economic identity, including her right to the franchise, into that of her husband or male relatives. Coverture for women was also the *de facto* law in the U.S. until the state-level Married Women's Property Acts challenged it, from the 1840s to the early twentieth century.[16] As we shall see, however, coverture as a theory extended well beyond women's suffrage.

Coverture was imposed on Indians for many of the same reasons it was imposed on English women. Indians allegedly had an "irrational" antipathy toward European settlement. Therefore, they needed to be physically confined—in their case, to particular geographic areas. In many ways, that prescription violated Enlightenment principles of choice, social compact, and reason; rather, it reflected a religious, cultural, and racial understanding of nationhood closer to "power structures defined by [medieval] titles to estates . . . than [to] commitments to self-governance," as Rogers Smith explains. The prescription contrasted sharply with the political foundations of other new nation-states of the period, including Britain, France, Spain, and Holland.[17] But considering Indians unsuited to the "natural" political community of white men did not violate Enlightenment cultural interpretations of women as mired in their bodies and so dependent on "natural affinities" that they had no political identities or agency. Even the putative Father of the Enlightenment, John Locke, made clear that political membership based on choice and social compact applied only to *men*.[18] The "natural" gender order, mandated by women's irrationality, passions, and God-ordained dependence, required female confinement to the domestic sphere and submission to male control over their property, persons, and prospects.

Prescribing natural rather than rational political communities for Indians simply expanded that gender blind spot and made clear that the American Enlightenment was reserved for white men. If policy makers regarded such paternalism toward Indians as containment for the good of the contained, as it allegedly was for women in their own families and in white society at large, they were mistaken on both counts. If they thought they would meet no resistance, they were wrong again, since Indians rebelled ceaselessly against efforts to contain them, especially in the face of massive European westward migration.

Coverture began for Indians with the Proclamation Act of 1763, which followed the French and Indian Wars (1754–1763). That Act transferred the control of most Indian lands to the British and drew a kind of "Maginot line" across the crest of the Alleghenies.[19] It continued as eighteenth-century recognition of Indian sovereignty and treaties based on that recognition were replaced by Jacksonian policies in the 1830s that not only declared the joys of westward movement for all but also subjected Indian tribes to federal law.[20] The Indian Removal Act of 1830 and other measures of the period required Indian peoples to move west of the Mississippi River under military threat. Treaties followed during the 1850s which identified retained tribal lands, or reservations, to be held under federal protection. During the 1870s, tribal lands were seized and held in lease to the government. By the 1880s, Indians were defined as wards of the state, given parcels of land on reservations, and educated to become as non-Indian as possible. The Code of Religious Offenses or Religious Crimes Code, issued by the Office of Indian Affairs in 1883 outlawed many Indian religious and kinship ceremonies and prompted numerous arrests before it was rescinded in 1924. Such laws were accompanied by educational programs that included gendered strictures about bodies—clothing and hair—as well as about language and culture. Even as late at 1906, all personal conduct of Indian citizen allottees was declared subject to state regulatory authority in the Burke Act.[21]

This gendered oppression never racialized Indians to the extent it did other groups, especially Africans, as we shall see in more detail in Part III. But it did facilitate Indians' ignominious confinement by white Europeans, which had its own dire consequences.

Distinction and Control of African Bodies: Gendered Race Beyond Chattel Slavery

The growing population of Africans in the New World also challenged white English rule in the colonies. That many Africans were slaves did not entirely reduce their threat to European dominance, since slavery was typically temporary and having been enslaved was not yet the automatic mark of inferiority that it would soon become. Freed slaves with well-developed work skills presented a daunting form of competition. Although neither racism nor "race" in the modern sense existed before perpetual bondage was associated with black Africans in the late seventeenth century, the intense competition with Africans by the English was exacerbated by the continuous importation of dark-complexioned Africans to the New World, on the one hand, and by the proto-racial British sense of Teutonic superiority, on the other.[22]

The journey from English racialist susceptibility to their actual racialism was gradual in the colonies, however, even with regard to Africans. This section of Chapter 4 explores the gendered distinctions and measures of control developed in English colonial culture along the way, from the years before race-based chattel slavery was codified to well afterwards, in the eighteenth century. Throughout that time, gender ideology shaped evolving definitions and classifications of race and racial difference. Men's and women's laboring and sexual bodies, as well as gendered prerogatives and norms, were focal points of racial definitions and hierarchies.

Women's Laboring Bodies

The first proto-racial distinction in the colonies between Africans and the English was based on codified differences between women. The Virginia Assembly passed a law in 1643 that classified all female English servants as domestic workers and all female African servants as laborers, regardless of their bonded status or actual work. That labor distinction was artificial, given the fact that "domestic" was rarely an adequate job description for any woman in the New World. Few of the already few English women throughout the new colonies engaged solely in domestic work, including in Virginia, where the Assembly had even voted in 1619 to allot English men shares of land for their prospective wives in order to entice more women to the colony.[23] Rather, colonial women worked in varied occupations, depending on their location as well as on the nature of men's work in their region, the need for subsistence labor, the relative health of men and women, the typical age of widowhood for both sexes, and related inheritance laws, among other factors.[24]

So why did the Virginia Assembly mandate a bogus distinction in women's labor? For at least two reasons. First, they wanted to establish "Englishness" as the basis of colonial rule, and gender conventions were a sign of English superiority. Second, they were uneasy with having their women in the fields, and they wanted to make it look temporary.[25] The presenting issue involved taxing or "tithing" male householders and their workers to support the colony's government. Initially, all women were excluded from the tithe, but in 1629, the Virginia Assembly observed that many women, bond and free, English and African, were hoeing tobacco and pounding corn, just like men. After debating the female exclusion for years, the Assembly decided in 1643 to extend the tithe to African women only. That decision codified the first arguably racial distinction in the colonies at a time when slavery was not yet solely race-based. It defined Africans and English as distinct groups based on the symbolism of work—not the actual work—assigned to women's bodies. All female English servants were tithe-free domestic workers (and/or dependent wives), as they had been defined at home, even if their backs were breaking over the hoe. All female African servants were tithe-able manual laborers.[26] Period.

By 1658, all Africans over the age of 16 who were imported to the colony were pronounced tithe-able. Free African women already in Virginia remained in a limbo state until 1668, when the Assembly ruled that they were also subject to tithes, regardless of their occupation. That law effectively ended legal recognition of class distinctions between free and bonded labor, thereby replacing class with race as defined by women's bodies.[27]

The tithe on free African women was overturned in 1705, briefly distinguishing them from their enslaved sisters and endowing free African women with the same status as white women. But such equal treatment was short-lived. The tithe exemption for free African women was overturned by the 1723 Assembly, which also imposed a tithe on Indian women and prohibited any free Negro, mulatto, or Indian man from voting in elections. In addition to enhancing Virginia's tax base, the reinstatement of the tithe on free African women identified a person's cultural body as a primary qualification for social, political, and economic status.[28]

Women's Sexual Bodies

Women's sexual bodies were also instrumental in justifying what became racial distinctions among free persons. From the seventeenth to the eighteenth century, the sexual reputations of English and African women, slave and free, were differentiated and categorized, especially in the southern and middle Atlantic colonies. Changing definitions of the term "wench" were symptomatic of that differentiation. In the early seventeenth century, contrasts drawn between "good wives" and "nasty wenches" had few racial connotations, according to Brown. All women—English, Dutch, African, or French—could acquire either label, depending on perceptions of their sexual reputations. Gradually, however, distinctions between chaste and wanton women gave way "to racial opposition in which women of English descent embodied the privileges and virtues of womanhood while women of African descent shouldered the burden of its inherent evil, sexual lust."[29]

The meaning of "wench" shifted as English wives were increasingly defined as domestic workers in the 1640s, and their burdensome field labor was transferred to servants, both male and female. At that point, a woman's relegation to outdoor work, according to cultural lore (incited by the greed of white masters and careless gossip) was a sign of her moral depravity, since only "nasty, beastly" wenches who were unfit for domestic employment would be assigned backbreaking tasks.[30] (A master who had to "put up" with such wenches also felt entitled to obscure their contributions to his profits.) By the early eighteenth century, "wenches" connoted only black female African slaves. By the mid-eighteenth century, "wench" came to mean a single "breeding" female slave. African women gradually shouldered the economic and symbolic burden once carried by English serving women from then through the nineteenth century.[31]

As work and moral value was assigned differently to different women, through laws passed between 1643 and 1662, African women's bodies became increasingly associated with sexual availability, lust, and licentiousness; and white women's bodies with sexual purity and chastity. Those associations helped to establish a hierarchy between the races and, therefore, to justify race-based slavery.[32]

Free Men's Bodies

Male bodies and the prerogatives attached to them were also useful in constructing race in the English colonies beyond the realm of slavery. Deliberate de-masculation of free African men began as early as 1639, when laws started excluding them from conventional masculine rights and privileges, including the right to government subsidy for guns and ammunition, on the basis of their "complexions" (a term that became increasingly somatic).[33] Property ownership and guns went hand in hand in the colonies (more so than in England), since guns not only signified patrilineal continuity over generations as they were passed from father to son, but also enabled men to fulfill the masculine roles of protecting their households and provisioning their tables. In addition, guns allowed men to participate in militias for the defense of their communities. Therefore, being deprived of guns significantly reduced a man's social status and threatened his manhood.[34]

The process of withdrawing guns was gradual in the colonies. Virginia laws, for example, recognized the importance of having all men available to defend the community against increasingly inhospitable Indians. So they started with slaves, whose gun subsidies were taken away in the 1670s. Free African men kept their guns until 1723.

Throughout the period, however, gun laws were worded to allow local authorities to exclude free African men from participating in county militias. Parallel laws, starting in 1705, chipped away at other masculine rights for free African men, including their right to serve as witnesses in court.[35]

Rescinding free black men's right to own property—another masculine prerogative—took a bit longer. Indeed, no laws before 1675 actually prohibited property ownership for free African men, but their economic condition in Virginia and elsewhere tightly circumscribed their access to land. Because so many free African men were ex-slaves who had purchased their own freedom, they had fewer chances to amass property and goods than their indentured white peers. That situation worsened in 1705, when the Virginia Assembly began legislating distinctions between the property rights of former English servants and those of former African slaves. The law granted acreage (and a musket) to freed white men, but prohibited black freedmen from taking with them any property or livestock they had acquired during bondage. Without those possessions, a man lacked a major source of patriarchal social power—the ability to support a family through hunting, farming, and animal husbandry. According to both colonial and traditional African values, then, even free African men were thereby legally defined as not-men, a distinction, like the tithe on women, that effectively stratified the races in gendered terms beyond the institution of slavery.[36]

The final masculine prerogative denied to African men was access to white women.[37] It is clear that such access was not always an issue, since inter-racial couples were permitted to marry in several early colonies, even southern ones, according to court records from North Carolina, Maryland, and Virginia. There was not yet a fixed concept of race or antipathy between groups. "Illicit" or unmarried sex in general was the primary target for punishment in the colonies because of the economic impact of pregnancies and motherhood on employers/masters of female servants or slaves. Most punishments for illicit sex by African-English couples were the same as those inflicted on English-English couples, and differences in the severity of punishment typically followed the economic status rather than the skin color of the offenders (although they could be related). Those who owned property were fined; those who didn't were whipped.[38] An unintended consequence of the Virginia tithing laws also demonstrates that black men were not always prohibited from marrying white women. Indeed, the laws actually reduced the number of marriages between free African men and women and increased marriages between free

African men and English women because an English wife incurred no tithe. Possibly for that reason, half the free African male population in Northampton, Virginia, married English women between 1664 and 1677.[39] By the end of the seventeenth century, the focus of colonial laws would turn to married rather than unmarried sex, as we shall see in more detail in Part III. Legal sexual access to English women became "an important component of free adult white male status," according to Brown, so sharing such a prized proto-racial resource could not last.[40] Indeed, preventing such sharing in inter-racial marriage would become a key theme of American culture.

The construction of cultural bodies discussed in this chapter either preceded the codification of race-based chattel slavery in the English colonies in the 1660s or accompanied its full flowering in the early decades of the eighteenth century. While not directed at slaves, such laws and policies helped to demonize the cultural bodies of black Africans and to justify race-based slavery. From the labor tithe to laws regulating property, guns, and eventually marriage, the idea of "race" evolved, and blackness was disparaged, by manipulations of the gender identities and entitlements of free, indentured, and temporarily enslaved persons.

5

Enslaved Bodies and Gendered Race

Many European and African slaves landed in the New World directly, to increase their owners' profits. Others arrived serendipitously, often as diverted cargo on Portuguese ships. The very first African slaves in North America were captured on the high seas on their way to the Caribbean, a form of kidnapping permitted by maritime laws. Those brought to Jamestown in 1619 were indentured servants destined for eventual freedom, as were the first African slaves in New England.[1] There were also Indian slaves, usually captured in war, such as the Pequots taken in Connecticut during the Pequot Indian War. Those captives were divvied up by a 1638 treaty between the English in New England and other Indian tribes. In such instances, Indian men were often taken to Africa and traded for black slaves, but men, women, and children were also kept in the colonies as servants.

Early colonial slaves held in bondage from Massachusetts to the Deep South, including those in Jamestown, were typically bound for limited terms, more like indentured servants than chattel. They faced lengthy periods of servitude and had restricted opportunities to marry, acquire property, or conduct fulfilling lives, but they were not condemned to their subjugated status for life, and neither were their descendants.[2] In only a few instances in the early colonial period, and mostly for Indians, was slavery considered a permanent, inheritable condition. Even slaves held in lifelong servitude were seldom deprived of their basic rights.[3]

Overall, neither skin color nor geographical origin alone was sufficient to determine a person's status in the early English colonial labor force. Free persons, indentured servants, and chattel slaves could be English or otherwise European, Indian, or African and either male or female, although all groups were not equally represented in all categories. A Virginia law from 1641 demonstrates the variety since it lists slaves of all types in authorizing the branding of recaptured runaways. A Massachusetts Bay Colony case from 1659 even condemned an English family to slavery because the father was both indolent and a supporter of the dissident Quakers.[4] Being African was a disadvantage for early conscripts, however, especially after 1650, because Africans had no status under English law, could not make contracts, and had dark skin that made them easier to spot and likelier to be recaptured if they ran away.[5]

That slavery was varied and temporary in the colonies does not mean colonists considered it an unacceptable source of labor, as had much of the world for millennia. Indeed, slavery offered such abundant economic advantages that even New England Puritans found it hard to resist. Their infamous Massachusetts Bond of Liberties, passed in 1641, both condemned and welcomed slavery by leaving open the possibility of enslaving "lawfull captives taken in just warres, and such strangers as willingly selle themselves or are sold to us."[6] Other colonies embraced slavery more directly and eagerly. Virginia, for example, blatantly bolstered the international slave trade in 1659 by passing a law, known as Act XVI, that imposed an equal tax on all tobacco produced by slaves, whether they had been imported by Virginians, the Dutch, or any "other foreigners."[7]

What distinguished American slavery from all other types throughout history was both its inheritability and its eventual association with only black African bodies.[8] "By legislating black chattel slavery," Rogers Smith explains, "Americans went beyond any explicit provisions in English law and gave legal expression to an increasingly racialized sense of their identity so powerful that the very humanity of these outsiders was denied." The colonists' equation of black bodies with enslavement was so extreme that the highest common law court in England disavowed it in 1772, in *Somerset v. Stewart*. In that decision, the Chief Justice of the King's Bench decreed absolute slavery so odious that it had no place in England, a decision many colonists interpreted as further evidence that the Crown disregarded their interests.[9]

Gender-blind laws were instrumental in establishing and promoting the connection of black bodies with chattel slavery, including laws that permitted and then eliminated baptism as a criterion for freedom both in the colonies and in England. Until the late 1620s, African slaves who agreed to be baptized were typically freed after a specified number of years. That opportunity began to erode in 1667, when the Virginia Assembly proclaimed, in Act III, that *"baptism does not alter the condition of the person as to his bondage or freedom."*[10] By the time the Massachusetts legislature weighed in on the same side of the issue in 1694, the foundation for slavery in the colonies had effectively shifted from an issue of culture or religion to one of racial destiny—a bodily fate. The process was complete by 1705, via a widespread and "comprehensive legal framework for mediating between the state's interests—support of the slave system and protection of all white people from slaves—and the interests of individual masters."[11] Men's and women's bodies were equally ensnared in that framework.

At the same time, many laws and policies establishing black chattel slavery in the colonies were gender-specific. Some feminized or emasculated African men and drew distinctions between the labor and sexual value of African and English women, as we have seen. Others justified slavery by denying that Africans shared in the gender distinction that marked whites as a civilized people. And in areas dependent on slavery for their local, colonial, or state economies, particularly in the South, slavery thrived on stratified gender roles and male dominance in white society.

Defining Race-Based Slavery: Enslaved Women's Sexual and Reproductive Bodies

The gendered foundations of racial ideology underlying rationales for black chattel slavery can sometimes be found in the contexts surrounding apparently gender-neutral discourse about the inferiority of black bodies. Thomas Jefferson's *Notes on the State of Virginia* (1781), considered the "most intellectually prestigious statement of inherent black inferiority" of its time, provides an example. Jefferson recognized that Negroes' alleged inferiority, not only to whites but also to Indians and to Greek and Roman slaves, reflected the harsh conditions under which they lived, but he argued that such conditions were not sufficient to explain it.[12] Rather, Negro inferiority resided in black bodies: "color, hair form, secretion, less physiological need of sleep but sleepiness in work, lack of reasoning power, lack of depth in emotion, poverty of imagination."[13] Jefferson apparently thought that Negro inferiority justified his ownership of slaves, despite his public condemnation of slavery, and he warned that racial segregation was necessary to prevent the dilution of whiteness through racial mixing.

Such statements seem gender neutral or gender inclusive, but actually they camouflage a complex and self-serving gender ideology that was so convoluted that it allowed Jefferson to engage in sex and racial mixing with his slave Sally Hemmings. According to Winthrop

Jordan, it was possible for Jefferson to overlook the inferiority of black women's bodies because he related to them solely as instruments of white men's sexuality. For Jefferson, all women were sexual predators, potentially disgusting and dangerous to men, unless proven otherwise. That's why his preferred white partners were married women who were already sexually contained. Even his wife Martha was a widow when he married her. His famous affair with the married Maria Cosway also illustrates that preference. Contained white women assuaged Jefferson's anxieties about women and about his own sexual passions. Black women, on the other hand, could be used to express those passions freely yet still manage his sexual anxieties. Enjoying the lascivious delights of an "innately" sexually aggressive black woman whom he owned simultaneously meant "disciplining" threatening female passions. His ownership of a slave woman's body allowed him to attribute his sexual desire and actions to the exercise of his duty as master.[14] This gendered sleight-of-hand left many a white man feeling innocent as he routinely exploited female sexuality. Justifying their sexual "attentions" to slaves as both fulfilling and disciplining the women's insatiable passions not only lessened white men's guilt for rape but also detached them from the sexual demands or threats of their white partners.

Harriet Jacobs's recently authenticated autobiography, *Incidents in the Life of a Slave Girl* (1861), exposes the white male self-deception embedded in that scenario. Emblematic of many other such narratives, *Incidents* clearly illustrates Jacobs' conclusion that "slavery is terrible for men; but it is far more terrible for women." Using the pseudonym, Linda Brent, Jacobs recounted her struggles to escape the sexual demands of her master. She also demonstrated the hazards faced by slave women who resisted their masters' sexual assaults, as well as the lengths to which such masters would go to control a slave woman they fancied. To escape her master's vengeance, Jacobs was forced to hide in an unheated attic crawl space, where she could not stand up, for nearly seven years before she was able to escape to the North and be reunited with her children. Jacobs's recapture was not finally foreclosed until her northern white employer paid $300 to her "owner."[15]

Status-of-the-Mother Laws

Such sexual exploitation of black women was codified as a premise of slavery in late seventeenth-century laws of *partus sequitur ventrum* ("progeny follows the womb") or "status-of-the-mother" laws. The first such law, passed by the Virginia Assembly in 1662, proclaimed "that all children borne in this country shalbe held bond or free only according to the condition of the mother." Status-of-the-mother laws were passed in Maryland in 1681 and in Massachusetts in 1670. South Carolina codified the inheritability of bondage based on the status of the mother in 1740.[16]

Those laws, which were passed throughout the colonies, violated the English and early colonial custom linking legitimate children's social and legal status to that of their fathers. The laws thereby classified all slave children by white fathers as illegitimate while sanctioning fornication that would otherwise be prohibited. The laws essentially admitted that the production of progeny between slaves and masters was simultaneously shameful and acceptable, as well as an expected outcome of slavery. In rewarding white men's illicit sexual activity, the laws also defined race via women's bodies, naturalized the concept of race-based slavery by making it an inheritable condition, and identified the exploitation of African women's reproductive capacity as the mainstay of slavery and its racial distinctions. Status-of-the mother laws were the lynchpin of slave proliferation in the U.S. from the seventeenth century to the Civil War.

Status-of-the mother laws did not allow white women to bestow their (free) status on their mixed-race children, however, and any white woman who tried to do so faced harsh penalties.[17] Such laws thereby manipulated white women's reproductive capacities in the institutionalization of race-based slavery, which was clearly their intent. For white women, the important status to be bequeathed was that of the father. The Maryland assembly established this principle in the first anti-miscegenation law in the colonies, passed in 1664, before perpetual chattel slavery was well established and before its own status-of-the mother law was passed. The law forbade marriages "between 'freeborn English women' and 'Negro slaves,'" and condemned to slavery, for her husband's lifetime, any English woman who married a black slave. The law also defined children resulting from such unions as slaves like their fathers.[18] When it was passed in 1681, Maryland's status-of-the mother law also applied only to black women. Virginia eliminated the possibility that a white woman could transmit her racial status to her mixed-race children in 1723, by declaring that any woman who bore mixed-race children would become legally black. Once again, racial differences hinged on definitions of women's cultural bodies.

Slavery and Gendered Fears

Such hypocritical controls of women's reproductive capacities in the context of slavery reflected a long-standing fear among white men that free mulattoes and white women would rise up against white masters in solidarity with slaves and free blacks, and that such danger would only increase if mixed race children could be free. Virginia's Act XXII, which was passed in 1660, before chattel slavery was fully codified in the colony, was perhaps the first to address the fear of class solidarity between white female servants and slaves, free blacks, and/or mulattoes. The law required English servants who assisted a slave's escape to serve out the time of the "Negroes' absence."[19]

Fears of inter-racial and cross-gender collusion were not entirely unfounded. Servant and slave unrest boiled over in the English colonies during the 1660s and 1670s, including a rebellion by servants in Virginia's York County in 1661 and Birkenhead's Rebellion in Gloucester County in 1663. The most violent rebellion of the period, Bacon's Rebellion, was fomented in 1676 by an outsider, Nathaniel Bacon, along with other relative newcomers to the colony. The conflict forged alliances among elite English men and women as well as between white and Negro servants and slaves and newly freed Africans. Bacon's death and the Crown's intervention ultimately quelled the rebellion in 1677, but it had lasting effects on Virginia's social order. It shattered all illusions that servants and slaves were "deferential, docile, and stable." It also politicized the lower orders of freemen and raised hopes for the eventual freedom of bound laborers, by giving some of them a taste of power. Some English women were also politicized, as they became the principal agents of the rebellion's spread by word of mouth, spokespersons for their imprisoned husbands, and temporary protectors of their homes. At the same time, the defeat of Bacon's Rebellion solidified the power of the white gentry, who noted that the last Baconians to surrender were groups of black slaves and white servants, many of them female.[20]

"Slaveholders' anxiety over potential revolts brought out their anxiety over the union of white women with black men," argues Karen Getman. For example, "an eighteenth-century Maryland planter, upon hearing that a white woman failed to report her slave's warnings about a possible uprising, replied: '[B]ut perhaps, She had a mind for a black husband.'"[21] And despite scant evidence of rape or rampant consensual sex during the slave revolts that did occur, "in the years after Bacon's Rebellion, sexual regulations became an increasingly important means of consolidating white patriarchal authority and defining racial difference," according to Brown.[22]

Women's Gendered Racial Sexuality

The codification of slavery at the end of the seventeenth century only increased the representation of black women's bodies as appropriate objects of white male lust, as we have seen in the evolving term "wench" and the sexual self-deceptions of Thomas Jefferson. At the same time, female chastity increasingly became a white characteristic and even a qualification for racial membership. Prejudicial distinctions between the sexual proclivities of African and English women were no longer limited to upper-class Englishmen who feared that lower-class English women and free and enslaved Africans might conspire against them.[23]

Martha Hodes's study of legal cases in the mid-Atlantic colonies and early states reveals that even the courts began ascribing sexual excess to the bodies of Negroes, male and female, and sexual purity to the bodies of white women. (White men's sexual bodies received little official attention.) Southern divorce laws were even liberalized in the early nineteenth century in recognition of white women's sexual virtue and the likelihood that they could become victims of less virtuous men, including their own husbands. Such "gains" were rather tenuous, however. Poor white women had less legal protection for their virtue than wealthy ones, even in conflicts with black men, and even elite white women could lower their racial status in the eyes of the law to that of a "Negress" if they displayed any "indecent" behavior.[24]

No laws or courts recognized sexual virtue for female slaves, however. According to the law, their cultural bodies were inviolable. White slave-owners were not punished for "commerce between the sexes." Slaves were legally defined as property, although even Southern courts struggled until the 1850s to balance slaves' legal status as chattel with their rights as people. And when it came to slave rape, judges typically claimed that such crimes were outside their jurisdiction. Some even denied that enslaved black women had the right to claim rape.[25] As one Maryland lawyer explained in 1767, "A slave is not admonished for incontinence, or punished for fornication or adultery; never prosecuted for bigamy or petty treason, for killing a husband being a slave." Likewise, if a white man raped the female slave of another white man, the law considered it a property crime against the owner, not a crime against the woman. Indeed, masters sometimes offered the sexual services of their female slaves to other white men as a sign of hospitality. The law eventually recognized no sexual offenses against black female slaves, since any form of sex simply satisfied their "insistent" biological urges.[26] Without the protection of law or family, female slaves were, as Deborah Gray White explains, the "most vulnerable group of antebellum Americans."[27]

Many white women who benefited from being defined as pure in custom and law, relished the contrast between themselves and their slaves. Others recognized their own humiliation implicit in that contrast. Some took that humiliation out in the vicious treatment of their female slaves; others sought to reduce their own humiliation by reducing their slaves' sexual abuse. The latter failed, according to Getman, because few Southern white women had "sufficient social, economic, or political power" to intervene. As evidence she notes that one Southern court dismissed "discussions between a slave and her mistress regarding the plantation overseer's sexual advances as mere 'tittle tattle.' "[28]

Dismissing women's agency in their own sexual bodies helped to solidify white men's power. White women's obedience and fidelity bought them the protection they allegedly needed against black men. Black women had no bargaining power at all, since even their protests did little to contradict the widespread belief in their need and desire for white men's sexual advances.

"A Negroe and a Passionate Woman": White Masculinity vs. Black Men

The degradation of black female slaves was only part of the gendered story of racial formation accomplished in the name of slavery. Black men also suffered, not only from ideas about their specific deficiencies, but also from analogies between their biological inferiority and white women's. Jefferson, for example, regarded white women and male slaves as equally inferior and equally immature.[29] He thought that black men should therefore forever be excluded from political rights and activities, just as "women should be neither seen nor heard in society's decision making councils."[30] Both groups' welfare was entirely dependent on the generosity of their superiors—white men. Another Virginia planter named Landon Carter agreed. In 1777 he wrote in his diary that "A negroe and a passionate woman are equal as to truth or falsehood; for neither thinks of what they say."[31]

Such gendered equations fueled the American ideology of race and made de-masculation a key mechanism for enforcing the enslavement of black men. The prohibition against marriage, for example, made clear as it had in ancient Rome that enslaved men did not share in the masculine prerogatives of heading a household or determining the domicile of their wives and progeny. (The prohibition also saved white masters from irate husbands as they violated female slaves.) As notions of Negro racial inferiority became more entrenched between the 1830s and 1850s, masters and slaves increasingly competed over the prerogatives of masculinity, and slaves increasingly received harsh punishments for any violation.

The constant threat of violence held over the heads of slaves was another way that whites robbed black men of their manhood. Although slaves of both sexes cowered under that threat, reducing all black bodies to subservience, there was an undercurrent of masculine competition in the violence of slavery. According to Drew Gilpin Faust, even if the lashes were delivered by the white mistress, as many were, slaves of both sexes often regarded the blows as an assertion of white male power against black male power. White women's violent acts were seen as proxies for the white master's rage, since "no gendered code of honor celebrated women's physical power or dominance" and "a contrasting yet parallel ideology extolled female sensitivity, weakness, and vulnerability ... A white woman disciplined and punished as the master's subordinate and surrogate. Rationalized, systematic, autonomous, and instrumental use of violence belonged to men." So clear was that distinction to slaves that the master's absence during the Civil War undermined the mistress's authority. It was apparent that the power structure that oppressed slaves was gendered as well as raced, so many slaves refused to work or obey white women's orders. That left some mistresses eager to free their slaves (with the exception perhaps of a single household servant) rather than struggle for their control.[32]

Some violence against slaves deliberately offended their gendered sensibilities. Toni Morrison's historically rooted novel, *Beloved*, illustrates that effect as it juxtaposes two forms of gendered torture. While Sethe is being "milked" by two "mossy teethed" white boys, Paul D, who witnesses that violation, is prevented from helping her "because the iron bit was in his mouth."[33] Sethe's torture was obviously unique to a woman, but the bit in Paul's mouth was also a specifically patriarchal assertion of racial control. In addition to animalizing anyone who was forced to wear it, the bit was "used in early modern England to silence women."[34]

Ironically, perhaps, such gender-specific punishments and tortures were also accompanied by intimations that the African race was without distinct gender differences. Since whites considered sharp gender distinctions as a mark of high civilization, their use of a gender-neutral term for slaves, such as "our Negroes," was another gendered insult. So was the claim that men and women had equal capacity for hard physical labor. That such labor was imposed on pain of death did little to complicate white slaveholders' view that Africans' gender neutrality justified denying "uncivilized" slaves gender-related privileges, especially male privileges.

Before the 1850s, however, being male did offer slaves some advantages. Indeed, a "passionate [white] woman" (particularly a poor one) could lose out to "a Negroe," even in rape or illicit sex cases, if the slave was considered a productive worker. Such judgments reflected lingering suspicions about the chastity of lower-class white women, but even elite white women did not always prevail in those cases. Convictions of slaves accused of actual, intended, or attempted rape were also less likely if they were considered good workers. Hodes discovered many instances in ante-bellum rape trials in which a white woman's accusation of rape did not stand up in court, including a Maryland case from 1823.[35] Getman also reports that between 1789 and 1833, sixty Virginia slaves were sentenced to death for the rape or attempted rape of white women, but twenty-seven of those were recommended for mercy on the grounds that the white woman had consented. The mercy recommendations "reflected tension between the need to assert white racial superiority and the desire to control white women's sexual behavior."[36] In addition, except in cases of insubordination or insurrection, lynching and other violent punishments of male slaves were rare before the 1850s.[37]

As late as 1860, at least one "suspect" white woman's testimony was insufficient to convict a black slave for rape. In a case from Florida in that year, the state Supreme Court vacated the conviction of Cato, a slave, and remanded the case for new trial on the grounds that the plaintiff was a prostitute who could not convincingly demonstrate her resistance to Cato's advances.[38]

Free black men shared in this gender advantage. They were also protected against allegations of inter-racial sex or adultery prior to the 1850s if they were considered valuable workers. Free blacks were typically called into court in adultery cases only if they were suspected of violence against a white husband. Black and white men were equally subject to private revenge for adultery, and such retaliation rarely befell a free man only because of his race, even when the act occurred between a white woman and a black man.[39] In the sexual arena, then, the prerogatives of male bodies could eclipse not only white women but also a man's own color and condition of servitude.

The 1850s brought a big change in this gender imbalance. Black men—free or slave—who were accused of raping a white woman were much likelier to be lynched or automatically convicted and executed, if they could not convince the court that they were really white.[40] As we shall see in Part III, for a time that was easier to do than it sounds.

"Contempt for Women, White and Colored Alike": The White Gender Code of Slavery

The culture of slavery depended not only on white patriarchal control of enslaved black bodies but also on white patriarchal control of the Southern household, including white women. According to Mary Beth Norton, slavery and the racial ideology that accompanied it were instrumental in confining a white woman to the domestic realm and subordinating her to her husband.[41] In short, white patriarchy blossomed most where slavery did. "As households enlarged and the plantation 'family' became the basic unit of Southern society," Norton explains, "the powers of male heads of household expanded and stabilized.... Southern men's conception of their authority over their white and black dependants (their wives, children, and slaves) was [absolute].... patriarchy became the norm in the South; and, although it did not achieve its fullest force until the early nineteenth century, white plantation women [always] felt the effects of unchallenged male dominance." Because racial categories were less central to the politics and economics of the North, Norton argues, patriarchy there became somewhat less entrenched.[42]

The economics and racial politics of slavery, then, required (some would say "forced") white women to focus on the "specialized" reproductive and domestic roles for which their bodies were "so obviously *biologically* suited." Those politics also required white men to exercise the control for which their bodies were also (obviously) biologically suited. The allegedly unspecialized bodies of black slaves offered further *ex post facto* evidence that Africans' inappropriate gender pre-destined *them* for slavery.[43]

The deep interconnection of white women's cultural bodies with the institution of slavery humiliated women of both races and supported male arrogance. As Alexis de Tocqueville observed in

1830, Southern aristocratic white men had "profound contempt for women, white and colored alike," and behaved like "haughty, hasty, and ardent tyrants" who expected to get their way. As a result, aristocratic ante-bellum Southern white women, after tasting sexual power during "their brief careers as eligible brides," spent the rest of their lives as insignificant drudges whose major role was to symbolize their husbands' social status. The trope of the pure white virgin not only demeaned black women, according to Beth Day, but also "segregate[d] the white woman from the power structure—as well as from interracial sexual activity. The main purpose of the virginity myth was to smother the white Southern woman in so-called sacred womanhood so that the white male could gently but firmly push her out of participation in a man's world." In such a system, degradation befell white wives, as they pretended not to notice their husbands' cross-racial promiscuity, and violation was the lot of black women, who had no protection from the lust of white slave-owners.[44]

6

Sexual Projection and Race

Science, Politics, and Lust

Arguments supporting white racial dominance in the U.S. have rarely acknowledged their own political and economic motivations, relying instead on proclamations of "natural" racial superiority and inferiority. Such arguments have been even less revealing about the excitement of racial dominance "in the groin," as William Pinar says, preferring to obscure the insidious connection between racial domination and prurience. W.E.B. Du Bois recognized that element of racism when he observed in 1917 that it is "not simply the rational, conscious determination of white folk to oppress us," but rather the result of "age-long complexes sunk now largely to unconscious habit and irrational urge."[1]

Those "complexes" have produced repeated and varied "sexual projections" over the centuries, from white men's displacement of their own sexual urges onto the libidos and bodies of female slaves, to the sex crimes associated with lynching, to racially motivated murders in contemporary America. Castrations and penis souvenirs were common features of lynchings in the decades surrounding 1900, where bodies were so much meat, and manipulating or decimating the sexual power of victims was often the point of the violence. Lawrence Russell Brewer, who tortured and killed James Byrd in Texas in 1998 by dragging him behind a pick-up truck, exemplifies a more recent case of sexual arousal through racial violence. "Well, I did it," he wrote, "and no longer am I a virgin. It was a rush and I'm still licking my lips for more." How much clearer can it be, as Pinar argues, that, "in America, terror and enjoyment [have often] converged on the site of the black body?"[2]

Sexual projection may be as old as humanity itself, but it did not appear as a concept in scientific literature until the 1920s, as Freudian psychoanalysis began framing sexuality in new ways. Laplanche's notion of the "fantasmatic," or the structuring scenario behind social action, underpins the idea. The fantasmatic refers to "over-determined actions structured by transferences and other forms of repetitive behavior."[3] These transferences include projections of one's own shameful desires onto the desires and bodies of others.

Western history is replete with examples of sexual titillation and projections of sexual desire by dominant peoples over degraded "others," as we have seen. But such projections became increasingly explicit (if not admitted) and increasingly racial (rather than geographical) in the nineteenth century, especially as the legal cover and economic advantages of slavery disappeared in the U.S. That change made the gendered mechanisms of racism more important to the assertion and maintenance of white supremacy. By the 1870s and 1880s, according to many scholars, several interrelated forms of racialized sexual projection rose to fever pitch and continued swirling through the twentieth century.[4] The emerging "sciences" of eugenics and sexology both fueled and were fueled by linkages of certain racial characteristics and ambiguities with various forms of sexual deviance, including homosexuality.

Chapter 6 analyzes the sexual prurience, voyeurism, and projection—each with its own kind of violence—that were strong undercurrents in nineteenth-century racial ideology. The chapter begins with the voyeuristic interests of white European "scientists" in black female bodies, and continues with analyses of white hysteria in the U.S. over non-white men's alleged sexual danger to white women. Sexual projection was inherent in the lynching and mass murder that accompanied and manipulated such hysteria, as is evident in the sex crimes that exacerbated the horrors of lynching (especially of black men). The chapter also explores sexual projection in conflicts between white and non-white men over the definition and prerogatives of masculinity, which seemed purely economic. Ironically, sexual projection reinforced white men's belief in their own "disembodied" power, in part by "embodying," and therefore feminizing and humiliating, the men of color—Mexican, Chinese, and African American—who were its prime targets. Starting at the end of the nineteenth century, accusations of "sexual inversion" or homosexuality against non-white men exacerbated that humiliation and further distanced racial "others" from the mythic white male (heterosexual) norm.

Heterosexual Projection: The Role of "Science"

As if Sethe's assault by the mossy-toothed white boys in *Beloved* were not bad enough on its own, Morrison includes a pseudo-scientist in the scene—known as School Teacher—and portrays his fake "objectivity" as he simply watches and takes notes rather than intercedes to stop the attack. That cold-hearted gathering of "data" exemplifies the voyeurism of much "scientific" interest in the bodies of black women in the nineteenth century, which spread beyond slavery and only increased as emancipation disturbed the social hierarchy that kept whites on top.

School Teacher's real-life predecessors included the European scientists who repeatedly scrutinized so-called "Hottentot" women over a 200-year period, starting with John Ovington's *Voyage to Suratt, in the Year 1689*. Ovington labeled such women primitive and sexually deviant and identified them as the "missing link" between ape and man. Edward Long spiced up that diagnosis in his 1774 *History of Jamaica* by accusing Hottentot women of actually fornicating with the orangutan. (Long also claimed that the women's eyes, lips, and nipples signified their tribe's low intelligence, immorality, primitivity, and laziness.) By the nineteenth century, according to Gillman, comparative anatomists carried on the tradition by "repeatedly locat[ing] racial difference through the sexual characteristics of the female body," which they studied enthusiastically.[5]

Indeed, voyeuristic scrutiny from afar, as in the works of Ovington and Long, gave way in nineteenth-century Europe to more hands-on analysis of the black female body. The scientific treatment of Saartje Baartmann, the infamous "Hottentot Venus," is a primary example. Baartmann (rechristened Sarah Bartmann in England) first came to the attention of English naturalists in 1810, when she was transported to London from the British colony on the Cape of Good Hope.[6] Apparently, the ship's doctor told Bartmann that she could get rich by displaying herself in the capitals of Europe. After adverse publicity undermined her popularity in England, she was taken to Paris as part of an animal show. France's premier comparative anatomist, Georges Cuvier, insisted on classifying Bartmann with the animals even though he recognized her lively personality and good memory and knew that she spoke three languages. In Paris she was subjected to physical examination by French zoologists and physiologists and displayed in public, until her death in 1815 from "inflammation" (read: overexposure) at age 25 or 26. Prurient exploitation of Bartmann's body continued even after death, since Cuvier performed an autopsy and presented her genitalia to the French Academy.[7]

Of particular interest to naturalists was the elongation—up to four inches—of the labia minora, or inner vaginal lips, among the Hottentots, which became known as the "Hottentot apron." There was much speculation over the centuries about the function of the "apron," as we have seen, starting with Ovington's pronouncement that it was a sign of hermaphroditism and Voltaire's claim in the eighteenth century that it proved the Hottentots belonged to a separate human species. Later in the eighteenth century, Sir John Barrow declared the apron nature's perfect defense against rape. But nineteenth-century physiologists, physiognomists, and phrenologists further sexualized African women's bodies by claiming that the apron was a malformation caused by concupiscence and other sexual excesses, which could also be found in lesbians and prostitutes. In all cases, they claimed, unusual genital size was symptomatic of the women's degeneracy.[8] By the 1930s, some German anthropologists decided that the apron resulted from masturbation.[9]

Male genitalia did not entirely escape scrutiny, although white men seemed less interested in it. If size indicated a libidinal surfeit in African women, they reasoned, then it must also indicate wanton and savage sexuality in African men. Thus, greater penis size was not necessarily better. (What a relief that must have been to white male scientists!) Rather, Africans' large genitalia suggested "the body's animal excess."[10] Whites could conveniently project their own sexual urges and shame onto that excess without guilt. (Those scientists did not apparently see a contradiction in their opposite assessments of large genitals and large skulls.)

By the end of the century, as Robyn Wiegman explains, comparative racial anatomists were determined to find evidence of the racial hierarchy they already believed in, and sexual deviance became an important measure of men's racial fitness. As they fractured "the universalism of the masculine . . . to reveal an anatomized African (-American) male," they reinforced Africans' lowly feminine status in the schema of racial value. Throwing universal male superiority to the wind, comparative anatomists also defined African men as intellectually feminine and increasingly relied on the discourse of sexual deviance "to forge the corporeal particularities on which [the association between] 'blacks and women' would subsequently depend."[11] By the turn of the twentieth century, even progressive whites characterized the Negro race as "the feminine race of the world" or the "lady of races," which was not meant as a compliment.[12]

Heterosexual Projection: Racial Politics and Gendered Bodies

Scientists were not alone in reinforcing their racial judgments through sexual projection. Indeed, sexual projection formed the core of Jim

Crow politics in the U.S., which were dedicated to ensuring a racially segregated society. To that end, much racial discourse in the decades following Reconstruction presumed that all black women were sexually degenerate—"prostitutes . . . thieves and liars," in the words of James W. Jacks, president of the Missouri Press Association, in 1895. Although Jacks's controversial condemnation of black women to "whoredom" sparked immediate resistance and inspired the founding of the National Association of Colored Women's Clubs the following year, it would take almost a century for black women to refute such judgments and to "educate the public mind to a just appreciation of us," in the words of Josephine St. Pierre Ruffin, the group's founder.[13]

Anti-Chinese sentiment also presumed that Asian women were "prostitute[s] of the basest order." Such accusations started in the 1850s, when many of the few Chinese women in the U.S. were imported for sex. The women's deviance made them a perfect match for Chinese men, however, since they too were considered "lustful and sensual in their dispositions."[14] Mexican women in the Southwest were also routinely accused of promiscuity, and the darker their skin the more "disgusting" (and alluring) whites found the "tawny visaged creatures."[15]

White women were also objects of sexual projection. At times, notions of sexual purity were projected onto their bodies as women of other races suffered from projections of sexual evil onto theirs. That formula faltered after the Civil War, however, as Southern white men became more open to defaming white women's sexual reputations in order to share their guilt for racist sexual aggression. The release of testimony given to the American Freedman's Inquiry Commission provided a catalyst for their change of view. Suppressed before the War as potentially damaging to the cause of abolition, the testimony contained stories of voluntary sex between black men and white women. Almost overnight, the sexually innocent Southern Belle was replaced with a flesh and blood woman who was accountable for her sex appeal, especially to black men. To Northerners, Southern white women began to seem as profligate as male slave-owners. Not to be outdone, Southern whites accused the Northern white female teachers who came South after the Civil War of promiscuity with black men. They held such women responsible for the increase in mulatto children, which conveniently obscured white men's contributions to the mixed race population.[16]

The new projection did not serve the ideology of white supremacy, however, which had long depended on the myth of white female sexual purity and on the unnaturalness of sexual relationships between black men and white women. Many whites, especially members of the Democratic Party, believed that such relationships would destroy the white race.[17] The once-regional sexual paradigms now assumed national importance: without white female sexual purity, white dominance was in jeopardy nationwide. For political purposes, white women's cultural bodies could not be connected with sexual agency. So an informal bargain was struck. If white women limited themselves to white sexual partners, believed in the sexual purity of their own persons, and perhaps most importantly, bought into the sexual danger of non-white (especially black) men, they could continue to stand on their pedestal and enjoy the protection of white men.[18]

That bargain reinforced an even more repressive form of sexual projection. White men could continue to project their sexual shame, desire, and guilt onto the bodies of women of color, as they had long done, while also keeping the lid on the sexuality of the newly "fallen" white woman. The bargain also strengthened the myth of the black male rapist and fueled the lynching craze, which peaked in the 1880s and terrorized non-white men into the 1930s. This new form of sexual projection also enhanced the role of the Ku Klux Klan, which was established in Tennessee in 1866 by six returning Confederate officers. Despite its underground organizational structure, the Klan's violent tactics, including castration and murder, primarily of black men, and rape of "degenerate" white women suspected of fornicating with black men, were familiar to most Americans by 1871.[19]

This form of sexual projection united white men and women in racial bigotry and violence. According to Grace Hale, white women now "shared a racial power that contradicted the supposed inferiority of their gender." Lynching sealed the deal, as it de-masculated black men (and other men of color) and simultaneously empowered and "limited white women as it signified their need for protection."[20] As we shall see, courts of law reliably recognized that the racial distinction so crucial to white dominance required the presumption of a white woman's sexual purity and subjection to a white man's control.[21]

Homosexual Projection: Black Male Lynching

The rape/lynching scenario of the late-nineteenth and early twentieth centuries is a primary case study of the fantasmatic underlying violent sexual projection in the construction of racial ideology. Because of its association with rape accusations, lynching is typically understood as a matter of heterosexual projection, as described in the previous section (and in Chapter 10)—accusing a black man of rape or thoughts of rape and eliminating that threat to white women by eliminating the man. This heterosexual rationale projects lasciviousness and aggression on one side of the racial ledger and gendered racial innocence and victimization on the other. Because protecting the white woman's cultural body was the alleged object, white women were often enthusiastic supporters of the act that defined them as innocent. Hale recounts story after story of white women calling for the torture of black suspects, rabble-rousing the crowd, or even stabbing a black corpse's heart with a knife.[22] The post-war lynching of black men was also a sexualized replacement for white men's flagrant rape of black women during slavery.[23]

That perspective is undoubtedly accurate. But some historians see an even more complex phenomenon lurking beneath the surface. For them, there is an inescapable homosexual logic to lynching. Trudier Harris explains: "If the white man can attribute his own basest sexual desires to the black man, then he can remain clean, pure, and morally superior in the eyes of his society." Having projected his desires onto black men, the white man becomes libidinally invested in the object of that projection and learns to hate "in the groin" both his own desires and their secret object. Harris compares the process to the Christian practice of denying one's own sins, attaching them to others, like the Devil, and then despising both the sins and the "other" sinner.[24]

William Pinar goes even further to explain that "the fantasy of black male bodies violently penetrating white female bodies" allowed "the white male ego to place himself, identify himself, with white supremacy and political dominance while enjoying, albeit via disavowal, a masochistic, self-shattering sexual ecstasy of being penetrated by a powerful (evil and black) man, in oedipal terms, an absent, loathed, longed-for father."[25] The sexualized gloating of Lawrence Russell Brewer illustrates such homosexual projection as a feature of racially motivated violence. From Pinar's perspective this process created a "homosocial racial economy," in which white men [eventually] felt compelled to kill those whom they desired."[26]

Grace Elizabeth Hale takes a slightly different tack to reach a related conclusion. She finds, first, that some of the goriest sex crimes associated with lynching had homosexual overtones. For example, one of the last victims of a public-spectacle lynching, in Florida in 1934, was forced by the white crowd to eat his own penis and testicles after being castrated, and to say that he liked it. Second, Hale explains that the "lynching narrative moved white women toward masculinity even as it subtly shifted white men away from the maleness embodied in the black beast."[27] This exchange of sexual identity neutered whites as a collective and allowed both sexes to project all sexual desire onto the insatiable black predator.

The violence and mob murders that occurred before the Civil War, when race was not the primary motivation, reinforce the role of homosocial economies in the lynching phenomenon. From 1834 to the 1850s, when the hanging of slaves was not called lynching, the term referred to hangings and mob murders of free men, including free blacks and white abolitionists. Pinar and others argue that masculinity and "situational homosexuality" in mining camps and on ranches were important catalysts for such violence and that asserting masculine prowess against men judged "substandard" or feminine often motivated it. From 1836 to 1856, 300 white men were lynched in such attacks.[28]

Race became a more common motivation for lynching in the 1850s, reached epic proportions between the 1880s and 1900, and continued at a lesser rate through the 1930s. Approximately 3400 African American men were murdered by mobs between 1882 and 1930, representing the vast majority of lynching victims overall. (Other estimates range between four and ten thousand African Americans, including from a handful to more than 100 women and children.)[29] Overtly homosexual projections seem evident in the lynching of freed Negro men during those years, as their new rights infuriated the white male population in the South, Midwest, and other regions of the U.S. Not only were many of the crimes accompanied by sexual mutilations and the taking of genital souvenirs, but they also excited crowds who took delight in those gruesome acts. Ida B. Wells, the anti-lynching crusader of the 1890s, exposed what she called the inversions of manliness entailed in the "lynch for rape scenario." She argued that white men "were the real embodiments of lust" and that members of lynch mobs were "vile, unmanly cowards, hiding their own rampant lusts with sanctimonious calls for chastity."[30] It is possible that many of those white men projected their own sexual aggression onto handy black men, became libidinally invested in them, and despised them for it. For some at least, a homosexual rape fantasy could have been included.

Lynching also displaced onto the bodies of black men the humiliation Southern white men felt from their defeat in the Civil War. According to Drew Gilpin Faust, the war that unleashed the pent-up power of so many black men also vanquished white men's masculinity, along with the patriarchal plantation system, and destroyed their ability to provide for or protect their families. They were ashamed that women had assumed men's roles during the war and that there was now no place for them in the new economy. Even men who stayed home from the war often felt de-masculated. Faust recounts stories of male students who did not enlist and sometimes expressed their humiliation by cross-dressing, which suggests their "anomalous position in a society where almost all young men had gone off to war."[31] White Southern women who colluded in the myth of the black male rapist to salvage their own reputations, simultaneously bonded with white men over the issue of racial privilege and "expressed their contempt for their husbands' failure to perform their manly responsibilities."[32] The hatred that ensued from that compounded defeat festered "in the groin," as lynchers reasserted their lost masculinity against the bodies of black men whose new potency they both coveted and despised. As we have seen, the sexual energy expended in lynching for some men undoubtedly displaced the sexual energy formerly expended on female slaves.

This complex gendered and sexualized scenario, publicly suppressed, was powerful in constructing the black-white racial paradigm for another half-century. Courts colluded with its deeper purposes by applying special doctrinal rules to black defendants accused of the rape or attempted rape of white women. For example, the Georgia Supreme Court ruled in 1899 that race alone was sufficient to "rebut any presumption that might otherwise arise in favor of the accused that his intention was to obtain the consent of the female, upon failure of which he would abandon his purpose to have sexual intercourse with her." From the 1890s through the 1930s and beyond, juries in such cases across the U.S. were allowed to assume that all black men desire to rape white women and that no white woman would consent to sex with a black man. A white woman was presumed virtuous unless proven otherwise. By then, even white prostitutes benefited, as their sexual backgrounds could be ruled out of order if the accused man were black, as it was in a 1912 case in Alabama (*Story v. State*): "The consensus of public opinion, unrestricted to either race, is that a white woman prostitute is yet, though lost of virtue, above the even greater sacrifice of the voluntary submission of her person to the embraces of the other race." One Justice in the Scottsboro cases in the 1930s called a white woman's rape by a black man "worse than death by an assassin." As late as 1964, the Georgia Supreme Court called the rape of a white woman by a black man "more horrible than death" and suggested that it had "soil[ed] for life her purity, the most precious attribute of all mankind." Conviction rates reinforce such logics, since thirty-six percent of black men convicted of raping a white woman were executed between 1930 and 1967, but only two percent of defendants convicted of rape involving other racial combinations were executed. Courts paid little attention to the rape of black women by either black or white men, on the continued assumption that women devoid of all sexual virtue could not be raped.[33]

Sexualized Lynching of Mexican and Chinese Men

Black men were not the only lynching victims in the United States. Hundreds of other men and a few women of color were lynched or murdered from the mid-nineteenth through the early twentieth century for reasons that also suggest homosexual projection masked by the "protection" of white heterosexual norms. As with African Americans, those acts of violence entailed accusations or suspicions of sexual misconduct—or the propensity for it—as they both constructed racial difference and incited racial hatred. Embedded within such accusations and suspicions were homosexual projections that needed to be avenged on inferior cultural bodies in order to purify the men who pulled the ropes. That nooses were tied in the name of white women—near and far—whose racial/sexual honor could allegedly be saved by an act of violence was again not the full story.

Mexicans and Chinese—presumptuous "foreign" men on the loose—were popular lynching targets in the West. Mexicans were especially victimized in the Southwest Territories, including southern California, where border disputes and land ownership were often settled by the rope from the 1840s to the 1870s and beyond.[34] Between 136 and 163 Mexican men were lynched in California alone between 1848 and 1860. Christopher Waldrep even claims that the lynching of Mexicans in the "lynching belt" from Montana through Wyoming, Colorado, New Mexico, and Arizona "outdid most of the South" between 1882 and 1902.[35] Overall, nearly 600 Mexicans were lynched in the U.S. from 1848 to 1928.[36]

Fewer Chinese men were lynched, but they were killed in greater proportion to their numbers. Twenty-nine were lynched in California after 1850, not counting those killed in a massacre in 1871.[37] Chinese men were victimized by racial violence even outside coastal states where their numbers were miniscule. For example, two died and many more were injured in a four-day protest and riot against Chinese laundrymen in Milwaukee, Wisconsin, in 1889, according to Victor Jew.[38] Overall, 143 Chinese men were murdered in the American West from 1852 to 1908, although race riots against them displaced more than 10,500. Most of the murders occurred in Oregon.[39]

Precipitating Gendered Causes

Murder and theft were the primary offenses that brought victims of all racial groups to the attention of incensed mobs. Indeed, more than a third of black male lynching victims were accused of murder, not rape or any of 80 other possible crime categories. Mexican lynching victims were most often accused of property crimes, horse theft, and murder. Murder accusations also accounted for most lynchings or murders of Chinese men. But the official charges alone were not necessarily what agitated a crowd. Mob violence against men of color usually entailed explicit or implicit suspicions of sexual aggression, perversion, or intention; and implications that all competition between men of color and white men—over land or horses or sex—somehow threatened white manhood and white women's virtue. Often charges of rape or inappropriate sexual advances toward "innocent" white women erupted through other criminal charges, and incited white crowds to kill in order to protect the social order.

The characterizations of race that swirled around these crimes further expose the possible homosexual projections involved in lynching. Although black men's allegedly insatiable sexual appetites were what fueled white male sexual fantasies, the more common representation of Mexican and Chinese lynching victims as unmanly or perverted is what triggered the displacement of white sexual fantasies. Mexicans were dangerous in part because they were incapable of the "manly virtues of honesty, honor, and loyalty" and therefore "unprincipled, conniving, and treacherous," like women.[40] Sometimes their bodies substituted for the erotic dark *Mexicanas* whom whites lusted after. At other times, they reminded white men of their own "weak," feminine tendencies or dependencies. In such cases, the alleged "sinners" must be killed to protect the real sinner. Of course, most Mexicans' actual "crime" was owning land in territory whites wanted to control.

Chinese men were often accused more directly of sexual designs on white women, including underage girls. Newspapers from San Francisco to New York alleged that they enticed girls with opium to their "morally dangerous dens" (actually laundries). Any conversation between a Chinese man and a white woman or girl might signify illegal trafficking in prostitutes or wives.[41] The "herd mentality" of sexually frustrated Chinese "bachelors" allegedly promoted conspiracies against white American women, as if their bachelorhood were not caused by immigration and anti-miscegenation laws that deprived the men of both "sexual expression and potential fatherhood."[42]

Without noticing any contradiction, white pundits also portrayed those same heterosexual predators as effeminate homosexuals. Some emphasized the Asian body's unmanliness—short stature, slight frame, and feminine hairstyle—and taunted the men's affinity for women's work in laundries and willingness to accept low wages (as if they had a choice). But Asian men's timidity did not mean they were not also treacherous. "They have a keen sense of fear, but a dull sense of honor," opined an editor of the *Albany Evening Journal* in 1859. Rosewell Pettibone Flower's words from 1882 were representative of the epithets that feminized "the Orient" in general and Chinese men's cultural bodies in particular, well into the twentieth century: "depraved, 'lacking control,' 'degenerate,' 'weak,' 'silent,' 'passive,' 'submissive,' and an 'object' to watch and examine." Today's image of Asians as the "model minority" developed from this stereotype of passive, malleable, and feminine Chinese men.[43]

Of course, Chinese men's real "crime" as the nineteenth century progressed was competing in business in an increasingly industrialized economy that already threatened white masculinity and racial dominance. Retaliation against that threat entailed projections of whites' gender anxieties onto the hyper-sexualized and/or emasculated bodies of Chinese men. That libidinal investment could only be resolved through direct assault. Often, the "women" being protected through such crimes were the vulnerable aspects of the white men's own selves in changing economic times. Chinese gender ambiguity also paralleled their ambiguous place in the black-white racial paradigm—neither black nor white, neither male nor female. For that reason, they were a gendered racial threat.

Whites enforcing what they regarded as frontier justice often denied that racism had anything to do with their animosity toward their Chinese or Mexican victims. But such denials are belied both by common sense and by the details of the attacks. The Mexican men most vulnerable to mob violence were the darker ones, and much early antipathy toward the Chinese emanated from whites' alleged inability to distinguish them from Negroes. In 1860, the Chinese area in downtown Los Angeles was called "Nigger Alley," and one white Californian argued that Chinese and African physiognomy were only slightly different.[44] Mississippi whites also initially identified Chinese immigrants as black.[45] By the same token, lynchings of Mexicans attracted white men, women, and children who wanted to view the "dead greaser"—a racial epithet if ever there was one.[46]

The gory details of lynching and other racially motivated killing suggest how important it is to understand lynching as a "gendered form of racial politics and violence" that could involve white men's regression "to their 'negative' Oedipal complex," as Pinar claims. In one form or another, whites' "repressed, racialized homosexual desire expressed itself" in sexualized acts.[47] Even for the many lynching victims not explicitly charged with rape, the pretense of protecting white women stirred for some the "white male fantasy of interracial heterosexual rape" and obscured an even deeper, repressed homosexual desire for or dread of the "other" male body.[48]

Homosexual and Homosocial Sexual Projection: The Science of Manliness

As the lynching scenario suggests, economic and political competition in post-Civil War American society undermined white men's sense of masculinity and increased their antipathy toward men of color.[49] The self-reliant entrepreneurial spirit promoted by small-scale, competitive capitalism, which had formed the core of middle-class white masculinity, eroded steadily from 1800 to 1880 and was all but gone by 1890, according to Gail Bederman.[50] In its stead were large-scale industries, in which men who were formerly their own bosses worked as clerks with few prospects or competed as small farmers against corporate landowners. In an increasingly "bureaucratic, interdependent society, the manly codes of self-restraint began to seem less relevant."[51] Bederman concurs with Pinar, Faust, and LeeAnn Whites that black men in the North soon became scapegoats for displaced white masculine pride.[52] In the West and Southwest, this displacement fell on Mexicans and the Chinese.

Lynching and mob rule were the draconian forms of sexual projection whites used throughout the country to handle competition over masculinity. But sexual projection also had a less violent role in constructing racial categories and hierarchies in the form of intellectual and cultural assaults and accusations of homosexuality. Starting in the late nineteenth century, with the growth of sexology, non-white bodies began to be "scientifically" associated with sexual pathology. Observations of "inverted" sexual identity or pathological object choice, called "Urnings" or "Uranism," actually began in the 1860s with the work of Karl Heinrich Ulrichs, James Murie, and Carl von Westphal. But so-called sexual inversion did not gain credibility until studies began appearing in medical journals in the 1880s and 1890s. By then, eugenic sexologists like Richard von Krafft-Ebing and Havelock Ellis were emphasizing the physiological differences among "sexual inverts" and linking racialized bodies with sexual "abnormalities." For example, sexologists linked the darker races with lesbians, since both groups were allegedly less sexually differentiated than the white norm. In the 1920s they noted that clitoral enlargement, alleged evidence of female homosexuality, was especially pronounced in women of color. Intermediate (or mixed) races were called "sexual half-breeds."[53]

Such "heightened surveillance of bodies in a racially segregated culture demanded a specific kind of logic," according to Siobhan Somerville, "which . . . gave coherence to the new concepts of homo- and heterosexuality." Literature, film, and popular culture became powerful mechanisms for projecting race onto homosexuality in new ways, particularly by connecting inter-racial sexual relations and culturally taboo sexual desires. Literary figures of the mulatto, as in the work of Pauline Hopkins from 1900 to 1904, were often linked with the homoerotic, possibly because interracial homoeroticism was more acceptable than inter-racial heterosexual relationships. Films, such as "A Florida Enchantment" (1914), portrayed characters whose sexual inversion or sex change, represented by cross-dressing, was linked to miscegenous desires. When Jean Toomer claimed that he was neither black nor white but American in 1930, he was automatically accused of questionable masculinity.[54] As gendered stereotypes increased from the late nineteenth through the early twentieth century, "the new discourse of sexual pathology was intertwined with these racialized images."[55]

The analogy between mixed race and homosexuality had particular effects on white perceptions of Mexicans and other Latinos. Their varied skin tones signified for many white Americans a muddied mess with analogies to sexual deviance.[56] The presence of multi-colored Mexicans on the American frontier was an insult to white men who associated manliness and civilization with whiteness. The best recourse, some imagined, was to appropriate such men's symbols of manhood—especially land—in order to show them where masculinity really resided.

"Yellow" Asian men also increasingly became feminized foils to white masculinity. David Eng argues that white views of Asian men, beginning in the 1870s, amounted to "racial castration." If they weren't seen as effeminate closet queens like Charlie Chan, Asian men were considered "homosexual menaces like Fu Manchu." In early films, the small stature of Asian men was routinely associated with homosexuality and contrasted with "cinematic images of whiteness and heterosexuality." Reaction to those images shaped Asian American literature for decades, as writers like Frank Chin and Lonny Kaneko expressed and portrayed heterosexual norms, desires, and behavior with a vengeance in order to recuperate Asian manhood.[57]

Undifferentiated gender roles and identities signified sexual deviance and questionable masculinity well into the twentieth century. Cultural discourses from editorials and films to contemporary cartoons depicted black men as "pansies," "weak and henpecked [men], dominated by their robust and overbearing wives."[58] Mexican men, according to one Texas cotton grower, were "just like . . . the nigger, but not so much."[59] Laziness became the sign of Mexican men's mixed-raced sexual lack. Asian men's menial natures and sneaky "mole-like" ability to "creep" into and corner any markets they entered were indicataive of their shrunken manhood.[60] Racializing homosexuality via the cultural bodies of men of color paralleled physical violence in shaping racial categories and racial difference throughout the twentieth century.

Conclusion

Embodying Race

All of the mechanisms analyzed in Part II—from feminizing laws and rhetoric about American Indians to the violent projection of white lust onto black bodies—reinforce *The Specter of Sex's* argument that presumed gender identities and characteristics often underlie—even form the core of—racial identities. Part II has focused on the most obviously gendered locus of racial difference—the body—and demonstrated how abstract qualities, such as masculinity and femininity, sexual power, and patriarchy, as well as apparently un-gendered attributes, such as skin color and head size, were interpreted and inscribed on gendered cultural bodies to differentiate and stratify the races.

Racial, ethnic, and national identities defined in terms of gender often sparked contests between groups of men that turned women into pawns or spoils. Sometimes white women were enthusiastic about their roles in such contests, but they also recognized that definitions of white women's cultural bodies constrained them in order to enhance white masculine power. They repeatedly learned that the primary racial subject was male and that the protection of masculinity rather than of women motivated the racial definitions, hierarchies, and mechanisms of social control—including violence—that even women upheld. Minority-race women also learned that the imperatives of masculinity, and not women's priorities and identities, were the defining feature of their race.

The gendered foundations of race in the U.S. do not end with the interpretation and disposition of cultural bodies, however. Indeed, the American story of gendered race was even messier in the service of something hidden from the eye but lurking dangerously beneath the skin. By the early twentieth century, "blood" became the dominant metaphor for race in American culture, and it is to that hidden gendered determiner of race that we turn in Part III.

PART III

Blood

Introduction

"Off women com owre manhed"

At the Paris Exposition of 1900, W.E.B. Du Bois displayed hundreds of photographs of African Americans in an exhibition entitled *Types of American Negroes, Georgia, U.S.A.*[1] Du Bois assembled the pictures to demonstrate that "typical Negro faces . . . hardly square with conventional American ideas" about race.[2] One black-and-white photograph of a clearly blue-eyed baby girl with shining blond ringlets and fair skin epitomized the extremes of coloring and features that were classified as "black" in the binary racial thinking of American culture, as they are still today. Taken together, Du Bois's pictures exposed the severe disconnect between American racial categories and the realities of human bodies on which centuries of racial mixing had been physically inscribed.[3] The photos graphically revealed to the world that the division of Americans into "black" and "white" stubbornly endured even though racial differences had become so physiologically ephemeral as to be virtually meaningless.

Many white Americans viewing Du Bois's exhibit would have felt fear rather than contrition in response to the wide array of "Negro" bodily possibilities it contained. That a beautiful white-looking child could harbor invisible blackness—in her "blood"—would only verify the extent of racial contamination rather than suggest the irrelevance of racial difference to such viewers. It would motivate them less toward racial acceptance than toward vigilance against the further dilution of the white race.

White Americans paid some attention to racial blood before the Civil War, but it was the demise of slavery that truly heightened the distrust of bodily appearances and incited fears of hidden blackness lurking in the blood to threaten "Teutonic whiteness."[4] Such paranoia evolved gradually and arrived at the point of hysteria after the eugenics movement gained credibility in the early twentieth century. By then, even a hint of blackness terrified many whites, who were obsessed with detecting the barest presence of so-called black blood in order to maintain (the illusion of) the black-white racial binary. Obsession with that binary sometimes erased the racial and ethnic specificity of other groups, including Indians, Latinos, and Asians. Thus the pale Chinese could be classified as black "because of their willingness to work in conditions akin to slavery, their incapacity to handle freedom, and their distinctive physical appearance."[5] "Distinctive" apparently equaled "black."

Locating the source of racial identity primarily in the human interior rather than on its exterior surface entailed a gradual shift in racial thinking, although parallel attention to bodies continued into the twentieth century. This new thinking is evident in judicial rulings issued during the key period of transition between the 1830s and the 1850s. A North Carolina case from 1834 reflects the earlier understanding of a shared humanity beneath differently hued skin. The court found a male slave guilty of manslaughter rather than murder for killing his overseer as he tried to thwart the slave's escape. The judge reasoned that slaves, who were clearly distinct from whites on the outside and absolutely bound to submit to their masters, nevertheless had a right to defend themselves against death. The court concluded that slaves were "degraded indeed by slavery but yet have 'organs, dimensions, senses, affections, passions' like our own."[6]

By the 1850s, court decisions reflected a different attitude, although debates continued throughout the nineteenth century, even in the South, about slaves' humanity, with varying and inconsistent results. In an 1853 case contesting the right of free black men to own slaves, for example, Georgia Supreme Court justices determined that there were absolute internal differences between whites and blacks "resulting from the taint of blood [that] adheres to the descendants of Ham in this country, like the poisoned tunic of Nessus." Whether slave or free, a Negro "must necessarily feel [his] degradation. To him there is but little in prospect, but a life of poverty, of depression, of ignorance, and of decay.... His fancied freedom is all a delusion," and any Negro would be better off as a slave "under the protection of a tolerable master." Since slavery was allegedly justified by blacks' inherent racial inferiority, the court ruled that there could be no discrepancy in racial value between free black men and their slaves and, therefore, no justification for black slaveholding in Georgia.[7]

The metaphor in the court's decision reveals the slippery belief system that came to characterize the American preoccupation with racial blood for all groups. The Georgia justices not only conflated the invisibility of blood with a tangible garment, but they also equated it with the social consequences of whites' racial judgments. This explanatory sleight of hand still functions in the notion of race as an inheritable, transmittable, but sometimes hidden characteristic that will, nevertheless, ultimately be revealed. Such reasoning ignores the fact that racial blood is "poisoned," like Nessus' tunic, only because of an external curse.[8]

Part III of *The Specter of Sex* traces the history, development, and significance of "blood" as a gendered metaphor for race in the U.S. from the colonial period through the mid-twentieth century, which functioned alongside but increasingly overwhelmed visible characteristics as a criterion for rewarding, disciplining, and controlling human beings on racial grounds. Chapter 7 first examines the relationship between kinship metaphors and "racial blood" and then analyzes evolving racial blood definitions, aimed primarily at distinguishing between blacks and whites, which appeared gender-neutral. Chapter 8 analyzes the gendered foundations of these policies and exceptions to them, many of which were based on gendered variants of reputation. Chapter 9 analyzes the gendered foundations of anti-miscegenation laws that were the primary mechanism for preventing the mixing of white and other racial bloods, including eventually the blood of "Mongolians" and Malays. Chapter 10 analyzes two additional mechanisms used to preserve white racial blood: accusations of rape, primarily against black men; and the intense scrutiny of white motherhood.

At first glance, racial blood appears the most un-gendered of the categories explored in *The Specter of Sex*. Bodies are obviously gendered, and citizenship has been a gendered, raced concept for most of American history (as we shall see in more detail in Part IV). Nevertheless, despite the language and apparently gender-neutral focus of laws and policies designed to regulate it, racial blood has not historically been a gender-blind concept. As Part III reveals, the control of racial blood was typically understood as a male prerogative exercised via women's bodies. Exceptions to blood definitions and measurements were also gendered, as were prohibitions against miscegenation and the very concept of white racial blood superiority.

7

Defining, Measuring, and Ranking Racial Blood

The Un-gendered Surface

That "blood" still seems an appropriate metaphor for racial membership and identity demonstrates the enduring use of Nature to endorse the American racial system. Blood is a biological symbol that continues to obscure the social underpinnings of race. For almost a century, the American racial system relied heavily on the notion of racial blood to determine the social status of millions of U.S. citizens and immigrants. Chapter 7 traces the public narrative about racial blood that became much more significant after 1830 and dominated the discussion of race after Reconstruction. That narrative was typically couched in gender-neutral terms, but their gendered foundations, which will be analyzed in detail in Chapter 8, are apparent nonetheless.

Race and Blood

First, a caveat. Before exploring the public epistemology of racial blood in the U.S., we should note the dubious link between the concepts of "race" and "blood." Despite its crucial role in naturalizing race as an identity and a criterion for assigning individuals and groups to racial categories and status, "racial blood" is an inaccurate metaphor for the workings of the natural world it is designed to evoke. If "blood" is meant to signify "genes," it masks the fact that genetic similarities and differences among human groups cannot be neatly mapped along the lines of racial categories. Superficial physiological similarities, like skin or eye color, can mask enormous genetic differences between individuals and groups. Moreover, roughly ninety percent of human genetic variation occurs *within* populations living on a given continent, including such apparently racially homogenous regions as Africa and Asia, and only ten percent occurs *between* continents. Individuals' DNA can link them with their ancestors but only insofar as those ancestors can be traced to a particular geographic region, preferably to an isolated area that has been subject to little outside genetic influence. That location may or may not correspond to a racial category.[1]

Recent linkages between certain diseases and groups defined as races or ethnicities only testify to the sharing of a small gene pool rather than to the existence of a gene for race.[2] The elimination of racial categories might actually improve the scientific study of population differences in disease distribution, since it is DNA and genetic variation with no relationship to racial bodily form that unlocks the processes of certain diseases.[3]

In short, racial genetics are about as far from the "single genetic switch," implied by the black-white racial blood distinction, as it is possible to get. Up to six pairs of genes are involved in the production of skin color alone.[4] People labeled as members of the same race may embody more genetic difference from than similarity to one another, and people of different so-called races may be more alike genetically than members of the same racial group.

If racial blood is meant to signify literal blood, then the concept becomes even more ridiculous. Blood types, like genes, are distributed geographically around the world, but visible "racial" characteristics have nothing to do with the distribution. The inaccuracy of "blood" as a metaphor for race is further reinforced by the fact that even close relatives can have incompatible blood types.[5]

There is, perhaps, one valid way to interpret the racial blood metaphor, but it is often lost on white people, according to James Baldwin. That is, "racial blood" accurately connotes racial violence throughout American history, as in blood spilled over racial relationships, conflict, and competition. Baldwin criticizes whites' desperate belief "that all the effort and carnage" involved in defending the alleged purity of their racial blood has been worth it. To him, blackness has become a metaphor for the bloody racial history that whites don't want to see.[6]

If blood says so little about race, then why is it such a powerful metaphor? The answer lies in the connection we have seen before— racial theorists and politicians have needed convincing "natural" evidence to make a case for the significance of racial distinctions and hierarchies. As we have also seen before, that natural evidence is typically related to the notion of allegedly natural and immutable gender differences, in which physiology both predicts and requires differences in mental capacity, moral character, political rights, and other traits and entitlements. Chapter 8 will analyze the deeply gendered origins and connotations of "racial blood," but in the meantime Chapter 7 explores the apparently un-gendered surface of American blood measurement and ranking, which also hints at its own gendered underbelly.

Measuring American Racial Blood

Difficult as it now seems to believe, measurements of racial blood only slowly came to define racial divisions in the U.S. Establishing race-based chattel slavery did not depend on the concept of racial blood, as we saw in Chapter 5. Geographical origins and skin color—"black or graduated shades thereof"—are what linked certain bodies to bondage and others to freedom, starting in Virginia and Maryland in the 1660s.[7] When African slaves were officially assigned to a racial category—Negro—in the 1680s, racial blood was not a defining factor.

The only colonies to use blood quanta to define race, Virginia and North Carolina, did not do so until the eighteenth century. The Virginia Assembly first mentioned blood as an indicator of race in 1705, when it declared that all children of Indians and anyone with one Negro grandparent or great-grandparent—or one-eighth "Negro blood"—was mulatto and could not claim the rights and privileges of whiteness.[8] North Carolina declared that anyone with African ancestry in the last three generations would be considered Negro. Everywhere else in the colonies, race, especially the Negro race, was understood primarily as a visible bodily characteristic with cultural implications. Both were broadly defined.

Only after the Revolutionary War did the republic's white citizenry become zealous about, even obsessed with, defining race. At that point, blood measurement joined geographic origins and skin color as mechanisms for constructing racial definitions in the support of slavery and the protection of white privilege, especially against the claims of a growing population of mixed-blood Americans. Virginia was perhaps the most strident of the states in using racial blood quantum for that purpose, as it tinkered with the percentages that constituted blackness.

The Virginia Assembly took a "step backwards" in 1785 by declaring that persons with one-quarter Negro blood—or one grandparent—were mulatto. Whether that step reflected the expansive spirit of the Revolution or the diminished role of mulattoes, who were thereby subjected to laws regulating free blacks, remains a matter of debate.[9] Regardless, the 1785 legislation provided an early lesson in the arbitrariness of racial blood measurement, as well as its impact on human experience. People whose "blackness" had circumscribed their identities and opportunities acquired the rights of white people overnight, with no change in the identities of their great-grandparents.

In 1866, the Virginia Assembly reaffirmed the "one-quarter" rule, and it remained in effect until 1910. In that year the proportion of black blood needed to define a Negro in Virginia decreased to one-sixteenth, or one great-great grandparent, which reversed the earlier "reprieve" by identifying as "colored" many people who had previously been defined as legally white.[10]

Other states also codified racial blood measurements over time. Arkansas, Florida, and Mississippi adopted Virginia's definition of blackness as one-quarter "Negro blood."[11] South Carolina, Missouri, Nebraska, and North Dakota all eventually enforced one-eighth rules, and Kentucky adopted a one-sixteenth rule. Oregon, Utah, and Oklahoma also enacted specific fractional rules about racial blood.[12] A few Eastern states held out for a while. From 1819 through the 1840s, South Carolina, Delaware, New Jersey, Ohio, and the District of Columbia avoided using blood measurements to determine an individual's racial status and relied on skin color and factors other than blood (such as reputation—a gendered idea) as primary signifiers of race and status.[13]

In the midst of such precise blood measurement, however, a less mechanistic definition of race was also brewing—the "one drop rule," which defined persons with any Negro ancestry as black. The one-drop rule began appearing in about 1830 and was regularly imposed by courts after 1850, especially after the 1857 *Dred Scott* Supreme Court decision that recognized "no distinction . . . between the free Negro and mulatto and the slave." All were equally tainted by stigma "of the deepest degradation . . . fixed upon the whole race," opined the court.[14] The 1896 *Plessey v. Ferguson* decision upheld racial segregation based on a single drop of black blood.

Although South Carolina adopted the one-drop rule in 1895, it was not actually legislated in Virginia until 1924, with the passage of the Preservation of Racial Integrity Act (RIA). Alabama and Georgia quickly copied Virginia's law. The one exemption allowed by the RIA was known as the "Pocahontas exception," which classified as white all of that famous Indian's progeny with John Rolfe, as well as their descendants and other Virginians of no more than one-sixteenth

Defining, Measuring, and Ranking Racial Blood   117

American Indian blood. The Virginia assembly reiterated the one-drop rule for blacks in a 1930 statute.[15]

Ranking Racial Blood

One obvious purpose of measuring racial blood was to rank the races. Starting in the 1830s, political and scientific narratives about the value of various racial bloods began converging to empower or disempower individuals and groups on the basis of internal rather than external racial qualities and characteristics.[16] Over the next three decades, those narratives built a system of racial hierarchy in the U.S. that would long outlive slavery.

Narratives about inferior and superior races infused Jacksonian politics in the 1830s. As they sought to justify the increasingly vexed institution of slavery and the removal of Indians to western lands, Jacksonians declared the United States a "white republic" in which people of other races could be governed without their consent.[17] Racial blood soon surpassed enslavement as a determiner of political position, property rights, and individual freedom.[18] Jacksonian policies were reinforced by the precepts of "scientific racism," which anticipated the theory of *polygenesis* and combined interests in bodies and blood to obfuscate the social origins of power divisions in American society. By naturalizing the domination of one racial group over all others, the evolutionary observations of scientific racism allowed white Americans to believe that American. society was "ordered around the natural divisions of race, not the artificial distinctions of class."[19]

Scientific racism also vindicated the isolation of Indians and the enslavement of Negroes by connecting both with the biological destiny of inferior peoples and claiming that domination was the biological destiny of whites. Scientific racism ultimately targeted the degenerative effects of "inferior" racial blood on a "superior" race. According to its precepts, the children of parents belonging to different races were assigned to the one that was biologically (and, not coincidentally, politically) subordinate. By the turn of the twentieth century, that idea would be known as "hypodescent."[20]

Scientific racism achieved its greatest influence during the 1840s, 50s, and 60s. The school of American ethnology, which was based on phrenologist Dr. Charles Caldwell's measurements of skulls, was founded in the 1840s. In 1844, Josiah Nott, the polygenesist and scholar of hybridity introduced in Chapter 2, published his influential *Crania*

Aegyptica, which promoted a theory of permanent racial hierarchies based on men's cranial measurements and argued vehemently against the mixing of racial bloods. Indeed, Nott overlooked abundant evidence of inter-racial reproduction as he initially insisted that blacks and whites, as different human species, could not reproduce. He also celebrated the white origins of civilization and defended European and American colonialism, imperialism, racial extermination policies, and race-based slavery on the grounds of his hierarchical racial categories. Eventually Nott conceded that white men and black women could produce mulatto offspring, but he adamantly denied that white women and black men could ever reproduce.[21]

In the 1850s and 60s, proscriptions against mixing racial blood gained even greater credibility in the U.S., as the racial narratives emerging from the American school were reinforced by racist interpretations of Darwin's *Origin of the Species* (1859) and *Descent of Man* (1870), even though the latter refuted the premise and debunked the idea of polygenesis. Particularly influential during that period was Samuel George Morton's 1854 *Types of Mankind* (co-authored with Nott), which declared Caucasians the superior race because of white men's large brains and powerful intellects (a blatantly gendered judgment). Morton's work was incorporated into religious and states' rights arguments for maintaining racial hierarchies and enforcing segregation to prevent racial mixing. Josiah Nott also remained influential throughout the 1860s, partly because he conceded that Negroes and whites were "permanent varieties" of mankind (like permanent genders) rather than distinct human species.[22]

It was also during the 1860s that the term "miscegenation" was coined in the context of a political election. Indeed, politicians embraced scientific racism and its concept of the black-white racial binary, based on blood, to argue against miscegenation, as if there were no other races or mulattoes in the U.S. population, including Asian immigrants and Mexican *mestizajes* in the Southwest territories. As the blood binary gained in ideological prominence, even European immigrant groups, such as Jews from Eastern Europe and the Irish, were classified as "black," thereby thrusting almost everyone into the racial dichotomy. As a consequence, the concept of a distinct mixed race or mulatto racial category lost traction in everyday life, even though the U.S. census started using it in 1850 (only to abandon it in 1920 as the one-drop rule took over).[23] "Other races," like Asians and mixed-race Latinos, were classified as both/and or neither/nor black/white.

Tracing Negro blood, especially in the South, became increasingly important. Anyone with a single drop was considered black, and if discovered, was constrained and restricted like any full-blooded African American (should there happen to be one). What resulted from that obsession was mass racial double-think. For example, a Pennsylvania judge ruled in 1867, apparently with a straight face, that blacks and whites had been mixing for 250 years "and yet the law still recognize[s] only two distinct races each of which ha[s] many members of mixed ancestry."[24] His opinion reflected an 1842 ruling in the Ohio State Court of Appeals: "whether a man is white or black is a question of fact . . . to break . . . the barriers, fixed by the Creator himself, . . . shocks us as something unnatural and wrong."[25]

Reconstruction's "Radical Hour," from 1866 to 1876, briefly provided egalitarian counter-narratives about race on the national level that were rare in 1860. During that period, some in the Republican Party argued for racial equality on moral and religious grounds, despite what many conceded was the racial inferiority of blacks. They simply argued that inferior racial blood did not justify denying rights. That same period produced the Thirteenth, Fourteenth, and Fifteenth Amendments to the Constitution; the Civil Rights acts of 1866, 1870, 1871, and 1875; the Expatriation Act of 1868; and the Naturalization Act of 1870, which extended naturalization rights to immigrants of African descent.[26] But the egalitarian momentum ebbed as both Reconstruction and the Radical Hour sputtered to a close. State interpretations of racial binarism soon overtook democratic federal efforts. The goal of Reconstruction to unravel the principle of racial hierarchy had proven "dauntingly complex and costly." The radical changes entailed in the laws of Reconstruction threatened many white Americans, particularly on the local level. Even the Reconstruction President, Andrew Johnson, ultimately expressed his own fear that the ascendancy of the inferior black race would threaten American civilization.[27]

In an ironic backlash, Reconstruction's coercive national agenda actually reinvigorated scientific racism "and refreshed the legitimacy of racist beliefs that had been partly discredited by the war's moral fervor," according to Rogers Smith. States' rights republicanism, "racism's old ally," also gained new credibility by the mid-1870s, and hastened both the official retreat from Reconstruction and the proliferation of new policies hostile to Chinese immigrants. "Finally, not even the bloody flag could sustain political support for radical reforms."[28] At the same time, belief in natural racial hierarchies based on blood "justified renewed paternalism toward native tribes," and predictably "undercut the much weaker efforts to liberalize the status of women." Thus, renewed support for stratified racial blood spurred support for gender hierarchy. According to Smith, "white commitments to racial hierarchy [ultimately] emerged as even more pivotal than capitalism in explaining the end of America's radical hour."[29]

Once the tenets of scientific racism were revived, there was no stopping them in post-Reconstruction America. The scientific community in both England and the U.S. pumped out ever more prejudicial racial analyses. In the 1880s, the new "science" of eugenics—meaning "well-born"—first appeared in Britain, founded by Charles Darwin's cousin, Francis Galton. In 1884, Galton explained that character is an ancestral heirloom and that racial differences are biological determiners of both physiology and innate moral and intellectual qualities. More strongly than the scientific racism that spawned it, eugenics transcended the discredited idea of polygenesis, blended the concepts of culture and biology, and convinced a gullible public that intelligence and moral character in different racial groups were biologically determined and carried in the blood.[30]

Eugenics slipped into the U.S. around the turn of the twentieth century, initially promoting the bogus idea that even a person's experience and acquired personality traits could cause him or her to produce defective offspring. That idea emboldened the state of Indiana, for example, to perform mandatory vasectomies on prisoners beginning in 1899, even though scientific challenges to the inheritance of acquired traits were already more than a decade old. Eventually most American eugenicists simply absorbed such critiques into their ideology and switched their attention to genetic reproductive fitness, located especially in the hereditary differences between races contained in racial blood.[31]

The eugenic focus on race and the prevention of miscegenation in the U.S. both advanced Galton's particular agenda and perfectly suited the American race system. Organizations such as the American Breeders Association, the Race Betterment Society, the Eugenics Record Office, and the Galton Society sprang up before 1920 from New York to Michigan. Some groups were financed by scions of industry, such as W.K. Kellogg, Mrs. E.H. Harriman, and the Carnegie Institution.[32] All were dedicated to promoting the same basic eugenic idea, expressed in 1916 by Madison Grant of the Galton Society (later called the American Eugenics Society): "The laws against miscegenation must be greatly extended if the higher races are to be maintained."[33]

Eugenics achieved the status of a science in the U.S. despite its unscientific origins and political purposes. Its acceptance was energetically promoted by the New Haven-based American Eugenics Society in 1925. The AES sponsored numerous contests—including Fitter Family contests and eugenics exhibits at state fairs—promoting what it called genetic fitness and convincing many if not most Americans that racial blood was a key determiner of people's intellect, morality, social position, and physical capacities. After 1914, college courses in eugenics could be found at Harvard, Columbia, and Cornell Universities, and by 1928, the majority of colleges offered such courses. High school textbooks identified eugenics as a legitimate science from 1914 to 1948 and trained students to believe that unrestricted immigration, racial integration, and unmonitored reproduction threatened American society.[34]

The Gendered Underbelly

Some gendered foundations for definitions and measurements of racial blood are already apparent in this chapter's analysis, undermining the apparently gender-neutral history of scientific and political influences on the regulation of racial blood. For example, measurements of racial value focused on the male racial subject, and support for racial hierarchy reinforced support for gender hierarchy. Such gender bias did not of course mean there were no gender-inclusive ramifications of the nation's focus on racial blood. Definitions, measurements, and judgments about racial blood affected both sexes, as did the texts (if not the enforcement) of anti-miscegenation laws.

Nevertheless, inclusive guidelines and consequences often obscured the gendered structures and motivations of such laws and policies as well as the race-specific and gendered nature of their enforcement and impact. Chapter 8 explores the gendered foundations of racial blood as a concept and a system of social stratification. In so doing, it reveals the many ways in which American white "manhed"—understood as race-based status, power, wealth, rights, and privileges—was achieved "off women," particularly white women, who were held primarily responsible for the protection and transmission of legitimate white racial blood.

8

Hardly Gender Neutral

Although laws and policies regulating racial classifications typically made no mention of it, gender was instrumental in defining whose blood was white and whose was not, in authorizing exceptions to racial blood rules, and in regulating the transmission of white racial blood and its privileges from one generation to the next. Even the concept of white supremacy itself was gendered, since whites' social power, rights, and privileges were coded masculine and applied unevenly to white women, who often attained their status through the racial and class positions of men.

Why is Blood Gendered?

One of the reasons that racial blood became such a powerful metaphor, as we saw in Chapter 7, was the connotation that Nature approved of the American race system. That alleged natural connection was awash with gendered associations because of its connection to the much older concept of "familial blood," which is a key symbol of the Euro-American kinship system. In this system, familial blood signifies the biological element of family relationships, which says more about DNA than about literal blood. Nevertheless, blood (which is thicker than water) signifies the permanent and indissoluble bonds, deep feelings, mutual obligations and responsibilities of family relationships, as well as social expectations about the passage of property, status, and wealth between generations. Familial blood can also signify either the legitimacy or the illegitimacy of sexual unions and reproductive acts.

So how is familial blood a gendered concept? For one thing, sex distinction and gender hierarchy are what legitimate the passage of familial blood and the establishment of nuclear families.[1] To qualify a familial unit as legitimate, reproductive partners must *lack* a natural connection, symbolized by blood, which would taint sexual unions with an aura of incest. (Homosexual unions signify to some the *presence* of that natural connection because of the partners' shared sex category.)[2] The "normal" family that such unions create is also characterized both by gender-specific roles and by male dominance.

Both of those gendered familial characteristics seem ordained by Nature because of the ancient gender associations discussed in Chapter 1. Femaleness has long signified the immanent or natural realm—in which actions and behaviors are self-evident, automatic, and instrumental—while maleness signifies the cultural or transcendent realm—in which actions are guided by reason, intentionality, and rational choice. That distinction identifies men as Cultural agents and women as a force of Nature. Reproductive roles reinforce that same apparently natural gender distinction. Women's reproductive work is tangible and physical (natural)—pregnancy, parturition, lactation. Men's biological contribution is less evident and more abstract (cultural). So, women's traditional role in the household—childcare and domestic work—is not always considered work, since it seems a natural extension of their reproductive biology and, more recently, of their chromosomal differences from men (though there is little evidence that a Y chromosome renders an individual incapable of caring for children, cleaning toilets, or making lasagna). That association of biology with domestic roles makes women the key symbols of reproduction in patriarchal familial systems, even though fathers may simultaneously be regarded as the primary parent for purposes of custody and inheritance, as they were in England and the U.S. before the late nineteenth century.[3]

The second reason that familial blood is a gendered concept in the American kinship system is its connection with men's control over the passage of family lineage between generations. That is, women legitimately transmit familial blood only by men's authority. Such patriarchal control probably emanated originally from the incest taboo, which historically orchestrated exogamy, or marriage between unrelated kin groups, via men's exchange of women rather than women's exchange of men. In order to identify new blood as "unrelated," the exchanged woman was seen as transmitting the familial blood of her male reproductive partner with male approval from her kin group, which legitimized the couple's offspring. This chain of control made tangible men's abstract reproductive role, reinforced perceptions of men's rational, transcendent cultural identities, and established male authority over household patterns and economic activities. In other words, it created the patriarchal family.

The metaphor of racial blood was opportunistically, if unconsciously, superimposed on the metaphor of familial blood in the U.S. Racial blood appropriated to itself—but also reinterpreted—familial blood's requirements of male dominance over female reproduction and the patriarchal family's gender distinctions and hierarchies. Especially as visual evidence of racial differences became unreliable, racial separatists increasingly defined race using the blood metaphor that had worked so well in rationalizing and manipulating gender distinction and stratification in the family.

The values of gender difference and hierarchy, as well as male dominance, implicit in the Euro-American kinship system allowed powerful men to define racial blood to suit their political and economic purposes. Recognizing that incest, although banned, was never an absolute taboo in the kinship system, for example, some white American men also considered the taboo against mixing racial blood open to interpretation. They felt empowered to manipulate definitions of racial blood and related anti-miscegenation rules as a patriarchal right. Because they were accustomed to male control over women's transmission of familial blood in the Euro-American kinship system, they could rationalize their own sexual and reproductive excursions over racial lines and justify manipulating women's transmission of familial blood depending on race. It seemed entirely appropriate for white men to choose which of their reproductive acts would bestow legitimacy on their children and which would not transmit racial and familial privilege to the next generation.

Thus, a large chunk of American racial history depended on a kind of reproductive deception, in which white men were able to disassociate their rape and impregnation of black women from the act of transmitting white familial/racial blood and to orphan their own mixed-race offspring with impunity. Even after slavery ended, white men's inter-racial progeny flew just beneath the radar of kinship, and their inter-racial sexual liaisons constituted an acceptable and convenient form of exogamy. Such duplicity defined, controlled, and preserved black, white, and (for a limited time) mulatto racial blood in the U.S. for more than a century.[4]

To explore how this system played into American racial politics, we turn now to the gendered precepts involved in measuring and ranking racial blood. Gendered interpretations of mulattoes and gendered exceptions to racial blood rules are key topics in that discussion.

Mulattoes

When Earnest Sevier Cox, co-founder of the Richmond-headquartered Anglo-Saxon Clubs of America, declared "the mulatto . . . the principal cause of nearly all the trouble of the poor Negro in America" in 1922, he was expressing both the fundamental fears and the contradictory messages that had motivated the measurement and control of racial blood in the U.S. for many decades.[5] Cox's assessment was also a misstatement, however. Even half a century after the Civil War, mulattoes' existence was a principal cause of trouble for *whites*, which is why they were a problem for Negroes.[6]

Mulattoes embodied the contradictions of race-based slavery and post-Reconstruction segregation. Both their skin color and their racial blood challenged white supremacy, but blood was by far the bigger concern. Passing for white on the basis of appearance had limited benefits; the "passer" still needed to compete socially and economically with other whites, and his/her racial origins could be exposed at any moment. But descendants with large percentages of white racial blood could feel entitled to white property and privilege. Therefore, as their numbers grew, mulattoes' blood was a greater threat than their skin to whites' exclusive hold on social, economic, and political privileges and rights.

Despite the general threat of mulatto blood to white racial purity and power, not all mulattoes were considered equally menacing. During slavery, white men's mixed race children with black women were relatively un-threatening to white dominance, since the law helped to hide them in the slave quarters (and later on the "wrong" side of the tracks) with their mothers. Such children were classified as black on the basis of blood as well as social status, thanks to the long-lasting effects of seventeenth- and eighteenth-century "status of the (black) mother" laws that condemned to slavery (or servitude) all children of slave or indentured women, regardless of the race of the mother or the status of the father. As we saw in Part II, Virginia led the colonies in that regard, passing its "condition of the mother" statute in 1662.[7] "Status-of-the-mother" laws also exempted white men from responsibility for white blood transmission when they engaged in inter-racial reproduction. These laws, accompanied by rapes of black women, expanded the enslaved population exponentially and profitably.

That the laws did not automatically bestow the status of white women's racial blood onto their children ensured that paternal blood alone could make the next generation white. To emphasize the point, some colonies, like Virginia and Maryland, actually reclassified offending white women as black in order to deny white status to their mixed-blood progeny. Anti-miscegenation statutes further reinforced white women's obligation to transmit white paternal blood to their children, as we shall see in Chapter 9. In addition to reinforcing white men's reproductive control, such measures addressed a problem caused by conventional gender roles. Because women were children's primary caretakers, their children were more socially visible than men's. So, the children of white women and black or mixed-race men, including African slaves, were more obviously linked to white families and white privilege than were white men's offspring with black women, slave or free. Therefore, white women's mulatto children with black men most threatened white rule, starting in the seventeenth century. In this way, the conventional gender roles that made white women's mulatto children so obviously dangerous were a primary culprit in the history of racial classification.

The gendered difference between mulattoes helps to explain why no post-slavery colony or state sanctioned a white man for impregnating a black woman, as long as he didn't marry her and thereby disturb property rights. It also helps to explain why "free mulatto" was such a problematic racial category during slavery. Those free children of black men and white women had the best reason to rebel against the effects of racial classifications and to claim white rights, privileges, and property on the basis of their white blood. Given that frightening prospect, controlling white women's reproductive behavior and choices and limiting non-white men's access to white women seemed the best way to preserve white men's control over the privileges of white racial blood.[8] Controlling black women—or women classified as black—was less important, since the only racial status they could convey was black. That white males benefited most from the economic, political, and social privileges being protected by such machinations, and white females could transmit but not generate the blood that achieved those privileges, further exposes the gendered foundations of white racial dominance and racial blood regulation.

Gendered Indian "Middle Bloods"

Before the wholesale containment of Indians in the Jacksonian period and beyond, discussed in Part II, Indian racial blood was sometimes a special case in American racial politics. By all accounts, Indians did not regard themselves as a people or race distinguished by either physiology or blood before European contact. Even after the arrival of whites, many tribes welcomed intermarriage, especially between European men and Indian women. Since those gender arrangements coincided with the idea that white men controlled white blood privilege, many early English settlers also welcomed white male-Indian female intermarriage as a way to expand English rule.[9] Only North Carolina and Virginia among the early English colonies banned such intermarriage, although a few states eventually did so. Some prominent English leaders of the eighteenth century, including William Byrd of Virginia, John Lawson of North Carolina, and the anti-miscegenist Thomas Jefferson himself, promoted white male-Indian female intermarriage as a mechanism for creating an invincible, truly American "team." Jefferson even lamented the fact that Indians had not blended into the winning white tribe: "They would have mixed their blood with ours [but not ours with theirs], and been amalgamated and identified with us within no distant period of time," he wrote in 1813.[10]

Indians were often treated in those years as bearers of a "middle blood" with special privileges—as in the Pocahontas exemption in Virginia—and a special intermediary role. "It was almost as if whites needed Indians to become fully white, and to make blacks fully black," suggests Scott Malcomson.[11] Another law passed in Virginia in 1833 makes Malcomson's point. It allowed people with English and Indian ancestry to be certified as "persons of mixed blood, not being free Negroes or mulattoes."

But perceptions of Indian middle racial blood waxed and waned over time, depending on the ever-changing needs and ideologies of whites. Some colonial governments resented the metaphorical allure of Indian blood for many white men who wanted to "become Indians" and live like hunters and warriors, for example. A few even executed white men who succumbed to that allure, starting in 1612. Perhaps because of that precedent, the white female writers of eighteenth- and nineteenth-century captivity narratives were more circumspect. They celebrated the survival skills and independence training they learned from their "hosts" only after expressing their earnest desire for rescue.

Eighteenth-century commentators like Crèvecoeur recognized Indians as symbols of the primitive hunting state that allowed "men to be men" instead of immobile cultivators of the soil, but he also found their appeal to white men a sign of "white degeneration." Some nineteenth-century writers, like James Fenimore Cooper, romanticized the attraction of Indian blood to white men. Since Indians faced imminent demise by that time, primarily at white hands, Cooper expressed nostalgia in 1823 for the loss of "part of white Americans' self-understanding," but he also accepted that loss as "a necessary stage in 'the march of the nation across the continent,' " in the last words of *The Pioneers*. Cooper's longing for westward movement was the literary equivalent of Manifest Destiny politics, a primarily male-driven enterprise, as many historians have documented. That white male political fantasy, projected onto the Indian, helped to romanticize male Indian blood but also to rationalize its complete obliteration.[12]

Jacksonian politics and scientific racism erased most vestiges of Indian blood's privileged middle status, a result that lasted into the twentieth century. For Jacksonians, the racialization of Indians became an important rationale for taking their lands with impunity. They applauded Supreme Court Justice Joseph Story's proclamation in 1828 that the "red" man was ultimately inassimilable and doomed to extinction. The only way to preserve their "bold, but wasting race," Story wrote, was through the white society that replaced them. Massaging that rationale, Jackson testified to Congress in 1830 that Indians were lucky to have the government's help in relocating, since their welfare, like that of whites, depended on moving West.[13]

Scientific racists like Josiah Nott reinforced such political judgments in the 1840s by calling Indians a specific species of "worthless and corrupt" savages with very limited reasoning power in their inferior skulls. Anything good that could be said about Indians, Nott contended, was attributable to infusions of white blood. But he was not recommending cross-racial reproduction. Rather than envisioning a "winning" tribe through the improvements white (male) blood could offer to red, such scientists predicted serious hypodescent for whites.[14] All intermarriage would be risky, but intermarriage between Indian males and white females was especially so, since without white male control, women's white blood would be lost. Their children would "become Indian" in every way. Such reasoning led the U.S. government to reject a bold request by the Cheyenne nation in 1854 that the tribe's annual payment be made in "four thousand dollars in money; [with the] balance of their annuity in guns and ammunition, and one thousand white women for wives."[15]

Whites had no reason to lament the demise of Indian blood, according to Senator Thomas Hart Benton. He argued in 1846 that it was up to them to choose civilization or "extinction . . . the fate of all people who have found themselves in the track of the advancing Whites." Nott agreed. He wrote in 1854 that "human progress has arisen mainly from the war of races," and someone has to lose.[16] Indians' doom was at least partially gendered, since their male blood allegedly carried both uncivilized barbarity and feminine deficiencies. In short, it was seriously out of whack on the gender scale. That's why Indians were deemed incapable of improvement and necessarily subject to strict monitoring and confinement for their own good.

"A Man's Reception into Society": A Gendered Exception to Racial Blood

Although the alleged deficiencies of Indian racial blood had important political and material consequences, it was black racial blood that became the primary focus of racial blood measurement, starting in the 1830s. Indeed, the measurement of black blood remained an American obsession for at least another 150 years. But even with that intensity of purpose, the process of determining black and white racial categories was more challenging than lawmakers had anticipated. Racial classification was always an uncertain and unstable enterprise, in part because whites—whose black ancestors might come back to haunt them—could suffer as much as blacks from the strict application of racial blood percentages. Moreover, the narrower the laws became, the more contradictions they contained. Things became progressively complicated as the *de facto* "one-drop rule" bumped up against legal mandates for *de jure* percentages. For example, North Carolina's fractional rulings in 1901 and 1908 contradicted a 1903 statute that prevented a child from attending a white school if he had any "Negro blood in his veins, 'however remote the strain.'" By 1910, Louisiana also interpreted its Jim Crow laws in terms of the "one-drop rule" but simultaneously excluded from such laws persons "in whom there is only an admixture of Negro blood," especially if "the admixture is so slight that even a scientific expert could not be positive of its presence."[17]

Given the inherent disconnect between strict blood definitions and lived experience, courts were continuously asked to rule on exceptions, and legislatures repeatedly refined racial definitions in order to advance social functioning. Cases from the late seventeenth century through the 1930s reveal that the concept of "reputation" was perhaps the most important basis for granting exceptions and for redefining racial blood. "Reputation" was a gendered concept because the relationships and behaviors most likely to trump strict measurements of racial blood involved activities in the male-dominated public arena, where men met and took one another's measure. Most exceptions to racial categories based on blood accommodated men's economic and political interests.[18] To serve those interests, legislatures and courts adjusted many a racial classification on the basis of reputation, especially during the racially volatile years at the turn of the twentieth century. Those adjustments, paradoxically, actually helped the emphasis on racial blood to distribute more rights to mulattoes than light skin color had ever done. Indeed, the long history of exceptions based on blood probably reduced the impact of the "one-drop rule," as Teresa Zackodnik explains.[19]

South Carolina was among several Southern states that considered a man's reputation more important than blood to his social status. Lawmakers there resisted using racial blood percentages to determine a man's race until the 1840s, as we saw in Chapter 7. An 1835 state court opinion expressed the state's attitude concisely: "We cannot say what admixture of negro blood will make a coloured person, and by a jury, one may be found a coloured person, while another of the same degree of blood may be declared a white man ... The condition of the individual is not to be determined solely by distinct and visible mixture of negro blood, but by reputation, by his reception into society, and his having commonly exercised the privileges of a white man."[20]

Likewise, reputation played an important role in black and white racial classification in the few Southern states, such as Alabama and Louisiana, which maintained a separate mulatto or Creole category until Reconstruction, based on West Indian or Arcadian racial definitions. That category benefited both blacks and the many self-defined whites who did not want to lose the status-enhancing effects of white blood. As the concept of impure black blood gained greater credence in the 1880s and 1890s, however, Louisiana increasingly sought to determine which Creoles were white and which were black and, therefore, of "impure blood." White Creole organizations formed to protect their threatened social status and to distinguish their members from imposter black Creoles. Reputation and association influenced where the all-important, albeit arbitrary, line could be drawn between black and white, when neither appearance nor blood could be counted on. Louisiana courts still accepted association as evidence of racial status into the 1930s, and Alabama courts did so into the 1920s.[21]

White men throughout the South also used their patrimonial wealth, associations, and reputations to protect their racial identities in cases where mixed blood was suspected. In the ante-bellum period, for example, an upstanding white man who suddenly produced a dark child with his white wife could accuse the wife of adultery with a black man rather than survey his own family tree to see if it contained "Negro blood."[22] Or, if he had the social status to protect his wife as well as his own reputation, he might invoke *vis imaginativa*, an ancient fiction accepted by many eighteenth- and early nineteenth-century American doctors, which claimed that a woman's active imagination could "disrupt the proper patriarchal transfer of historically constituted 'blood' as metonym of racial genius and with it the intergenerational transfer of patri-racial culture (patrimony)," as Brackette Williams explains. In other words, men transmitted race through women's wombs, but a woman's imagination could explain a racially "distorted" fetus.[23] On the surface *vis imaginativa* might seem to empower women as definers of race, including their own, beyond legal restrictions on racial blood, but such manipulations of legal proceedings really depended on men's reputations and status.[24] Moreover, even a positive ruling could cast doubt on a woman's background and morality and compromise her reputation.

After 1850, when racial blood became a stronger determiner of racial identity, black men continued to benefit from their positive reputations, even if they were accused of raping a white woman. Although executions of black men convicted of raping white women increased significantly at that time (as we saw in Chapter 6), courts still had the task of determining the racial category of the accused. According to Martha Hodes, men were judged in such cases on their appearance and blood lineage as well as on their "reputation,... reception into society, and... exercise of certain [male] privileges."[25] A black man's successful exercise of white male privilege could whiten his blood and reduce the severity of his punishment.

Into the twentieth century, reputation and association continued to shape racial categorization in Southern states, as illustrated by a 1907 North Carolina case in which a man accused of "passing" for white countered the charge with a parade of "reputable white Carolinians" who attested to his white identity. Because "the threat of the 'white nigger'... was used as a justification for effectively controlling those whites whose commitment to white Southern economic, political, and social interests was questionable," as Zackodnik explains, those given a racial reprieve undoubtedly knew how to maintain their privilege by curbing their behavior and choosing their friends.[26]

Other non-white groups also found reputation significant in defining men's racial blood. After the U.S. annexed formerly Mexican territories to the Southwest in 1848, for example, *mestizos* of Mexican origin could invoke reputation to whiten their racial status. Although treaties had promised the privileges of American citizenship—that is, of whiteness—to former Spanish and Mexican citizens, in practice that status was highly contested, as we shall see in Chapter 14. Fears about a "takeover" by mixed-raced persons dogged *mestizos*, and those with darker skin were dependent on the support of Anglo allies and their lighter-skinned *compadres* to affirm their manly worthiness and thereby nudge them into the white category. In contrast to American

Indians in certain periods, *mestizos'* blood never occupied an honored "midway position."[27]

Mixed-race Japanese Americans also found that their blood could seem "whiter" during World War II if they proved not only that their veins carried less than fifty percent Japanese blood but also that their associates before the war were mostly white. Men were the likely beneficiaries of this variation on the reputation theme because the whitening of Japanese blood was designed to cement loyalty to the United States, and women's political loyalties were considered mere functions of their husbands' or fathers' affiliations.[28]

Women's Different Reputations

Because of women's socially mandated dependence on men, the concept of reputation had a different impact on their racial classification. That is, a woman's history of private associations with men was often more important than her individual blood heritage in determining her racial fitness for marriage to white men, her inheritance or property rights, and sometimes the racial classification of her children. Denied access to the public sphere in which reputation functioned to whiten men, a woman depended on the racial status of her husband: if he was accepted as white, she was likely to be seen as white herself. This equation is evident in a North Carolina court case from 1892, a Texas case from 1894, and an Alabama case from 1903.[29] Women whose male companions were considered black, on the other hand, were likely to be classified as black or mulatto for public purposes, even if their own lineages were white.

Women had a virtually exclusive claim to still another kind of gendered reputation with regard to racial blood classification, however, and that was *sexual* reputation, which could darken or whiten their blood (usually the latter). White or apparently white women of the lower classes typically found their blood darkened by questionable sexual reputations. They "could not count upon white ideology about white female purity and black male aggression to absolve them of illicit sexual activity," as Hodes argues.[30] Thus, their racial classification was often shakier than that of their upper-class white sisters (but not always).

Free mulattas in some Southern states, such as Mississippi, Alabama, and Louisiana, which recognized a separate mulatto racial category, had a different experience. Their reputation for sexual allure actually promoted their acceptance in white ante-bellum society in such states, which, not coincidentally, imposed fewer miscegenation restrictions than elsewhere in the South.

The lore about mulattas' attractiveness to white men had a national reach, as evident in the 1853 opinion of Supreme Court Chief Justice Joseph Henry Lumpkin in *Bryan v. Walton*: "Which one of us has not narrowly escaped petting one of the pretty little mulattoes belonging to our neighbors as one of the family?"[31] But mulatta sexual allure was nowhere more thoroughly institutionalized than it was in New Orleans, whose annual ante-bellum Quadroon Ball was a kind of coming out party for each year's new crop of young, beautiful mulattas, raised intentionally by their mothers, aunts, and grandmothers to be the concubines of white men. Only white men were allowed to attend the ball, and the wealthiest and most eligible among them paid the $2 gate, selected their quarry, and began negotiating contracts with either the girl or her female guardian that were "formal, businesslike, and as openly conducted as other business transactions, with stipulated residences and incomes," according to Beth Day.[32]

The benefits of such a reputation and its attendant economic boon were, of course, illusory. The unintended but inevitable consequences no doubt inspired the trope of the "tragic mulatta," which became a staple of late nineteenth- and early twentieth-century literature and contrasted starkly with literary depictions of mulatto men as "brave, honest, intelligent, and rebellious."[33] Reality tended to bear out mulattas' tragic destiny, especially as the Civil War deprived many ante-bellum gilded quadroons of both their white lovers and the resources and protection they promised. Many found themselves reduced to domestic work or forced to marry whatever black men would rescue them after white lovers disappeared or their ardor dimmed. Such marriages were also typically doomed. In 1864 alone, six young quadroon women were murdered in New Orleans by their black husbands in cases involving rivalries with other men. Many others committed suicide as the only apparent escape from the perils of racial "passing" or an ignominious life in the black community.[34]

Illegal Blood

If the variability in and multiple exceptions to defining racial blood discussed in this chapter somehow suggest that racial categories based on blood were frivolous or irrelevant, such an idea should be dispelled immediately. As we shall see in Chapter 9, even flawed judgments about racial blood, like those about raced bodies, could be deadly serious. Anti-miscegenation laws that dictated racial blood qualifications for marriage were especially threatening. They created a reign of terror for many decades, particularly for the black men and white women who were their primary targets.

9

Gendered Anti-Miscegenation

Laws and Their Interpretation

The term "miscegenation" was coined during the 1864 presidential election, when a few Democrats disguised themselves as Republicans and distributed leaflets that linked political freedom for blacks with rampant sex between black men and white women, which they called "miscegenation." The spirit of anti-miscegenation was much older, however, dating to the 1660s, when some colonies prohibited "abominable mixtures," especially within the servant class.[1] Those early laws were less concerned with race or with interracial fornication or reproduction per se than with property rights and status, as we saw in Part II. That concern would remain compelling even beyond slavery, as marriage remained the target of such laws from the seventeenth through the mid-twentieth century. They were dedicated to preventing the birth of the most dangerous mulattoes—the progeny of black men and white women.

By 1915, 28 American states had prohibited and declared invalid all marriages between Negroes and whites, classified according to their blood. Leading the bandwagon were eugenicists like Madison Grant, who declared in 1916 that interracial marriages were a crime that would lead to "racial suicide" through the principle of hypodescent.[2] The eugenics movement also promoted the standard pre-marital blood test to prevent inadvertent interracial marriages (later to diagnose the dangers of sexually transmitted diseases).[3] By the 1930s, 41 states had outlawed marriages on the basis of eugenics categories. Another 14 states passed and repealed anti-miscegenation statutes in the 1940s and 50s. Thirty states kept their hateful laws on the books until the civil rights movement of the mid-twentieth century.[4]

Court decisions provided an hospitable environment for these laws. As Peggy Pascoe explains, "Judicial justifications reflected the momentum toward racial categorization built into the nineteenth--

century legal system and buttressed by the racialist conviction that everything from culture, morality, and intelligence to heredity could be understood in terms of race." From the 1880s until the 1920s, an individual's only official defense against anti-miscegenation laws was to dispute the racial category to which he or she had been assigned. The categories were malleable and inconsistent, as we have seen, but they were enforced in their inconsistency "by judges and juries who believed that setting racial boundaries was crucial to the maintenance of ordered society." No court declared miscegenation laws unconstitutional until 1967, when the Supreme Court, in *Loving v. Virginia*, finally found Virginia's miscegenation laws in violation of the Fourteenth Amendment. Their primary purpose, the Court declared, was "to maintain White Supremacy."[5]

Throughout their history, American courts reinforced the fiction that anti-miscegenation laws applied equally to both sexes and to all races, as they repeatedly declared them constitutional. As Chapter 9 discusses, however, seemingly neutral and inclusive anti-miscegenation laws were rarely applied equally to all races or to members of both sexes. Their phrasing obscured their gendered intentions and mechanisms of enforcement, which helped to assuage white men's historic fear of political collusion between white women and black men.

Gendered Anti-Miscengenation Laws and Policies in the Colonies and New Republic

As we saw in Part II, the earliest regulation of sexual activity in the American colonies was not motivated by race. Only the Dutch of New Amsterdam mentioned skin color in their prohibition of adulterous intercourse. That their law outlawed intercourse between *whites* and blacks and "heathens" but not between the latter two groups foreshadowed the unequal application of such laws to racial groups. English colonies worried most about regulating fornication in all its guises within the indentured and enslaved classes. Such regulation was designed to reduce employers' and masters' financial losses from the missed work time of pregnant female servants and slaves (of all colors and geographical origins) and from the forced support of their resulting "bastards."[6] To mitigate that risk, masters and employers in most English colonies acquired rights in the progeny of their female servants and slaves, starting in the 1650s.[7] The early regulation of marriage, which began in Virginia in 1634, was also only tangentially about race. The intent of those laws was to reduce elite English men's competition for scarce marriageable English women. The harshest anti-miscegenation laws developed when whites became alarmed about the economic threat of the dangerous mulattoes produced by English women and Negro or mulatto men.

At every stage, anti-miscegenation regulations racialized gender issues. The unintended consequences and repeated reformulations of early laws demonstrate how ineffective they were in preventing targeted mixed-race marriages and eliminating mulatto progeny. That same struggle plagued the regulation of racial blood for almost a century, which makes it worthwhile to examine the sputterings of a few early laws in detail.

Maryland

Maryland's 1664 statute, mentioned in Chapter 5, was the first anti-miscegenation law in the colonies. It preceded the first colonial status-of-the-mother law, in Virginia, by 18 years. The ostensible purpose of its prohibition against marriage between an English woman and a Negro slave was to deter "freeborne women from such shamefull Matches," not only with slaves but with "all Negroes," as we saw in Chapter 5.[8] The Maryland law also established the principle that white women could not bequeath their whiteness to their children unless the fathers were white. In reality, both laws protected white property and power via women's bodies.

To many slave owners, Maryland's 1664 law appeared to encourage—even coerce—marriages between male slaves and white serving women, since their children would enlarge their enslaved workforces. It seems that mulattoes were not so repugnant if they enhanced profits. This unintended consequence of the law inspired the Assembly to rule in 1681 (the year it passed the colony's status-of-the-mother law) that an English woman forced by her master into marriage with a slave would be free "Instantly upon her Intermarriage . . . And all Children borne . . . shall bee free." In addition, both masters and marrying ministers would be fined ten thousand pounds of tobacco.[9]

The Assembly's effort to establish race-based social norms was an uphill battle.[10] The 1681 law stopped neither the mixed marriages nor the mixed-race progeny, because female servants used the new law to conclude their terms of service through miscegenation. So, the Assembly passed another law in 1692 that indentured "any free born English or white woman be she free or Servant" who intermarried with "any negro or other Slave or to any Negro made free." The penalty was seven years of service "to the use and benefit of the Ministry of the Poor" by both the English woman and the man "if he be a free Negro." Children of such matches were condemned to servitude until the age of 21. The law included other conditions depending on the circumstances of the interracial marriage, and for the first time it applied, at least on paper, to white men who intermarried with or impregnated a Negro woman. There is no evidence, however, that the latter provision was ever enforced.[11] Maryland's anti-miscegenation law was revised slightly in 1728, after which it remained unchanged—and woman-focused—until 1859.[12]

Virginia

Virginia embraced miscegenation legislation after deciding that interracial fornication threatened the colony's economy. The Assembly was already fining all fornicators 250 pounds of tobacco, but in 1662 it doubled the fine for Christians (whites) found guilty of fornicating with a Negro man or woman. That change promoted the racial distinctions that supported the codification of perpetual chattel slavery, which was then beginning and already exacerbating concerns about the marriages and progeny of white women. So, in 1691 the Virginia Assembly passed an anti-miscegenation law designed "for the prevention of that abominable mixture and spurious issue which hereafter may encrease in this dominion, as well by Negroes, mulattoes, and Indians intermarrying with English, or other white women, as by their unlawfull accompanying with one another."[13] Virginia's law was thereby the first in the colonies to use "white" as a racial term and to make clear that the primary white miscegenation offenders were women.

The punishment phase of the 1691 law appeared a bit more gender inclusive: "Be it enacted . . . whatsoever English or other white man or woman being free shall intermarry with a negro, mulatto, or Indian man or woman bond or free shall within three months after such marriage be banished and removed from this dominion forever." But that apparent inclusivity was contradicted by the law's emphasis on marriage as the violation. That focus virtually eliminated white men from punishment, since they had little incentive to marry free Negro women, who were subject to labor tithes, and fornicated freely with their slaves. In addition, the law's punishment phase excluded blacks, Indians, and mulattoes. Thus, its strong language and harsh punishment were really reserved for English women, the only miscegenation partner left standing.[14] The targeting of English women is also evident in the law's requirement that any English woman who produced a bastard child by a Negro or mulatto would pay a fine and be forced to indenture the child for 30 years. In addition, since only English female servants could bear bastard mulattoes (all black women's children being black), only they were subject to the punishment of an extra five years of indenture.[15] In short, the law further enriched planters on women's backs.

Virginia's anti-miscegenation laws became even harsher for women in the eighteenth century. The ban on marriages between English and Negroes or mulattoes was extended in 1705, but banishment was replaced by six months in prison for whites (which, as we have seen, meant women) and hefty fines for ministers performing the ceremonies. The 1723 law that condemned female servants' children to 31 years of servitude and declared their children legally black further legalized the expansion of Virginia's captive labor force via women's bodies. As white blood gained in legal value, liaisons between white women and black men were even further discouraged. In 1786 Thomas Jefferson successfully revised the colonial marriage law to nullify existing unions between free and bond, English and Negro, or mulatto and English, thereby exposing long-married interracial couples both to prosecution and to challenges against their estates and property rights. Such nullifications again targeted the free white women and black men most likely to marry. The racial blood definitions of 1785 were used to enforce Virginia's anti-miscegenation statutes until 1910.[16]

Other Colonies

Many Southern colonies also prohibited interracial marriages before the Revolution, and their laws also shared the property emphasis and gender bias prevalent in Maryland's and Virginia's anti-miscegenation legislation. North Carolina's 1715 statutes imposed a fine on all whites who married non-whites but required only English indentured women found guilty of interracial bastardy to serve an extra four years in servitude or to pay a fine (which few could afford). Laws passed in North Carolina in 1723 and 1741 and in Georgia in 1750 (the same year that colony legalized slavery) seemed more gender neutral. North Carolina specified the blood quanta necessary for the legal marriage partners of whites, and Georgia prohibited marriages between whites and blacks and nullified existing interracial marriages. Georgia did not again address interracial sex or marriage until 1852, when the state banned interracial adultery and fornication as well as marriage. An 1861 law renewed the ban on interracial marriages.[17] Despite their neutral appearance, however, all such laws had a gendered focus and imposed gendered punishments.

Parts of the South influenced by West Indian patterns of race relations remained less concerned with miscegenation for longer and gave free mulattoes special status as an intermediate race. Mississippi and Alabama did not legislate against miscegenation prior to the Civil War. Louisiana passed a Code Noir in 1724 that banned interracial marriage, but its effect was primarily to promote interracial concubinage between mulattas and French or English men, as we have seen. The alternative history of miscegenation policy in Mississippi, Louisiana, and Alabama encouraged a "keener awareness of the complexities of color," according to Peter Bardaglio. In addition, separating free mulattoes from the majority black population through a "porous racial boundary" kept the black majority from growing even larger in those states.[18] The Civil War would eliminate such racial subtleties. The demise of slavery's social controls prompted such states to pass strict anti-miscegenation laws which, among other consequences, reversed the fortunes of previously protected mulattas.

Several New England colonies and early states also prohibited miscegenation with laws that sounded gender neutral but were not. Massachusetts was the first Northern colony to follow Virginia's lead by passing its own "Act for the Better Preventing of A Spurious and Mixt Issue, Etc." in 1705. The law banned fornication and marriage between English or other Christian people and Negroes and mulattoes. Slavery was abolished in Massachusetts in 1780, but in 1786 an act prohibiting and nullifying marriages between whites and Negroes, Indians, or mulattoes became law. (Blacks and Indians were lumped together because the small number of Negroes in the region made Indians seem blacker.) As in Virginia, the whites most likely to engage in prohibited marriages in Massachusetts were women. Abolitionists started agitating for the repeal of this ban in 1830, and their efforts were successful in 1843.[19]

Rhode Island imitated the 1786 Massachusetts law almost verbatim and passed "An Act to prevent clandestine Marriages" in 1798. Maine was the only other New England state to pass a miscegenation law, as it separated from Massachusetts in 1821 following the Missouri Compromise. Maine's law replicated the 1786 Massachusetts law, although it was aimed primarily at white women's intermarriage with Indians, who were much more numerous in the state than Negroes and mulattoes.[20]

The apparent gender neutrality of those Northern laws, as well as others in Delaware and Pennsylvania were again contradicted by the different realities of men's and women's lives. Both slavery and white assumptions about black female sexual virtue (or its lack) disqualified most black women from the realm of interracial marriage, so they and any offspring they produced were mostly unaffected by the laws. Their children were routinely defined as Negro and subject to their mother's legal constraints, property, and status regardless of their father's identity. White men's interracial sexual and reproductive activity occurred primarily outside of marriage, with the approval of custom if not of law, so they too were effectively excluded from most enforcement clauses.[21] Therefore, white women and black men bore the brunt of anti-miscegenation prohibitions and punishments, either explicitly or by default, despite the fact that white men continually produced the most mixed-race children.[22]

Gendered Anti-Miscegenation After the Civil War

Anti-miscegenation mania increased in the South and West after the Civil War, accompanied by a heightened focus on white women as the primary transmitters of racial blood. Their liaisons with black men or other men of color were increasingly targeted by anti-miscegenation policy and enforcement clauses well into the twentieth century.

Convinced by Radical Republican arguments that anti-miscegenation laws were an offshoot of slavery and deserved to die along with that institution, all Northern states east of the Mississippi, except Indiana, repealed their anti-miscegenation laws by 1887. Some Northern states even added anti-miscegenation bans to their constitutions after the war. Most Southern states, on the other hand, strengthened their existing laws or passed new ones. Mississippi, Louisiana, Alabama, South Carolina, and West Virginia passed their first anti-miscegenation laws after the war, while Georgia, Missouri, Kentucky, Florida, Arkansas, Tennessee, North Carolina, Delaware, Texas, and Maryland amended their existing laws.[23] A few states also added prison terms as punishment for miscegenation violations. In interpreting those laws, Southern judges were particularly determined to differentiate between Negro men's begrudgingly conceded political rights and any semblance of their social equality, which interracial marriage would signify.[24] (Only Alabama, Georgia, Tennessee, and Texas made cohabitation for unmarried persons of different races a separate crime.)

Fourteen states, including many that entered the Union after the war, adopted or revised anti-miscegenation statutes to apply to "Mongolians" or "Maylays" in general or to the Chinese in particular.[25] Gender was also paramount to western lawmakers as they determined that the "blacks" white women were most likely to marry were Chinese men.[26] No state officially banned white-Latino intermarriage, however, presumably because treaties accorded white status to former Spanish and Mexican citizens.[27] As we shall see in Part IV, that official status was by no means automatic in practice, and *mestizo* blood could seem threatening to some whites.

A good illustration of the gendered focus of Western United States' post-war laws can be seen in an 1880 amendment to the 1879 California constitution that prohibited intermarriage by "a white person with a negro, mulatto, or Mongolian." Like most Western laws, California's amendment was more effective in conveying the idea of racial inferiority than in preventing already unlikely interracial relationships, especially given the small Negro population and Asian men's nearly total segregation from white society. Nevertheless, hypothetical mixed-race couples, which almost necessarily meant men of color and white women, were denied marriage licenses by constitutional decree. After 1905, lawmakers contemplating an influx of Japanese immigrants also criminalized existing interracial marriages involving whites.[28] Though blatantly *not* racially inclusive, the new law's language appeared gender inclusive, but its eugenic concerns about Asian "lawless sexuality" and depraved way of life were clearly coded male. In addition, the law's subtext was the control of white women's sexual and reproductive behavior in order to control the passage of white racial blood. California political leaders were particularly horrified by the prospect of white girls "sitting side by side in the school rooms with . . . Japs, with their base minds, their lascivious thoughts."[29]

The ultimate purpose of post-war anti-miscegenation laws across the board was to restrict the privileges of white racial blood exclusively to the progeny of white men and white women. In pursuing that goal, the laws made white women explicit pawns in political and sexual competitions among men. The absence of anti-miscegenation laws in Hawai'i demonstrates that the real purpose of such laws was to prevent white women's from bestowing white privilege on mixed-race children. There were very few white women in Hawai'i.[30]

Anti-miscegenation laws were in some ways superfluous, however, since there were many ways to eliminate men of color from competition with white men. False accusations of rape, particularly but not exclusively against black men, gave that effort a substantial boost starting in the 1850s, as we saw in Part II. Although motivations for such accusations were complex, involving whites' sexual projections onto black male bodies and class-based assumptions about white women's sexual propensities, they acquired yet another purpose as the nation increasingly turned its collective attention to racial blood. Rape accusations served as gendered agents of anti-miscegenation fervor and enforcement. The perhaps unexpected corollary to such accusations was the heightened scrutiny of white motherhood to detect any hint of white racial contamination.

10

Preserving White Racial Blood

Rape Accusations and Motherhood

As we saw in Chapter 6, rape accusations against black men increased in the late nineteenth and early decades of the twentieth century as the racial controls of slavery faded away. Such accusations helped to promote racial antagonisms that, in turn, discouraged the dreaded black male-white female reproduction that eugenicists would ultimately identify as the key source of white racial deterioration. Anti-miscegenation laws alone could not prevent hypodescent; rather, the entire social system needed to "protect" white women from sexual assault and from their irrationally passionate selves. Many women who bought into that protection racket made a bargain they came to regret. If they accepted their roles as bastions of whiteness dedicated to the preservation of white racial blood, then white society would watch their reproductive lives like a hawk. Like rape accusations against black men, the scrutiny of white motherhood reinforced anti-miscegenation laws, particularly in the South.

Specious Rape Allegations

To many whites, inter-racial rape signified "a direct assault on [white men's] domination and control over blacks and over white women." Rape fears were a handy way to incite panic over the "sullying" of white women, as we saw in Chapter 6, but they also evoked white panic over the possibility of vengeful mixed-race children. Rape fears offered a pretext for retaliating against even imagined assaults or sexual innuendo.[1] White women were both targets and perpetrators of this form of miscegenation control. Some made up for their own lack of civic agency by exerting power over black men with cries of rape, but they risked being accused of lasciviousness themselves. It wasn't easy for a raped "sexual paragon" to navigate her identity as natural conservator of Christian morality and guardian of household and children while newly aroused suspicions about white women as wanton temptresses lurked just beneath the surface of patriarchal families and social institutions, particularly after the Civil War.[2]

Perhaps it was the strain of that balancing act that kept so many white women from empathizing with their black sisters, who were effaced almost entirely by their undeserved licentious reputations among whites and had no legal standing to make rape charges against the white men who had historically committed the most inter-racial rapes. Most white women ignored pleas by Mary Church Terrell to "arise [with black women] in the purity and power of their womanhood to implore their fathers, husbands, and sons" to stop the spilling of innocent black men's blood in the lynchings that increasingly resulted from rape accusations or convictions. As if their erasure in the white world were not enough, black women also suffered isolation *within* their racial group as black men increasingly insisted that their own manliness was the primary antidote to racism and lynching. "We are men and our aim is perfect manhood, to be men among men," as Frederick Douglass wrote in 1892.[3]

Instead of pursuing gender solidarity, many white women, particularly in the post-war South, instigated or supported accusations of actual, attempted, or intended rape, often with male encouragement, on the slimmest of pretexts. Black men who seemed likely to vote Republican were favorite targets. Jourdan Ware's story is a case in point. Ware, a successful Georgia freedman, moved out of the state after being warned by the Ku Klux Klan (KKK) not to vote the "radical ticket." The KKK had him killed anyway for being "big, mighty forward, [and] pompous," after accusing him of speaking to a "white lady." Ware's political and sexual offenses were interchangeable to the KKK. Since he was capable of casting the wrong ballot, he was as good as guilty of polluting white blood.[4] The "lady's" position was not much more secure. If she had consented to conversation, let alone to sex, with Ware, she would have forfeited her white racial status as well as her right to protection from the KKK.

The conflation of sex and politics rose to fever pitch between 1882 and 1900, and for the first time reliably ensured black men's conviction and execution for allegations of rape, no matter how specious. Despite (or, perhaps, because of) post-war revelations about the sexual aggression of white mistresses toward black male slaves in hearings of the American Freedman's Inquiry Commission, and despite Ida B. Wells's painstaking analysis of lynching statistics (which demonstrated a fair number of consensual adulteries by white "ladies" among alleged rape cases), the idea of a consensual union between men of color and middle- or upper-class white women became increasingly difficult for whites to admit or tolerate.[5] When Alexander Manly, editor of the black newspaper, the *Wilmington* [North Carolina] *Daily Record*, dared to suggest in 1898 that sexual liaisons between white women and black men were no worse than those between white men and black women, the resulting outrage catapulted the Democratic Party into power in the state (although not in Wilmington). Nevertheless, a riot ensued there, and Manly was forced to leave the city.[6]

Although there were always whites who protested the rape-lynching scenario, it wasn't until the 1930s, when lynching was increasingly associated with the "backwards" South and white women's cultural luster was fading, that Southern white women organized against it. The Association of Southern Women for the Prevention of Lynching argued quietly on local levels that white women didn't need the mobs' protection. Even when they were successful in particular cases, however, they could not end the segregation that fueled lynching in the first place.[7]

As we saw in Chapter 6, rape allegations were also hurled at other men of color, especially the Chinese, with occasionally deadly results. Those allegations never achieved the same level of hysteria as those against black men, although fears about Asian and Mexican men's sexual creepiness or predation certainly incited sometimes vicious violence against them and their unacceptable blood. Accusations of sexual offenses against Mexican men often occurred after the fact, even in the goriest lynchings, which were initially inspired by economic or property concerns.[8] Filipinos came closest to inciting comparable rape fright in white communities, much later and only in the West. Filipino men's American citizenship and English language skills made them more confident than other Asian men, so they struck some whites as "strutting Asian peacocks" seeking the attention of young American and Mexican girls. Some Filipino men did openly defy anti-miscegenation laws and resist controls on their sexuality. One group of white men started a race riot in California in 1930 to protest such "flagrant" socializing with white women. In 1933, the legislature amended California's anti-miscegenation law to include "Malays," after an appeals court ruled that the original law did not apply to the Filipino racial group.[9]

White women who played the rape scenario like a violin in post-Civil War America, whether willingly or in a desperate attempt to protect their social status, endorsed with their conduct the suspect doctrine of white women's sole responsibility for the preservation of white racial blood. This doctrine made them, rather than white men, " 'the great stronghold, the vital point' of creation," dismissed white men's inter-racial sexual transgressions as "individual and limited," and maintained that those of white women struck "mortally at the existence of the family itself."[10] It also held white women responsible for the "defilement of the white race" if mulatto children were born (*vis imaginativa* having been discredited by then).[11] In so doing, white women set themselves up for heightened scrutiny of their reproductive lives as a means of conserving white racial blood and promoting white supremacy, especially (but not exclusively) in the South. The devil's bargain some white women made to protect their racial status and reputations in cases of inter-racial sex came back to bite them, as legal and cultural controls on their reproductive lives went well beyond anti-miscegenation prohibitions.

Preserving White Racial Blood: Motherhood

Where the concept of white racial supremacy flourished, laws increasingly regulated white women as mothers, starting in the latter decades of the nineteenth century. Such laws revealed the intensely gendered motivations and effects of eugenic thinking. Instead of protecting white women according to the Southern code of chivalry, they undermined white women's cultural value and social power and isolated them within their own racial group. By the 1930s, the scrutiny of white motherhood in the South rivaled attempts to control black men as a means of advancing the cause of white supremacy.

Black women might well say, "Welcome to the club," since their reproductive capacity had long been exploited in the name of preserving the purity of white blood. During slavery, no laws shielded black women from recurrent rapes or the sale of their children. Masters figured that slave mothers "were less likely to escape than slave men because of their attachment to their children," as Dorothy Roberts explains. And they were mostly right. Few women escaped with their dependent children, although some escaped because of their children, if they could run toward friends or family.[12] Between 1850 and 1860, only 19 percent of the runaway slaves advertised in North Carolina were women, a pattern that was consistent throughout the South. Slave mothers typically did "everything they could to ensure their [children's] ... safety and survival," even that of their mixed-blood children whom whites did not recognize. "Some worked extra hours in order to purchase their children's—especially their daughters'—freedom rather than their own."[13] After slavery was abolished, the legal system became less interested in black women or mulattas, since they could still transmit only black blood, as far as the law was concerned. White supremacists ignored black mothers because they figured very little in the calculus of white blood domination.

White women were another matter. Their reproductive capacity became their defining racial feature as the preservation and control of white racial blood became more urgent. Starting in the nineteenth-century, physicians, such as Charles Meigs, declared the female body a closed system of energy in which the reproductive organs are in constant conflict with the brain. Meigs promoted the idea that delicate women risked physical damage by "unnatural" acts of thinking, working, or engaging in vigorous physical activity (a concern that excluded women of color from the get-go). A white woman's goal should be to "maintain the purity of woman-the-field of nourishment for racial reproduction," Meigs said. As organisms centered on their wombs, white women needed to concentrate on their obligation to transmit the superior blood of the nation across the generations.[14]

By the end of the century, warnings to white women proliferated. Theodore Roosevelt urged white men to keep fighting wars and white women to continue breeding on behalf of their race.[15] Many white women embraced the primacy of their roles in racial reproduction. The Daughters of the American Revolution, for example, abandoned their historical role as "mothers of patriots" in 1894 and made paternal rather than maternal family lineage the preferred proof of a Revolutionary heritage. That change replaced women's cultural authority within the domestic sphere with the "racialized family bloodline" traced through men.[16] A mother's primary role became the transmission of unsullied paternal blood rather than her moral influence.

Although black dignitaries from Ida B. Wells, to Frederick Douglass, to Anna Julia Cooper were infuriated by the DAR's changed criteria, they too reinforced the idea that women of all races were "the source from which the life-blood of the race is to flow," as Cooper put it in *Voice From the South* in 1892. In expressing their outrage about the DAR's elimination of black men from the patriots' bloodlines, its perpetuation of a fiction of shared white patriotic paternity across the country from the Revolutionary period through the nineteenth century, its obfuscation of the race-based Southern caste system, and its erasure of African American military history, they unintentionally reinforced the organization's patriarchal message about mothers' service to racial blood. By insisting that Negroes should also be credited with patriots' "racial blood," their protests made black women into guardians and transmitters of the paternal blood that signified racial value.[17] Whether that new focus ultimately undermined or elevated black women's social status among African Americans is still subject to debate.

Eugenicists of the period worked hard to persuade middle-class white women of their responsibility for advancing the white race. Albert Edward Wiggam, journalist and eugenics popularizer, declared the white woman "the natural Conservator of the race, the guardian of its blood." "It is peculiarly to woman that America looks for the realization of eugenical marriages and motherhood," he explained. Starting in the 1880s, Francis Galton declared white women the guardians of their family's eugenic fitness. He persuaded many to maintain eugenicist "family albums" and participate in "eugenic-fitness" photographic contests in order to trace and advance the development of the white race (ranked first out of nine) and to discourage its debasement through intermarriage with inferior races, especially the Negro (ranked ninth out of nine). Galton particularly chastised the white, upper-middle-class, educated New Woman who seemed most in danger of devaluing or foregoing motherhood.[18]

Indeed, as the twentieth century got underway, white women's new freedoms and changing roles after World War I inflamed eugenic fears about racial order. Eugenicists were especially alarmed by a 1923 survey of female college students that showed 78 percent of respondents planning careers and only 50 percent planning to marry. Also alarming was the equal rights bill that started its way through both the Virginia legislature and the U.S. Congress in the same year. Eugenicists railed against higher education, careers, and birth control for middle-class white women. As Lisa Dorr explains, "Separation of the races matched a parallel system of gender role differentiation . . . social stability depended on controlling [white] women's sexuality as a means of assuring they were virtuous enough to raise virtuous children." The same control was never exerted on either white men or black women, for familiar reasons. White women alone were held responsible for white "racial suicide." Only their maternal role could maintain culture and civilization, which were equated with the dominance of the white race.[19]

Eugenic fears about racial decline motivated the National Immigration Restriction Act of 1924 and many state-level compulsory sterilization policies throughout the U.S. during the 1920s. Particularly in the South, targets of those sterilization policies were "feeble-minded" women, believed to be genetically possessed of powerful sexual desires and, therefore, insufficiently attentive to their obligation to maintain the purity of white racial blood. Virginia took the lead in legislating the control of undesirable mixed-blood populations by targeting impaired women.[20] Such women were subjected to two-thirds of the forced sterilizations performed in Virginia between 1924 and 1972.[21]

Virginia's 1924 Preservation of Racial Integrity Act, which was vigorously supported by nationally recognized eugenicists (who also testified in favor of the National Immigration Restriction Act) officially extended the burden of preserving white racial blood to all white women in the state. Ostensibly, the Act forbade any white person to marry a person of another race and defined race in terms of ancestry or racial blood. It codified the one-drop rule by restricting white status to persons having no "discernable trace" of non-white (Negro, Indian, or Asian) blood, which prevented near-whites from claiming the benefits of whiteness. As in most anti-miscegenation regulations, however, white women's relationships with black men were the real focus of the Act, which specifically required new white mothers to register the race of their children according to its definition of race. If the Bureau of Vital Statistics suspected miscegenation, the mother received a warning letter exhorting her to "see that the child is not allowed to mix with white children, it cannot go to white schools and can never marry a white person." The letter concluded by declaring blood mixing "an awful thing." Since letters were sent only to mothers, white men were again held harmless for producing mixed-race children.[22]

The law's concentration on white mothers reflected what *Richmond Times-Dispatch* journalist John Powell defined in a 1926 as the crux of the race problem—"the increasing frequency of the birth of mixed breed children to white women." Given that "the race of illegitimate children is determined by that of the mother," Powell claimed that "[white men's] amalgamation [with black women] is more controlled by the color line. Where the mothers of mixbreeds are white, however, the danger is increased a thousandfold." Powell was most alarmed by the reproductive misbehavior of poor white women, whom he considered sexually depraved. With such sentiments, anti-miscegenation policies, like spurious rape accusations, lost all pretense of protecting white women. The issue increasingly became the protection of white society from white women's sexual excess and reproductive irresponsibility.[23]

The Anglo-Saxon Clubs organized during the same period also addressed that issue. The clubs started in Virginia in the early 1920s and expanded to 36 branches by 1925, including two in New York and one in Pennsylvania. The clubs disavowed the violence of the KKK but were equally dedicated to white supremacy. They wanted to strengthen Anglo-Saxon "instincts, principles, and traditions," restrict immigration, develop a "final solution" to the "Negro Problem" by reinstating an impenetrable boundary between the races, and preserve patriarchal families as the mark of civilization that distinguished Anglo-Saxon settlers in the New World from the bachelor conquistadors of Spain and Portugal (some ideas never die). Uppity white women were a particular threat to the Clubs' goals, since such women were most likely to use birth control and to enter universities and the labor force, thereby threatening the white birth rate. That women were excluded from club membership reflects the group's belief that "man-made and man-enforced laws should control women's sexual and reproductive functions because women were not able to do so on their own."[24]

Although the Racial Integrity Act was popular with members of the Anglo-Saxon Clubs and other white Virginians, some in the state realized that it was white men's failure to provide for their mixed-race offspring with black women, not white women's miscegenation, that created the greatest social problem. That failure not only allowed white men to hide their dalliances and adulteries across racial lines, but it also victimized black women, who were daily "insulted by some poor ill-bred white youth." A proposed amendment to the Racial Integrity Act in 1926 addressed white men's roles in miscegenation, but it was never passed.[25]

The amendment's failure reinforced the gendered agenda of legal and cultural prohibitions against the mixing of racial blood in American society over many years. All mixed racial blood was not equally abhorrent; all blood mixers were not equally guilty. That men "owned" racial blood did not mean they took responsibility for it. In different ways, black and white mothers and their children were the real victims of this specious blood taboo, not the white men who perpetrated the most racial mixing. Thus, many white women who bought into the concept of white racial blood superiority lived to regret it.

Conclusion

Miscegenation as Racial Reconciliation?

Perhaps because the prohibitions against the mixing of racial blood were so focused on women, several women writers, both black and white, took issue after the Civil War with the intentions of anti-miscegenation regulations. Instead of lamenting racial mixing, these writers envisioned a strong hybrid nation in which human value was not measured by blood or skin. White writers Lydia Maria Child, Anna Dickinson, and Rebecca Harding Davis produced novels between 1865 and 1868 that explored the positive possibilities of mixing racial blood via inter-racial romance and marriage and embraced racial mixing as a strategy to resolve racial conflict and achieve a better world. Their works unintentionally replicated the existing racial order, however, by depicting fictional interracial couples as white male and black female and thereby reinforcing white men's prerogative to pick women and to legitimate racial mixing on their terms. As Toni Morrison suggests in *Playing in the Dark*, such black characters in white literature typically fortify the boundaries of the white world and define whiteness rather than promote a new world order.[1] Given that phenomenon, white literature could not sustain America's Radical Hour any more than federal law could.

Black writer, Pauline Hopkins, offered more revolutionary novels about mixed racial blood between 1900 and 1904. For Hopkins, racial mixing was less about validating the strength of racial hybrids than about demonstrating the insignificance of racial blood in determining human quality. Good social institutions, not blood, made good people, she argued. In linking racially mixed characters with homosexuality, however, Hopkins also inadvertently reinforced racial stereotypes of the period.

Whatever their strengths or weaknesses, such literary efforts went mostly unnoticed. Measuring racial blood in gendered terms continued. Especially in the South, black men and white women were relentlessly targeted by efforts to keep racial blood borders inviolable. Controlling white women's reproduction remained particularly important to preserving white supremacy well into the twentieth century.

The nation's focus on racial blood promoted racism after slavery ended by arbitrarily disempowering some people and empowering others with ambiguous laws and extralegal force. Blood-based anti-miscegenation laws, rape accusations, and manipulations of white motherhood proved even more effective than body-based discrimination in generating fear about racial difference in the U.S. But such laws and practices were neither sufficient to that purpose nor alone in it. Citizenship definitions and policies—also gendered—were parallel partners in defining and controlling the nation's racial composition and in generating fear of the racial "other." Part IV explores the gendered foundations of citizenship, immigration, and naturalization, via federal laws and policies and other cultural narratives that combined American obsessions with raced bodies and racial blood and reinforced their meaning.

PART IV
Citizenship

Introduction

"My Folks Fought for This Country"

Laws, policies, and practices concerning American citizenship, from the late eighteenth through the mid-twentieth centuries, were preoccupied with both defining racial difference and controlling the racial composition of the U.S. The struggle over citizenship, especially as applications for immigration and naturalization increased after the Civil War, combined concerns about raced bodies and racial blood and mobilized conventional concepts of gender difference and hierarchy, as well as gender norms, in formulating restrictive definitions of an American. By that time, the very idea of democracy was linked with white masculinity, and many non-white men and all women had an uphill battle to qualify for full recognition as nationals. As a crucible for defining racial difference, citizenship reinforced the primacy of white male self-definitions and promoted conformity to white European gender standards as a mark of racial acceptability and assimilability. And even though blackness was *not* the primary racial issue with regard to immigration, conflicts over the admission and naturalization of immigrant groups ironically reinforced the black-white paradigm of American racial ideology.

Citizenship is, of course, a capacious concept. It can entail simple membership or belonging in a nation-state as well as the right to participate in politics and perform civic duties. It can also include social rights—such as the right to minimal economic security, education, and other social resources—as well as civil and political rights. Many feminist scholars have focused on the distribution of civil, social, and political rights between the sexes and on the denial of such rights on the basis of sex and race. For example, Alice Kessler-Harris notes that law and social policy by the last decades of the twentieth century produced different social commitments to different groups. Male breadwinners, for example, were given the rights of "economic citizenship," but married women and domestic workers were not.[1] In recent years, scholars like Eileen Boris have begun exploring "sexual, intimate, or reproductive citizenship."[2] Feminists have also debated whether the state is an enemy of gender justice, serving primarily "as the force structuring male dominance and white supremacy," or an oppressor as well as a resource for women. That question made citizenship a "terrain of struggle" for feminists by the end of the twentieth century.[3]

Part IV of *The Specter of Sex* does not address such questions, which deal with what Evelyn Glenn calls "substantive citizenship," or "the ability to exercise rights of citizenship." Rather, it explores formal citizenship as "embodied in law and policy."[4] Formal citizenship includes legal qualifications for citizenship, naturalization, and simple admission to the country, as well as the right to vote as the most concrete marker of citizenship status. Formal membership is "where the *politics* of citizenship begins," as Ruth Lister explains, the status from which rights and obligations emerge and from which individuals can develop relationships with both the state and other citizens. Without formal state membership, as Olaf Petersson notes, " 'equal possibilities to participate in the governing of society' " do not exist.[5] By the same token, formal citizenship reveals the "cultural process of 'subjectification' " underlying citizenship status. That process is rarely fully transparent or equal and often exposes the need to negotiate criteria for belonging to a nation, which, in turn, "depends on how one is constituted as a subject who exercises or submits to power relations."[6] Although enforcement (or non-enforcement) of formal citizenship rights by national, state, or local governments creates racialized and gendered citizenship disparities, the texts of and reasoning behind legislation and official policy also reveal a great deal about the construction of gendered racial ideology.

Gender has historically been so fundamental to formal birthright American citizenship (as opposed to naturalized citizenship) that sex difference not only preceded racial distinction among free native-born persons, but it also outlived that distinction in the country's citizenship standards. The primacy of gender with regard to formal birthright citizenship emerged almost immediately in the early republic. Although all free men and women were asked to accept or reject U.S. citizenship in 1776, and all free residents who declared their allegiance to the nation were defined as voluntary citizens, state constitutions soon eroded women's identities as American nationals. Most states replaced the concept of *consent* for women with the concept of *legal capacity*. Maleness alone qualified most free men, both black and white, for the rights of formal citizenship, legal protection, and the vote in many states in the nation's early years. The biggest obstacle men faced was property ownership, with its attendant class and racial connotations.

But women's alleged lack of legal capacity eliminated them from the "governed" who gave consent to their government. It also disqualified them for the franchise regardless of their class or racial status. Women could reach the age of reason, but they could never achieve full independence or adulthood. Except for a few decades in New Jersey, a *feme sole* could acquire some property rights throughout much of the nineteenth century, but married women were wards of their husbands. Women's citizenship capacity was considered so weak that even self-supporting, property-owning women could not vote in general elections.[7] As the decades passed it became increasingly clear that a married woman's formal citizenship status was "derivative," or dependent on that of her husband. In addition, from 1855 until 1934, native-born women of all races were stripped of birthright American citizenship (both *jus soli*—law of the soil—and *jus sanguinis*—law of blood) if they happened to marry the wrong foreign man.

Birthright citizenship for children has also historically been a gendered concept. Since *partus sequitur ventrum* determined racial identity in the U.S. for so long, it might seem logical that the "womb" also determined the citizenship of a child. But that was not typically the case, at least not before 1934, unless the child was illegitimate. Rather, in keeping with British Common Law, a child's *jus sanguinis* American citizenship rights were determined by the father's not the mother's citizenship status. In other words, citizenship based on family (blood) inheritance was *partus sequitur patrem*. It belonged to the cultural bodies of (white) men and was denied to "incapacitated females." A child's "legitimacy" made citizenship a patriarchal inheritance; its "illegitimacy" made blood a matriarchal curse. For much of American history, women were the means but not the agents of transmitting (white) American citizenship to children. The status to be inherited was men's. Only since the passage of the Fourteenth Amendment have children born on American soil automatically become American citizens, according to *jus soli*, without regard to either paternal or maternal descent.[8]

Free native-born black men gradually inherited women's second-class status as legal aliens in their own country by about 1830, as states that had allowed (or had not disallowed) free black men to vote gradually eliminated that right, often by questioning their gender credentials. As a result, by 1851 the "principle of universal suffrage" applied only to "white males of age."[9] But race figured more prominently in naturalization policy, which formally linked gender incapacity with race as early as 1790, when the country's first naturalization law was passed. Although it did not impose serious immigration restrictions, the law did limit naturalization to "free white males" with two years of residence.[10] That qualification presumed such men's capacity for independence and self-governance and excluded all women and men of color from that capacity.[11] Foreign-born free women were welcomed into the country primarily as dependent wives or servants for more than a century thereafter.

When immigration and naturalization became crucial issues after the Civil War, black men were not the initial targets of racist policies. Indeed, men of African ancestry were added to the short list of acceptable candidates for naturalization during America's brief Radical Hour. That list had previously included only white men of (primarily northern) European descent. Rather, the Chinese were the first real targets of immigration and naturalization restrictions. The first federal immigration law, the Immigration Act of 1875, explicitly excluded Chinese "coolie" laborers and prostitutes from the U.S., thereby defining the racial "other" in gendered terms. As both the Democratic and Republican parties developed anti-Chinese planks designed to prevent the further immigration of the "Mongolian race," in 1876 and 1880 respectively, the politics of race were already the politics of gender. The two parties justified disallowing Chinese immigration by portraying both sexes as hyper-(hetero)sexualized and, without noticing the contradiction, by impugning the masculinity of Chinese men.

Part IV of *The Specter of Sex* analyzes the ways in which gender characteristics and stereotypes influenced formal American citizenship status for native-born Americans and immigrants and thereby defined racial difference and shaped the racial composition of the American polity. The discussion is based on proceedings of political parties and legislative bodies, state constitutions, newspaper accounts, editorials, texts of laws, court opinions, and historical interviews. Chapter 11 begins Part IV by analyzing the masculine nature of citizenship theory in Western nations in general and in the United States in particular. Chapter 12 then defines and analyzes American women's second class citizenship status up to and beyond their acquisition of the franchise, since the vote alone did not automatically eliminate the principle of "derivative" citizenship for American women. The chapter also establishes the gendered principles of partial citizenship that became a template for restricting citizenship rights for men of "undesirable" races, both native and foreign. Chapter 13 analyzes the ways in which inappropriate gender and alleged moral unfitness, including contradictory accusations of homosexual tendencies and heterosexual aggression, became explicit or implicit standards for limiting the citizenship rights of native-born Negro and Indian men and for restricting the entry, residency, and naturalization of Chinese men. Chapter 14 explores for the first time how the interconnection between mixed race and suspect gender, as discussed in Chapter 6, became a premise for denying formal citizenship rights to Latinos, specifically Mexican and Puerto Rican men whose right to American citizenship was promised by treaties. In that discussion in particular, it becomes apparent that formal citizenship, while ostensibly a matter of national policy, was also constructed by state and local laws and policies.[12] Part IV concludes with an analysis of homosexuality as a form of gendered race that disqualified sexually suspect immigrants for citizenship for most of American history.

11

What is Citizenship?

Gender and Race

Understanding American gendered racial citizenship policies requires understanding the theoretical underpinnings of state membership in the Western cultures that preceded it. Most important in that heritage, perhaps, are the sexual and racial contracts in such cultures that enable white men of European descent to do much less negotiating about national membership or citizenship rights than all other groups.

The Sexual Contract, which Carole Pateman defines as fundamental to contractarianism itself, has "generate[d] political right in the form of relations of domination and subordination" that are inherently gendered.[1] As we saw in Chapter 1, patriarchal domination was the "normative logic" of classic contract theorists, who then rationalized the "inconsistencies, circumlocutions, and evasions" necessary to promote and justify it.[2] This "logic" extended from Greek and Roman definitions of the polis through Lockean and Kantian notions of politics and the state. In particular, contract theorists promoted the idea of men's and women's complementary roles and relationships to the state: men have nature's blessing to dominate politics; and women have the natural "right" to men's domination.

The Racial Contract inherent in Western political systems entails white citizens' tacit consent to a "*racially hierarchical* polity, globally dominated by Europeans," according to Charles Mills. Following Pateman, Mills documents the racial deficiencies of normative theories of both political and moral citizenship contracts, which help explain how slavery, racial oppression, and colonialism could coexist with the Enlightenment principles of modern states. Because white supremacy is a fundamental precept of the Western political contract, whites do not see it. "The whole point of establishing a moral hierarchy and juridically partitioning the polity according to race," Mills notes, "is to secure and legitimate the privileging of those individuals designated as white/persons and the exploitation of those individuals designated as nonwhite/subpersons."[3]

The Specter of Sex links these two interpretations of citizenship and exposes the ways in which the racial contract succeeded but did not supersede the sexual contract in the U.S. context. Citizenship remained highly gendered in the name of race-conscious citizenship standards, and gendered notions of citizenship—such as women's inherent dependency and passionate natures as markers of political incapacity—continued to define racial difference and to delay racial inclusion in the U.S. through the feminizing of non-white men. The two contracts together made native-born women and non-white men undesirable internal "others" and combined gender ideology with racial ideology to define inadmissible foreigners as threats to political harmony.

The "We vs. They" Gendered State: Outsiders and Insiders

The perceived threat posed by immigrants and internal "aliens" had material as well as psychological components. Economic competition was an important reason for restricting aliens' rights and access to resources and opportunities, but so was the possible disruption of an "imagined" national community. A sense of belonging is essential to successful political entities, and nations capture the imaginations of their citizens by persuading them that the world their laws describe is the only one attainable.[4] Such communities have an "insatiable need to administer difference" between themselves and unacceptable "others." That need sometimes entails "violent acts of segregation, censorship, economic coercion, physical torture, [and] police brutality," but more often it depends on a concept of *alterity*, a sense of "we vs. they," with continual reference to various definitions of others that are different from one's own national self. In other words, nations know both who and what they are and who and what they are not.[5]

The English colonists in North America pursued that "we vs. they" notion of community and nationhood with a vengeance by defining themselves in contradistinction to other national groups, such as the Dutch, Spanish, Portuguese, and Africans. From the get-go, being non-English meant being "alien." The English settlers' relatively even-handed disparagement of all national others, including lesser Teutonic Europeans, was well entrenched before they attributed absolute racial inferiority to Africans. Perpetual chattel slavery helped their judgment along.

It is important for our analysis that the "we" in many nationalist ideologies, as George Mosse explains, was implicitly masculine—a strong people able to control energies and (female) passions without the use of brute force. In the American case, the primacy of guns and hunting as signs of national vigor and the manhood of the nation was expanded in the late nineteenth century by the masculine sports of football, baseball, crew, and track. Women's role in that same nationalist discourse was primarily supportive and static. They were seen as the immutability underlying the dynamic, progressive, masculine state, in which they could never be more than "insiders/outsiders." The healthiest nations contained the most feminine women and the most masculine men. Diseased nations contained unfeminine women and unmasculine men. In healthy societies, masculine men controlled feminine women. Women on the loose threatened the continuity of the social order.[6] "Female access to public space [even] ... compromised women's symbolic value to men, jeopardizing the fiction that men imprinted ... public identities upon the persons of their wives," according to Kathleen Brown.[7]

Homosocial male bonding has historically been a logical corollary of the sexual dichotomy implicit in nationhood, according to Mosse and Benedict Anderson. Such bonding both naturalizes male dominance over women and creates a sense of fraternity that motivates men to fight and die for their country. As we saw in Chapter 1, conceptualizations of homelands as female bodies, vulnerable to violation and penetration by foreigners, also helps to cement the homosocial bond. As this feminine trope inspires men to defend and or invade other nations, however, it does little to empower actual women. Rather, the concept of the feminine homeland typically constructs a paradoxical symbol of womanhood as both devoted mother and chastely dutiful daughter. Thus the nation becomes a "fantasmatic female" who somehow secures "male-male arrangements and an all-male history." Actual "empirical women," who inevitably fall short of the symbol, play their political roles through obedience to men.[8]

Feminine national symbolism also prevents empirical women from being completely identified with the body politic and exacerbates the difference between men's and women's relationship to the nation-state.[9] Even when women play significant political roles, as they did in the American and French revolutions, they are usually re-relegated to obedient daughterly and maternal roles once the political turmoil ends.[10] In such ways, the symbolic submissive woman often eclipses the agency of her living, breathing counterparts.

The homosocial bond that engenders nationhood should not be confused with state approval of male-male sexual relations, from which nations typically disassociate themselves in the strongest possible terms. Indeed, most national discourses exclude all non-reproductive sexualities, although lesbians seem less threatening to national identities than do sodomy and male transvestism. Such homosexual aversion explains why sodomy today functions as a "question of national interest," according to Jonathan Goldberg.[11] The real mission of the nation has historically been, and remains, a heterosexual mission in which national interests depend on conventional coupling and reproduction among its citizens.

From Gender Dichotomy to Racial Hierarchy

Taken together, as Brackette Williams suggests, such gendered nationalist narratives—the Sexual Contract—became "the vantage point from which the visibility of [national] difference as race and gender was sharply focused"—the Racial Contract. In the processes of nation-formation, narratives about the importance of gender dichotomy to both the modernity and the superiority of the "higher" races converged with narratives about "subordinated forms of masculinity" and blurred gender distinctions of older, decaying "inferior" races. As the older races were associated with women, they also became natural enemies of culture—containers for but not producers of culture "as a civilizing process." If left to their own devices, these older races, like women, threatened the social order "created by the true manhood of the dominant/modern race." They undermined majority men's agency and, by extension, the viability of the nation. Therefore, like women, they were "insiders/outsiders" in terms of national identity and citizenship.[12]

When immigrant men displaying "other" forms of masculinity presented themselves, they were "dead on arrival," according to Williams. "The less noble races were [seen as] forms of either obsolete nature or inappropriate juxtaposing of nature and agency." In other words, they were considered "inappropriately gendered." Their forms of aggression were called degenerate, as opposed to the allegedly "genuine" aggression exercised by racially dominant men seeking rational control of society. That difference within masculine character provided another rationale for exclusive citizenship and immigration policies. The alternative masculinities of racialized men both problematized "the coherence of masculine prototyping" in the nation-state and justified excluding such men from "nationalist projects."[13] They were judged inassimilable to American culture, which required both rational, "can-do" attitudes of masculine citizenship and assurances that white women would be submissive only to white men.[14] In another tricky syllogism, the alleged male deviance of inferior races demonstrated the superior rationality of the dominant race, at least to themselves.

"Other" men could sometimes redeem their "inferior" racial status, however, through displays of masculinity. After all, the "Other-as-racialized-male" still had his "Other-as-female," and he could be recognized in the national narrative if he asserted his power over her, as we saw in Part III. By mimicking "insider" men's relationship to womanly virtue and submitting to "patterns of respectability," including hard work, control over sexual passions, dominance over women, and athletic prowess, he could achieve the appropriate gender status to qualify him for citizenship. "The Other-as-his-female" had no such opportunity. Demonstrations of appropriate femininity only further condemned her to perpetual insider/outsider status and to the constraints of her female nature—passionate, irrational—as well as of her marital status and mothering responsibilities.[15]

In these ways and others, sexual difference and conventional gender norms became basic tenets of racial hierarchy within nation-states. Gender binarism and hierarchy linked women of all races to particular symbolic roles in evolving nationalist discourse, even as other forces stratified their social value on the basis of race. Racial difference signaled variations in the quality and degree of women's passions, particularly with regard to excessive sex and reproduction. But as far as states were concerned, all women were, to a greater or lesser degree, resident aliens—irrationally passionate, torn by divided loyalties, and incapable of the independence and commitment that citizenship requires. Even a woman of refined sexual behavior was, by nature, meant to submit to state controls via marriage and dependence on men. In a classic Catch-22, the state's requirements kept women in the very condition that disqualified them for full citizenship.

This brief overview demonstrates the important role that gender and/as race has played in what Aihwa Ong calls the "self-making and being-made by power relations that produce consent" to the nation-state.[16] In most Western nations, including the U.S., white men of European descent have done most of the "self-making" and consent-giving, while all women and most minority men—understood for much of American history as equally dependent and unreliable— have been relegated to "being-made" and excluded from consent. Over time, various racial groups gained or lost rights and status in the American polity in gendered terms, as issues of sexual morality, domestic stability, and levels of male dominance figured in judgments about the citizenship worthiness of each new "alien" group.

12

Engendering Citizenship

Dependency and Sex

Following patterns in other post-revolutionary societies, American citizenship became an increasingly gendered concept after the Revolutionary War, as egalitarian promises receded, and gender conventions reasserted themselves. State constitutions, like the one drafted in New York in 1777, typically specified "male" as a qualification for suffrage. Throughout the new states, women were more quickly and absolutely denied full citizenship rights and the franchise than were free black men, even in the South, as we shall see in Chapter 13.[1] And by the mid-nineteenth century, American women's second-class citizenship became the template for the second-class citizenship status of native-born men of color. In ensuing decades, it would also help define and constrain the citizenship prospects of immigrant men.

The nineteenth-century doctrine of Manifest Destiny intensified the country's focus on manliness as a qualification for American-ness and reaffirmed women's primarily supportive role in the country's growth. Congress codified this hierarchy in 1855 by declaring the "capacity for full citizenship inherent in the self-governing man only and not in any person encumbered by bonds of dependence."[2] With few exceptions, women were seen as too encumbered for citizenship, but free black and Indian men were only gradually deemed like them and, therefore, unworthy of citizenship. By 1830, free black men were systematically identified, state by state, as innately dependent, incapacitated, and unmanly. At the same time, Indian men were on their way to becoming wards of the U.S. government. Later in the century, Mexicans in annexed territories and male Chinese immigrants would join their feminized ranks. The Supreme Court made the connection between women's and marginalized men's second-class citizenship explicit in an 1875. In deciding a case brought by suffragist

Virginia Minor, the Court ruled that black men could be excluded from juries and denied voting rights in Jim Crow America because women were.[3]

"Trafficking in Women": Coverture and Forced Dependence

American women's second-class citizenship emerged from the concept of *coverture*, which was inherited from British Common Law but taken to a new extreme by the American legal system. In England, coverture made women the economic and political dependents of their fathers or husbands, but it did not preclude their independent relationship with the state. In the U.S., coverture imposed economic and legal dependency on women by preventing them from purchasing land without the consent of their husbands or fathers, owning property in their names only, holding power of attorney, gaining custody of their children, or testifying against their husbands, among other restrictions. Coverture also gave husbands ownership of their wives' labor and control over their wives' wages.[4] Men in both nations represented women's political interests and controlled their economic lives, but only in the U.S. was a wife's citizenship status dependent on her husband's. As marriage became the primary criterion for defining women's derivative citizenship, the U.S. became increasingly guilty of what Anne Marie Nicolosi calls "trafficking in women."[5]

Before the codification of women's dependent or derivative citizenship in 1855, a woman who married a foreigner could retain her American citizenship. An 1830 Supreme Court decision, in *Shanks v. Dupont*, confirmed that principle, explaining that "marriage to a foreigner does not *ipso facto* contravene an American woman's allegiance." Writing for the majority, Justice Joseph Story stated that "marriage with an alien . . . produces no dissolution of the native allegiance of the wife. It may change her civil rights, but it does not effect [sic] her political rights or privileges," miniscule as they might be.[6] But even as Married Women's Property Acts began to redress property-rights restrictions starting in the late 1840s, laws and legal opinions began tightening the noose of coverture around women's necks with regard to citizenship. Those Acts addressed equity procedures before the Civil War and limited husbands' rights under coverture afterwards—by granting wives the right to draw their own wills, control their own wages, maintain separate estates, and achieve *feme sole* status in case of abandonment, among other reforms. But independent and complete American citizenship for native-born women remained elusive.[7]

Manifest Destiny and Money

The frontier mentality of Manifest Destiny reinvigorated the idea that men's dominance of both women and society was necessary to social well-being. It also valorized brute force and patronage as foundations of civic and political rights and privileges. The male military hero became the model citizen in a nation increasingly consecrated by the blood that women did not (allegedly) shed.[8] The hero's counterpart—the Republican Mother—was exhorted to perform her patriotic duty by producing loyal soldiers.[9] Female bodies seemed increasingly inadequate to the physical might required for full participation in the polis. Some Northern women offered to exchange their "protected" status for the vote, with no results. Nationwide, women's "manifest destiny" was to enact their role as the "weaker sex."[10]

Once again citizenly responsibilities seemed intrusive upon women's attachments and loyalties to husbands and children. Citizenship rights for women also seemed to negate the alleged social benefits of men's power over women's public status.[11] Full citizenship might allow women to own their domestic labor, for example, or keep their own wages. How then could husbands hold families together as a social unit? Conservatives even argued that it was the husband's right to control the "person and labor of [his] wife, and the benefits of her industry and economy" in order to prevent wives from functioning in their own "pecuniary self-interest," as Charles O'Conor argued at the 1846 New York state constitutional convention. Besides ruining both the family and the nation, such female self-interest might give some wives the idea that they could demand specific cash amounts as their legal right to maintenance.[12] To forestall both public and private ruin, courts routinely ruled that women were too dependent "by nature" to be full citizens, despite the fact that their dependency was an artifact of the law.[13]

Widespread protests in the 1830s, 40s, and 50s derided coverture as an "anomalous" remnant of the "dark ages" that violated American constitutionalism, created more hardship for the so-called incapacitated, and made married women into virtual political slaves.[14] But the alleged hazards of allowing married women to manage their own money prevented the passage of earnings acts for women prior to the Civil War except in Massachusetts, where such a law was passed in 1855. New York gave women the right to control their wages in 1860, but control of their own domestic labor took longer.[15] Women's property rights and citizenship prospects faced even greater hurdles on the national level, since "even more than in regard to the 'lower races,' the [Supreme] Court had no strong proponents of women's equal rights, economic or otherwise," as Rogers Smith explains.[16]

Coverture, Slavery, and Race

Slavery provided yet another obstacle to women's full citizenship. Pro-slavery advocates in the 1840s argued that maintaining women's secondary citizenship status was necessary to the survival of slavery, since free women's ineligibility for birthright citizenship rights justified denying such entitlements to enslaved men.[17] The "civic death" of free married women was hardly analogous to the legal erasure of slaves, of course, since free women had choice about most aspects of their lives, including marriage, and could claim at least some legal protections. But those differences did not prevent Southern leaders from offering parallel reasons for withholding basic citizenship rights from both groups.

Legal commentator Edward Mansfield explained in 1845, for example, that slaves and wives needed the guardianship (or "custodianship") of white males for their own good as well as for social stability. The language differed a little—wives lost "personal control," and slaves lost "personal independence"—but the effect was parallel. Some husbands even argued in court that their legal custodianship of their wives should give them the same right of peaceful "reception" of runaway wives as the Fugitive Slave Law gave them for runaway slaves. Although that argument did not entirely fly with trial judges, it did support the notion that wives who left their husbands lost their rights to alimony, child custody, and property.[18]

Through such reasoning, free women's bodies were seen as analogous to enslaved bodies, as equally inappropriate containers for civil and political rights. Indeed, this idea outlived the end of slavery as the courts and legislatures shied away from the term "citizen," which was too contestable, and began talking about "person." One could be a distinct person without having the full rights of a citizen. Black men and all women were persons who needed partial state custody. An 1873 Supreme Court ruling in *Bradwell v. Illinois* held, for example, that women could not practice law or assume the mantle of state power for two reasons: God had ordained that they were subordinate to man; and their bodies were not those of a sovereign citizen. Also like slaves', women's "words and actions" could not "defend their bodies."[19]

Free Black Women

There were few discussions of free black women's citizenship status in ante-bellum America, but it is clear that they had at least two chances to lose their rights. If the law associated them with free black men, as it did in states like Ohio that had Black Codes, then their rights were circumscribed by race and sex simultaneously. If the law lumped them together with free white women, as in New Jersey and Massachusetts, where free black men's rights for a time resembled those of white men, then their rights, like white women's, were circumscribed primarily by their sex.[20]

Whatever their locale, however, free black women's racial classification never saved them from the taint of their gender with regard to political rights or citizenship. As women, they were not among the former slaves granted the franchise by the Fifteenth Amendment, for example. When African men gained the right to naturalization in 1870, the exclusion of African immigrant women went beyond their race and geographical origin.[21] At the same time, being female did not protect black women from the same assaults on their citizenship rights as those endured by black men. In Jim Crow America, black women were also subject to race-based lynching, and after 1920 they also faced race-based poll taxes and literacy tests. And when it came to the privileges American society associated with femininity, free black women rarely qualified as sufficiently female. They were granted no "first place" or special care in public arenas—quite the contrary—and for centuries they had no legal protection from rape or sexual assault. On the whole, then, African American women, before and after the Civil War, were doubly disadvantaged in terms of citizenship. Neither race nor gender offered any refuge.

Derivative Citizenship and Race

Derivative citizenship, or the idea that American women's citizenship depends on that of their husbands, appears on the surface equally applicable to all women. But despite that appearance, the concept was designed to control women's reproductive role in generating racial difference. That intention became clear with the passage in 1855 of a federal law to "secure the right of Citizenship to Children of Citizens of the United States." The children referred to in the law were men's, not women's, and the spouses eligible for automatic citizenship were only the wives of American men, not the husbands of American women.[22] Since most blacks before the Civil War were already excluded from full American citizenship, the law reinforced primarily white women's contingent citizenship status (*jus sanguinis* and *jus soli*) and demonstrated that only white men could transmit citizenship to others.[23]

The significance of the 1855 law for native-born American women's citizenship status was quickly revealed in judicial rulings that revoked women's American citizenship when they married foreigners. Marriage to a non-American was *ipso facto* evidence that a woman (but not a man) had voluntarily disavowed U.S. citizenship. That idea was reinforced by the Expatriation Act of 1868, which established for the first time that American nationals *could* disavow their citizenship.[24] The 1855 law also reveals a deep connection between coverture, as a principle of American female citizenship, and the concept of racial control in American society.

In 1907, with the passage of another Expatriation Act, women's derivative citizenship became both more explicit and more directly related to race. The new law made explicit what was only implicit before: an American woman who married a foreigner voluntarily renounced her American citizenship and assumed her husband's nationality. The law did not distinguish among the foreigners an American woman might marry, but it did distinguish among the women to whom American citizenship might be restored if the marriage ended. In that event, exapatriated ex-wives would become naturalized rather than birthright American citizens, so any restrictions affecting naturalization—racial and otherwise—would apply. If the expatriated wife were racially ineligible for naturalization herself, she would not be naturalized, even if she were native born. Since all Chinese people had been excluded from naturalization in 1882, the law was especially targeted at Chinese American women.

Obviously, the 1907 Expatriation Act discouraged American women from marrying immigrants or foreigners, prevented the wife of an immigrant husband from being naturalized independently, and punished American women "who introduced foreign elements into the body politic."[25] The Act also further institutionalized women's role as the creators of race, since it empowered the government to differentiate between racially desirable and undesirable native-born women and their children. The Supreme Court upheld the 1907 Expatriation

Act in 1915, reaffirming that marriage to a foreigner constituted a voluntary renunciation of a woman's, but not a man's, American citizenship status.

The Cable Act, also called The Married Women's Independent Nationality Act, which Congress passed in 1922, made the racial implications of women's derivative citizenship status even clearer. Congress was actually trying to revisit the rules in the 1907 Expatriation Act, which governed the repatriation of non-resident American women upon the termination of their marriages to foreigners. The Cable Act's "alias" was ludicrous, however, since the law's result actually mocked the idea of married women's independent citizenship by tightening the link between women's marital status, the construction of race, and American citizenship. The Act specified that "any woman citizen who marries an *alien ineligible to citizenship* shall cease to be a citizen of the United States." That italicized phrase was code for undesirable racial groups, especially Asians, as well as for anarchists and polygamists.[26] Given that foreign women married to American men automatically became American citizens, the Cable Act was a slap in the face to native-born American women with regard to citizenship.[27]

The Cable Act did have some benefits, however. It established the principle that marriage and citizenship *could* be separate and thereby signified the erosion of coverture. Other tenets of the law signaled the demise of protective labor legislation. But only women who had previously lost their citizenship by marrying an alien "eligible for citizenship" were helped by the repatriation clause of the Cable Act, and then only if their racial identities made them eligible for citizenship. Since they could only become naturalized citizens in any case, however, all women repatriated under the Act's auspices could still have their citizenship papers revoked or be deported at the government's whim.[28] Those whose own racial classification was "ineligible to citizenship" might never regain their citizenship, as mandated by the 1907 law. In short, the Cable Act continued to make clear that a woman's marital choices shifted the relationship between her racial identity and her citizenship status.[29]

Many Asian American women were denied repatriation under the Cable Act on racial grounds. Huang Cuilian, for example, was born and raised in San Francisco but married a Chinese national in 1917 and lived with him in China. Although abandoned by her husband after thirteen years of marriage and five children, Huang was denied re-entry to the U.S. in 1930. Her marriage made her an alien and her race made her ineligible for citizenship.[30] Such policies allowed the government to cull the American polity of women as both embodiments and progenitors of racial undesirability. Male American citizens never faced such restrictions.

The provisions of the Cable Act demonstrate that "arguments for sexual equality were rooted in racial hierarchy and arguments for racial determinism often had sexual fears at their root," according to Martha Gardner. The Cable Act also reinforced the courts' view that a woman's eligibility to enter the U.S. was not meant to recognize her individual rights but rather to reinforce men's right to spousal company and services. The Act kept alive "traditional ideas of marriage as a moral necessity [for men] and women's roles as wife and mother."[31] The Cable Act was amended in 1930 and 1931, but it wasn't until the 1934 version, known as the Equal Nationality Act, that "the discriminatory consequences of marrying an 'alien ineligible for citizenship' were eliminated and [native-born] women's citizenship fully separated from marriage consequences," according to Nancy Cott.[32]

The Racial Connotations of Women's Independent Citizenship

We should note that the Cable Act continued to reinforce American women's derivative citizenship for fourteen years after the passage of the Nineteenth Amendment to the Constitution that granted American women the right to vote. This time lag suggests that independent citizenship was in some ways a greater gendered sticking point than the vote, possibly because of the connection lawmakers made between restricting married women's reproductive rights and controlling the racial composition of the U.S. This reasoning is reinforced by the fact that women's final acquisition of the right to independent citizenship also served racial purposes, since the new freedom continued to link race, reproduction, and gender difference.

Because the 1934 Act was passed in the midst of the Depression, men's unique right to bestow their citizenship status on any children and any wife had begun to seem problematic. Congress, labor unions, and civic leaders were all agitating to limit the influx of immigrants, including white Europeans, in the early 1930s. Blame for poverty and indigence shifted from unskilled men to poor immigrant mothers who produced public charges. That shift made men's ability to bestow their citizenship and racial status on their children with foreign women seem no less risky than allowing American women, especially white ones, to do the same.[33]

This racist reasoning produced the Equal Nationality Act of 1934, which expedited the naturalization process for American women's alien husbands and allowed the foreign-born children of such unions to apply for American citizenship for the first time, provided they had entered the country before the age of 18 and resided in the U.S. for five years.[34] With the Nationality Act, the U.S. abandoned marital expatriation but did not automatically restore the citizenship of previously expatriated women. Although it equalized naturalization, expatriation, repatriation, and immigration for the two sexes, the Equal Nationality Act did not remove discrimination against individuals because of race, color, or national origins. The Chinese remained an exception, for example, as we shall see in Chapter 13. The law just no longer focused this aspect of discrimination solely on women. Indeed, by allowing American mothers to bequeath their citizenship to either their *legitimate* or their *illegitimate* children but prohibiting American fathers from bequeathing their citizenship to their *illegitimate* children, the Equal Nationality Act in some ways favored women. As Gardner explains, "a child was her mother's by birth but her father's only by law. Paternity outside of marriage . . . could not be assumed."[35] Enforcement, of course, was uneven, and the law was modified by subsequent legislation, including the Nationality Act of 1940, which complicated the transmission of citizenship to children of American citizens born abroad.

Like the Nineteenth Amendment, the Equal Nationality Act did not fully establish American women's equal citizenship status. Women's service on juries remained contested, and New Deal policies revived the male definition of the principal citizen. The majority of New Deal benefits accrued to white men as husbands, fathers, or potential providers for families and to women only if they were widows or wives. Thus, even though marriage to a foreigner no longer deprived a woman of her American citizenship, her marital status still compromised her capacity to inhabit her citizenship fully. "Formal inclusion in the political arena is never as decisive and determinative as formal exclusion," as Cott observes.[36]

As Gender Goeth, So Goeth Race

Racism kept coverture's grip on American women's citizenship intact through the passage of both the Fourteenth and Fifteenth Amendments to the Constitution, in 1868 and 1879 respectively, even as African American men's citizenship status was officially (if not practically) divorced from race. The adjudication of those amendments made clear that both equal protection of the law and suffrage remained privileges of male inhabitants, as the concepts of "male," "citizenship," and "suffrage" were conjoined in the Constitution for the first time. Coverture even outlived women's right to vote. Indeed, the "persona ficta" of the rights bearer was not completely divorced from the concept of the "universal and reasonable man" until the 1970s.[37]

At the same time, white women's pursuit of citizenship rights for themselves also had racial consequences. Perhaps they were passive beneficiaries of the Equal Nationality Act's racist attitudes, but they were more active in arguing during the suffrage movement that votes for educated, responsible (read: white) women would counteract the negative influence of votes by uneducated, irresponsible, "alien" (read: non-white) men. Fortunately, that tactic did not succeed in disenfranchising women of color or reducing their chances for citizenship, but it has had lasting effects on inter-racial relationships among American women. It also demonstrates how deeply and on how many levels gendered citizenship rights have been interconnected with issues of race.

13

"No Can Do" Men and Their Others

Dependency and Inappropriate Gender

After the passage of the Fifteenth Amendment, Susan B. Anthony predicted that once the courts established that U.S. citizenship did " 'not carry with it the right to vote in every State, . . . there is no end to the cunning devices that will be resorted to, to exclude one and another class of citizens from the right of suffrage.' " She was right, of course, but her analysis was incomplete. Anthony failed to note that the denial of full citizenship rights to native-born American women had already become a template for denying citizenship rights to non-white men. Its use only increased in the late nineteenth century, as judges repeatedly upheld states' right to withhold privileges and immunities of citizenship for Negro, Indian, and Asian men because they could withhold them for women. As Joan Hoff observes, in the last quarter of the nineteenth century, "sex paved the way for increased racial bias within the American legal system."[1]

The New Jersey Compromise

Long before the Supreme Court heard Virginia Minor's case and ruled on the gender precedent for Jim Crow, the state of New Jersey provided a clear example of sex paving the way for racial bias. New Jersey's constitution of 1776 (fourth draft) was the only state constitution of the period that deliberately enfranchised all adults "worth fifty pounds," who had resided in the state for one year, without either gender or racial exclusions. (Coverture meant that female voters were necessarily single or widowed.) Although the initial omission of "race" as a voting qualification in New Jersey may have reflected the unlikelihood that free black men could meet the property qualifications, the omission of a gender qualification was intentional. State politicians thought large numbers of female voters could "spirit up their countrymen" for the Revolution and expand electoral support for the ruling party.[2]

The political winds began to shift in 1800, however, and those same politicians began to see a political advantage in disenfranchising certain voters. Moderates began wrangling with liberals within the Republican Party, Republicans began competing with Federalists (who had eagerly enlisted women voters starting in 1789), and both parties faced the challenge of an upstart third party. Women, "aliens," and black men were the targets for disenfranchisement, but the early debates concentrated on women.[3] Lawmakers who had once celebrated the justice of universal suffrage and reaped the benefits of women's political support began spouting old saws about "female delicacy and reserve [as] incompatible with the duties of a free elector." The slippery slope of disenfranchisement started with women's "unsuitability"—as "too genteel"—and soon focused on Negro inferiority and alien "untrustworthiness."[4]

After the debates, a compromise was struck in 1807 that limited the franchise to taxpaying white male citizens and omitted equal numbers of Republican voters (non-taxpayers and aliens) and Federalist voters (white women and Negroes). Trumped up deficiencies attributed to all disenfranchised groups, but allegations that they were responsible for corruption in state elections masked the *realpolitiks* of the situation: the excluded groups tended to vote for the wrong party. The election law compromise meant that New Jersey voters were no longer seen as individuals who did or did not meet particular standards. Instead, they were members of interest groups "for whose allegiance ... parties competed," according to Judith Klinghoffer and Lois Elkins. (A change that is still with us.) Because immigrants had no standing to protest, and black men were afraid to rock the fragile boat of gradual emancipation (enacted in 1804), the new election law not only passed handily despite its clear unconstitutionality, but it also escaped court challenge until the state constitution was revised in 1844.[5]

White women's support of the bogus law foreshadowed the unholy alliance that would emerge in a slightly different form in the national fight for woman suffrage. White women voters in New Jersey agreed to disenfranchise black men and immigrants because they secretly regarded them as their inferiors. They were willing to sacrifice their gendered political self-interest in order to assert their racial superiority. Many women who might have opposed this sacrifice were disenfranchised themselves by their marital status, since coverture was alive and well, even in liberal New Jersey.[6]

The Ultimate 'No Can Do' Males: African American Citizenship

Full citizenship for American-born and immigrant men of color was variously restricted by analogy to the political incapacities of all women. Many groups were characterized at one time or another as "no can do" men whose lack of skill, virtue, and economic productivity not only contrasted to the "can do" spirit of the model (white male) citizen but also rendered them suspiciously like unruly feminine "weaker vessels."[7] In the late ante-bellum period, free native-born African American men were the primary analogs of women as incapacitated citizens. And again after the Civil War, before the ink was dry on the Fifteenth Amendment, narratives about black men's pre-industrial, erotic, and economically careless identities resurfaced to undermine their new political and social rights, especially in the South. Black men also seemed increasingly inassimilable to white American culture because they could intervene in white men's control of white women and, therefore, of white racial blood.[8]

When Gender Eclipsed Race

The case of free African American men's evolving citizenship rights illustrates the initial primacy of gender in defining American citizenship status. Black men's right to vote did not begin with the Fifteenth Amendment, nor was it limited to New Jersey prior to the Civil War. Rather, during the colonial period, the British government's complaints about "complexion"-based rights influenced eleven of the original thirteen colonies not to exclude free black men in the enfranchised electorate.[9] There were other barriers, however, that interfered with universal male suffrage in some colonies. In Massachusetts and Connecticut, for example, voters had to be members of the Congregational Church. In many other colonies, they had to own property. Tax-paying was a requirement for voting in still others (and remained so in many states until 1810).[10] But all free men who met such qualifications were typically granted suffrage, at least on paper, although often with harsh restrictions.

Eight original states, including a few in the South, also did not exclude Negro men from the franchise, provided they met other qualifications. (Whether all black men could actually exercise that right was another matter.) Only gradually did those states insert "white" to modify "male" in allocating suffrage and other rights of citizenship. Virginia, for example, allowed all freemen (except religious "recalcitrants") to vote with a tax-paying requirement until 1723, when Negroes, mulattoes, and Indians were all excluded from the franchise.[11] Rhode Island allowed black freemen to vote from 1776 onward, although they were singled out for property qualifications before 1842 and subjected to a poll tax after that.[12] Maryland did not exclude black freemen from voting until 1801.[13] Free black men could vote in Pennsylvania after 1790 and before 1838, in Delaware before 1792, and in New York after 1777.[14] North Carolina allowed free black male suffrage until 1835, the last of the original southern colonies to do so.

None of those states allowed women to vote because of the alleged deficiencies of their sex. It seems that sex differences and hierarchies were still perceived as more serious than differences of race, which was not yet considered an absolute biological category. New Jersey was a special case, as we have seen, since all adults who were worth fifty pounds, including women, could vote there until 1807. It was the only state to enfranchise women in all elections before Wyoming entered the Union as a women's suffrage state in 1890.[15]

Several new states added to the Union under the Ordinance of 1787 also permitted free black men but not women to vote, including: Vermont, starting in 1790; Kentucky, from 1792 until 1799; Maine, starting in 1820; and Tennessee from 1796 until 1834. Vermont and Maine were the only two states in that group that did not subsequently prohibit voting on the basis of race. Among territories acquired under the same Ordinance, Indiana and Mississippi made no racial distinction in defining male suffrage until 1808. The Illinois Act of 1809 was the last territorial act that did not prohibit Negroes from voting.[16] By 1855, only Massachusetts, Vermont, New Hampshire, Maine, and Rhode Island did not discriminate against free Negro men in voting, but those states contained only four percent of the free black population.[17]

In some cases, particularly in the North, the extension of suffrage to free black men honored the fact that they had fought for their country and were "born as free as [white men], natives of the same country, and deriving from nature and our political institutions the same rights and privileges which we have," in the words of Peter A. Jay of New York in 1821. Although that logic escaped most southern lawmakers, as it had the colonial Virginia Assembly, many northern politicians believed that all free men shared male privilege. So, Jay

"No Can Do" Men and Their Others 185

asked, why should free black men "remain forever aliens among us?" Why should black men be considered more subject to the influence of money than were the "many thousands of white fawning, cringing sycophants?" Former New York state Attorney General Abraham Van Vechten pointed out that black and white men worked together and served together in the militia. How then, he asked, "can distinctions justify us in taking from them any of the common rights which every other free [male] citizen enjoys?" Such arguments helped to retain the franchise for black men in New York, although they did not prevent lawmakers there from imposing more stringent property, tax, and residency requirements on black than on white male voters in 1821.[18]

Race Matters

As the nineteenth century progressed, egalitarian arguments like Jay's were overwhelmed by growing racialist thinking and political exigencies within states that had enfranchised black male voters. As the Southern economy became increasingly dependent on slavery, Southern lawmakers calculated that disenfranchising free black men would help to save that sad institution. Northern lawmakers wanted to eliminate black voters in order to give whites an advantage in increasingly competitive labor markets. To that end, even New York began eroding black male suffrage rights in 1811, by requiring Negro voters to present proof of their freedom in order to vote. That cumbersome and expensive requirement discouraged many from exercising their suffrage rights.[19] Other Northern states that allowed black men to vote imposed similar restrictions by the 1830s, both to serve whites' economic interests in their region and to compensate for perceived innate racial deficiencies, which were becoming clearer as time (and racialist thinking) went on.

Whatever their true motivation, arguments for restricting or eliminating black men's voting rights often impugned their masculinity, which remained the primary qualification for citizenship. Indeed, depriving a man of citizenship rights was increasingly seen as tantamount to denying that he was a man at all, let alone manly enough to engage in the political sphere or the workplace—that "central proving ground for the Self-Made Man," according to many nineteenth century whites.[20] Such a Man must be an achiever, a man of action, a gentleman. But black men were increasingly seen as primitive, even savage. It was okay for a tough white man to display forceful even brutal masculinity, but in an African American man, toughness seemed threatening, vengeful, and a sign of uncontrollable lust.[21]

Such stereotypes kept most white men from understanding that reducing some men to non-citizenship status diminished all men. Representative David Wilmot of Pennsylvania was one of the few to recognize, as he did in 1847, that free men needed "a fair country" for all. Wilmot explained that Negro men's degradation brought disgrace upon whites too.[22] To most white men, however, eliminating as much male competition as possible from the economic and political realms seemed unequivocally advantageous. To justify their own superiority, whites projected the taint of slavery even on blacks who had never experienced it and defined the dependent status of slaves as a norm of black masculinity.[23]

Even as legislators and civic leaders decried the evils of slavery, in both North and South, they increasingly justified its existence on the grounds that black men were insufficiently manly to interact with white men. Northern Free Soilers (early Republicans), for example, who supported abolition but not racial equality, claimed that even the free Negro was not "fully a man."[24] Many Southern critics of slavery agreed, and for that reason argued that black men were better off as slaves "in the midst of a community of white men, with whom [they have] no common interest, no fellow feeling, no equality"—that is, no shared manhood.[25]

Freed slaves were particularly subject to such judgments. They were most frequently depicted as "feminine"—dependent, weak, subject to their passions, and "beset with temptations, 'strong, nay, almost irresistible,' to the force of which in most cases he may be expected to yield.' " Temptations included sexual liaisons with white women and alliances with black men still in chains for the purpose of exterminating the entire white race.[26] Such sentiments guaranteed that every new Southern state—Louisiana, Mississippi, Alabama, Missouri, and later Arkansas, Florida, and Texas—as well as many new states in the West, would enter the Union with constitutions that prohibited Negro suffrage. Even the Tennessee Constitution, which granted "every freeman" the right to vote, was eventually construed to apply only to white men. By 1835, North Carolina was the only slave-holding state in which free Negro men could still vote, a distinction that disappeared that same year with the state's new constitution.[27]

Such arguments also help to explain why many Northern states, including New Jersey, Connecticut, Ohio, and Indiana, initially balked at the idea that black manhood suffrage was the logical extension of emancipation after the Civil War. Because black men were "emasculated," primitive, and incapable of progress (like women), the idea of black male suffrage, even for free men, became increasingly unthinkable. "The negro is satisfied if he can appropriate one or two acres of land," wrote Frederick Grimké in 1848. "All he cares for is to obtain just enough to satisfy the wants of animal life. He has the name of freeman only: for liberty is of no account, unless it absolves us from the yoke of our own propensities and vices."[28] Men who lived to indulge their senses and petty desires, like women, would only abuse the freedoms of citizenship.

Whites who argued that free Negroes should form their own internal colony or emigrate to Liberia also equated citizenship with manliness. Blacks should not rest until their children could "grow into the dignity of a noble manhood," argued an editorial writer for the *National Era* (a prominent anti-slavery, free soil journal). In the early 1850s, publications like the *Era* praised Negroes for their admirable "patience, contentment, and fidelity"—conventionally feminine qualities—but warned that, without the manly, entrepreneurial spirit of the Anglo Saxon race, such qualities suited them only for slavery, not citizenship.[29]

Beyond the Franchise

Black men's allegedly feminine inferiority inevitably eroded their citizenship rights beyond the issue of the vote. Some impediments were blatant. For example, the State Department started denying black men's passport applications in the 1840s and 1850s on the grounds that free Negroes were not citizens under the Constitution. The Department's reasoning was reinforced by the Supreme Court decision in *Dred Scott v. Sanford* in 1857, in which Chief Justice Taney concluded that Negroes were of such an inferior order that they were "altogether unfit to associate with the white race, either in social or political relations . . . and . . . had no rights which the white man was bound to respect."[30]

Other objections to and denials of black male citizenship rights were subtler, reminiscent of the inconsistencies and machinations involved in defining and enforcing women's second-class citizenship status. Even black men's intelligence could be used as evidence that they did not qualify for full citizenship. Postmaster General Gideon Granger notified Congress in 1802, for example, that he was worried Negro mail carriers might put two and two together and figure out "that a man's rights do not depend on his color." Equipped with that information as well as access to the postal system, they could plan and execute an uprising. To avoid that possibility, Congress prohibited black men from carrying the mail in 1810 and did not revisit that restriction until 1862, at which time it was tabled.[31]

Through such manipulation, free black men were "nominally admitted by the law to the privileges of citizenship," according to Attorney General (later Chief Justice) Roger Taney in 1831, but they had no standing to defend those rights—like women. Moreover, free black men enjoyed whatever rights they had only at "the sufferance of the white population," just as free women's rights depended on the sufferance of men. In 1843, the then-Attorney General Hugh Legare modified Taney's stance by arguing that free Negro men occupied an intermediate position between white male citizens and aliens. He agreed with Taney, though, that black freemen, like all women, had citizenship rights but not necessarily full-fledged political status.[32]

Such varied interpretations continued into the early years of the Civil War, even as free Negro men were allowed to vote, mostly with restrictions, in all New England states, except Connecticut.[33] In 1861 the Massachusetts legislature decided to grant passports to any male citizen, "whatever his color may be," and in the following year U.S. Attorney General Edward Bates ruled that "free men of color, if born in the United States, are citizens of the United States." His ruling meant that "citizenship was 'not dependent on nor coexistent' with color, race, 'the degradation of a people,' or the legal right to vote and hold office."[34] But it also meant, as Susan B. Anthony said, that there were classes of citizens and that race, like sex, could disqualify a denizen citizen from full citizenship rights. That changed for black men officially, if not practically, with the passage of the Fourteenth Amendment six years later and the Fifteenth Amendment in 1870. (Women's second-class status was not changed by those amendments, however, since neither was ever successfully used to achieve women's full citizenship status.)

Gendered Racial Citizenship after the Civil War

Reconstruction brought significant changes in native-born black men's official citizenship rights and expanded naturalization rights to African men after 1870. The Reconstruction Act required Southern states not only to hold conventions to re-write their racist constitutions but also to allow all men (except for whites connected with the Confederacy) to vote for delegates, a requirement that contributed to black majorities in some states and major cities, such as Baltimore. During Reconstruction, black men could not be denied the legal right to vote, and from 1865 to 1875, black men were elected to state legislatures and county offices (although some states did whatever they could to prevent such victories). For a brief time, a district along the

Sea Islands of South Carolina allowed black men to elect their own Congressional representative.[35]

With the defeat of Reconstruction, such progress came to a halt, suddenly and violently. White male voters gained control in state after state and eliminated black men from state legislatures and from the national Senate and House. Their efforts were aided by the Ku Klux Klan, whose members did not hesitate to murder a black man to keep him from voting Republican. In the "Tidal Wave" of 1874, Southern states elected a nearly solid Democratic delegation to the House, which could only have been accomplished by the suppression of the black vote. In 1876, Rutherford B. Hayes struck a deal with Southern Democrats: if they helped him get elected, he would withdraw federal troops from polling places.[36] The success of that deal marked the end of America's Radical Hour.

Even though states were prohibited by the Fifteenth Amendment from passing statutes or constitutional amendments that directly denied black men the vote, many did so one way or another—South Carolina in 1895, Louisiana in 1898, North Carolina in 1900, Alabama in 1901, Virginia in 1902, and Georgia in 1908. In addition, Jim Crow laws that imposed poll taxes, mandated secret ballots, and established white-only primaries in many Southern states continuously undermined black men's official citizenship rights for decades.[37] Race-based lynching and anti-miscegenation laws denied black men the male prerogative of choosing either their politics or their spouses. Arguments justifying such vicious measures often focused on the childishness and dependency of black men, who were routinely called "boys" regardless of their age. Deprivations of education and of political participation created some of the very incapacities that racial bigots claimed were inherent in the race, making their victims appear innately unprepared for citizenship, just as women presumably were.

Rather than challenging the gender terms used to deny their citizenship rights, many black leaders reinforced the idea that manliness was an appropriate criterion for citizenship by claiming that black men were sufficiently manly to qualify. John Russwurm (one of the first African American college graduates in the antebellum period) started the trend before the Civil War by touting the manly achievements of rebellious slaves as emblematic of black men's qualification for citizenship. Abolitionists, both black and white, also accepted manliness as a symbol of racial freedom and independence. Even Maria Stewart argued in the 1830s for the Masculine Achiever "ideal of manhood that incorporated achievement, autonomy, and 'intensive competition for success in the marketplace' " as the foundation of citizenship rights for black Americans.[38] After the Civil War, freed slaves reiterated the theme: masculinity was their primary qualification for the right to "independence, citizenship, engagement in the marketplace, mastery over self and the environment, and patriarchy." Without such rights, as W.E.B. Du Bois argued in 1903, "submission to civic inferiority . . . is bound to sap the manhood of any race in the long run."[39] Without black manliness the race would not survive.[40]

Women also continued to accept separate and unequal feminine and masculine capabilities as the paradigm for black citizenship. Black women were morally upright, many argued, and black men had the intellectual and physical capacity for citizenship. Such arguments positioned men as the true racial subject and fueled both male bravado and patriarchy. Any black woman who violated such gender conventions or asserted women's rights despite them risked being called a traitor to her race.[41]

To the nation's shame, black voting rights were not again guaranteed by federal law until 1965, after more than a decade of civil rights protesting, dangerous and violent voter registration drives in the South, and floor-fights and filibusters in the U.S. Senate. The Voting Rights Act of that year outlawed all voting requirements, such as poll taxes and literacy tests, which had kept blacks from exercising their right to vote. And for the first time there was federal legislation guaranteeing the voting rights of Indians, Asians, and Latinos as well as African Americans.

A State of Pupilage: American Indian Citizenship

American Indian men were excluded from full American citizenship for a variety of reasons, not the least of which was white interest in their vast territories. Even more than for African American men, however, reasons for excluding Indians from the franchise were racialized by being feminized. In addition to their allegedly irrational passions and civic incapacity, Indian men were accused of dependency and divided loyalties, which pegged them as alien insider/outsiders.

Even during the relatively friendly seventeenth century, English settlers refused to give Indians the right to govern their own affairs, despite the fact that tribes had ceded authority to the British king in matters involving the colonies. By 1831, Indians existed in "a state of Pupilage" to the U.S. government, in the words of Chief Justice John Marshall, a status that remained essentially intact into the twentieth century.[42] As discussed in Chapter 4, this view of Indian dependency led to a kind of coverture that had both economic and political implications in the American context. Like women, American Indian men became virtual wards of the United States government, which placed much of Indian land into a government-controlled trust and physically removed whole tribes to reservations. But unlike women, Indians received occasional offers of American citizenship and the franchise over the years. Those offers, too, reveal the gendered foundations of citizenship, since even when relations with whites were good, Indians' best chance to attain American citizenship status over many years was to adopt "civilized" gender norms.

Gendered Indian Citizenship

The offers began when a few colonies invited Indians to form "praying societies" and become their affiliates. The invitations came with a catch, however, which would characterize white-Indian relations for centuries. That is, affiliation depended on the Indians' conformity to English ways, including patterns of "civilized" patriarchal family life. When the Indians declined to abandon their traditional cultures, the English transformed the "praying societies" into quasi-reservations, and no Indians became citizens no matter how long they lived in the colonies. After the Revolution, Congress used treaties to deal with Indians outside of English territories. There was some thought of admitting Indian territories into the Confederation, but it was never acted upon.[43]

Throughout the nineteenth century, as pundits from Thomas Jefferson in the 1810s to anthropologist Lewis Henry Morgan in the 1870s called for intermarriage between native women and white men (although not the other way around) on the theory that Indian blood could toughen the winning white race, the government continued to use the promise of citizenship to entice Indians to assimilate on white terms. After Chief Justice Marshall's landmark decision in the 1830s basically declared Indians resident aliens, even if they were born in the U.S., and after the 1857 *Dred Scott* decision affirmed that interpretation, it briefly seemed as if Indians could become citizens by naturalization. But the Attorney General ruled at about the same time that Indians could only become citizens by treaty or an act of Congress, even if they did live among whites and pay taxes. What resulted was a hodge-podge of efforts, from attempts by Congress to naturalize whole tribes, to the formal disenfranchisement of Indians by some states, to the enfranchisement by others of "civilized" Indians who did not belong to tribes. As a result, citizenship remained mostly an unrealized possibility for Indians throughout the ante-bellum period, but it was a possibility.[44]

After years of battle, the U.S. government became more interested in the 1870s and 80s in turning Indians into white people than in eliminating them.[45] So, officials made new offers of citizenship to promote pseudo-racial assimilation. Most such offers were gendered. The government wanted to undermine the tribes' communal values, transform collective childrearing practices, and reduce the alleged sexual availability of Indian women. To combat "sexual lawlessness," the government's offer also promoted marriage, the family, and the primacy of the individual. It threatened to punish adultery, polygamy (especially polyandry), and cohabitation. The Dawes Act in 1887 promoted property ownership along with patriarchal families and linked Indian prospects for citizenship to conventional gender norms. Congress was so intent on promoting these norms that the Dawes Act even reinforced men's status as heads of household by denying married Indian women the right to receive property when the government distributed reservation lands to families. In another effort to subordinate Indian women, the government made a direct offer of citizenship in 1888 to any who married white men.[46] Because the offer recognized white men's control of white racial blood, it did not extend to Indian men who married white women.

The Indian boarding school system begun in the 1870s was part of the effort to transform Indians into acceptable citizens via white gender norms. Children were removed from "debased" fathers and "degraded" mothers in order to encourage individualism and discourage unmanly "habits of aimless living, unambition, and shiftlessness." "Throughout the decades of federal intervention to reform Indian families," according to Rachel Moran, "officials used policies about sex, marriage, and childrearing to preserve racial difference as a biological matter while eradicating its social and cultural significance."[47]

For women, the imposed gender norms were chastity and subservience. For men, they were family dominance, individualism, and a willingness to fight for their country (not their tribe).[48] The U.S. did not regard Indian men as legitimate property owners despite their vast territories, as we saw in Chapter 4, so Indian manliness, unlike white masculinity, could never be proven on the basis of land. The Act of November 6, 1919, demonstrated what the American government really valued by offering citizenship to Indian men who enlisted in World War I.[49]

Gender or Race?

This history of the government's efforts to impose white gender norms on American Indians—chastity, subservience, domesticity, and marriage for women and manual labor, warfare, and the elimination of tribal dependency for men—suggests to several scholars that the concept of Indian "race" created by American citizenship laws was in many ways more gendered than raced. Why else, they argue, were Indian men excluded from the only Constitutional Amendments designed to eradicate race-based discrimination—the Fourteenth and the Fifteenth? Interpretations of those Amendments routinely lumped Indian men together with women rather than with black men and denied both groups suffrage rights and equal protection under the law.[50] Moreover, American Indian men were denied birthright citizenship in part because they, like women, were suspected of divided loyalties. White lawmakers and judges believed that Indian men owed their allegiance elsewhere than the state and could not, therefore, develop sufficient national loyalty for full citizenship. The "elsewhere" in the case of Indian men was not the family, as it was for women, but the tribe.

Proposed solutions to the problem of Indian men's divided loyalties also resembled the bargain offered to native-born American women. Women could only retain their birthright citizenship if they abandoned their right to marry prohibited spouses. Indian men could only acquire full citizenship status by giving up their tribal affiliations. Throughout the nineteenth century, U.S. citizenship was available only to male heads of household who were willing to "break away from the tribe."[51]

Such a deal was struck with the Cherokees in 1817 and 1819 and with the Choctaws in 1830. Refusal to accept citizenship under those terms resulted in a man's (or a tribe's) removal to a reservation. The government's offer of citizenship to an entire tribe "generally entailed the destruction of the tribal organization and government," as it did for the Wyandots in 1855 and the Ottawas in 1862. Indians who maintained their tribal affiliations were defined as alien domestic dependents of the U.S. government, a status that resembled free women's during the same period. The government wanted tribal nations to recognize the higher civic authority of the U.S. and come under the protection of that more powerful nation, according to Justice Marshall in 1832.[52] American wives also had to recognize their husbands' "higher" power to represent them under coverture and subsume their independent civic identities for their own good.

Indian men's feminized status was also evident in treaties signed in the 1860s that gave the President and the courts the power to determine "when adult, male alottees had become sufficiently 'intelligent and prudent' to conduct their [own] affairs and interests." Unmarried Indian women could also qualify for such a release of dependency. A treaty with the Pottawatomies in 1867, for example, even allowed single adult women who were heads of a family to be declared eligible to conduct their own affairs.[53] That such a status exceeded what an American *feme sole* could achieve at the time in many states suggests a concession to Indians' "inappropriate gender": feminized men meant masculinized women. Such an interpretation did not last long, however, as U.S. laws soon imposed mainstream gender values on both sexes.

Indian Emancipation

The termination of the treaty period in 1871 did not eliminate Indians' state of pupilage to the U.S. government. Statutes that replaced the treaties still required "de-tribalized" Indians to vacate their land, adopt civilized habits, become self-supporting, and learn English. The Dawes Act of 1887 even prolonged Indian pupilage by empowering the President to allot reservation land and the government to hold land titles in trust for 25 years. Although citizenship was initially offered as compensation for relinquishing property rights, that offer expired in 1906, when Congress passed the Burke Act that allowed the government to withhold Indian citizenship until after the trust period ended.[54] The Burke Act reinforced the idea that American Indian men "could not be quickly improved and must still be firmly controlled."[55] Like women.

Not all Indians wanted citizenship, of course. Many men held tightly to their tribal memberships, and few wanted an option that would end their tribal governments. Women in many tribes understood that American citizenship would deprive them of their ability to own and control property, initiate divorce, prevent warfare, exercise public and political authority, and participate in consensus building within their tribes and in treaty negotiations with outsiders. As William Stone explained in 1841, "in the adjustment of weighty and difficult matters, no other people are in the habit of treating the opinions of their women with greater deference than the America [sic] Indians." That's why Dr. Peter Wilson, a Cayuga chief, encouraged American men as early as 1866 to give everyone the vote, "even the women, as in his nation," and why a Dakota woman exclaimed in 1891 that she "would not be a white woman." Many whites, including suffragists Lucretia Mott and Matilda Joslyn Gage, recognized that Indian women had more political rights and more liberty than American women and that American citizenship would be a terrible come-down from their egalitarian heritage.[56]

It wasn't until June 2, 1924, that the Indian Citizenship Act finally granted birthright citizenship to American Indians. That law did not eliminate governmental control over Indian affairs, however, since both the principle of wardship and the trustee relationship remained in effect while tribal lands were held in lease to the government. The Bureau of Indian Affairs continued to regulate the personal conduct of allottees, as we have seen, which badly undercut their citizenship status, and many government-sponsored boarding schools operated into the 1930s (and beyond). Congress finally passed the Indian Reorganization Act in 1934, the same year that American women achieved independent rather than derivative citizenship status. The Act recognized that American Indians had three simultaneous citizenships—tribal, state, and federal—and finally put them on a par with other native-born and naturalized Americans.[57] The coincidence of female and Indian citizenship rights did not mean that gendered race no longer constrained American citizenship rights for other groups, however, as we shall see in the next section.

Prostitutes and Bachelors: Gender Complementarity in the Exclusion of Chinese Immigrants from American Citizenship

The long and torturous story of Asian American citizenship exemplifies many of the stringent and contradictory gendered rationales that excluded various racialized groups from full American citizenship. This analysis will focus on the gendered citizenship struggles of the Chinese, who were the earliest large-scale Asian immigrant group in the U.S. and, therefore, the test case for Asian immigration and naturalization policies. Since citizenship was a male province, exclusionary laws focused primarily on Chinese men, but Chinese women were official pawns in that process to a greater extent and for a longer time than were women in most other groups.

Slave-like Conditions and Citizenship Exclusions

Chinese men began arriving in the U.S., without spouses, in 1848, seeking employment in the California Gold Rush. In the 1850s, some tried to apply for naturalization, only to be told that they were not white, as required by the 1790 naturalization law. After 1870, when men of African birth or ancestry were granted naturalization rights,

Chinese men already in the country tried again. This time a federal court quickly made clear that Chinese persons were neither white nor African and were therefore still ineligible for citizenship.[58]

The slave-like conditions under which male Chinese workers were admitted to the U.S., from California's mining industry, to Southern post-war cotton plantations, to Eastern and Mid-western commercial laundries, also undermined their citizenship prospects. Indeed, the situation was so bad in the South that American authorities halted the recruitment of Chinese workers as early as 1867, unless the men themselves swore they had come voluntarily and had willingly signed labor contracts. California businessmen hired Chinese men to work longer hours than white workers for less than half the pay. Despite Chinese workers' crucial role in completing the transcontinental railroad, its owners excluded them from the photographs taken when the two halves of the tracks met and refused to pay the men's passage back to California, as promised in their contracts. As a source of cheap labor, they were valuable to employers for short-term economic growth but threatening to white workers as long-term competition. That competition caused many white Americans to demonize the Chinese as undesirable racial invaders of a country to which whites alone were entitled. So, when the owner of the Passaic Steam Laundry in Belleville, New Jersey, replaced his Irish female employees with Chinese laborers brought from San Francisco, riots broke out and the unions created a panic throughout the Eastern states.[59]

Because of their value as workers, the government did not initially want to eliminate Chinese labor entirely, but they did want to discourage long-term Chinese settlement and, heaven forbid, U.S. citizenship. Because the admission of Chinese women might encourage such settlement, Congress decided to limit or eliminate their admission to the U.S., even though, as women, they were already ineligible for independent citizenship. Without wives, went the logic, or the possibility of marrying white women (covered by anti-miscegenation laws), Chinese bachelor men would more likely want to return home. Deprived of prostitutes, went the same reasoning, they might even hurry on their way back to China.

To realize both goals, the first exclusionary immigration law in the U.S., the Page Act of 1875, prohibited the importation of Chinese prostitutes or "lewd women." Despite its stated focus, the law effectively prevented the immigration of all Chinese women since it required any woman seeking to emigrate to the U.S. to undergo interrogation by U.S. officials stationed in China. Because few "decent" women would subject themselves to such intimate and potentially intimidating questioning, the Page Act drastically reduced female immigration. The number of Chinese women of any kind entering the U.S. between 1876 and 1882 declined sixty-eight percent from the previous seven-year period. Therefore, by 1880, Chinese men outnumbered Chinese women in the U.S. by twenty to one (100,686 men to 4779 women). Only about 150 Chinese women entered the U.S. legally between 1906 and 1924.[60] Even in its heyday, Chinese women's immigration was miniscule until after World War II.

There was a whiff of truth in the Page Act's choice of prohibition, since many Chinese women who emigrated to the U.S. before 1875 entered the country as prostitutes. Some were smuggled in to service Chinese workers in the mines, since ordinary Chinese women did not travel, and Chinese workers (as opposed to merchants) already in the U.S. could not import their wives and families. Most of those female émigrés were basically chattel, even those employed by wealthy men. They could be covered with jewels one day and stripped and auctioned to the highest bidder the next. None received regular wages, and those imported under a contract system, which included initial compensation, typically found that the contract never ended. If they failed to work the requisite 320 days per year or became pregnant, an entire year might be added to their work obligation. Compounding their night-time burdens, many prostitutes were forced to sew for sweatshops during the day for no wages. Some were actually purchased outright, in which case they were literally slaves. They had little hope of repurchase by a sympathetic friend because of the exorbitant interest that entailed.[61]

With the Chinese so tainted in the public's mind, as economically and sexually dangerous bachelors or contaminated prostitutes, Congress decided to prevent further Chinese immigration and naturalization. They passed the Chinese Exclusion Act in 1882, which prohibited the importation of all Chinese laborers—including wives of laborers—for a ten-year period and barred all states and federal courts from naturalizing any Chinese person. That Act began a decades-long process of denying entry and naturalization to the Chinese, which was very effective in reducing the Chinese presence in the U.S. Between 1851 and 1880, approximately 229,000 Chinese entered the country, but between 1891 and 1900, fewer than 15,000 did.[62]

The racial implications of that exclusion became increasingly clear as Congress extended the geographical reach of exclusion laws. An 1884 amendment to the Exclusion Act targeted Chinese people from Hong Kong, and subsequent legislation—in 1888, 1902, and 1904—expanded "China" to include the Philippines and Hawai'i.[63] In 1892, the Geary Act extended the exclusion of laborers for another ten years and required certificates of residence for all "Chinese" immigrants. In 1902, Congress passed another ten-year extension to the 1882 Act, and in 1904, the exclusion was made indefinite. The federal Immigration Act of 1917 finally prohibited "all Asiatic immigration" but exempted the Chinese because they were already excluded.

Numerous gendered precepts fueled the laws limiting Chinese immigration and naturalization. One was the wish to discourage family formation. To achieve that result, California lawmakers even decided to exclude Chinese children from state funded education between 1871 and 1875.[64] Congress attacked the family formation problem directly with the 1888 Scott Act, which applied to immigrants seeking re-entry to the U.S. after a brief absence. Readmission was possible, but it required meeting nearly impossible measures of masculine achievement, such as owning property or having family in the country. Laws like the California Alien Land Acts, which prohibited land ownership by "aliens ineligible for citizenship" (meaning Asians) and restricted their opportunity to lease land from 1907 to the 1920s made land ownership virtually impossible for Chinese men. Thus 20,000 immigrants were denied Certificates of Return because of the Scott Act. The 1924 Immigration Act (or the National Origins Act) reinforced the gendered strictures of the 1922 Cable Act, which had targeted Chinese American women in particular.

Exceptions to Chinese exclusion also illustrate the gendered aspects of citizenship policies focused on the Chinese. The 1882 Exclusion Act, for example, did not apply to government officials, teachers, students, merchants, and travelers, in keeping with an 1880 Sino-American commercial treaty. Thus, "Chinese resident merchants" were allowed to import wives and families into the U.S. on the grounds that a man has a right to his " 'body and household servants,' " which included his wife. That privilege stayed in effect until World War II.[65]

After the war, Congress added gendered exceptions to Chinese exclusion and citizenship eligibility. The War Brides Act of 1945, for example, allowed foreign spouses of war veterans to enter the U.S. It brought several thousand Chinese women into the country between 1945 and 1948, but only as dependent wives. Similarly, the Fiancées and Fiancés of the War Veterans Act of 1946 (which, for Asians, meant fiancées) temporarily admitted Chinese and other foreign women into the U.S., but only because of their prospective marital status. Chinese American men were also given the right to bring their wives to the U.S. as non-quota immigrants by the Act of August 9, 1946. Chinese spouses only qualified for full citizenship rights after the repeal of the Chinese Exclusion Acts in 1947. Even then, despite the McCarran-Walter Act of 1952 that eliminated overt racial bars to citizenship, the national origins quota system continued to limit Chinese women's independent admission to the U.S. Throughout the period, improvements in Chinese citizenship prospects primarily benefited men, thereby calling into question the U.S. government's credentials as a post-World War II standard-bearer for equal justice.[66]

A Gendered Racial Dilemma

Chinese men in twentieth-century America faced a by-now familiar dilemma. If they were to overcome racial obstacles to their acceptance as full American citizens, they often felt compelled to denigrate all things feminine, position themselves as the official "racial subject," and emphasize their own masculinity as a mechanism for redeeming the Asian race.[67] They also noticed that "cutting off their social ties with blacks, invoking racist representations of blacks, and culturally imitating the white community" could raise their status, as we saw in Part III.[68]

At the same time, the Chinese community worked to position its women to counter stereotypes of moral depravity, opium addiction, and rampant prostitution in filthy ghettos. To that end, they organized beauty contests in Chinatowns across the U.S. starting in the 1920s. The contests echoed (white) Miss America contests which started in 1921 and put a public face on Chinese heterosexuality by showcasing conventional femininity and gender norms. The contests attracted multiracial audiences, raised money for good causes, and introduced Chinese women to the American mainstream.[69] The downside of such conformity was the creation of new stereotypes about tough—anti-black—Chinese men and hyper-feminine, submissive Chinese women. Sadly, such stereotypes made the Chinese appear more eligible for citizenship.

Other Asians

Immigration exclusion laws targeting the Chinese racialized and restricted the citizenship prospects of all Asians, even before specific laws including non-Chinese groups were passed. In 1905, for example, the U.S. attorney general ruled that the Japanese, like the Chinese, were neither white nor black, and therefore equally ineligible for citizenship. The Supreme Court reinforced that ruling in its 1923 decision in *The*

United States v. *Thind*, which defined Chinese, Japanese, and Asian Indian peoples as neither white nor black for purposes of naturalization. With that decision, skin color rather than Caucasian ancestry became the official criterion for citizenship.[70]

Just as Asians suffered for decades from being neither black nor white and, by association, neither genuinely male nor female, so too did mixed-race Latinos suffer from allegations of inappropriate "both/and" gender. In Chapter 14, we shall see how such gendered interpretations of mixed race restricted citizenship opportunities for Latinos.

14

Mixed Race, Suspect Gender

Both White and . . . Whatever

In 1842, the U.S. Chargé d'Affaires to the Republic of Texas, Joseph Eve, described Mexicans as "that feeble, dastardly, superstitious priest ridden race of mongrels composed of Spanish, Indian and negro blood."[1] Although last on the list, racial "mongrelism" was a key reason that many white Americans disparaged, even hated, Mexicans and other Latinos. Like black-white biracial mulattoes, Latino mixed-bloods embodied the hazards of white "hypodescent" via the dilution and pollution of a white—Spanish—heritage. Their very existence "foreshadowed the end of whiteness" in the era of scientific racism, as Rosa Linda Fregoso explains.[2] Moreover, "both white and . . . whatever" racial status violated the macho ethos of the Western frontier in the period of Manifest Destiny, linked as that era was to white male prowess. Racial ambiguity for these mulattoes also violated the neat black-white racial paradigm of American life and reminded Anglos of their other "Indian problem," since both Latinos and American Indians had what whites considered dubious claims to precious land resources. Though the U.S. government had promised annexed Mexicans citizenship in the Treaty of Hidalgo that ended the U.S.-Mexican War in 1848, reneging on that promise became a kind of patriotic duty. General Winfield Scott suggested as much in 1852, when he declared, "As a lover of my country, I [am] opposed to mixing up that race with our own."[3]

Puerto Ricans joined Mexicans as another racially "mongrel" Latino group in the minds of many Anglo Americans after 1898. Their mixed race also represented both white hypodescent and economic competition, although not for land resources. They, too, had citizenship claims because of a negotiated treaty—in their case, the one that ended the Spanish-American War. Despite the very different origins of the two groups, they shared a mixed-racial profile and, eventually, similar migration patterns. Both groups included many unskilled workers seeking jobs in the low-wage sector of U.S. economy, and they were also concentrated regionally in the U.S., albeit in different regions.[4] Their social isolation also set up both groups for Jim Crow-like treatment that denied or robbed them of economic independence, herded them into dead-end work, and manipulated them into competition among themselves for even minimal opportunities. Because both groups were predominantly Catholic, they also made many American Protestants anxious on religious grounds.[5]

Given Latinos' shared economic and political disadvantages, it is not surprising that Anglo Americans easily lost sight of particular groups' ethnic specificity and geographic origins and lumped them together as one race. Indeed, when Puerto Ricans first entered the country in 1917, whites often mistook them for Mexicans, and by 1930, actually classified them as Mexican. In addition, even though treaties and U.S. government policies defined them as white, unless they were clearly Negro or Indian, it took years before Latinos were included in the census category "white."[6] Even when the "white" classification was bestowed, however, it did little to improve Latino status. On the one hand, whiteness was never permanent or clear-cut, regardless of skin color; on the other, white status could actually create disadvantages. For example, because white status excluded Mexicans from the remedies promised by the 1954 school desegregation decision in *Brown v. Board of Education*, their segregated schools and classrooms remained untouched in Texas and elsewhere. Only in the 1970s did courts recognize that "Hispanos" were "an identifiable ethnic minority with a past pattern of discrimination."[7]

Chapter 14 traces processes of racialization for Mexicans and Puerto Ricans and analyzes the policies and arguments that demeaned and impeded their citizenship rights on racial grounds. It argues that Latino racial ambiguity—which was often couched in terms of inappropriate or exaggerated gender characteristics—explains why both groups could only achieve, at best, second-class citizenship status in the U.S until the late twentieth century.

"Ill-clad, Unclean, and Immoral": Gender Constructs "Mongrel" Mexican Citizenship

The Treaty of Guadalupe Hildago, which concluded the U.S.-Mexican War of 1846-1848, is the oldest treaty still in effect between Mexico and the United States.[8] Through its negotiation, the U.S. acquired more than 500,000 square miles of territory and ensured its own status as a world power in the nineteenth century.⁹ For a mere $15 million, Mexico ceded half of its territory, including the current states of California, New Mexico, Nevada, and parts of Colorado, Arizona, Utah, and Oklahoma. But the annexed acreage quickly grew, after later negotiations in the U.S. Senate omitted Article X of the original treaty that guaranteed protection of "all prior and pending titles to property of every description." This omission allowed the federal government to seize an additional 1.7 million acres of communal land in New Mexico alone.¹⁰

Approximately 100,000 Mexicans were attached to the ceded territories, and they were given one year to decide whether to remain in "occupied Mexico" or to leave. About 2000 decided to leave, but the rest chose to stay on what many believed was *their* property. For all but those residing in Texas, American citizenship would be delayed; they would be "admitted, at the *proper time (to be judged of by the Congress of the United States)* to the enjoyment of all the rights of citizens of the United States according to the principles of the Constitution; and in the meantime ... maintained and protected in the free enjoyment of their liberty and property, and secured in the free exercise of their religion without restriction."¹¹ With the elimination of Article X, however, the pledge of property protection was effectively nullified. Indeed, even Article X had called the legality of Mexican land ownership into question. Because the courts decided that the "proper time" for citizenship would coincide with statehood for annexed territories, most Mexicans waited for citizenship status until statehood was achieved. For *Californios* that meant 1850, but for New *Mexicanos* it meant 1912, despite repeated attempts to achieve statehood starting in 1850. Congress's real intentions regarding Mexican citizenship and property rights are revealed by that delay, since New Mexico was the only territory to honor all articles of the Treaty.¹²

The Treaty of Guadalupe Hidalgo did not apply to Texas because it was already a state, and *Tejanos* already had U.S. citizenship. But their status was also contested. Lawmakers even tried to add "white" to voter eligibility in the state constitution in order to exclude them (since the original constitution excluded only Africans and their descendants). That the attempt failed had less to do with accepting Mexicans as either white or as citizens than with recognizing the benefits of their votes in tight elections. Prejudice against the "grovelling yellow race of Mexico" persisted, however, and constrained *Tejanos'* participation in Texas politics up to and beyond the Civil War. There was virtually no representation of Mexican Americans at the constitutional convention or, by the 1850s, in state offices, except in San Antonio where they were concentrated. The selection of Austin rather than San Antonio as the state capital further disadvantaged *Tejanos*.[13]

Mexican Indians residing in the ceded territories fared even worse at the hands of Anglo officials who believed that their vicious ancestors, the Aztecs, "sacrificed 30,000 victims a day."[14] For that and other reasons, indigenous tribes were denied both Mexican and American citizenship until the 1930s. Pueblo Indians who had occupied their villages for centuries did not get constitutional citizenship rights in New Mexico until 1953.[15]

Official attitudes toward annexed Mexicans' citizenship rights were fueled by years of tense interaction between Anglos and Mexicans, particularly in California.[16] By the 1840s, for example, many Anglo Californians thought of Mexico as "a nation of mestizos not . . . predisposed to democracy" and unfit to occupy American territory.[17] G.B. Tingley, a legislator from Sacramento who thought all mined gold belonged in Anglo hands, supported this bias by claiming that Mexicans were "devoid of intelligence sufficient to appreciate the true principles of free government; vicious, indolent, and dishonest, to an extent rendering them obnoxious to our citizens; with habits of life low and degraded; an intellect but one degree above the beast in the field, and not susceptible of elevation; all these things combined render such classes of human beings a curse to any enlightened community."[18] Not coincidentally, such racial epithets—inherently dull, incapable of elevation, a curse to civilization—were implicitly feminine.

Westerners who clung to the myth of a once-homogeneous American population and the belief that white pioneers had single-handedly "won" the West considered "tempest-tossed" peoples like Negroes, Asians, or Mexicans an obstacle to developing the true "American race." Landless and nomadic Mexicans, despite U.S. policies that made them so, seemed especial exceptions to the great American melting pot motif. Such people were so inferior, so ignorant of democracy, and so subject to "charismatic autocrats" that citizenship for them seemed almost unthinkable.[19]

Migrants or Citizens?

Problems for Mexican Americans' citizenship prospects were exacerbated by successive waves of migrants from Mexico that poured into the ceded territories and states starting in the 1880s. Most were lured by railroad jobs and the growth of agriculture in the Southwest. By 1900, the Mexican-born population in the U.S. was over 100,000, concentrated primarily in Texas, Arizona, and California. An additional

50,000 arrived by 1910. The immigration rate quadrupled from 1910 to 1920, in part because of the Mexican Revolution, and arrivals included members of the middle and upper classes. In the 1920s almost 460,000 Mexican immigrants entered the U.S. Numbers dipped during the Great Depression but rose again substantially from 1942 to 1964 with the *bracero* program for Mexican workers, who were prohibited from becoming citizens.[20]

The recruitment of Mexican workers by U.S. businesses and industries during times of labor shortages encouraged such waves of Mexican migration. In 1917, for example, railroad, farming, and mining interests successfully lobbied Congress to exclude Mexicans from the limitations of the Immigration Act, which denied entry to non-English speaking groups. Labor surpluses had the opposite effect. Business leaders were successful in getting that exclusion reversed six months later, when workers were plentiful, and then re-instated in 1920, when a new shortage developed. Mexicans, along with Canadians, were also exempted from immigration quotas imposed by the Johnson Act of 1920, in the mistaken belief that both groups would always return home. Lawmakers with that preconception were undoubtedly stunned when Los Angeles became the second largest Mexican community in the world by 1925, as many Mexicans overstayed their six-month work permits. Such illegal settlement actually delighted American businesses seeking cheap labor, which is why the influx of both legal and undocumented workers from Mexico soon rose into the hundreds of thousands.[21] In the first three decades of the twentieth century, about ten percent of the Mexican population—about one million people—crossed the border seeking a better life.[22] What they found is another story.

Those staggering numbers, as well as other factors, kept most Anglo Americans from making clear distinctions between Mexican immigrants and Mexican Americans or *Mexicanos*. Anglo settlers moving into the new territories after the U.S.-Mexican War tended to regard all people of Mexican descent as foreigners. As Mexicans' affiliations with the U.S. fluctuated with changing economic and political circumstances, both immigrants and citizens were sometimes regarded as white enough to escape restrictions on entry to the U.S. or to qualify for American jobs, opportunities, public offices, and even intermarriage. At other times and in other places, immigrants and citizens were equally racially unacceptable. They might be called red, as they were in a special census in Los Angeles in 1927, or yellow, as they were in parts of Texas, or brown, as they were during the Brown Scare in West Texas in 1900 that led to the segregation of Mexicans from "interracial contact [that] would lead to other relationships." In many locales, Mexicans were never considered white no matter what the government said. In such places, they were placed in separate schools because "they learned more slowly" than whites.[23]

Both immigrants and citizens were also subject to deportation at various periods. In the late 1840s, for example, the U.S. and Mexican governments worked together to send about 1000 Mexican nationals eligible for U.S. citizenship back to Mexico, a process of "repatriation" that continued until the 1880s, when deteriorating conditions in Mexico tipped the scales the other way. Whether it was called repatriation or deportation, the departure of Mexicans was clearly welcomed in Texas, California, Arizona, and other areas of the U.S. during the early decades of the twentieth century. Deportations increased during the Depression, known as *La Crisis* among Mexicans, even though by then fifty-seven percent of the Mexican American population was American-born. In southern California, federal immigration agents began knocking on doors, demanding documentation and pressuring even naturalized U.S. citizens to repatriate to Mexico. In Texas, scores of Mexicans were deported by a single judge, including sixty percent of Austin's Mexican residents, by January 1931. Between 1929 and 1939, up to two million Mexicans and their U.S.-born children were deported. Propaganda supporting that effort, including President Herbert Hoover's call for a homogenous (white) American population, rarely distinguished between legal and illegal immigrants or citizens and non-citizens.[24]

From the mid-nineteenth century until well into the twentieth, Southwestern states, including California and Arizona, used racial ideology to deprive eligible Mexicans of citizenship rights and status, mostly by drawing a distinction between "white" and "Indian" or "mestizo" Mexicans. Since all Indians were already disenfranchised in those states, Mexicans who fell into that category were disenfranchised too. They were also subject to segregation and other forms of discrimination. In Texas as well as California and Arizona, *Mexicanos* were victims of Anglo land grabs, inferior educations, and low wages, as well as poll taxes, electoral shenanigans, voter manipulations, and/or outright exclusion from the political process. Even in New Mexico, where most adult *Mexicanos* could vote and hold political office, they were often landless, poorly educated, underpaid, and segregated from whites and lighter-skinned Hispanics and were not, therefore, recognized as full citizens. Thus, at best, they had the "illusion of inclusion."[25]

Throughout this shameful history, Mexicans were constructed racially in gendered terms. Mexican women's alleged reproductive excess, Mexican men's alleged innate criminality, and both sexes' alleged propensity to spread venereal disease were seen as racial characteristics that justified Anglo opposition to full citizenship for *Mexicanos*, whether native-born, naturalized, or immigrant. Moreover, all Mexicans were suspected of divided loyalties and un-Americanism, a charge that cast the whole "motley race" into the feminine mold of "insider/outsiders" who could never be fully assimilated into the American polity.

"Licking the Greaser": Feminizing Mexican American Citizenship

Charges that people of Mexican descent were innately un-democratic camouflaged racist fears of the mass miscegenation they embodied. Some eugenicists claimed that further mingling of white blood with Mexicans' already-diluted racial blood would not only spread their "innate" wildness, lawlessness, ignorance, and instability, but it would also terminate human reproduction altogether. That is, Mexicans' less robust constitutions would eventually lead to sterility, a racial weakness perceived as a feminine fault that threatened civilization itself: "Conceive for a moment the difference it would make in future ages," challenged Louis Agassiz, "for the prospect of a republican institution and our civilization generally, if instead of the manly population descended from cognate nations, the United States should hereafter be inhabited by the effeminate progeny of mixed races, half Indian, half Negro, sprinkled with white blood."[26]

Exacerbating this threat was the *Mexicana*, the generator of mixed race. At best, she was a symbol of Mexican "exclusion from a national identity based on racial homogeneity," according to Fregoso, and an icon of passionate sex who needed white male control. D.W. Griffith depicted such women in two of his films, the three-minute long *Mexican Sweethearts: The Impetuous Nature of Latin Love* (1909) and the horrifically-titled *Licking the Greaser* (1914). According to these films and other popular lore, attractive but wayward *Mexicanas* needed rescue from their own culture and/or from Mexican men, who deserved a "licking."[27]

At worst, *Mexicanas* were personifications of the wantonness, reproductive excess, and sexual debauchery of Mexican *barrios*, where "one meets . . . idleness, hordes of hungry dogs, and filthy children with faces plastered with flies, disease, lice, human filth, stench, promiscuous fornication, [and] bastardy," in the words of one immigration restrictionist in 1930. *Saturday Evening Post* writer Kenneth Roberts took such abjection as a sign that "pauperized Mexicans" had no interest in the community, as he wrote in a 1928 article about *Mexicanos* in Los

Angeles and other cities. Their women brought "countless numbers of American citizens into the world with the reckless prodigality of rabbits." Licentious, excessively reproductive, civically indifferent "lazy squaws" attracted equally indifferent "lounging, apathetic peons." Together they wallowed in "beans and dried chili, liquor, general squalor, and envy and hatred of the gringo." Why would whites clamor for "more of this human swine to be brought over from Mexico" or welcome them as citizens?[28] The Secretary of California's Board of Health concluded that Mexicans of all kinds exemplified the "sexual and depraved" nature of mixed races and their "hereditary vices and engrafted peculiarities," one of which was syphilis.[29]

De-landed and De-masculated: The Anglo Land Grab

Some Anglos decided that appropriating Mexican-owned property in the ceded territories was a fitting response to the hazards *Mexicanos'* mixed race represented to the white population. Land ownership had already begun replacing mining as a symbol of American masculine power by the time the Treaty of Guadalup Hidalgo was signed. Racial violence directed at Mexican men was one way to enhance this power, as we saw in Chapter 6. But there was also another way. More than a few Anglo men set out to marry the daughters of lighter-skinned, upwardly mobile *ricos* (rich landowners) on the theory that a white son-in-law would be welcome as a ticket to protection for the family and acceptability in white society. The Anglo men were motivated by the fact that Mexican women inherited property on an equal basis with their brothers. Suitors tried to Mexicanize themselves, often by converting to Catholicism, and fed their egos with fantasies about the special passions such women had for men like themselves. They were, indeed, welcomed as suitors who valorized the Spanish heritage of the fair-skinned women. Apparently, the *ricos* were so dazzled that they seldom recognized the handsome men for what they were—"lazy, worthless, dissolute vagabond Americans whose object of marriage was to get rich without work."[30]

The marriage scheme was so successful that Anglos in nineteenth-century New Mexico were able to acquire some significant Spanish land grants, including the Maxwell grant. In California, Anglo suitors were assisted by high taxes and land laws, like the California Land Act of 1851, which challenged the legality of Mexican land titles. As a result, *Californios'* vast landholdings dwindled to virtually nothing between 1860 and the 1880s.[31] While advancing Anglo economic supremacy in the state, the land grab also removed a key symbolic basis of citizenship from Mexican hands and reinforced the white masculine symbolism of land ownership in the American West.[32]

Anglo-Mexican intermarriage seldom followed other patterns because of the gendered nature of land ownership and the unwritten rule of white blood transmission—only white men could whiten *mestizo* blood. Anglo women did not typically marry the sons of wealthy Mexican landowners, and there were very few unions between other Mexican males and white females. Scholars have documented only five such unions in San Antonio, Texas, between 1837 and 1860, for example, while "at least one daughter from every *rico* family in San Antonio married an Anglo."[33]

The marriage-for-land scheme temporarily affected *Mexicanos'* racial categorization in the U.S., since intermarriage with Anglos elevated Mexican landowning families to "Spanish" or "Castilian," while mere workers were disparaged as "half-breeds" or simple Indians and discriminated against as a result. The plight of the lower, darker classes was also exacerbated by their own *compadres*. Some *ricos* supported the Ku Klux Klan's brand of white supremacy, for example, and upper class New Mexicans cherished the designation *Hispanic* because it emphasized their alleged Spanish origins and distinguished them from Mexicans who arrived in the twentieth century. This internal snobbery overlooked the extensive intermarriage that occurred between their sixteenth-century *Hispano* ancestors and Pueblo and Mexican Indians in the area. But such internecine competition ultimately did little good. Although New Mexican Hispanics retained some land and political power, by the turn of the twentieth century, Anglos lumped once-landed *Tejanos* and *Californios* together with workers and immigrants as dark, undesirable, and manipulable, especially by white candidates on both sides of the border. By the 1930s, all people of Mexican descent were classified in the U.S. census under "other races."[34]

Race-based segregation also increased in California, Arizona, and Texas in the early twentieth century, when there were "Anglo market towns" and "Mexican labor towns." That phenomenon eased after World War II, as agribusiness passed into corporate hands and production became mechanized, farm workers migrated to cities, and the Mexican American middle class was born. That internal migration led to the "Chicano Movement," with its civil rights protests and labor organizing, in the 1960s and 1970s.[35] Like other liberation movements we have seen, however, the Chicano Movement was plagued with internal sexism as Chicanas were pressured to support the masculine prerogatives of their men as the key to racial justice.

Mixed Race, Divided Loyalties

Mixed-race Mexican Americans were also feminized by accusations that they were uncommitted to the U.S. and suspiciously un-American. Starting in the nineteenth century, Mexicans in annexed territories were accused of divided loyalties as whites noted their continued affection for and attachment to their homeland despite its political upheavals and "inferior culture." Celebrations of Mexican holidays, mandated in part by *Mexicanos'* segregation and exclusion from Anglo society, offered additional evidence of their split affiliations. Some Anglos in Texas were so worried about disloyalty to the U.S. that they formed militias during the Spanish American War to protect themselves from *Mexicanos* who might rise in solidarity with Spain and attack border towns. (None ever did.) Allegations about *Mexicanos'* disdain for American culture also included their "constitutional prejudice... toward school attendance" and view of welfare as a "pension," according to a 1910 Report of the federal Immigration Commission. By 1930, arguments supporting the ultimately unsuccessful Harris Bill—designed to reduce the number of Mexicans admitted to the U.S. to below 2000—included pointed accusations of un-Americanism. As the 1930s progressed, Mexican immigrants were routinely subject to surveillance as suspected German spies.[36] Given the feminized history of "insider/outsider" citizenship status, such suspicions offered yet another gendered mechanism for withholding citizenship from *Mexicanos*, even from those legally entitled to it.

The Racial Construction of Puerto Ricans: Gendered Economic Policies

The U.S. government could not completely deny American citizenship to Puerto Ricans, as it could not to Mexicans, but it could create obstacles and take advantage of their "foreign" origins. The Treaty of Paris (or Treaty of Peace, December 10, 1898), which ended the Spanish American War and delivered the territory of Puerto Rico to the U.S., promised Puerto Ricans U.S. nationality and "civil rights and political status" as determined by Congress.[37] But the fulfillment of that vague obligation was once again slow in coming, retarded by racial stereotypes and fears of economic competition. Like Mexicans, mixed-race Puerto Ricans were characterized as inferior and threatening to whites of European descent. As the government doled out citizenship rights to island-based Puerto Ricans in piecemeal fashion, it imposed paternalistic economic and social controls that promoted the business interests of mainland whites. Not coincidentally, those policies manipulated Puerto Rican gender identities and roles, defamed the Latino "race," and helped to control the racial composition of the American polity.

Paternalistic Occupation

Although most Puerto Ricans initially welcomed American occupation as liberation from Spanish oppression, they soon saw the ominous underside of its positive reforms.[38] Among the detractions of American rule, besides the threat of military force, were economic policies that de-masculated the men by reducing their employment opportunities, and both expanded and limited economic opportunities for women, whom the government courted as natural allies of American rule.[39]

The 1900 Foraker Act that established U.S. occupation provided Puerto Rico with its first civilian government in 400 years and promised free trade, but it also revealed the mainland government's paternalistic and imperialistic intentions toward the island. The Foraker Act imposed a restrictive (albeit civilian) governance structure on the island and defined its citizens as virtual wards of the U.S. government with minimum rights. Things went downhill with the 1901 Supreme Court decision in *Downes v. Bidwell* that defined Puerto Rico as an unincorporated territory with no prospects of becoming a state and no guarantee of constitutional protections offered to incorporated territories like Arizona. Puerto Ricans achieved American citizenship status in 1917 with the passage of the Jones-Shafroth Act (or the Federal Relations Act), which was an improvement over the ward status offered by the Foraker Act. But the citizenship it promised was statutory rather than constitutional.[40] It also made Puerto Ricans into a second-class category of citizen because their legislature's laws were subject to U.S. Congressional monitoring. Even the Nationality Act of 1940, which extended *jure soli* citizenship to Puerto Ricans born on the island on or after January 13, 1941, did not guarantee Puerto Ricans an absolute right to U.S. citizenship by virtue of birth on the island. That right is still subject to Congressional discretion, although Puerto Rican citizenship "cannot be regulated or terminated in violation of due process of law, and equal protection of other fundamental rights." Congress declared Puerto Rico a Commonwealth in 1952, but its citizenship problems continued. Puerto Rican residents still cannot run for president, because they do not meet the constitutional requirement of birth in the U.S. proper, and they cannot work for federal or state governmental agencies.[41]

Today Puerto Ricans can elect their own governor and participate in a state-like commonwealth administration. As inhabitants of a federal territory, they pay no U.S. taxes, but they also have only a non-voting representative in Congress. That means they remain subject to U.S. laws formulated without their formal consent.[42] When emigration to the mainland began in large numbers after World War II—amounting to 1.6 million people over the age of sixteen by 1966—whatever citizenship rights various laws and policies did not deny Puerto Ricans living in the U.S., racial discrimination helped to restrict. That Puerto Ricans are not really immigrants has not guaranteed their inclusion in mainland culture. Even today, children born on the mainland suffer the effects of segregation, inferior schools, and structural underemployment.[43]

From Class and Gender Differences to Race

Considering Puerto Ricans a race is really absurd, of course, since the island population is as racially varied, if not more varied, than the population of Mexico. But as for Mexicans, racial formation for Puerto Ricans reflected the white American dread of "mongrelism." In their case, that term demonized not only racial mixing but also the ordinary Latin American perspective on "race . . . conceived of as a continuum with no fixed demarcation between categories," including black and white. Nomenclature for race in the region included *blanco, indio, moreno, negro,* and *trigueño* (wheat colored), with *negro* often used as a term of endearment, even for the light-skinned.[44] Since most white Americans at the time considered such "flexible racial relations and identities . . . unintelligible," the prospect of such a spectrum was horrifying. It suggested unrestrained sexual behavior and the "unconsciousness of the obligations of morality," according to an American official in 1900. Puerto Rican "peasants" needed the guidance of the U.S. to awaken them from their "premoral natural state" into civilized adulthood.[45] The process of civilizing the "natives" would be gendered, as we shall see in more detail later in the chapter.

Puerto Ricans themselves evaluated their racial spectrum through class issues, which were also gendered. After centuries of Spanish colonial rule, Americans arrived on the scene in the late nineteenth century to discover that power relations in Puerto Rico involved what Eileen Findlay calls a fluid combination of gendered "cultural competencies, sexual practices[,] . . . material resources and physical phenotype," in which lighter complexions took precedence over darker ones. But a family's "social complexion" was not identical to its members' skin color. Rather, social complexion depended on a family's reputation for respectability, and women's behavior was a primary determiner of that respectability. Thus, women's sex lives were (and still are) policed in the name of a family's honor. A woman's respectability could "distance [a family] from poverty and blackness." The Puerto Rican nationalist movement reinforced that gendered racial linkage by arguing for a "virile nation," freed of "dangerously African, feminizing, and sensual popular classes," especially dark-skinned "unruly plebian women, who were labeled 'prostitutes.' "[46]

The arrival of U.S. forces strengthened the role of gender relations in upward mobility by emphasizing the importance of marriage, including male control over women, as a discipline for the "popular classes." Gender "continued to be a particularly powerful marker of difference for . . . male political actors . . . even as they and their female allies gave gendered power relations new meanings and devised new political projects around them," according to Findlay.[47]

Many of the new meanings and projects resulted from U.S. governmental policies for Puerto Rico that offered self-fulfilling gendered racial prophecies. Most such policies were designed to create economic advantage for the mainland. American businesses needed a malleable workforce, not a new crop of American citizens with rights and demands of their own (especially since those citizens were more likely to vote Democratic than Republican).[48] When Congress exempted mainland-owned businesses in Puerto Rico from U.S. taxes in 1921, exploitation of local labor helped qualifying "possessions corporations" to make billions of tax-free dollars.[49] Interestingly, the U.S. government still declines to call its relationship with Puerto Rico colonial.[50]

Needless to say, gender tensions increased on the island as such policies produced unemployment and underemployment for men and more (but exploitative) employment for women. The resulting gender imbalance helped to construct Puerto Ricans as a people who fulfilled Anglo American stereotypes of the Latin "race," defined less by particular physiology than by inferior blood, male resistance to progress and hard work, and inappropriate female power. In addition, U.S. policies made middle class economic status harder for Puerto Ricans to achieve, thereby exacerbating the importance of various symbolic systems related to social class, of which gender was a crucial one.

Gendered Racial Citizenship

The capacity of islanders to own local businesses and to amass economic power virtually disappeared under American rule. Farmers were also displaced by the American government's interest in sugar cane, which replaced traditional coffee and tobacco farming in mountain areas.[51] Island men could work for wages, but they could not compete as business owners with the mainland-based beneficiaries of U.S. tax policies. Like *Mexicano* victims of the land-grab in annexed territories, Puerto Rican men were forced to work for others, in their case in low-level jobs in the sugar cane industry, which was controlled by mainland corporations. Predictably, they found such opportunities demeaning and de-masculating, especially in their historically *macho* culture. As men's earning capacity diminished, so did their labor force participation. The number of males fourteen years and older in the labor force declined from almost ninety-four percent in 1909 to seventy-five percent in 1940. According to Maria del Carmen Baerga-Santini, those threatened, underemployed men became increasingly *macho* and violent toward women, whom they blamed for their lost social power.[52]

Puerto Rican women had a different experience under American rule, especially between 1900 and 1952, but it also backfired for them. Their labor force participation increased, but their work did not enhance either their independence or their economic power. Indeed, women's economic success was really illusory, because they qualified mostly for low-level jobs in the tobacco and needlework industries, often as homeworkers, and were hired primarily as temporary or secondary workers who could be paid less than men.[53]

Increased employment for Puerto Rican women escalated tensions between the sexes, exaggerated gender differences, further devalued Puerto Rican labor and racial value, and undermined Puerto Rican prospects for full citizenship. In short, women's employment under U.S. auspices did more to "[integrate] women in subordinate positions than to [establish] more equitable social and gender relations. Occupational segregation, pay differentials, the 'double day,' and ideological structures that perpetuated the notion of domestic and childrearing work as women's responsibility . . . kept women sexually subjected to the control of men," according to Alice Colón-Warren, Idsa Algría-Ortega, and Altagracia Ortiz.[54]

The gendered results of U.S. policies in Puerto Rico—what we might call the "egg"—increasingly seemed like their cause—the "chicken." Mainland whites developed a narrative about a "Latin mentality" that produced a "race" of submissive wives, who were dependent on men and the state and had too many children but also threatened their families and their men's masculinity by working. Meanwhile, "lazy" Latin men were only too happy to let their wives work while they lounged at home.[55] Such a race threatened to drag down the American economy, if left to its own devices, as well as further pollute the true (white) American race, if given a chance. U.S. policies ensured that little chance would be given.

Needlework

The needlework industry exemplifies the U.S. government's attempt to manage the gendered racial characteristics it associated with Puerto Ricans. The industry promoted women's economic productivity at minimal expense while maintaining their traditional roles at home. The needlework industry blossomed in Puerto Rico in the early twentieth century because American businesses wanted to control the large American market for embroidered linen items traditionally supplied by China, Ireland, France, and Switzerland. The government was so eager to shift needlework production into Puerto Rico that it reinstituted needlework training as part of the public school curriculum for girls from 1909 to 1926, despite American policy prohibiting such training in 1898 because the close work threatened female eyesight and health. As the outbreak of World War I cut off other sources of the world's needlework supply, Puerto Rico was therefore well positioned to corner the market. Its dominance continued for a decade.[56]

By 1935, needlework was the principal source of employment for a woman in sixty percent of Puerto Rican towns, and forty-four percent of the female workforce was in the needlework industry. Seventy-two percent of all needleworkers were homeworkers, and ninety-nine percent of those were women.[57] By keeping them tied to their families and husbands, needlework employment at the industry's low rates of pay did little to provide women with either independent income or a worker's identity. They had no share in whatever boon needlework brought to the Puerto Rican economy. Indeed, home-based female needleworkers were so marginalized that they were counted as housewives, and when they lost their jobs, they were not classified as unemployed.[58]

Such outcomes may have suited the American vision of Puerto Ricans' "racial" inadequacies, but they did little to elevate the island economically and much to exacerbate gender tensions, as women's meager employment oppressed them yet threatened the many men already disempowered by policies that siphoned tax-free profits to mainland corporate culture.[59]

Reproduction

As time went on, the U.S. government decided that controlling the island's high birthrate, which was blamed on women's reproductive excess as a racial (and Catholic) characteristic, would really improve the Puerto Rican economy by stretching resources on the island (rather than increasing them). Smaller families would also civilize the race and, not coincidentally, reduce the mass of Puerto Ricans demanding full American citizenship. To accomplish its purpose, the government formulated two plans.

The first entailed forced sterilization for women and increased access to contraception, which was authorized for Puerto Rico in 1937, a year before it was legalized anywhere else in the U.S. The combined strategy would ostensibly allow more women to work (albeit in limited government-sponsored jobs) and increase family incomes.[60] (That sterilizing men might do even more to produce the same result did not, apparently, occur to these lawmakers.)

To that end, the U.S.-sponsored Puerto Rican government passed Law 116, also in 1937, which placed the sterilization effort under the auspices of a eugenics board and provided government subsidy for "la operación" from public funds. Employers began to favor female employees who could show evidence of sterilization. By the time Law 116 was repealed in 1960, thiry-five percent of Puerto Rico women of childbearing age had been sterilized, and two-thirds of sterilized Puerto Rican women were still in their twenties.[61] Despite the law's repeal, the government continued to emphasize mass sterilization into the 1970s as a means of expanding resources. Women were not informed of their rights or required to give prior consent to the operations until 1979. After that date, participation in the program plummeted, from 25,000 sterilizations between 1974 and 1977, to eighty-five in 1985, to zero the following year.[62]

The second approach to Puerto Rican women's excessive childbearing was a short-lived government-sponsored program to train young women for careers as domestic servants in the homes of mainland white Americans. From February 1948 to October 1949, the New York State Employment Service arranged for the placements, primarily in Scarsdale. Donald J. O'Connor, chief economist of the Office of Puerto Rico, estimated that "300 jobs on the mainland per week for the next decade or so would halve the projected population figures" by preventing the birth of five children per worker. "If Ireland could depopulate itself by emigration, Puerto Rico can," he concluded. Officials also believed that the "girls" would be "invisible migrants" who would demand little from American society, send money home, and advance to hotel work or, preferably, improve their skills for eventual marriage and housekeeping back home. The program was terminated because the number of placements was not high enough for policy makers. It was replaced with a training program for the hotel industry and then with a contract labor program for male agricultural workers. In the end, men's employment was more important to the government than women's, since women's work was less about exporting needed skills than about population control.[63]

As bizarre as the domestic servant training program might seem today, it made a certain kind of sense in the context of Operation Bootstrap, which was instituted by the U.S. government in Puerto Rico in 1948. Operation Bootstrap was dedicated to improving the Puerto Rican economy by employing islanders to manufacture products for export on a commercial scale that had not been manufactured in Puerto Rico on that scale prior to 1947. Mainland businesses employing a sufficient number of island residents and incurring a specified percentage of labor costs in Puerto Rico could qualify for exemptions from income and property taxes, as well as from certain municipal taxes, for periods ranging from ten to twenty-five years.[64]

In some ways, Operation Bootstrap improved the conditions of American occupation for Puerto Rican women by increasing their educational opportunities, expanding maternity leave, and recognizing that "needs related to the domestic sphere ... were a public responsibility."[65] Nevertheless, Operation Bootstrap was primarily a reprise of the familiar use of off-shore workers in mainland businesses that dominated U.S.-Puerto Rican relations from the start. It also took advantage of the already sex-segregated labor market and introduced new female occupations, like clerical work, that kept most Puerto Rican women at the lower levels of the administrative and professional economic sectors for decades.[66] That Operation Bootstrap also temporarily included the export of female domestic workers to the mainland as part of its economic plan for the island exemplifies the gendered racial foundations of U.S. policies for Puerto Rico.

Mixed Race, Suspect Gender

Racially stereotyped Mexican "greasers," "squaws," and "peons," along with Puerto Rican "*machistas*" and "hot tamales" were mixed-race reminders to many white Americans of the eugenic consequences of "mongrelism." Being "both white and other" made Latinos an undesirable, even if indefinable, race. Few white Americans recognized that their own attitudes and their government's policies created the self-fulfilling prophecy of mixed-race abjection. Instead, they delivered tepid offers and delayed promises of American citizenship as a means of maintaining racial differences and controlling the alleged racial fitness of the American polity. Limiting immigration and restraining economic, political, and even reproductive rights of "inferior" peoples were all designed to keep their inner deficiencies as well as their visible physiological characteristics from further contaminating white American society.

Gender judgments formed the core of public debate and official doctrine about the Latino "race." The lazy men did not deserve masculine prerogatives, and the women needed rescue from reproductive and sexual excess. Together, they were better off as (feminine) dependents of white Americans and their government for the racial and social good of the United States.

Conclusion

Homosexual Citizenship

The Naturalization Act of 1855, which was so important in establishing American women's derivative citizenship, sent a clear if unspoken message to anyone who was paying attention: American citizenship is a hetero-normative affair. It helped to cement the interconnection of citizenship and marriage for women and paved the way for preferences that would be given to wives and other dependents of male American citizens. Added to the feminizing of men of allegedly undesirable races, the law further reinforced hetersexual norms and made heterosexuality a core identity of the model American citizen. That message, combined with other laws and policies directed at racial "others" and homosexuals in the nineteenth and twentieth centuries, strongly suggests that homosexuals constituted a variation on the theme of gendered race with regard to American citizenship. To explore this idea, Part IV concludes its analysis of the gendered foundations of racialized citizenship standards, qualifications, and exclusions in the U.S. with a brief analysis of the relationship between homosexuals and the modern American state. This section demonstrates how suspect sexuality was historically interpreted as racial inferiority.

Implicit in American citizenship policies was an analogy between the nuclear family model—specifically Christian marriage pacts and monogamy—and the concept of national fidelity.[1] Perhaps that is why a woman's marriage to a non-U.S. national, especially one who was racially inadmissible, nullified her American citizenship. A foreign marriage suggested national disloyalty. Excluding homosexuals from the U.S. as immigrants or naturalized citizens extended that gendered racial analogy.

The exclusion began in the nineteenth century, although the term "homosexual" did not appear until 1930, and homosexuality was not specifically mentioned in immigration statutes until 1952. Racial associations with homosexuality were foreshadowed by the exclusion of Chinese prostitutes in the Page Act in 1875 and of polygamists (assumed to be Asian) in the Immigration Act of 1891. Those laws associated persons displaying or harboring "alternative sexualities" with undesirable races.[2] In addition, from about 1891 until 1979, when the American Psychiatric Association removed homosexuality from its list of mental disorders, homosexuals were suspected of carrying frightening and population-destroying diseases, just like Asians and persons of mixed race.

The link between homosexuals and undesirable races is even more evident in the government's use, in the late-nineteenth and early twentieth centuries, of the same Class A certificate to exclude homosexuals that it used to exclude the Chinese, as well as "idiots," "imbeciles," "epileptics," "insane persons," and persons with "a loathsome contagious disease," such as ringworm, yaws, leprosy, or the "Oriental sore" (a racial metaphor for syphilis). Homosexuals were diagnosed with "constitutional psychopathic inferiority" and other mental defects listed as disqualifications for admission to the U.S. The list got more specific with the passage of the Immigration and Nationality Act (or the McCarran-Walter Act) in 1952. Then it included anyone who displayed "psychopathic personality," "moral turpitude," and/or "sexual deviation." Because foreign women were ineligible for independent immigration and naturalization for so much of U.S. history, gay men were by default the initial targets of exclusion on the basis of sexuality.

Also starting in the late nineteenth-century, the Public Health Service (PHS) administered performance tests to help immigration officials determine who possessed inadmissible traits. The government's *Manual of the Mental Examination of Aliens*, published in 1918, reveals that the questions asked included, "Do you have strange feelings?" and "Have you acquaintances of the opposite sex?"[3] Individuals responding inappropriately could be denied visas or refused entry or re-entry into the U.S., just like American women married to "foreigners ineligible for citizenship." Homosexuality was also a justification for an immigrant's deportation once he was admitted to the country. Although the PHS stopped issuing Class A certificates to exclude homosexuals in 1979, lesbians and gay males seeking naturalization as U.S. citizens can still be denied that privilege if their sexual behavior suggests that they are not of good moral character.[4]

After World War II, as race became a less acceptable reason to deny admission or naturalization, American policies directed toward homosexuals kept alive race-like criteria for excluding undesirables from the U.S. Congress "unceasingly" exercised its plenary powers to restrict the naturalization of lesbians and gay men, even though such restriction defied principles of individual autonomy and freedom of association underlying democratic citizenship.[5] The McCarran-Walter Act's definition of sexual orientation as an innate identity rather than a set of behaviors effectively racialized homosexuals in gendered terms from 1952 up to and beyond 1979. Understood as an identity, sexual orientation resembled a racial characteristic harbored in the "blood"—poised to explode onto the "healthy" majority to disastrous effect. Cold War paranoia in the mid-twentieth century further pathologized homosexuality as innate inappropriate gender. Homosexuals could not only disrupt conventional gender roles, which looked particularly precious to the public right after World War II, but they could also subvert the government. Their secret sexuality made them perfect pawns of the subversive Communists allegedly hiding under every bed. (That the government itself was creating secrecy and denial among homosexuals did not occur to legislators or the general public.) At best, homosexuals were reduced to insider/outsider citizenship status, doubly or triply so if they were lesbians or gay Asian or Latino men. Many scholars believe that the "don't-ask/don't-tell" policies adopted by the U.S. Armed Services in 1994 have constructed a similar insider/outsider model of homosexual citizenship.[6]

The treatment of homosexuals because of their inappropriate gender and sexual "pathology" exemplifies many principles that also shaped women's and non-white men's citizenship struggles. Feminized by law, homosexuals were also defined as untrustworthy citizens. Considered innately deficient, they were also deemed incapable of improvement. But unlike women and non-white men, homosexuals had no apparent redeeming or compensating qualities. Without specific reproductive or productive skills, there was little to support homosexuals' acceptance or even toleration as a group in American society. In citizenship terms, they were a throw-away class.

PART V
Implications

Introduction

Patterns for a New Bridge

Part V of *The Specter of Sex* considers the implications of this book's analysis for feminist theorizing and anti-racist politics as well as for the comparative study of racial formation. It is designed to stimulate dialogue about how to reconfigure and perhaps even heal racial divides and how to create new alliances across the race and gender boundaries so often considered insurmountable in American life. New thinking seems imperative on many levels and in many arenas, including politics and policy making as well as the academic study of women, gender, and race, where misunderstandings and defensiveness have too often been the unintended consequences of discussions about race and gender intersectionality. *The Specter of Sex* was inspired in part by the frustrations I have witnessed and experienced in such discussions.

Reexamining the concept of coalition is a key theme of Part V. I say "*re*examining" because, as we shall see, there have been other moments when coalitions have formed across race and gender boundaries to address issues of social justice. Although alliances inevitably have their difficulties, coalition building seems a logical and appropriate extension of this book's primary point that racial categories are constructs built in part on ideologies of gender—from the earliest distinctions between English colonists and Africans based on women's laboring bodies, to the repeated insistence that women are the reproducers of racial difference, to the patriarchal foundations of America's race-based chattel slave society, to the contradictory feminizing and hypersexualizing of allegedly racially undesirable men, to the regulating of all women's citizenship rights in order to define racial difference and control the racial composition of the American polity. Since gender has both motivated and been a proxy for racial judgments and control systems, and since gender dichotomy has been a marker of racial value for all groups, it seems appropriate for those who share in such overlapping systems to collaborate in exposing and redressing the gendered racial patterns that persist even today.

Women of different races and women and men who have been denied power for racial reasons can identify such structural linkages among their very different experiences. Even those who have been empowered by the gender/race systems in American culture must consider the structural hazards of their positions, not only for the others they harm but for themselves. White men and women have been both advantaged and disadvantaged by definitions of racial superiority that mandate, regulate, and stratify clear distinctions between their acceptable behavior, roles, personalities, and qualities. By the same token, men and women of all races have suffered from the common "wisdom" that tells a man to prove his racial worthiness by controlling "his" woman. Women of all races can compare notes on the cultural manipulations of motherhood that have enhanced (or undermined) the value of their racial categories. In different ways and to different degrees, all women have been defined in instrumental terms, presumed incapable of public life, relegated to demeaning symbolic roles in racial definitions (albeit of different races), and subjected to men's control. In addition, as the "done to" rather than the "doers," women of many groups have been denied agency and manipulated as racial subjects. These structural linkages and patterns do not obliterate the varied material effects produced by them for different groups and individuals, but even such differences can be clarified by exposing shared underlying causes and specific triggers that transform disadvantage for one group into structural abjection for another.

The historical alignment of racial discrimination with misogyny also argues for coalition. That alignment has not only increased misogynistic views of actual women, but it has also created deep-seated fear of "the feminine" by maligning minority-raced men in terms used to demean women. Marginalized men, like women, have been degraded because of their "embodiment"—that is, their bodies' allegedly greater identity with physical particularity—in contrast to white men's allegedly abstract and disembodied "natural" state. Contesting such associations could benefit women, whose identities have so often been reduced to their reproductive physiology, as well as counteract a potent source of misogyny and fear of the feminine within men. Collaboration between women and men on this subject might even ensure that the remedy for men of color's insulting "embodiment" is not simply to reinforce the tenets of conventional masculinity and male dominance. Collaboration might produce a new resolve to eliminate the gendered metaphors that have so long perpetuated racism. It might also allow white men to accept and occupy fully their own bodies and vulnerabilities, including their origins in the bodies of women.

Evidence in *The Specter of Sex* of sexualized violence as a corollary of gendered racial judgments and discrimination definitely calls for coalitions, since sexualized racial violence transcends groups and eras. The uncontrolled rape and involuntary impregnation of female slaves and the lynching of men of color were both fueled by sexual fantasies and sexualized notions of white racial power. Those same factors also motivated sometimes violent discrimination against homosexuals, who were excluded from the country for years as diseased and sexually deviant, like the despised Chinese. People across the racial spectrum were taunted and condemned for mere "suspect sexuality." Gay men's exclusion in particular gave heterosexuals the illusion that they were stamping out the allegedly sexual origins of racial inferiority and allowed them to proclaim their own sexual and racial superiority.

Many people are wary of attempting to construct dialogues and alliances across racial and gender boundaries because of difficulties they have experienced in the past. Others are resistant because they are fearful of making false assumptions about all women on the basis of those who control the discourse about women's oppression. They understandably want to emphasize the historically rooted particularities of gendered/racial experience. Indeed, the concept of *intersectionality* emerged from that response. It encourages groups to define their own particular experience of simultaneously raced and gendered social and personal identities. But this book's analysis seeks to avoid such dangers. Its exposure of overarching patterns and surprising commonalities within vastly different experiences of gendered/racial discrimination follows a somewhat hidden parallel trajectory in feminist theory and politics, which we will see in a moment, and offers another approach to the concept of coalitions. The alliances it suggests are structural, and they do not obscure or mute the experiential differences underlying them.

For example, African American and white women have clearly had very different cultural histories of motherhood. On the one hand, as Laura Briggs explains (and we have seen), white women have typically been criticized for being overly civilized and disinterested in procreation. Their low fertility rates compared with immigrant and poor women of other races have historically vexed supporters of white racial supremacy and generated endless admonitions to reproduce with white men as a patriotic duty, instead of risking their reproductive health by too much thinking or achieving in the world. On the other hand, black women have been both excoriated and exploited because of their alleged reproductive prowess and sexual voracity.

Their reproductive fitness has never been considered anything but a reason to oppress them.[1]

The material effects of these contrasting reproductive narratives have been dramatic, yet a common pattern also appears within them: few women have escaped cultural pressures, scrutiny, disparagement, or governmental interventions directed at their reproductive rates and motherhood practices. (The Puerto Rican sterilization program provides an additional example.) Race, ethnicity, and class have created very different degrees of harm and suffering for mothers, and these should be addressed and repaired. But it is also reasonable to protest the patterns of reproductive manipulation that have helped to establish and maintain the racial paradigms that produce those harms and power differentials. By exposing that connecting thread, women of all races may avoid having their reproductive lives determined by artificially concocted racial demands, such as those fueling controversies over abortion even today.

The challenge is to turn this history of shared patterns into guidelines for contemporary action. The first step, to which Parts I-IV of *The Specter of Sex* are dedicated, is to disseminate information about the patterns of gendered racial formation that link women of different races as well as women and certain men. The next step is to consider how to mobilize that knowledge into productive alliances and coalitions for theorizing about and working for social justice. Part V outlines some theoretical and political possibilities for taking that second step.

In preparation for that discussion, we should learn whatever we can from previous attempts to create coalitions across racial and gender barriers. There is an impressive history of such attempts, which is sometimes overlooked in favor of probing the unique experiences of women and men of color in their own racial histories. Many historical cross-racial coalitions emerged as members of different racial groups identified their own self-interest in goals that were larger than any one racial community. Temperance offered such a goal to many nineteenth-century women. Founded by white middle-class women in the 1870s, the temperance movement included black women by 1881. (Frances E. W. Harper joined in 1883). Eventually the coalition devolved to separate organizations as racial barriers were revived, but Cynthia Neverdon-Morton concludes nevertheless that many black women of the period (more than black men) were willing to participate in interracial organizations, such as the NAACP, the Urban League, and the Commission on Inter-racial Cooperation, even when they were not treated as equals. Interracial coalitions also formed around compelling local issues. For example, black and white women in Baltimore organized a Women's Cooperative Civic League in 1911 to work for the improvement of housing conditions for all racial groups. The League argued that the city's segregation order, aimed at "colored people," "proved a boomerang and hit the white property owner harder than the colored purchaser" because there was a shortage of housing restricted to black buyers and a surplus available in white neighborhoods.[2]

Black and white women also found enough common ground to form a few coalitions around the cause of suffrage, even in the South. Shared membership in the Methodist Women's Missionary Society was the catalyst for one such alliance in Nashville, Tennessee, in 1919. According to Anita Shafer Goodstein, it began with white women's support for improved social services for the African American community. In working on that cause, black women became convinced that supporting suffrage and achieving the vote for women would advance racial progress.[3]

More recent history of inter-racial feminist organizing reveals mixed success, but success nonetheless. Becky Thompson has reexamined the history of the 1970s and 1980s radical women's movement and discovered more interracial and international coalitions among women than are generally recognized. Such coalitions organized primarily around the interlocking oppressions attributable to white supremacy and imperialism, both within the U.S. and around the world. In addition, the women sometimes confronted male dominated revolutionary movements, such as Students for a Democratic Society and the Black Liberation Army, about their sexism. Thompson argues that the radical coalitions had more staying power than groups engaged in what she calls bourgeois and reductionist analyses based on sexism alone. They did not die out in 1974, as some historians have contended, but rather flourished into the 1980s, a decade historians typically see as a period of decline for feminist groups. For the radical alliances, 1981 and the publication of *This Bridge Called My Back*, which exposed both the blatant and the unconscious racism of white feminists, simply provided a "new political subject" for radical action, although it took many white feminists by surprise.[4]

There are lessons to be learned from this history. The Tennessee suffrage coalition succeeded in part because it focused on specific, attainable goals and in part because the women shared a similar social status within their communities, had similar capacities for political organizing and rhetoric, and had leaders who were willing to take risks.[5] But it is also evident that the activists had an abstract understanding of the advantages to both sides of breaching the racial wall between women. A concrete focus may initially be more compelling than abstract discussion, but effective coalitions must reach an abstract level of analysis in order to identify the deeper issues behind specific problems and oppressions.

A variety of interracial coalitions have succeeded because they emerged in locales where women could witness gender discrimination first-hand, such as churches, places of employment, or labor unions. Susan Hartmann observed that phenomenon in her study of the "other feminists" who worked for social justice outside of any specifically feminist organization during the 1950s and 60s. She credits black women with recognizing that "projects to advance racial justice were incomplete if they did not embrace an attack on sex discrimination and that feminist projects were deficient if they did not contain an anti-racist component." Hartmann also notes that logistics play a role, since women are more likely to attend meetings when they have already carved out time from family responsibilities to be where they occur.[6]

Based on her 1995 study of inter-racial women's groups, Winifred Poster argues that concepts like "justice" work better as themes for coalition than feminist-sounding concepts like "equality." Poster also notes that tensions within inter-racial coalitions can arise because women of color tend to emphasize differences among women while white women prefer to overlook those differences. This disparity can be mitigated somewhat by a parallel phenomenon: women of color are more likely to mobilize around "big issues" that subsume feminist interests within them—such as the "Up and Out of Poverty Campaign" and the National Welfare Rights Conference—than around explicitly feminist causes, like abortion rights, even though they might support reproductive rights.[7] Identifying larger issues can be a catalyst for exploring commonalities within difference and for strengthening coalitions.

Both past and recent inter-racial coalitions have clearly benefited from women of color's leadership initiatives. A recent study of attitudes toward sexism in various racial groups reinforces this historical reality. Andrea Hunter and Sherrill Sellers conclude from their 1995 study that "minority group membership may be a catalyst for the development of feminist attitudes." Depending on income, education, employment, contact with the welfare system, "racial ecology," and contact with the police, members of minority groups are more likely than whites to recognize and critique gender inequality, support egalitarian gender roles, and endorse political activism for women. In particular, African Americans of both sexes are more likely to express support for feminism than are whites of either sex. Black men who have struggled with unemployment or the police typically support feminism because they can understand the impact of structural inequities on individual choices.[8] (Although they might still be misogynist at home.)

Such insights clearly suggest that white women need to turn more often to women of color for leadership in the pursuit of social justice. They also suggest that feminists should broaden their focus and see feminist issues within larger contexts. Many so-called Third Wave feminists, such as Rebecca Walker, Jennifer Baumgardner, and Amy Richards, have made the same point.[9] But there is also a danger in that approach, since feminist causes and a gender focus can easily be subsumed by the larger issues, as they so often were in the radical feminist movement of the 1970s. The socialist feminist group Bread and Roses, for example, hitched their feminist wagons to the agendas of radical black groups, especially the Black Panthers. They also worked primarily with male leaders. It turned out, however, that those men had little interest in gender issues and did not support a feminist perspective, according to Winifred Breines.[10] It would be better, perhaps, to work on the model *The Specter of Sex* offers, from gender concerns to general issues rather than the other way around. Instead of starting with poverty, for example, we start from women's greater likelihood to be impoverished and move toward the ideological and practical linkages between their situations that construct the larger issue.

Becky Thompson suggests that progressive, feminist, antiracist struggles should form coalitions based on respect for identity-based groups, pay attention to process as well as products, and emphasize specific action. Groups must work for racial parity from the beginning, recognize that race is not binary, and concede that racism is everywhere. Thompson adopts Mari Matsuda's phrase "jurisprudence of antisubordination" as a rubric for this work.[11] Thompson's analysis may stop a bit too soon, however, since it is also the case that successful historical coalitions that pursued attainable goals also understood those goals in abstract enough terms to see self-interest as well as the collective good within them. Nevertheless, Matsuda's concept of *antisubordination* as an ultimate feminist goal is a useful and complementary next step beyond *intersectionality*. Antisubordiantion activism brings attention to the linking concepts of hierarchy and dominance that are both the cause and effect of race-gender interdependence throughout history.

The chapters of Part V continue this discussion of inter-racial coalitions by considering possibilities in two overlapping categories.

Chapter 15 offers a novel perspective on *intersectionality* as the primary analytical term in feminist theories of the race-gender relationship by expanding it to incorporate commonalities and shared patterns, both among women and between women and men of color. Chapter 16 offers a novel perspective on racial formation theories and comparative racial politics, both of which have typically minimized the role of gender. It suggests ways to reconceptualize racial identities and race-based activism by foregrounding gender's role in racial formation. Discussions in both chapters temporarily dissect race and gender as concepts only to reconnect them in terms of structure and meaning.

15

Implications for Feminist Theories of Racial Difference and Antisubordination Politics

Race has been is a problem for American feminism since well before the term "feminism" was coined and the suffrage movement began to give it life. The problem boils down to this: How can gender be disaggregated from the many other identities, including racial ones, both imposed upon and claimed by individuals and groups? Centuries of racialization and race-based discrimination have complicated what it means to be a man or a woman. There is no such thing as a generic "woman" or "man" at the heart of feminist claims.

But as true as those statements are for recent times, at least since the nineteenth century, it is also the case that the gender-race interconnection has a history that requires attention. This history does not suggest that gender is more important or more basic than gender or that gender and race can or should be approached separately, but it does suggest a causal, formative relationship that contemporary intersectionality theory does not fully acknowledge. The challenge presented by that history is to consider what it might mean for feminist theorizing about difference and diversity to recognize the historical construction of racial ideology on the basis of gender ideology.

Examining those implications today is complicated by a damaging legacy of deliberate or inadvertent misunderstanding of gendered racial formation that still haunts feminist theorists and gender justice movements. That legacy has valorized the idea that the "woman" most feminists were fighting for is white and middle-class and that her status and problems are the standard for all. Otherwise, how could white women have so often pursued what they called women's causes by separating themselves from or disparaging women of color? Black women started protesting that irony in the nineteenth century— reflected famously in the line attributed to Sojourner Truth, "ar'n't I a woman?" But women of color really began holding white feminists accountable for their solipsism in the 1980s, after the publication of *This Bridge Called My Back*. Some white feminists were genuinely shocked by the stark evidence that they had so egregiously failed to account for all women in their analyses of and claims for justice, and women of color were disturbed by their myopia. After that, except in radical circles, it was not at all clear how to heal the rift caused by years of misrepresentation and neglect or whether it was possible to rally all racial groups around feminist causes.

Since then, feminist theorists of all ideologies, ethnicities, races, geographical locations, economic classes, sexualities, and religions have been struggling to formulate both a more accurate account of their separate and related issues and better mechanisms for analyzing sexism and pursuing gender justice without obscuring the many chosen and imposed differences among women, including their different experiences of and perspectives on gender injustice. Chapter 15 takes a fresh look from the perspective of this book's analysis at some feminist approaches to racial and ethnic diversity among women that emerged from that period and suggests a possible model for thinking anew about feminist racial politics.

The theoretical approaches discussed in this book's introduction provide a context for that fresh look. The most influential among them is *intersectionality*, a term popularized in the 1980s by legal scholar and critical race feminist, Kimberlé Crenshaw. Like other critical race feminists, Crenshaw exposed the inherent combination of racism and sexism within the American legal system. Through the 1990s and early decades of the twenty-first century, theorists like Bonnie Thornton Dill, Jacquelyn Grant, Leela Fernandes, Evelyn Nakano Glenn, and Laura Gillman expanded Crenshaw's work into *integrated frameworks* and *conjunctural approaches* that probe the nuances of gendered race and its differential impacts on various groups of women. Their approaches inform implications of *The Specter of Sex* for feminist theorizing, but the book's *consistent historical analytic* also reveals a limitation within them. Intersectionality, integrative frameworks, and conjunctural approaches emphasize the differences, especially between white women and women of color, that impede communication, complicate issue identification, reduce interpersonal understanding, and interfere with political coalition. But they underemphasize or overlook the constructedness of the categories they discuss as well as the gender-based commonalities or structural connections, such as those summarized in Part V's Introduction, that exist across racial, ethnic, class, and other boundaries. It is hard to deny, for example, that women in all groups have been victims of misogyny.

Political Play

Feminist theorizing about racial and ethnic difference can begin by simultaneously interrogating the validity of racial, ethnic, and gender categories and recognizing the material effects such categories have on people's lives and opportunities. Feminist theory and politics can inhabit that tension by refusing to reify or reinforce artificial constructions or take them at face value even as it continues to elaborate and expand knowledge about the differences those constructions make in people's lives.

The theory and practice of "political play" offer opportunities to do both together. Such play can be whimsical or serious, self-conscious or unintentional as it shifts paradigms and forces confrontation with the complexities and contradictions within and between categories of difference. Political play offers possibilities for transforming basic premises of feminist analysis by challenging basic understandings of race, gender, ethnicity, class, and other identities.

Racial "passing" is a venerable form of political play that has long disrupted identity categories. Recent scholarship expands the concept of passing from a secret and dangerous intervention in racial categorization to a powerful disruption of all identities, including gender. For example, Stephen Knadler has recently analyzed the passing narrative as "a trope that defines the very process of all identity formations," making all identities inherently products of passing. Since "one cannot deviate from an identity that was never natural," Knadler argues, "passing ... is 'the only way in which a subject can take up a position of identity in terms of race.' "[1] Knadler's work parallels Paul Gilroy's ideas about race as performance in *Against Race*, where he argues that race in contemporary society has become primarily a matter of particular looks, style, and "trangressive stance," especially for young black men who seek "visible difference from an implicit white [male] norm." In "passing" for "true" black, such men do more to enrich transnational corporations, Gilroy claims, than to validate the authenticity of racial or gender difference.[2]

Both Knadler and Gilroy owe a debt to Judith Butler's work on gender performativity in *Gender Trouble*, which undermines the "naturalness" of gender itself.[3] If gender identities are products of socially mandated scripts that are so internalized they *seem* natural, rather than of internal compulsions that cannot be helped, then no racial identity based on gender ideology can be free of performativity.

When the reality of lesbian motherhood leapt onto the feminist radar screen with the publication of Adrienne Rich's *Of Woman Born* in 1976, another form of political play emerged to expose the performativity of a seemingly natural feminine act and to turn a truism about femininity into a conundrum. For the next two decades, writers like Gloria Joseph and Jill Lewis, Jean Renvoizé, Jane Price Knowles, and Ellen Lewin revealed the intricacies and implications of a life experience that many thought of as an oxymoron.[4] The very idea overturned categorical assumptions about motherhood, as defined by heterosexual norms and patriarchal marriage. Lesbian motherhood paralleled the high American divorce rate in challenging the value of male role models for healthy children. It also challenged the relationship between sex acts, technology, and reproduction, the source of maternal "instinct," and the role of motherhood in creating racial value. Even Freud's theory of the Electra complex, penis envy, and women's libidinal desire for a male child needed emergency revision. Seen in conjunction with Butler's ideas about gender performativity, lesbian motherhood also upset gendered racial categories based on women's reproductive subordination to male control.

Disability studies have had a similar disruptive effect. Rosemarie Garland-Thomson's work on disability, for example, challenges naturalized intersections of gender and race by confronting "the limits of the ways we understand human diversity . . . multiculturalism, and the social formations that interpret" the most gendered of all foundations for race, the body. Who a woman is, what she can do, how she relates to the world and to other people, and what race means in the context of her gendered physical identity are all complicated by disability as a "category of analysis and a system of representation."[5]

More intentional forms of political play have emerged from theatrical productions. Toward the end of the 1990s gendered racial-bending theater and musical performances extended and elaborated a tradition that Amy Seuyoshi calls "mindful masquerades." Gender impersonators like Mary Marble were part of the tradition. Her man-drag performances in San Francisco at the turn of the twentieth century delighted audiences as they blatantly flouted gendered racial boundaries. Marble's performances were especially popular with immigrant Asian men, whose lives required them to impersonate Western masculinity by adopting its trappings in order to appear assimilable to American culture. The men understood that their masquerades paralleled Mary's, although they might not have characterized the two performances as "coexisting ideologies of passing and privilege . . . along the axes of gender and race," as Seuyoshi does.[6] Contemporary drag queens and kings are part of the same tradition. They too expose coexisting ideologies, as their talent for tricking audiences into believing that male is female or vice versa and for subverting race-related gender conventions make viewers wonder what their own gender and race really signify.[7]

The theater productions of playwright and performer Anna Deavere Smith and the troupe Culture Clash, also a product of the 1990s, offer another form of mindful masquerade that disrupts gendered racial expectations. In their cases, the disruption occurs via unique characterizations. For example, Smith's play, "House Arrest," which opened in 1997, toyed provocatively with gendered racial norms by casting a black woman as Bill Clinton. Two plays by Culture Clash, *Culture Clash in Border Town* and *Radio Mambo*, also challenged audience expectations by casting a Chicano-Latino male trio as a group of elderly African American women, a Jewish art dealer, and Shamu the whale, among other surprises. The point in such performances was neither to ridicule the actors and the characters nor to recreate the humiliating race-imitations of minstrelsy. Rather, they were designed to free audiences from knee-jerk reactions and automatic acts of self-protection and to de-center the gendered/raced body from the cultural power of famous or iconic people (or animals). Such de-centering encourages viewers to "rethink enduring political inequities and possibilities for political alliance and social justice," according to Dorinne Kondo. Performing "others" directly or vicariously allows us to transcend the boundaries of race, gender, sexuality, and age.[8]

Such theatrical play might mean little for feminist politics if it did not also suggest an important starting point for political transformation. The invitation to inhabit another or to imagine inhabiting another can allow us to adopt the "other's" perspectives. Articulations of difference can connect as well as separate. Sojourner Truth's alleged question in the 1850s, "Ar'n't I a woman?," was powerful because it both captured the essence of an enslaved woman's life and invited other poor and immigrant women who were not slaves to expand their gender worlds and see their own disadvantage in a new context. Asian American feminist Karin Aguilar-San Juan accomplished something similar in 1997 when she defined "home" and "family" as not only domestic sites that white women fight to escape but also as synonyms for the American "nationhood" and "nationality" that Asian women cannot fully inhabit.[9] Her redefinition can resonate with Latinas because gendered racial stereotypes and cross-border family ties also hinder their full acceptance as Americans. It can also resonate with anyone whose home is a political site, where the state both protects and intrudes for various gendered/racial reasons. For example, same-sex couples live parallel private and public lives in homes that are both domestic centers and arenas of political ambiguity and contradiction. The state may forbid the couple to marry but still require marriage for economic benefits and children's social legitimacy. The homes of welfare mothers are also simultaneously private spaces and continual sources of political contestation.

To supplement integrative frameworks and intersectional or conjunctural approaches to social change, feminists need mechanisms like political play that go beyond honoring and comprehending existing differences. Disrupting those differences is an important step in achieving political progress based on race-gender intersectionality. The consistent historical analytic offered by *The Specter of Sex* provides guidance in the process by deconstructing and complicating naturalized heterosexuality, gender dichotomy, and male dominance, as well as its corollaries in racial ideology—the patriarchal foundations of white supremacy, gendered racial hierarchies, and the gendered foundations of the black-white racial dichotomy, among others.

From Historical Analytic to Feminist Politics

The next step for feminist theorizing about difference entails translating political play and conceptual disruptions of difference categories into possibilities for political alliance and social justice. Such a translation involves turning the historical *causes* of gendered racial formation into as inspiring and practical a basis for political action and coalition as the divisive *effects* of the process have typically been. As in the realm of theory, a two-pronged, apparently contradictory approach to gender/racial justice may be most appropriate. A way must be found both to inhabit difference and to collaborate across differences to challenge the politics of difference.

Howard Winant's 1994 observation that race must be treated as real because its effects are real informs the first prong of feminist antisubordination politics. Winant recommends forming and maintaining racial identities and race-based collectives and communities in order to resist hegemonic influence. He encourages "alternative, emancipatory account[s] of the virtues of racial difference and racial diversity." Those accounts should emphasize the "links between the fate of racially defined minorities and the fate of U.S. society as a whole," as well as of the world at large, where white identity is less transparent.[10] Winant's program seems like a recipe for a politics of racial division, but perhaps unintentionally it also offers a rationale for a unifying form of feminist politics consistent with this book's historical analytic. That is, revised emancipatory accounts of racial diversity by individual groups could also reconsider the particular forms of misogyny, patriarchy, and sexism that have helped to construct racial communities and incorporate women's contributions into stories of racial strength and resilience. By the same token, race-specific emancipatory programs could link with other progressive movements in the U.S. and the world and transcend the politics of difference. Instead of linking oppressions, those programs could link gendered racial liberations among groups.

Renya Ramirez called for just such a revised emancipatory account in Native American communities in 2007. She explained that tribal sovereignty "can no longer mean that Native men have the right to control Indian women's lives . . . It must also involve respect, interdependence, responsibility, dialogue, and engagement with indigenous women's rights and claims . . . [R]ace and tribal nation can no longer be privileged over gender issues." Ramirez cites Elisa Laura Perez, who argued in 1999 that Chicanas can no longer work for the Chicana/o movement without addressing the sexism within it.[11] Perhaps *The Specter of Sex* can contribute to writing an emancipatory white history that holds both sexes accountable for their collusion in the doctrine of white supremacy and that tries to unravel the Gordian knot of sexual, reproductive, and misogynist ideology that has contributed to that doctrine.

A second, parallel prong of feminist politics based on *The Specter of Sex's* historical analytic seems to contradict the first, since it is skeptical about the validity of the very categorical differences the book emphasizes. But such skepticism really complements the embracement of new, more equitable racial identities within groups and avoids the pitfalls of identity politics that can reify difference categories as well as *difference* itself. The feminist politics of skepticism enacts political play while keeping an eye on the material difference that *difference* makes and emphasizing that identity differences are more rooted in cultural constructions than in facts of nature. Such politics can also challenge the value of the experiential knowledge underlying identity politics, which may underestimate the role of cultural factors, basic assumptions, and surrounding circumstances in constructing the meaning of experience.

The feminist politics of skepticism would also entail alliances across identity categories of race, class, religion, ethnicity, and even gender. Creating such alliances without relying on identity categories requires a rethinking of coalition politics. Iris Marion Young and Gayatri Spivak have provided related models for such alliances, based not on identity or experience but on relationships to key *material-ideological facts* that construct the concept of gender. Young and Spivak identify the sexual division of labor and the heterosexual norm (or heterosexism) as the most important "facts" historically circumscribing women's everyday lives and the milieus within which they are required to function.[12]

To adapt that model to the consistent historical analytic of *The Specter of Sex*, I propose a slight revision of Young's and Spivak's model. The history of gendered racial formation reveals an overarching "set of material-ideological facts" that long ago subsumed heterosexuality and the sexual division of labor in constructing cross-cultural gendered (racial) limitations. Clearly, heterosexuality and the gendered division of labor (as well as other definitions of gender roles and characteristics) preceded race as a concept, but gendered definitions of race in the U.S. brought those "facts" into their full oppressive force. It was only after race became a key defining measure of human value that heterosexuality and gender-specific labor norms became tools of white supremacy and indicators of non-white, especially black, inferiority and abjection. We have seen how much more powerful "the feminine" became when it demeaned not only women but also men of color in the name of protecting (white) civilization itself.

The feminist politics of skepticism would depend on political coalitions formed around the overarching material-ideological fact of gendered racial formation at the same time that racial communities were reconstructing identities on the basis of gender equity and inclusion. Such coalitions could utilize another of Young's ideas—*seriality*—which she first articulated in 1994. Young borrowed Jean Paul Sartre's definition of a "series" as a form of commonality created not by shared characteristics, which would constitute a group, but by shared proximity and entrapment within the "structured relations" of a particular social milieu. People waiting for a bus that does not come, for example, become a series constructed by a common inability to alter their material circumstances. They might coalesce around a particular solution—say, shared taxicabs—for a limited purpose. Since the past limits the ways women live within present material *practico-inert realities*, Young included shared histories as a motivation for serial coalitions. It is here that Young's approach deviates sharply from Spivak's, however, for instead of advocating a "strategic essentialism" of innate characteristics among commuters (or women) in order to address "scrupulously visible political interests," as Spivak endorsed for subalterns in 1985, Young suggests creating a social category based on a limited form of social unity for a specific purpose.[13]

Seriality could constitute a feminist politics both respectful and skeptical of identity as the basis of political action. Various groups could unite for limited times and purposes across racial and other differences, real and constructed, and work against the past and present practices, material conditions, and practico-inert realities that structure lives across boundaries of difference. Series could also accommodate the differences in goals and methods of political organizing and issue identification discussed in Part V's introduction. They would allow groups to address large issues in the context of difference as well as commonality.

As promising as Young's vision of *seriality* is for forming political coalitions around shared structural positions or past practices, it would be even better with the addition of one more point. Maya Goldenberg identified that point in 2007. She noted that members of a "serial" alliance could be more politically active if they recognized themselves as pluralists, or members of multiple series or political alliances formed around a variety of pressure points. Nothing about one practico-inert reality or oppressive past practice precludes the possibility that other realities constitute inequity for the same person or group.[14] By the same token, nothing about gender itself precludes the possibility of shared structural linkages. Serialized political coalitions can also cross gender boundaries.

With Young and Goldenberg as political inspiration, the consistent historical analytic of *The Specter of Sex* could motivate multiple "series" in various and overlapping configurations for various durations. Asian men might ally with Asian women on the basis of their shared histories of sexual misrepresentation, from characterizations as predatory bachelors and prostitutes, to hypersexualized caricatures, to the asexual "model minority" label that hounds them today. Their "series" could ally with gay activists of any race because of shared characterizations as inadequately or inappropriately gendered. Likewise, black women might serialize with women of other races to challenge cross-racial claims that restoring masculine prerogatives and prowess is the primary purpose of racial justice. Because working class white women and women of color share a history of official suspicion about their sexual behavior, they too might join in a series, possibly including black men whose sexual motives have also been suspect.

Members of such "series" need not embrace any particular identity, characteristic, or shared experience in order to mobilize on behalf of themselves and others plagued by similar historical constructions of racialized gender. Indeed, joining a coalitional series for political purposes would not prevent members from engaging with their own diverse identity groups or communities. By the same token, participation in series would be compatible with political activity in the first prong of feminist politics, in which racial groups identify non-sexist grounds for racial authority and subjectivity, as well as equity for all of its members.[15]

The two-pronged approach discussed in this chapter would never attract everyone, but it could become the foundation of a comprehensive feminist antisubordination politics that is both respectful and skeptical of all identities by defining the practico-inert realities, such as the patriarchy underlying white supremacy, that have affected both sexes across racial, class, and other lines. Such a politics could also offer possibilities for new and surprising alliances.

16

Gender Implications for Theories of Racial Formation

Gender has been a problem for the study of racial formation. In fact, gender has typically been omitted from such studies, starting with Winthrop Jordan's *White Over Black: American Attitudes Toward the Negro, 1550-1812*, published in 1969, and other early discussions of race-based slavery, and continuing with more recent scholarship, such as Michael Omi and Howard Winant's *Racial Formation in the U.S.—1960s-1990s*, and Tomás Almaguer's *Racial Fault Lines: Historical Origins of White Supremacy in California*, both from 1994; Richard Delgado and Jean Stefancic's *Critical White Studies: Looking Behind the Mirror*, from 1997, and Martin Bulmer and John Solomos's *Researching Race and Racism*, from 2004.[1] Even Martha Menchaca's 2002 *Recovering History, Constructing Race*, which notes gender stratification within Mesoamerican cultures, does not make gender an organizing principle of its investigation of race.[2] In most discussions of racial formation, then, the racial subject is either ungendered or male, which, as feminist theorists point out, amounts to the same thing. The consistent historical analytic of *The Specter of Sex* makes such omission and gender elision unacceptable in the full story of racial formation.

Like the question of racial diversity in gender studies and feminist politics discussed in Chapter 15, redressing the absence of gender in the study of racial formation calls for a two-pronged approach. On the one hand, for the purpose of reclaiming and revising racial history, gender must be recognized as a real category that has real effects. On the other hand, because both race and gender are suspect and/or contrived categories, they must be disrupted even as they are embraced. Chapter 16 analyzes one way of navigating the inevitable tension between the two prongs of a new racial formation narrative—reconfiguring the boundary between male and female as a "border identity."

Re-visualizing the Centrality of Gender

The overall project of the first prong entails acknowledging that gender distinctions are significant to the history of racial formation. That process requires a few steps. The first is interpreting the invisibility and "unspokenness" of women and gender in the controlling narratives of racial formation, whether by dominant or marginalized racial groups. Toni Morrison's method of decoding the unspoken presence of blackness in white American literature provides some guidance for that interpretation. Morrison reads the whiteness of Moby Dick, for example, as a signifier of the white privilege in American society that white men would sacrifice their lives for. She sees the novel's pairing of characters by race—Ahab with Fedallah and Ishmael with Queequeg—as an oblique inscription of unspecified but burgeoning racial hierarchies and intimacies in American society. "What Africanism became for, and how it functioned in, the literary imagination is of paramount interest," Morrison explains, "because it may be possible to discover, through a close look at literary 'blackness,' the nature—even the cause—of literary 'whiteness.' "[3] In the same way, a close look at the role of gender and the symbolic importance of women in racial formation discourse not only includes women's contributions and experience, but it also reveals the nature, even the cause, of racial distinction and hierarchy. Using Morrison's model, racial formation narratives can be rewritten to expose gender ideology in the story of racial formation. *The Specter of Sex* is part of that process.

The second step in redressing the invisibility of women and gender in racial formation narratives, related to the first, is recognizing how their absence promotes men's normalcy as human subjects and women's particularity and deviance from that standard. The absence of a gender focus thereby reinforces male dominance and reduces women to outsiders or tentative members of their own racial groups. It also excludes women from leadership roles and skews relationships between the sexes.

The lingering effects of women's historical invisibility in African American racial formation narratives are evident in Johnetta Cole and Beverly Guy-Sheftall's 2003 *Gender Talk: The Struggle for Women's Equality in African American Communities*. Cole and Guy-Sheftall critique what they identify as the prevailing symbolic system in contemporary black communities, in which men's experience still exemplifies racial suffering and women's contribution to the racial narrative is confined to their efforts to prevent men's further "emasculation." This symbolic system obscures black women's painful legacy of brutal rapes and enforced maternity, minimizes women's experience of lynching, and elevates men's victimization as the primary signifier of black suffering. It also obscures black women's suffering at the hands of violent or abusive black husbands, fathers, and ministers. No matter how painful, women's experience remains invisible and unrepresentative of racial experience. In addition, Cole and Guy-Sheftall argue that homophobia in African American communities results from the continuing expectation of hypermasculine sexuality for black men.[4] They call for ameliorative measures that embrace black women as racial subjects and increase honesty about sexuality in African American life.

Similar presumptions about the representative male racial subject afflict Asian American communities. Elaine Kim analyzed the "gender warfare" that resulted from such presumptions in 1990. She explained that Asian American men have punished women in their own community for the men's lack of patriarchal status in American culture. They have also disparaged Asian women's interest in feminism and asserted their own authority over the community and over women. Author Frank Chin is the veritable poster child for that phenomenon, since he has blatantly admonished women to take a back seat to men, especially in the creation of literature, so that men can develop a "muscular" vernacular that will "recuperate Asian American cultural integrity through a 'recognized style of Asian-American manhood.' " Maxine Hong Kingston and Amy Tan have been excoriated by Chin for their attempts to recuperate Asian American cultural integrity by reviving female-centered Asian heritages.[5] Leslie Bow concurred with Kim in 2001 and further exposed the ways in which presumptive maleness in the racial subject has reinforced the dominant culture's idea of women as Asian American insider/outsiders. Women allegedly threaten Asian American citizenship because they can seduce men, "corrupt their identification with other men," and undermine male allegiance to the nation or racial group.[6]

Homophobia and fear of "the feminine" have also resulted from presumptions of maleness in the Asian American raced subject. David Eng argued in 2001 that the dominant culture's longstanding construction of Asian men as "feminized, homosexualized, queer" fomented a homophobic backlash within the Asian American community that was also fueled by Frank Chin's male characters who were models of heterosexual Asian male norms, desires, and ideals. According to Eng, another symptom of the backlash can be seen in the "male hysteria" that has infected Asian American fiction (and culture), up to and including the postmodern story collection *Pangs of Love*.

Hysteria is exemplified in that collection by Asian men's panic over their impotence with white women. Given the longstanding importance of men's access to white women as a symbol of assimilation into American culture and citizenship, the male characters fear that their sexual incapacity will jeopardize their acceptance in the U.S.[7] The compulsion to prove manliness both within and between racial identities continues to paralyze male-female relationships and threaten women's self-esteem in Asian American communities.

Presumptions of maleness in the Puerto Rican racial/ethnic subject have also created gender backlash. Though rejecting a racial identity per se, Puerto Rican men have historically felt de-masculated by the racial constructions implicit in American colonialism. As we saw in Chapter 14, feelings of de-masculation fomented misogyny and gender conflict, as male anger at their deprivations in colonial policies spurred violence against women and further connected "Puerto Ricanness" itself with robust masculinity. What remains hidden in this scenario, however, is the degree to which the real targets of *machismo* are other men. The intensity of *machismo* typically depends on a man's place in the class structure and his degree of involvement in male competition. Thus exaggerated displays of strength, authority, invulnerability, and courage really express men's solipsistic desire to earn respect from their peers, often by dominating women, whose suffering—whether in relationship violence or lost economic opportunities—is only collateral damage. According to Rafael Ramírez, Puerto Rican men fear most being called *mongo*—weak, disrespected, the butt of jokes, having a "weak penis"—since the epithet itself can make a man "disqualified to assert his positions and ideas." He will begin to speak slowly, slouch, and fulfill the slur's prophecy by becoming ever more *esmongao*.[8] As we also saw in Chapter 14, the Puerto Rican nationalist movement adopted this gender war's rules of engagement by seeking to establish Puerto Rico as an independent, virile nation. Addressing the direct harm done to women by *machismo* and accepting that women deserve equal opportunities to work and to express their individual and national identities are necessary steps in redressing the Puerto Rican version of presumptive maleness in the racial subject.

An even larger specter of sex haunts such reparations for women's omission from and assumptions of maleness in racial formation narratives, however. That is, men's conflicts with other men of different racial or ethnic groups often entail seeing women as embodied signifiers of strife. We saw this phenomenon in the heterosexual rape/lynching scenario discussed in Chapters 6 and 10, and we can read about it almost daily in international news coverage. In Afghanistan and India, for example, especially in recent attacks on Muslims by the Hindu Right, women become the targets of inter-group violence and revenge not only to reinforce the manliness of the aggressors but also as proxies for the real source of the conflict.[9] One consequence of this substitution is the association of a group's own women with past injustices or threats. The women's claims for equity or justice for themselves are forever muffled or even obliterated by the anger that men feel on women's behalf as a burden of honor. Through a misogynistic irony, the women become the detritus of conflict instead of agents of the group. That is why a woman raped by an enemy can be spurned by her own family and why women of another identity group, race, or religion, although innocent non-combatants themselves, can be mutilated and murdered without remorse in so many conflicts around the world. Even at times when violence abates, its perceived underlying cause endures in disrespect for the feminine and disregard for women.

Revisions of racial formation narratives to redress the omission of women and gender and to contradict the assumption of maleness in the primary racial subject must account for the possibility that such displacement of conflict has occurred and created a curtain of non-recognition between men and women of the same racial group, as well as between groups. Indeed, that obfuscation is what erased women from racial formation narratives in the first place. Parting that curtain is essential to racial reconciliation, which cannot occur without addressing both the hidden and obvious gender issues lurking within and hovering between racial communities.

Borderland Identities

At the same time that the omission and misrepresentation of women and gender must be addressed in comparative racial studies, it is also necessary to recognize the inadequacy and potential danger of seeing both gender and race as necessary, absolute, or even viable distinctions between human beings. To the extent that racial discourse has equated racial purity or authenticity with gender purity or authenticity, both men's and women's lives, especially their sexual and reproductive lives, have been manipulated, aggrandized, or contained for the good of the race. But neither kind of purity or authenticity is possible, let alone desirable, in actual life. Certainly the genealogy of racial formation in the U.S. demonstrates that both forms of purity and authenticity are myths. What we have instead—from the lightest of Euro-American whites to the darkest of African Americans—is a nation of hybrids. Many Americans, whether they are called African Americans, Euro-Americans, American Indians, or Latinos, are racially and/or ethnically mixed. Even Asian Americans often have mixed heritages that have been obscured by the claims of racial purity constructed in Asian countries to differentiate populations from their political enemies or in the U.S. to categorize immigrants. Indeed, the racial hybridity of the national subject is the unspoken corollary of the American melting pot. That American story of race produces confusing and sometimes conflicting multiplicity within families, at the same time that sexual identities, political affiliations, occupational identities, sports interests, and geographic loyalties further complicate racial identities.

Latina writer Gloria Anzaldúa coined a phrase in the 1990s—"border identities"—that captures this racial complexity and ambiguity. She defined such identities as slightly uncomfortable but flexible modes of defining oneself and of relating to different communities across physical as well as cultural boundaries. Anzaldúa was thinking specifically of Mexican Americans' intersecting racial and national hybridity, but the term is also apt for other hybrid American racial histories and geographic origins. Anzaldúa eschewed the "hyphenated model" of African-American or Mexican-American, which attempt to fix the identity on each side of the hyphen. She preferred the unhyphenated version, which has prevailed, to indicate that both terms are constantly in flux, ambiguous, and dynamic. She explained that the two terms "define themselves as hybrid creations of distinct forces."[10]

I propose that we apply Anzaldúa's concept of "border identities" to the male-female dichotomy as the second prong of racial formation theory revision. Gender "border identities" would generally weaken the power of the male-female gender dichotomy to reinforce the imperatives of racial difference and would specifically reduce the power of the black-white racial binary. If the racial subject could be seen as *both* and *neither* male and/nor female, the two gender terms could also enrich and energize one another, as in Anzaldúa's model. Men and women could embrace and take responsibility for one another's pasts, and racial narratives could, in turn, stop reinforcing male dominance.

W.E.B. Du Bois offered a provocative prototype for cross-border thinking about gender in his fictional work, *Dark Princess*, published in 1928. In his text, Du Bois reconceptualized the "interstitial relationship between race, gender, nation, and art," according to Monica Miller. He also redefined African American masculinity in relationship to cultural nationalism. Reconceptualizing masculinity was actually a continuous strain in Du Bois's work, according to Miller, despite what Hazel Carby calls the "anxious masculinism" of his *Souls of Black Folk* from 1903. Indeed, Du Bois repeatedly explored and advanced the black "feminine man" who embodies the racial gifts of artistic ability, aesthetic sensibility, and "sensuous nature" and has the capacity to "soften the whiteness of the Teutonic." Du Bois elaborated this strain of thought in *Dark Princess*, where the beautifully dressed black dandy, Matthew, plunges into the political fray by running for office and dips into the diaspora by traveling abroad to assess African Americans' readiness to become involved in a world-wide revolution of people of color. Matthew's politicized dandy-ness elevated beauty and sensibility into the struggle for racial equality and contrasted with the apolitical European aesthete. The novel's reformed gender roles also feminized what counts as civilization and defined the aesthetic as political practice.[11]

There was a downside for women in Du Bois's novel, however. That is, actual women were eclipsed by the Negro dandy as agents of the ideal aesthetic/political form of blackness. The novel's class implications were also oppressive. But its combination of masculinity and femininity in a reformulated racial subject does address the "perennial crisis of black masculine leadership without restoring 'manhood' to its uninterrogated rights," according to Miller. It also nods toward the "anti-race man" developed in recent years by Paul Gilroy and Ross Posnock—a man who can free "race men" from the need to prove their racial authenticity. The anti-race man also deconstructs stereotypes, provides alternatives to a world defined by the color line, and embodies the postmodern reality that multiple forces construct individual, cultural, and national identities. As Du Bois's novel ends with the birth of a "multi-racial, multi-cultural, pan-African, and pan-Asian leader of the Darker People's revolution," Gilroy sees not a fusion of two pure essences but "a meeting of two heterogeneous multiplicities that . . . create something durable and entirely appropriate to troubled anti-colonial times."[12]

That is a pretty utopian vision in and of itself, albeit one of "heterogeneous multiplicities" rather than of purity. Still, if we tweak Du Bois's text a bit more, it might yield an even greater benefit for women and unite the two prongs of Chapter 16's analysis. In addition to feminizing civilization and humanizing masculinity, the anti-race man could become a catalyst for revealing, valorizing, and incorporating invisible womanhood into contemporary racial discourse. The suppressed, unspoken but actual *woman* in racial formation narratives could be the one to intertwine with the newly reconstituted anti-racial male subject. Given that possibility, *The Dark Princess* could be seen as a metaphor for recognizing that unspoken woman, calling her by name, and embracing her into a more fully formed racial subjectivity.

Conclusion

Interdependence

Section V has returned us to the beginning of *The Specter of Sex* by examining in more detail the contemporary theoretical and political discourses that dominate discussions of gender's relationship to race but have ultimately failed to interconnect them. Those discourses may even, ironically, have contributed to the analytical separation of race and gender. Section V has also suggested possible remedies to that conundrum in order to make feminist theoretical discourse, feminist political efforts, and racial formation discourse more deeply inclusive as well as more disruptive of racial and gender categories.

Intersectionality Redux

In providing the "backstory" of intersectionalilty theory, *The Specter of Sex* further complicates contemporary perspectives on race-gender interconnection. The genealogy of racialized gender reveals that the two concepts were separated or fused depending on context, motivation, and time period. Their intersection was also gradual. Until the early decades of the nineteenth century, for example, a man's gendered reputation could still eclipse his racial category, and a white woman's racially biased accusations did not automatically convict a black rape suspect. As the century progressed the concepts of race and gender became increasingly intertwined and seemed equally "natural," and by century's end, Asian women, black men, and white women exemplified in various contexts discreet gendered racial categories that many Americans regarded almost as different human species.

That was the nation's legacy for the twentieth century, although it took feminist analysis to articulate it as *intersectionality*. At the same time, perceptions of the inextricable fusion of gender and race that followed have tended to obscure the contradictions and inconsistencies in intersectionality theory that are evident today in continued struggles over the nature of race/gender interconnection within feminist and race theories. Overlooking or minimizing these struggles or contradictions may allow intersectionality theory to overlook the false assumptions on which each category was founded. Indeed, the two terms may never exist in perfect emulsion in part because they are unstable ingredients.

Foucault Redux

In exploring the complexity and ambiguity of intersectionality as both theory and lived reality, this book's genealogical method owes much to Foucault. His histories of prisons and sexuality provide a model for analyzing ideas and actions that are not what they seem on the surface and for probing deeper motivations that are invisible or suppressed. Foucault's work offers a vocabulary for exploring mechanisms of hegemonic power as both embedded in particular time periods and apparently timeless. Foucaldian analyses also expose the interconnection between ideologies and discourses of power and the lives of individuals.

At the same time, *The Specter of Sex* departs from Foucault in its particular focus on racial formation. Foucault conducted only a limited analysis of race, primarily in the final chapters of *The History of Sexuality* and in a series of lectures at the Collège de France in 1975-76. Most of his brief discussion reinforces this book's argument, since he defined race as a "fictitious unity" and identified racism as a mechanism of state normalization within the context of an emerging discourse of biopower. He also argued that race is connected with regimes of power targeted at the capacities, energies, and pleasures of bodies.[1] He further explained that technologies of sexuality created a "susceptibility and discursive field" for racism and eventually incorporated a racist logic. All such statements reflect major points in *The Specter of Sex*. However, Foucault deliberately avoided the primary project undertaken in this book—constructing a genealogy of the invention of race.[2]

The Specter of Sex also departs from Foucault's legacy in its focus on gender, which he did not isolate as a mechanism of hegemonic power. This book argues that the hegemonic power of racial formation cannot be fully understood without exploring its gendered motivations and effects. Indeed, it demonstrates that the nineteenth-century scientific discourse that Foucault explored was also able to exert its power so effectively by creating a sense of natural and timeless inevitability in the parallel development of race and gender in human evolution. For example, scientific discourse identified women as the primitive evolutionary stage of all racial groups and recycled ancient gender ideology that assigned primary responsibility for reproduction to women. Nineteenth-century doctors and anthropologists were thereby empowered to chide white women about their responsibility to procreate "correctly" and often in order to prevent white hypodescent. Hegemonic discourses about American citizenship also derived power from mechanisms of gender, without which they could not have been as effective as they were in defining racial groups and maintaining white supremacy. In addition, men of color maintained their own power within their racial groups by suppressing the voices and ignoring the rights of "their" women. Even as gender was suppressed, however, it remained a force in public epistemologies of race as they evolved, became internalized at personal levels, and repeated and adapted themselves to changing conditions.

Despite these differences, I would like to conclude with another of Foucault's most salient points: systems of power are never finite social totalities; every system entails intersecting circles of power and resistance. Even as racial ideologies appropriated the power of gender ideologies to stratify races, many other factors contributed to racial formation, including the economic, religious, scientific, and political issues this book examines. (Of course, many of those were also inherently gendered.) At the same time, the racialization of gender was never monolithic or consistent. For example, men and women were affected both together and separately as various racial categories and hierarchies were established over time. And even as patterns of gendered racial formation repeated themselves, no two processes were identical and not all minority races were equally disempowered or oppressed. By the same token, the concept of race was and is a slippery one. Only in the late twentieth century, for example, did "white" emerge as one racial category among others and "Latino" decline as a racial rather than an ethnic category, now characterized more by surname than physiology. Categories continue to merge, erode, appear, and vanish. Throughout it all, however, a gendered thrust has shot through centuries of racial formation in the U.S., and *The Specter of Sex* argues that it should not be ignored.

Notes

Introduction

1. For a longer discussion of "constructedness," see Judith Butler (1990), *Gender Trouble: Feminism and the Subversion of Identity* (New York: Routledge), especially 8–9 and 134–35.

2. Jane Flax (1990), "Postmodernism and Gender Relations in Feminist Theory," in *Feminism/Postmodernism*, ed. Linda J. Nicholson (New York: Routledge), 50.

3. See Mary Hawkesworth (1997), "Confounding Gender," *Signs* 22, no. 3 (Spring): 649–85 for such a parsing. Many theorists have argued that bodies take on particular shapes and affects according to the politics and tenor of their times. For a concise statement of that claim, see Butler, *Gender Trouble*, 129–32.

4. Evelyn Nakano Glenn (2002), *Unequal Freedom: How Race and Gender Shaped American Citizenship and Labor* (Cambridge, MA: Harvard University Press), 9.

5. See the use of those terms in Eileen Boris (1995), "The Racialized Gendered State: Constructions of Citizenship in the United States," *Social Politics* 2 (Summer): 160.

6. See Kimberlé Williams Crenshaw (1989), "Demarginalizing the Intersection of Race and Sex: A Black Feminist Critique of Antidiscrimination Doctrine, Feminist Theory and Antiracist Politics," *University of Chicago Legal Forum*: 139–67; and (1997), "Intersectionality and Identity Politics: Learning from Violence Against Women of Color," in *Reconstructing Political Theory: Feminist Perspectives*, ed. M. L. Shanley and U. Narayan (University Park: Pennsylvania State University Press), 178–93.

7. Critical Race Theory doesn't really deal with racial formation. See Kimberlé Crenshaw et al., ed. (1995), *Critical Race Theory: Key Writings that Formed the Movement* (New York: New York University Press); and Adrien Wing, ed. (2003), *Critical Race Feminism: A Reader* (New York: New York University Press).

8. See Leela Fernandes (1997), *Producing Workers: The Politics of Gender, Class, and Culture in the Calcutta Jute Mills* (Philadelphia: University of Pennsylvania Press); and Evelyn Nakano Glenn (1999), "The Social Construction and Institutionalization of Gender and Race: An Integrative Framework,"

in *ReVisioning Gender*, ed. Beth B. Hess, Judith Lorber, and Myra M. Ferree (Thousand Oaks, CA: Sage), 3–43.

9. Glenn, *Unequal Freedom*, 15–16.

10. Laura Gillman (2007), "Beyond the Shadow: Re-scripting Race in Women's Studies," *Meridians: feminism, race, transnationalism* 7, no. 2:120, 137, 128–29.

11. Evelyn Nakano Glenn (1992), "From Servitude to Service Work: Historical Continuities in the Racial Division of Paid Reproductive Labor," *Signs* 18, no. 1 (Autumn): 34.

12. Nancy Fraser and Linda J. Nicholson (1990), "Social Criticism without Philosophy: An Encounter between Feminism and Postmodernism," in *Feminism/Postmodernism*, ed. Linda J. Nicholson, 34–35.

13. Susan Bordo (1990), "Feminism, Postmodernism, and Gender-Scepticism," in *Feminism/Postmodernism*, ed. Linda J. Nicholson, 139.

PART I: ROOTS

Chapter 1

1. Nancy Tuana (1993), *The Less Noble Sex: Scientific, Religious, and Philosophical Conceptions of Woman's Nature* (Bloomington: Indiana University Press), 155. The quotation comes from Euripides' Hippolytos. The playwright was even harsher in Medea: "What we poor males really need/is a way of having babies on our own—/no females, please. /Then the world would be completely trouble free." Tuana, *The Less Noble Sex*, 155, quoting Euripides' *Medea*, lines 573–75.

2. Gerda Lerner (1986), *The Creation of Patriarchy* (New York: Oxford University Press), 15–53. Lerner argues that hunting/gathering societies were the root cause of patriarchy, as women opted out of the hunt because of childbearing and child-rearing burdens. Agricultural societies did not necessarily promote female power either, since "in the course of the agricultural revolution the exploitation of human labor and the sexual exploitation of women became inextricably linked." Lerner finds no solid evidence for pre-patriarchal matriarchal societies.

3. Genesis was written sometime before 1445 B.C.E., probably in stages. The entire Hebrew Bible is a compilation of Greek, Babylonian, Sumerian, and other texts and traditions dating as far back as the fifteenth century B.C.E. According to the *New Oxford Annotated Bible* (New York: Oxford University Press, 2001), the Hebrew Bible, including the Book of Genesis, was probably canonized around 586–538 B.C.E., well after the Theogony was written.

4. Tuana, *The Less Noble Sex*, 5–6.

5. Gregory Vlastos (1997), "Was Plato a Feminist?," in *Plato's Republic: Critical Essays*, ed. Richard Kraut (Lanham, MD: Rowman & Littlefield), 120–21.

6. Ibid., 123.

Notes

7. For details about the role of metaphor and analogy in science, see Nancy Leys Stepan (1990), "Race and Gender: The Role of Analogy in Science," in *Anatomy of Racism*, ed. David Theo Goldberg (Minneapolis: University of Minnesota Press), 38–57. For feminist analyses of the cultural roots of scientific inquiry, see Anne Fausto-Sterling (1985), *Myths and Gender: Biological Theories About Men and Women* (New York: Basic Books); Sandra Harding (1991), *Whose Science? Whose Knowledge?* (Ithaca, NY: Cornell University Press); Robyn Wiegman (1995), *American Anatomies: Theorizing Race and Gender* (Durham, NC: Duke University Press); and Nancy Tuana, *The Less Noble Sex*, cited in this chapter.

8. Tuana, *The Less Noble Sex*, 11–12.

9. Londa Schiebinger (1993), *Nature's Body: Gender in the Making of Modern Science* (Boston: Beacon Press), 147.

10. Tuana, *The Less Noble Sex*, 6–7, 18–19, 21–22.

11. Mary Magdalene's complaint is found in Pistis Sophia I-III, where it is clear that she is a primary interlocutor of Jesus and that Peter is jealous of her role. To counter Mary's influence, Peter disparages the "female race," according to most scholars of the text. For more detail, see Antti Marjanen (1996), *The Woman Jesus Loved: Mary Magdalene in the Nag Hammadi and Related Documents* (New York: E.J. Brill), 179–81.

12. Tuana, *The Less Noble Sex*, 13–14, 22–24; 17, 31, 34.

13. Roxann Wheeler (2000), *The Complexion of Race: Categories of Difference in Eighteenth-Century British Culture* (Philadelphia: University of Pennsylvania Press), 40.

14. Cited in David P. Barash (2003), "Believing is Seeing," *The Chronicle Review: The Chronicle of Higher Education* 49, no. 42, June 27: B10–11. Barash develops Thomas Kuhn's ideas in *The Structure of Scientific Revolutions (Chicago: University of Chicago Press, 1970)* about the need for a paradigm shift before anomalous observations can be recognized and interpreted. What Barash does not see, which Londa Schiebinger points out, is the role of gendered economic as well as anthropomorphic metaphors in sociobiology. Socio-biologist May Willson, for example, says that plants are investment bankers, who judge their "reproductive success" against the "cost of their mating investment and parental investment." Plants also have tactics, make choices, and engage in conflict. Quoted in Schiebinger, *Nature's Body*, 27.

15. Tuana, *The Less Noble Sex*, 156.

16. Charles W. Mills (1997), *The Racial Contract* (Ithaca, NY: Cornell University Press), 54.

17. Religious fundamentalism is keeping this idea alive into the twenty-first century. For example, in July 2003 jeering crowds kept a female judge from being installed in Iraq on the grounds that "women are always ruled by their emotions" (quoted in Neil Macfarquhar, "After the War: LEGAL SYSTEM; In Najaf, Justice Can Be Blind but Not Female," *New York Times*, 31 July 2003, http://www.nytimes.com (accessed July 31, 2003)). Haven't men's passions created most of the war and violence in the world?

18. Tuana, *The Less Noble Sex*, 156–57.

19. Ibid., 160–61.
20. The divinely ordained power that Locke wrested from kings and fathers in his *Two Treatises of Government* he bestowed solely on sons. See Nancy Isenberg (1998), *Sex and Citizenship in Antebellum America (Gender and American Culture)* (Chapel Hill: University of North Carolina Press), 9–10.
21. Tuana, *The Less Noble Sex*, 161–63.
22. Mills, *The Racial Contract*, 68–69.
23. Tuana, *The Less Noble Sex*, 163.
24. Ladelle McWhorter (2004), "Sex, Race, and Biopower: A Foucauldian Genealogy," *Hypatia* 19, no. 3 (Summer): 49.
25. Mills, *The Racial Contract*, 70–71.

Chapter 2

1. Ania Loomba (2002), *Shakespeare, Race, and Colonialism* (Oxford: Oxford University Press), 27.
2. Ibid., 17, 16, 15.
3. Ibid., 26–27, 56, 59.
4. Reginald Horsman (1981), *Race and Manifest Destiny: The Origins of American Racial Anglo-Saxonism* (Cambridge, MA: Harvard University Press), 10, 30. The visit is usually dated as 63 B.C.E., but 37 B.C.E. is also mentioned.
5. Wheeler, *The Complexion of Race*, 17.
6. Ibid., 12, 7, 14.
7. Hall and Loomba's arguments are documented below. See Wheeler, *The Complexion of Race*, 5, for the non-racist side of the argument: "*Black* had a range of meanings [during the Renaissance] unavailable to us today." It referred to the color of the body, which was not necessarily permanent, as well as to non-Christians, those who live apart from civil society.
8. Kim F. Hall (1995), *Things of Darkness: Economies of Race and Gender in Early Modern England* (Ithaca, NY: Cornell University Press), 9.
9. Loomba, *Shakespeare, Race, and Colonialism*, 27–28, 39, 43.
10. Jennifer L. Morgan (2006), " 'Some Could Suckle over Their Shoulder': Male Travelers, Female Bodies, and the Gendering of Racial Idology," in *New Studies in the History of Slavery*, ed. Stephanie M.H. Camp and Edward E. Baptist (Athens: University of Georgia Press), 25, 56.
11. Loomba, *Shakespeare, Race, and Colonialism*, 31.
12. Morgan is quoting Sharon W. Tiffany and Kathleen J. Adams (1985), *The Wild Woman: An Inquiry into the Anthropology of an Idea* (New York: Cambridge University Press), 65. See also Loomba, *Shakespeare, Race, and Colonialism*, 30.
13. Morgan, " 'Some Could Suckle Over Their Shoulder,' " 171.
14. Ibid., 173.
15. Morgan, " 'Some Could Suckle Over Their Shoulder,' " at n. 20, p. 58 cites Stephen Greenblatt (1991), *Marvelous Possessions: The Wonder of the New World* (Chicago: University of Chicago Press), 143.

16. Wheeler, *The Complexion of Race*, 17, 19–20.

17. Loomba, *Shakespeare, Race, and Colonialism*, 43. Loomba cites Pliny the Elder and John Mandevill as examples. In 1653, John Bulwer suggested that the breasts of Irish women would be perfect money bags for merchants, since they were "more than half a yard long, and as well wrought as ... leather." Irish women could also allegedly suckle babies over their shoulders (ibid.).

18. Morgan " 'Some Could Suckle over Their Shoulder,' " 42.

19. Ibid., 34–35, 38.

20. Ibid., 35–36. For more on Lok's narrative, see Loomba, *Shakespeare, Race, and Colonialism*, 47.

21. Felicity Nussbaum (1995), *Torrid Zones: Maternity, Sexuality, and Empire in Eighteenth-Century English Narratives* (Baltimore, MD: Johns Hopkins University Press), 73–74.

22. Morgan, " 'Some Could Suckle over Their Shoulder,' " 47–48.

23. Ibid., 49, 53–54.

24. Wheeler, *The Complexion of Race*, 26–27.

25. Ivan Hannaford (1996), *Race: The History of an Idea in the West* (Washington, DC: Woodrow Wilson Center Press), 191, 208; Schiebinger, *Nature's Body*, 118–119, 129–31; Winthrop D. Jordan (1969), *White Over Black: American Attitudes Toward the Negro, 1550-1812* (Baltimore: Pelican Books), 222–23. A few Renaissance thinkers questioned the influence of climate on skin color, including Jean Bodin, who explained in his 1565 treatise, entitled *Method for Easy Comprehension of History*, that nature permanently marked various groups, with no "conversion" possible; and George Best, who defined blackness, in his 1578 *A True Discourse of the Late Voyages of Discovery*, as a "natural inflection" that "neither the Clime" nor a white mother's "good complexion" could alter. Quoted in Loomba, *Shakespeare, Race, and Colonialism*, 39, 54.

26. Michael Banton (1977), *The Idea of Race* (Boulder, CO: Westview Press), 31.

27. Excessive blood produced excitability; excessive black bile produced melancholy; excessive phlegm made people apathetic; and excessive yellow bile made people jaundiced in both skin and temperament. Excesses of any humor could produce an unbalanced personality and stained skin. See Loomba, *Shakespeare, Race, and Colonialism*, 53.

28. Wheeler, *The Complexion of Race*, 15, 22–23, 25–26. Johann Blumenbach (1752-1840) favored the theory of humors well into the eighteenth century (ibid.).

29. Wheeler, *The Complexion of Race*, 5.

30. Ibid., 96.

31. Linnaeus classified American Indians as wild; Europeans as white, sanguine, brawny, gentle, inventive, governed by customs and blue-eyed; Africans as capricious, crafty, indolent, and negligent; Hottentots as single-testicled; Chinese as long-headed; and Canadians as slant-headed. Jordan, *White Over Black*, 218–23. None of the variations undercut the unifying single "chain of universal being," however (ibid.).

32. Schiebinger, *Nature's Body*, 119.

33. Banton, *The Idea of Race*, 201.

34. In Blumenbach's theory of humors, peoples in the temperate zone between the fortieth and fiftieth degrees of latitude (including Spain, Italy, Greece, France, southern Germany, Georgia, and the Caucasus mountains) were most beautiful. Unlike most anthropologists, he chose a Caucasian female skull to represent that most favored race, although he used a Caucasian male, Jusuf Aguiah Efendi, as his racial prototype. See Schiebinger, *Nature's Body*, 129–31, and Horsman, *Race and Manifest Destiny*, 46–47.

35. Schiebinger, *Nature's Body*, 122–24, 138, 133. Blumenbach's selection of female beauty in Caucasian women as a mark of racial value took no account of Bernier's conclusion, in 1684, that they were probably descendants of white female slaves brought into the Levant in thirteenth through late fifteenth centuries. Such women fetched a particularly high price. Schiebinger, *Nature's Body*, 129–31.

36. Ibid., 122–25.
37. Ibid., 133–36.
38. Ibid., 156–57.
39. Ibid., 124–25; Jordan, *White Over Black*, 221.
40. Schiebinger, *Nature's Body*, 119, 161–69.
41. Ibid., 164–65.
42. Ibid., 159.

43. Linnaeus himself recognized that his was an artificial approach. His classification of groups above the rank of genus has now been abandoned, but his binomial system of nomenclature remains, along with many of his genera and species. Though Linnaeus took England by storm in 1750s and 1760s, he had detractors, such as Georges-Louis Leclerc, Comte de Buffon and William Smellie, chief compiler of the first edition of the *Encyclopedia Britannica*. See Schiebinger, *Nature's Body*, 28–29.

44. Schiebinger, *Nature's Body*, 21–22; Jordan, *White Over Black*, 218–19.
45. Schiebinger, *Nature's Body*, 23.
46. Ibid., 37–39.
47. Ibid., 140.

48. Shawn Michelle Smith (1999), *American Archives: Gender, Race, and Class in Visual Culture* (Princeton, NJ: Princeton University Press), 48; Rogers M. Smith (1997), *Civic Ideals: Conflicting Visions of Citizenship in U.S. History* (New Haven, CT: Yale University Press), 203.

49. Wiegman, *American Anatomies*, 53.
50. Jordan, *White Over Black*, 227.
51. Ibid., 224–25.
52. Hannaford, *Race*, 232.
53. R. Smith, *Civic Ideals*, 105; Horsman, *Race and Manifest Destiny*, 99, 116–17.
54. Schiebinger, *Nature's Body*, 140.
55. Joseph Wenzel, one of Soemmering's students, understood the ambiguities of sexual and racial difference. Schiebinger, *Nature's Body*, 118.
56. Ibid., 115–16.

57. Theorists of the eighteenth and nineteenth centuries identified from two to sixty-three races: Julien-Joseph Virey—two; Honoré Jacquinot—three; Immanuel Kant—four; Johan Blumenbach—five; Georges Buffon—six; John Hunter—seven; Louis Agassiz—eight; Charles Pickering—eleven; Jean Bory de St-Vincent—fifteen; M. Charles Desmoulins—sixteen; Samuel Morton—twenty-two; John Crawfurd—sixty; and Burke—sixty-three.

58. Morton first "measured" skull capacity using seeds that were sensitive to cranial shape, but when he turned to buckshot, which minimized cranial contours, he did not alter his conclusions about race and intelligence. In fact, he threw out data on Indians that contradicted his claims of Caucasian cranial size. See Stephen J. Gould (1981), *The Mismeasure of Man* (New York: Norton).

59. S. M. Smith, *American Archives*, 48; R. Smith, *Civic Ideals*, 203.

60. Schiebinger, *Nature's Body*, 156.

61. Ibid., 118.

62. Banton, *The Idea of Race*, 31.

63. Horsman, *Race and Manifest Destiny*, 124; David Brion Davis (2006), *Inhuman Bondage* (New York: Oxford University Press), 64–67. It wasn't actually Ham whom Noah cursed in Genesis 9:18–27, but Canaan, Ham's son. The story is the first in the Bible to use slavery to condemn someone, proving that "slavery is the result of human sin" (albeit, in this case, the sin of the father). The harsh punishment may indicate that Ham actually sodomized his father, since "uncovering nakedness" can be a euphemism for sexual intercourse. But since Ham's brothers, Shem and Japheth, took great care not to view their father's genitals, Ham's offense was probably viewing his father and thereby, as believed at the time, gaining mastery over him. Ham's descendants via Canaan were seen as despised black peoples, even though they included Nimrod, the first great king on earth (Genesis 10:8–9).

64. Loomba, *Shakespeare, Race, and Colonialism*, 35–36. *The Travels of Sir John Mandeville* (1371) was not an accurate historical record; even its authenticity remains uncertain. However, as the most popular book in medieval Europe, its motifs and legends clearly influenced its many readers.

65. Horsman, *Race and Manifest Destiny*, 124.

66. Hannaford, *Race*, 129, 133; Jordan, *White Over Black*, 43.

67. Wiegman, *American Anatomies*, 54.

68. Schiebinger, *Nature's Body*, 156–58.

69. R. Smith, *Civic Ideals*, 273.

70. Ibid., 292. Spencer's Lamarckian claim that acquired characteristics might be inherited (rather than Darwin's natural selection among random variations) appealed to many Americans because it supported the notion that social conditions could become biologically transmissible traits. Such acquired characteristics would eventually allow higher cultures to produce better people.

71. Ibid., 292. Followers of Spencer and Darwin believed that their theories both promoted and linked concepts of absolute gender and racial differences and hierarchies and supported the idea that societies follow their own natural

evolutionary course rather than that they develop from the tug and pull of power in the hands of various peoples, classes, *gens,* or races (ibid.).

72. R. Smith, *Civic Ideals,* 292, 294.

73. Ibid., 294. For a discussion of "Othellophilia," see Celia Daileader (2005), *Racism, Misogyny, and the Othello Myth: Inter-Racial Couples from Shakespeare to Spike Lee* (New York: Cambridge University Press). Daileader defines Othellophilia "as a cultural construct [that] is first and foremost *about women*—white women explicitly, as the 'subjects of representation'; black women implicitly, as the abjected and/or marginalized subjects of the suppressed counter-narrative" (10). White men project their guilt for sexual transgression onto black men and then control white women to prevent inter-racial sex. *Othello* has been popular on American stages partly because "it has served well as a cautionary tale for white women who might besmirch either their (sexual) 'purity' or that of their race. In lynching, white female sexuality justifies racist violence: in Othellophilia the woman is lynched too" (8–9). (More on this in Chapter 6.)

Chapter 3

1. Davis, *Inhuman Bondage,* 32–33. According to David Brion Davis, the first documentation of slavery comes from Sumer in 2000 B.C.E., but other sources identify Mesopotamia, in about 4000 B.C.E., as the first slave-holding society. Davis says the domestication of animals in Mesepotamia in 8000 B.C.E. was a template for the treatment of slaves, but Kirsten Fisher has another view: "the connection between slaves and livestock was . . . predicated not on the belief that Africans were animals but rather in the evocation of a degraded but fully present humanity." Slaves were likened to animals to humiliate them, not to proclaim them insensate, which would make them incapable of humiliation. Kirsten Fischer (2002), *Suspect Relations: Sex, Race, and Resistance in Colonial North Carolina* (Ithaca, NY: Cornell University Press), 105.

2. This history of slavery combines information from David Brion Davis (1966, rpt. 1988), *The Problem of Slavery in Western Culture* (New York: Oxford University Press); "Slavery," *Encyclopedia Britannica* (1998), 289–93; Milton Meltzer (1971), *Slavery: From the Rise of Western Civilization to the Renaissance* (New York: Cowles Book Company,); and Scott L. Malcomson (2000), *One Drop of Blood: The American Misadventure of Race* (New York: Farrar, Straus Giroux).

3. Stepan, "Race and Gender: The Role of Analogy in Science," 42.

4. Davis, *Inhuman Bondage,* 31–34. Aristotle could never really define the "natural slave" and admitted that the wrong men could be enslaved by force. In effect, Aristotle's "natural slave" "was very close to what a human being would be like if subjected to a genetic change similar to that of domesticated plants and animals." But no slave population was held in bondage long enough to undergo "genetic neoteny" that would permanently alter their appearance or behavior. The marks of the "natural" slave were usually the result of his/her enslavement (ibid.).

5. Lerner, *The Creation of Patriarchy*, 76–87. According to Davis in *Inhuman Bondage*, Lerner "has argued persuasively that the archetypal slave was a woman and that the status of slaves as inferior dependents was closely modeled on the status of women in patriarchal societies," 38.

6. Davis, *Inhuman Bondage*, 29.

7. Ibid., 38.

8. Ibid., 46, 61.

9. Ibid., 38.

10. The medieval Catholic Church did support slave marriage, but Aquinas and other spokesmen for the Church never suggested that such marriages should supersede the supreme authority of masters. Davis, *The Problem of Slavery in Western Culture*, 105–106.

11. Note that the date for associating skin color with slavery preceded the date for equating skin color with race.

12. Malcomson, *One Drop of Blood*, 152–56. African leaders in many areas enslaved their own people for both economic and political reasons. In urban sub-Saharan Africa, slaves were important symbols of power. In rural sub-Saharan Africa, they provided labor for economic development and lived under conditions similar to those in the American South. See Chapter 6 of Murray Gordon (1989), *Slavery in the Arab World* (New York: New Amsterdam Books), 128–50.

13. Malcomson, *One Drop of Blood*, 152–56. Many have documented the positive or neutral views of the Spanish and Portuguese about Africans, such as Malcomson (this note) and Ann Pescatello (1980), "The *Leyenda Negra* and the African in Sixteenth- and Seventeenth-Century Iberian Thought," *Catholic Historical Review* 66, no. 2:169–83. But others note "less than complimentary" depictions of Africans by Portuguese writers before 1470 and distinctly anti-black attitudes and rhetoric after black slavery became entrenched in Portugal. Sixteenth-century writers often "excoriated not only the slaves' blackness, but their supposed savagery, their 'brutish ways,' their libidinousness, their moral degeneracy, and their unorthodox religious practices." See A.J.R. Russell-Wood (1978), "Iberian Expansion and the Issue of Black Slavery," *The American Historical Review* 83, no.1, Supplement (Feb.): 39.

14. Kathleen M. Brown (1996), *Good Wives, Nasty Wenches, and Anxious Patriarchs: Gender, Race, and Power in Colonial Virginia* (Chapel Hill: University of North Carolina Press), 110.

15. Davis, *Inhuman Bondage*, 56.

16. Malcomson, *One Drop of Blood*, 138–39, 142; Gordon, *Slavery in the Arab World*, 100–01.

17. Ibid., 142.

18. Davis, *Inhuman Bondage*, 51.

19. Ibid., 239.

20. Davis, *The Problem of Slavery in Western Culture*, 70.

21. Ibid., 104–06, 201.

22. Jordan, *White Over Black*, 42. This concern is reflected in *Holinshed's Chronicles* of 1578, according to Jordan. Note, however, that it had nothing to do with race.

23. Davis, *The Problem of Slavery in Western Culture*, 78, 200, 204, 208.
24. Davis, *Inhuman Bondage*, 189.
25. Loomba, *Shakespeare, Race, and Colonialism*, 24.
26. Other cognates include the Old French *rasse*. The Italian *razza* is of more obscure origin.
27. Hannaford, *Race*, 175.
28. Ibid., 111.
29. Tuana, *The Less Noble Sex*, 162.
30. Loomba, *Shakespeare, Race, and Colonialism*, 25.
31. Tuana, *The Less Noble Sex*, 101, 120, 149, 124.
32. Loomba, *Shakespeare, Race, and Colonialism*, 16, 24–25. Jews were seen as threatening to the emerging Spanish nation because they were considered wanderers with closer affinity to their religion than to any one place. In this case, religion was more important to the idea of nation than was bloodline, heritage, or race, since the word *race* was not typically used in reference to Jews.
33. Brown, *Good Wives, Nasty Wenches, and Anxious Patriarchs*, 111.
34. Davis, *The Problem of Slavery in Western Culture*, 218–82.
35. Hannaford, *Race*, 12, 35, 42.
36. Joan Kelly (1982), "Early Feminist Theory and the *Querelle des Femmes*, 1400-1789," *Signs* 8, no. 1:9, 10–11, 15–20, 23.
37. Ibid., 9.
38. Brown, *Good Wives, Nasty Wenches, and Anxious Patriarchs*, 14–15.
39. Hannaford, *Race*, 182–84.
40. Isenberg, *Sex and Citizenship in Antebellum America*, 27.
41. Ibid., 193.
42. Brackette F. Williams (1996), "Introduction: Mannish Women and Gender after the Act," in *Women out of Place: The Gender of Agency and the Race of Nationality*, ed. Brackette F. Williams (New York: Routledge), 2, 6–9.

PART II: BODIES

PART II: Introduction

1. The quotation in this paragraph comes from Robyn Wiegman (1995), *Sexing the Difference* (Durham, NC: Duke University Press), 48. For interpretations of Foucault, see McWhorter, "Sex, Race, and Biopower," 44.
2. For more about Butler's view of performativity, see Butler, *Gender Trouble*, 135–37.
3. Wiegman, *Sexing the Difference*, 48.
4. Barbara J. Fields (1982), "Ideology and Race in American History," in *Region, Race, and Reconstruction: Essays in Honor of C. Vann Woodward*, ed. J. M. Kousser and J. M. McPherson (New York: Oxford University Press), 143–77.
5. Ibid.
6. Paraphrasing Winthrop Jordan, *White Over Black*, 80, in William F. Pinar (2001), *The Gender of Racial Politics and Violence in America: Lynching, Prison Rape, and the Crisis of Masculinity* (New York: Peter Lang Publishers), 76.

Chapter 4

1. R. Smith, *Civic Ideals*, 51–52.
2. A. Leon Higginbotham, Jr. and Barbara K. Kopytoff (1989, rpt. 2000), "Racial Purity and Interracial Sex in the Law of Colonial and Antebellum Virginia," (Lexis-Nexis Academic Universe Document), 9.
3. R. Smith, *Civic Ideals*, 59–63. The Iroquois were one exception.
4. Horsman, *Race and Manifest Destiny*, 24, 15.
5. Ladelle McWhorter (2004), "Sex, Race, and Biopower," *Hypatia* 19, no. 3 (Summer): 48; quotation is from Michel Foucault's 1976 lecture in *'Society Must Be Defended': Lectures at the Collège de France, 1975-1976*, trans. David Macey (New York: Picador, 2003)
6. Brown, *Good Wives, Nasty Wenches, and Anxious Patriarchs*, 219.
7. Ibid., 221–22, 243. Although free Indians had advantages over free blacks, "mustee" and "mustizo" became derogatory labels for Indians of mixed parentage by 1800.
8. Thomas More was influenced by the democratic constitution of the Iroquois Confederacy in the composition of his *Utopia* in 1516. John Locke extracted from it some of his own views of tolerance, natural equality, and rights. Early historians of the New World were impressed with Indian ideas of liberty, as well as with the absence from their societies of crime, jails, and greed, which were all too familiar in Europe. The colonists' ideas for confederation, as well as for the eventual Constitution of the United States (and even later, the United Nations charter), were probably influenced by Iroquois and other Indian practices. Benjamin Franklin's Albany Plan of Union reflects years of talking with Indian leaders. See Donald A. Grinde and Bruce E. Johansen (1991), *Exemplar of Liberty: Native America and the Evolution of Democracy* (Los Angeles: American Indian Studies Center), 13–20; and Wilbur R. Jacobs (1992), "Commentary: The American Indian Legacy of Freedom and Liberty," *American Indian Culture and Research Journal* 16, no. 4:188. The new nation also chose the Iroquois symbol of the bald eagle for its Great Seal and for dollar bills. Grinde and Johansen, *Exemplar of Liberty*, xxi. Suffragists Matilda Joslyn Gage and Elizabeth Cady Stanton found inspiration for their principles of gender equity and women's sovereign control over their own lives in the practices of the Six Nations of the Iroquois Confederacy. They observed the equal division of power between the sexes, the primacy of the mother-child bond, and women's freedoms within marriage, among other egalitarian practices. See Sally R. Wagner (1992), "The Influence on Women's Rights," in *Indian Roots of American Democracy*, ed. Jose Barreiro (Ithaca, NY: Cornell University Press), 118–20.
9. J.G.A. Pocock defines Harringtonians and Neo-Harringtonians as followers of English political theorist James Harrington (1611–1677), whose theory of citizenship was based on the notion that property ownership conferred independence on owners and gave them power over those who depended on their property for subsistence. Guns for use in individual or "the public quarrel" were symbols of citizenship rights. Neo-Harringtonians believed that Parliament must "exercise a jealous surveillance of government" to prevent encroachment on those rights. See Pocock (1971), *Politics, Language and Time: Essays on Political*

Thought and History (New York: Atheneum) 124, 131–32. Whether Pocock's explanation is an accurate portrayal of Harrington's republican views is a matter of some debate. Michael P. Zuckert calls Pocock's explanation "Whig political science." See Zuckert (1994), *Natural Rights and the New Republicanism* (Princeton, NJ: Princeton University Press), 182. But Rogers Smith (*Civic Ideals*), confirms Pocock's explanation. In any case, Harrington was not popular with the Crown. He was charged in 1661 with conspiracy to overthrow Charles II, although he was never convicted. *Encyclopedia Brittanica*, s.v. "James Harrington," http://www.britannica.com/EBchecked/topic/255874/James-Harrington (accessed January 12, 2007); Margaret Drabble and Jenny Stringer (2003), "Harrington, James," *The Concise Oxford Companion to English Literature*, http://www.encyclopedia.com/doc/1O54-HarringtonJames.html (accessed January 12, 2007).

10. R. Smith, *Civic Ideals*, 54–55, 61.
11. Brown, *Good Wives, Nasty Wenches, and Anxious Patriarchs*, 55.
12. Ibid., 65–67.
13. Ibid.
14. Ibid., 49–53.
15. Wagner, "The Influence on Women's Rights," 123–25.
16. American wives had more basic rights than their British counterparts, including the right of support, protection from a husband's violence, and rights to one-third of their husband's estate for life. Unlike British coverture, American coverture tied a woman's citizenship to that of her father and/or husband, as we shall see in more detail in Part IV. American Married Women's Property Acts, passed state-by-state from 1839 to 1913, rectified some of coverture's ills, but many American wives only got the legal right to their own earnings or to joint custody of their children in 1860.
17. R. Smith, *Civic Ideals*, 41, 58.
18. Ibid., 78–79.
19. R. Smith, *Civic Ideals*, 53. Colonists were ordered to remain east of that line, and the tribes were given the region between the Alleghenies and the Mississippi River from Florida to 475 miles north of Toronto.
20. The term "Indian reservation" originally meant "any land reserved from an Indian cession to the federal government regardless of the form of tenure." The modern meaning of Indian reservation emerged during the 1850s, "referring to land set aside under federal protection for the residence of tribal Indians." This meaning was firmly established in the Indian Major Crimes Act of March 3, 1885. However, the earliest treaty referring to various lands as a "reserve" for Indians was the Treaty with the Choctaws of November 16, 1805. See Felix S. Cohen (1982), *Felix S. Cohen's Handbook of Indian Law* (Charlottesville, VA: Michie Co.), 34–35. See also Malcomson, *One Drop of Blood*, 82–91, for Indians' response to the alleged lure of the West.
21. Gary A. Sokolow (2000), *Native Americans and the Law: A Dictionary* (Santa Barbara, CA: ABC-CLIO), 1–18. Tribal sovereignty was re-recognized by the 1934 Indian Reorganization Act (Wheeler-Howard Act), which stopped further allotments of Indian lands and enabled tribes to buy back their own

land and rebuild their holdings. Public Law 280, passed in the 1950s, restored legal jurisdiction over tribes to the authorities of six states. Full Indian self-determination did not finally get established until the 1970s. Current U.S. policy promotes tribal self-government and respect for the sovereignty of Indian nations. (Ibid., 6–7.) See also R. Smith, *Civic Ideals*, 461–62; and Will Roscoe (1991), *The Zuni Man-Woman* (Albuquerque: University of New Mexico Press), 176 ff.

22. Historians disagree about whether racist attitudes preceded or followed the legal codification of slavery in the U.S. Kathleen Brown, *Good Wives*; Winthrop Jordan, in *White Over Black*; and David Brion Davis, in *Inhuman Bondage*, argue that slavery was the primary motivation for racism in the colonies, however, and I agree, since early definitions of race before slavery was codified were tangentially related to slavery. Considering racism primary may erroneously assume the existence of race as a psychological and genetic fact before exploring the cause-and-effect relationship. Brown, *Good Wives, Nasty Wenches, and Anxious Patriarchs*, 109.

23. Ibid., 80, 86.

24. Ibid., 20–27, 368; Mary Beth Norton (1984), "The Evolution of White Women's Experience in Early America," *The American Historical Review* 89, no. 3: 611. According to Norton, Northeastern English women whose husbands were relatively long-lived were also among the most domesticated of colonial women, since they were even subjected to arranged marriages.

25. Jennifer L. Morgan (2004), *Laboring Women: Reproduction and Gender in New World Slavery* (Philadelphia: University of Pennsylvania Press), 74.

26. Brown, *Good Wives, Nasty Wenches, and Anxious Patriarchs*, 126, 116–19.

27. Ibid., 108, 116–18, 119, 122.

28. Ibid., 123, 126, 218–19.

29. Ibid., 2.

30. Ibid., 102–03. A woman's role in influencing the lines between "good wives" and "nasty wenches" was complicated by the fact that her own moral standing was also under continuous scrutiny. Any woman could turn from a good wife to a nasty wench overnight.

31. Ibid., 369.

32. Beth Day (1972), *Sexual Life Between Blacks and Whites: The Roots of Racism* (New York: World Publishing), 44–45.

33. A. Leon Higginbotham (1978), *In the Matter of Color: Race and the American Legal Process, The Colonial Period* (New York: Oxford University Press), 21, 27–29, 32.

34. Brown, *Good Wives, Nasty Wenches, and Anxious Patriarchs*, 177.

35. Ibid., 182.

36. Ibid., 182–83.

37. Karen W. Weierman (2000), " 'For the Better Government of Servants and Slaves': The Law of Slavery and Miscegenation," Lexis-Nexis Academic Universe Document, *Legal Studies Forum*, 3.

38. Higginbotham and Kopytoff, "Racial Purity and Interracial Sex," 13; Karen A. Getman (1984), "Sexual Control in the Slaveholding South: The Implementation and Maintenance of a Racial Caste System," *Harvard Women's Law Journal* 7:122–23; Martha Hodes (1997), *White Women, Black Men: Illicit Sex in the Nineteenth-Century South* (New Haven, CT: Yale University Press).
39. Brown, *Good Wives, Nasty Wenches, and Anxious Patriarchs*, 116–19.
40. Ibid.

Chapter 5

1. Getman, "Sexual Control in the Slaveholding South," 120. It was possible to view the diversion of the first shipload of African captives to Jamestown as a "godsend," since they would have faced certain slavery in the Spanish colonies, while the English might make them indentured servants.
2. Higginbotham, *In the Matter of Color*, 75–77. In Virginia, as the labor supply waned in the 1660s, the Assembly lengthened the terms required of Christian servants imported to the colony before age 16 and increased the age of termination to 24. Unrest fomented by such changes undoubtedly hastened the establishment of slavery. Brown, *Good Wives, Nasty Wenches, and Anxious Patriarchs*, 150.
3. Higginbotham, *In the Matter of Color*, 75–77, 20. By the time of King Philip's War in 1675, Indian slaves, especially women and children, were a common sight across southern New England.
4. Ibid, 75–77.
5. Steven Martinot (2007), "Motherhood and the Invention of Race," *Hypatia* 22, no. 2 (Spring): 83–84.
6. Weierman, " 'For the Better Government of Servants and Slaves,' " 9.
7. Higginbotham, *In the Matter of Color*, 34.
8. Martinot, "Motherhood and the Invention of Race," 84.
9. R. Smith, *Civic Ideals*, 64.
10. Higginbotham, *In the Matter of Color*, 27–28.
11. Weierman, " 'For the Better Government of Servants and Slaves,' " 9.
12. R. Smith, *Civic Ideals*, 104–105.
13. Gunner Myrdal (1944), "Racial Beliefs," in *An American Dilemma: The Negro Problem and Modern Democracy*, eds. Richard Sterner and Arnold Rose (New York: Harper & Brothers), 90.
14. Jordan, *White Over Black*, 462–67.
15. Many historians have assumed that Jacobs's book was written as well as published by Lydia Maria Child, a well-known white anti-slavery writer, but Jean Fagan Yellin uncovered the historical details of Jacobs's work, which was published under the pseudonym Linda Brent, in 2004. Yellin's research confirmed the accuracy of the story and the identities of Jacobs's master, Dr. James Norcom, and of the white man, Norcom's bachelor neighbor Samuel Tredwell Sawyer, with whom Jacobs produced the two children she left with

her grandmother while she hid. Jacobs entered into an affair with Sawyer, a descendant of a colonial governor of North Carolina, in order to protect herself from Norcom, who was threatening to make her his concubine. She hoped that Sawyer's status could protect her from Norcom, but she was wrong. David S. Reynolds (2004), "To Be a Slave: Review of Harriet Jacobs: A Life by Jean Fagan Yellin," *New York Times Book Review* (July 11): 25.

    16. R. Smith, *Civic Ideals*, 63; Hodes, *White Women, Black Men*, 28–29; Weierman, " 'For the Better Government of Servants and Slaves,' " 7, 9.

    17. Brown, *Good Wives, Nasty Wenches, and Anxious Patriarchs*, 132–35; 196.

    18. Peggy Pascoe (1991-92), "Race, Gender, and Intercultural Relations: The Case of Interracial Marriage," *Frontiers* 12, no. 1:7. It is possible that there were two laws passed in Maryland, one in 1663 and one in 1664. Zackodnik cites two separate laws, but Alpert says that the 1664 statute, which matches Zackodnik's version of the 1664 law, is often incorrectly cited as 1663. See Teresa Zackodnik (2001),"The Mulatto, Southern Courts, and Racial Identity," *American Quarterly* 53, no. 3:427; Jonathan L Alpert (1970), "The Origin of Slavery in the United States—the Maryland Precedent," *American Journal of Legal History* 189:194–95; and Weierman, " 'For the Better Government of Servants and Slaves,' " 7.

    19. R. Smith, *Civic Ideals*, 52; Higginbotham, *In the Matter of Color*, 19, 21, 27–29, 32, 34–35, 67. The formal status of perpetual chattel slavery was defined in legal codes throughout the colonies in the 1660s-80s. Fear of black servants' rebellion fostered both the concepts of whiteness and the politics of white solidarity in Massachusetts. Starting in 1698, various provincial laws were passed that defined and regulated the behavior of non-whites, as well as non-white slavery in the state, although blacks and Indians were still able to petition the courts for their freedom in Massachusetts as late as the 1730s. Higginbotham, 75–77; Brown, *Good Wives, Nasty Wenches, and Anxious Patriarchs*, 198.

    20. Brown, *Good Wives, Nasty Wenches, and Anxious Patriarchs*, 60–179. For a discussion of slave unrest and white anxiety in Barbados and the Carolinas, see Morgan, *Laboring Women*, 166–78. The gender patterns she describes resemble those in Virginia.

    21. Getman, "Sexual Control in the Slaveholding South," 141.

    22. Brown, *Good Wives, Nasty Wenches, and Anxious Patriarchs*, 2, 196.

    23. Hodes, *White Women, Black Men*, 28.

    24. Ibid., 43.

    25. Before the 1850s, Southern courts did not always consider slaves subhuman. In *State v. Jones* [1 Miss. (Walk.) 83, 83–85 (1820)], for example, the court ruled that slaves were both chattel and men, with some rights but no freedom, and determined that a white person could be indicted for the murder of a slave. By 1859, both the Mississippi and Georgia Supreme Courts concluded that "masters and slaves cannot be governed by the same common system of laws: so different are their positions, rights, and duties."

Neal v. Farmer, 9 Ga. 555, 579 (1851), quoted in *George v. State*, 37 Miss. 316, 320 (1859), quoted in Mark Tushnet (1975), "The American Law of Slavery, 1810-1860: A Study in the Persistence of Legal Autonomy," *Law and Society Review* 10, no. 1:119–33.

26. Getman, "Sexual Control in the Slaveholding South," 121.

27. Deborah Gray White (1999), *Ar'n't I a Woman?: Female Slaves in the Plantation South* (New York: W.W. Norton), 15.

28. Getman, "Sexual Control in the Slaveholding South," 130, 143–44, 146, 148.

29. Myrdal, "Racial Beliefs," 103.

30. Higginbotham, *In The Matter of Color*, 41.

31. Brown, *Good Wives, Nasty Wenches, and Anxious Patriarchs*, 367.

32. Drew Gilpin Faust (1996), *Mothers of Invention: Women of the Slaveholding South in the American Civil War* (New York: Vintage Books), 63–70.

33. Toni Morrison (1988), *Beloved: A Novel* (New York: New American Library), 70–71.

34. Brown, *Good Wives, Nasty Wenches, and Anxious Patriarchs*, 352.

35. Hodes, *White Women, Black Men*, 58.

36. Getman, "Sexual Control in the Slaveholding South," 136.

37. Ibid. Runaway or insubordinate slaves were likely to be killed, tortured, or mutilated, without mercy. See Trudier Harris (1984), *Exorcising Blackness: Historical and Literary Lynching and Burning Rituals* (Bloomington: Indiana University Press), 78.

38. Getman, "Sexual Control in the Slaveholding South," 138–39.

39. Hodes, *White Women, Black Men*, 86, 90–91.

40. Ibid., 98.

41. For later sources that confirm Norton's hypothesis, see Brown, *Good Wives, Nasty Wenches, and Anxious Patriarchs*; Faust, *Mothers of Invention*; and Hodes, *White Women, Black Men*.

42. Norton, "The Evolution of White Women's Experience," 597–610, 613.

43. R. Smith, *Civic Ideals*, 293.

44. Day, *Sexual Life Between Blacks and Whites*, 44, 106–107.

Chapter 6

1. Thomas C. Holt (1995), "Marking: Race, Race-Making, and the Writing of History," *American Historical Review* 100:5.

2. Pinar, *The Gender of Racial Politics*, 7, 16, 42.

3. Ibid., 16.

4. See for example Robyn Wiegman (1995), "The Anatomy of Lynching," *American Anatomies: Theorizing Race and Gender* (Durham, NC: Duke University Press); Pinar, *The Gender of Racial Politics*; Londa Schiebinger, *Nature's Body*; Grace Elizabeth Hale (1998), *Making Whiteness: The Culture of Segregation in*

the South, 1890-1940 (New York: Pantheon); and Siobhan B. Somerville (2000), *Queering the Color Line: Race and the Invention of Homosexuality in American Culture* (Durham, NC: Duke University Press).

5. Somerville, *Queering the Color Line*, 26–27.

6. That British colony became the Cape Colony after the Dutch ceded it to the British in 1814.

7. Schiebinger, *Nature's Body*, 168–71. Different historians attribute different ages to Bartmann, but all agree that she died in 1815.

8. Francette Pacteau (1994), *The Symptom of Beauty* (London: Reaktion Books), 127.

9. Schiebinger, *Nature's Body*, 168–71.

10. Wiegman, "The Anatomy of Lynching," citing Winthrop Jordan, *White Over Black*, 58–59.

11. Ibid.

12. Pinar, *The Gender of Racial Politics*, 70–71.

13. Lillian Serece Williams (1995), "Introduction," *Records of the National Association of Colored Women's Clubs, 1895-1992* (University Publications of America), http://www.lexisnexis.com/documents/academic/upa_cis/1555_RecsNatlAssocColWmsClubPt1.pdf (accessed July 23, 2007). In direct response to Jacks's letter, Ruffin called a meeting of African American women in Boston in 1895, to which one hundred black women came from across the U.S. The NACWC was founded the following year. Among its leaders was Ida B. Wells, and among its causes was attacking the credibility of bigots like Jacks. Despite its class implications and concessions to hypocritical standards of morality, the NACWC was an important outlet for black women's pride (ibid.).

14. Rachel F. Moran (2001), *Interracial Intimacy: The Regulation of Race and Romance* (Chicago: University of Chicago Press), 30–31.

15. William D. Carrigan and Clive Webb (2003), "The Lynching of Persons of Mexican Origin or Descent in the United States, 1848 to 1928," *Journal of Social History* 37, no. 2:421.

16. Hodes, *White Women, Black Men*, 131–32.

17. Ibid., 147.

18. Ibid., 201.

19. Martha Hodes (1993), "The Sexualization of Reconstruction Politics: White Women and Black Men in the South after the Civil War," in *American Sexual Politics: Sex, Gender, and Race since the Civil War*, ed. J. C. Fout and M. S. Tantillo (Chicago: University of Chicago Press), 62.

20. Hale, *Making Whiteness*, 233, 235.

21. Ibid., 204.

22. See Harris, *Exorcising Blackness*, 203–54 for the truly horrifying details.

23. Pinar, *The Gender of Racial Politics*, 11, 14.

24. Harris, *Exorcising Blackness*, 91–92.

25. Pinar, *The Gender of Racial Politics*, 7.

26. Ibid., 85.

27. Harris, *Exorcising Blackness*, 224, 234.

28. The phrase "Lynch's law" dates from an 1834 newspaper account about a man who was tarred and feathered in Lancaster, PA. Before 1830, Lynch's law referred primarily to border disputes where there were few civil authorities and where "situational homosexuality" tended to prevail. Pinar, *The Gender of Racial Politics*, 165–66.

29. Estimates range between four and five thousand lynchings in the U.S. between 1882 and 1903, although the "lynching era" extended past 1930. Pinar estimates that between 2,400 and 3,500 African American lynchings occurred during those years and that three percent of those victims were women. Ida B. Wells estimated that more than 10,000 black lives were lost to "rope and faggot." A few historians regard the years between 1865 and 1880 as the most deadly 15-year period, but most consider the years from 1885 to 1900 as the heyday of lynching. If the statistical period were extended to 1968, the total number of documented lynchings would rise to more than 4700. Pinar, *The Gender of Racial Politics*, 51; Carrigan and Webb, "The Lynching of Persons of Mexican Origin," 414.

30. Gail G. Bederman (1992), " 'Civilization,' the Decline of Middle-Class Manliness, and Ida B. Wells's Antilynching Campaign (1892-94)," *Radical History Review* 52:12.

31. Faust, *Mothers of Invention*, 229, 260–61.

32. Pinar, *The Gender of Racial Politics*, 268.

33. Jennifer Wriggins (1983), "Rape, Racism, and the Law," *Harvard Women's Law Journal* 6:111–12, 112–13, 124–25, 127.

34. Michael Pfeifer (2004), *Rough Justice: Lynching and American Society, 1847-1947* (Urbana: University of Illinois Press), 85.

35. Carrigan and Webb, "The Lynching of Persons of Mexican Origin," 422; Ken Gonzales-Day (2006), *Lynching in the West 1850-1935* (Durham, NC: Duke University Press), 205–28; Christopher Waldrep (2005), "Section 8 Introduction," in *Lynching in America*, ed. C. Waldrep (New York: New York University Press), 160; Pfeifer, *Rough Justice*, 85.

36. Carrigan and Webb, "The Lynching of Persons of Mexican Origin," 413.

37. Gonzales-Day, *Lynching in the West*, 205–28.

38. Victor Jew (2003), " 'Chinese Demons': The Violent Articulation of Chinese Otherness and Interracial Sexuality in the U.S. Midwest, 1885-1889," *Journal of Social History* 37, no. 2:389–410.

39. John R. Wunder (1992), "Anti-Chinese Violence in the American West, 1850-1910," in *Law for the Elephant, Law for the Beaver: Essays in the Legal History of the North American West*, ed. John McLaren, Hamar Foster and Chet Orloff (Pasadena, CA: Ninth Judicial Circuit Historical Society), 214.

40. Carrigan and Webb, "The Lynching of Persons of Mexican Origin," 420.

41. Jew, " 'Chinese Demons,' " 391–92, 396; Arthur Bonner (1997), *Alas! What Brought Thee Hither? The Chinese in New York, 1800-1950* (Madison, NJ: Fairleigh Dickinson University Press), 45.

42. Chiung Hwang Chen (1996), "Feminization of Asian (American) Men in the U.S. Mass Media: An Analysis of 'The Ballad of Little Jo,'" *Journal of Communication Inquiry* 20, no. 2:59.

43. Chen, "Feminization of Asian (American) Men," 60, 61, 64, 68.

44. Ian F. Haney López (1998), "Chance, Context, and Choice in the Social Construction of Race," in *The Latino/a Condition: A Critical Reader*, ed. R. Delgado and J. Stefancic (New York: New York University Press), 12.

45. Jonathon W. Warren and Frances W. Twine (1997), "White Americans, the New Minority? Non-Blacks and the Ever-Expanding Boundaries of Whiteness," *Journal of Black Studies* 28, no. 2:200–18. The Chinese themselves played into the black-white paradigm and sought identification as not-black (which they hoped would mean white) as their ticket to prosperity. The were somewhat successful at that by the 1960s, when southern Chinese were allowed to join the White Citizens' Council and white churches, to intermarry with whites, and to be classified as white on their drivers' licenses—all privileges denied to blacks.

46. Pfeifer, *Rough Justice*, 86.

47. Harris also recounts numerous examples of sex crimes connected with lynchings and analyzes them as rituals in *Exorcising Blackness*. See especially Chapter 1, "Ritual and Ritual Violence in American Life and Culture," 1–28.

48. Pinar, *The Gender of Racial Politics*, 11.

49. Gail Bederman (1995), *Manliness and Civiliation: A Cultural History of Gender and Race in the United States, 1880-1917* (Chicago: University of Chicago Press), 18–19. "Manly" was the term widely used prior to the 1890s to denote "the highest conceptions of manhood." "Masculine," which meant any characteristic, good or bad, that men shared, later took over as a term to denote male power. Today, they are mostly interchangeable.

50. In 1800, over 80 percent of American men were farmers; by 1880, only fifty percent farmed. In the first decades of the nineteenth century, four-fifths of men were self-employed; by 1870, only one-third worked for themselves. The largest factory in the U.S. before the Civil War employed 300 to 400 workers. By 1892, Edison Electric alone (GE's predecessor) had over 10,000 employees. Pinar, *The Gender of Racial Politics*, 268–69.

51. Bederman, *Manliness and Civilization*, 7.

52. See LeeAnn Whites (2005), *Gender Matters: Civil War, Reconstruction, and the Making of the New South* (New York: Palgrave Macmillan).

53. Somerville, *Queering the Color Line*, 25–33.

54. Several of Hopkins's novels explore the mulatta as a sign of unstable racial categories linked to unstable sexual categories. James Weldon Johnson's fictional *Autobiography of an Ex-Coloured Man*, first published in 1912 and reissued in 1927, depicts homosexual object choice as interracial desire and feminizes the mulatto at the moment he discovers his biracial identity. Somerville, *Queering the Color Line*, 105, 119.

55. Ibid., 11, 131.

56. Clara E. Rodríguez (1996), "Challenging Racial Hegemony: Puerto Ricans in the United States," in *Race*, ed. Steven Gregory and Roger Sanjek (New Brunswick, NJ: Rutgers University Press), 131–45.

57. David Eng (2001), *Racial Castration: Managing Masculinity in Asian America* (Durham, NC: Duke University Press), 2, 94, 117.

58. Bederman, *Manliness and Civilization*, 28.

59. Frank Van Nuys (2002), *Americanizing the West: Race, Immigrants, and Citizenship, 1890-1930* (Lawrence: University Press of Kansas), 27.

60. Bonner, *Alas! What Brought Thee Hither*, 40–41, 49.

PART III: BLOOD
Part III: Introduction

1. The title of this introduction is adapted from an unnamed Middle English poem that reads: "off women come duke and kyng/I zow tell without lesyng/of them com owre *manhed*." Quoted in Brackette F. Williams (1996), "Introduction: Mannish Women and Gender after the Act," in *Women out of Place: The Gender of Agency and the Race of Nationality*, ed. Brackette F. Williams (New York: Routledge), 1.

2. W.E.B. Du Bois (1900), "The American Negro at Paris," *American Monthly Review of Reviews* 22, no. 5 (November): 577.

3. M. Smith, *American Archives*, 180–86.

4. Christine B Hickman (2001), "The Devil and the One Drop Rule: Racial Categories, African Americans, and the U.S. Census," in *A Reader on Race, Civil Rights, and American Law: A Multiracial Approach*, ed. Timothy Davis, Kevin R. Johnson and George A. Martínez (Durham, NC: Carolina Academic Press), 7.

5. Moran, *Interracial Intimacy*, 30.

6. *State v. Will*, 18, N.C. 121, 165 (1834), quoted in Mark Tushnet, "The American Law of Slavery," 143.

7. *Bryan v. Walton*, 14 Ga. 185, 198, 205–06 (1853), quoted in Tushnet, "The American Law of Slavery," 172–73. Free blacks were allowed to own slaves in other southern states, however, including Virginia. Tushnet claims that the Georgia court's racist language was rare.

8. According to Greek mythology, the tunic of Nessus was the poisoned garment that killed Hercules. The tunic's deadly effect came from Hercules' own poisoned arrows, one of which had killed Nessus in the act of raping his wife, Deianeira. As he was dying, Nessus gave Deianeira a cup of his own blood, which he said would give Hercules extra strength. Naively, Deianeria spread the poisoned potion on Hercules' cloak as he was heading off to a tournament. After he had left, she spilled some of Nessus's potion onto the ground, where it began to foam and bubble. She immediately realized what she had done, and she sent word to Hercules. But by then it was too late. Hercules died a long and agonizing death caused by his own poison.

Chapter 7

1. Michael J. Bamshad and Steve E. Olson (2003), "Does Race Exist?" *Scientific American* 289.6 (December): 80–83.

2. Nicholas Wade, "2 Scholarly Articles Diverge On Role of Race in Medicine," *New York Times*, 20 March 2003, www.nytimes.com (accessed January 15, 2007).

3. Director of the National Human Genome Research Institute of the NIH, Dr. Francis S. Collins supports the use of race as a proxy for genetic variation until another way of locating genetically identifiable groups is found. See Nicholas Wade, "Articles Highlight Different Views on Genetic Basis of Race," New York Times, 27 October 2004, www.nytimes.com (accessed January 15, 2007).

4. Paul Gilroy (2000), *Against Race: Imagining Political Culture Beyond the Color Line* (Cambridge, MA: Belknap Press of Harvard University Press), 49.

5. Naomi Zack (1993), *Race and Mixed Race* (Philadelphia: Temple University Press), 14–15.

6. James Baldwin (1965), "White Man's Guilt," *Ebony* (August): 320; cited in David R Roediger, ed. (1988), *Black on White: Black Writers on What It Means to Be White* (New York: Schocken Books), 22.

7. Zackodnik, "The Mulatto, Southern Courts, and Racial Identity," 427.

8. Brown, *Good Wives, Nasty Wenches, and Anxious Patriarchs*, 215. The same legislation declared slaves "real estate" that could be bequeathed to heirs of their owners and deprived all non-white persons—"negro, mulatto, or Indian, Jew, Moor, Mahometan, or other infidel"—from owning Christian servants or slaves. See Weierman, " 'For the Better Government of Servants and Slaves,' " 4.

9. Helen C. Rountree (1990), *Pocahontas's People: The Powhatan Indians of Virginia through Four Centuries* (Norman, OK: University of Oklahoma Press), 179–80; Peter W. Bardaglio (1999), " 'Shamefull Matches': The Regulation of Interracial Sex and Marriage in the South before 1900," in *Sex, Love, Race: Crossing Boundaries in North American History*, ed. Martha Hodes (New York: New York University Press), 118.

10. Lisa Lindquist Dorr (1999), "Arm in Arm: Gender, Eugenics, and Virginia's Racial Integrity Acts of the 1920s," *Journal of Women's History* 11, no. 1:145.

11. Ibid.; Bardaglio, " 'Shamefull Matches,' " 118. Alabama, Georgia, Tennessee, and Texas eventually decreased the proportion to one-eighth.

12. Jonathon W. Warren and Frances Winddance Twine (1997), "White Americans, the New Minority? Non-Blacks and the Ever-Expanding Boundaries of Whiteness," *Journal of Black Studies* 28, no. 2:118–19.

13. Zackodnik, "The Mulatto, Southern Courts, and Racial Identity," 436.

14. Lay, "Sexual Racism," 171.

15. Weierman, " 'For the Better Government of Servants and Slaves,' " 5–6; Rountree, *Pocahontas's People*, 191.

16. Higginbotham and Kopytoff, "Racial Purity and Interracial Sex," 7; Rountree, *Pocahontas's People*, 191.

17. Although the Jacksonians defied many ideas of their intellectual muse, Thomas Jefferson, who emphasized the consent of the governed, they were also encouraged by Jefferson's disparagement of Negro slaves.

18. R. Smith, *Civic Ideals*, 203.

19. Zackodnik, "The Mulatto, Southern Courts, and Racial Identity," 441.

20. Derryn E. Moten (1999), "Racial Integrity or 'Race Suicide': Virginia's Eugenic Movement, W.E.B. Du Bois, and the Work of Walter A. Plecker," *Negro History Bulletin* (April-September):6.

21. S. M. Smith, *American Archives*, 32–48; Moten, "Racial Integrity or 'Race Suicide,'" 2.

22. R. Smith, *Civic Ideals*, 203–05, 293.

23. Moran, *Interracial Intimacy*, 54.

24. Lay, "Sexual Racism," 169.

25. Helen Catterall (1968), *Judicial Cases Concerning American Slavery and the Negro*, Vol. 5 (Shannon: Irish University Press), 6–7. The Ohio appeals court judge was J. Read.

26. R. Smith, *Civic Ideals*, 286–88.

27. Ibid., 286–88, 291. Reconstruction began declining in the 1870s and was finally repudiated in the 1890s, although the Republican Party that started it stayed in power almost continuously from 1864 to 1912 (ibid., 286).

28. Ibid., 289, 304.

29. Ibid., 291.

30. Peggy Pascoe (2000), "Miscegenation Law, Court Cases, and Ideologies of 'Race' in Twentieth-Century America," in *Unequal Sisters: A Multicultural Reader in U.S. Women's History*, ed. Vicki Ruiz and Ellen Carol DuBois (New York: Routledge), 163.

31. Many responsible scientists protested against eugenics in the early days. In 1911, delegates from 50 countries, including W.E.B. Du Bois and Franz Boas from the U.S., gathered in London to proclaim that members of all races have "equal intellect, enterprise, morality, and physique." Their claim did little to stop the march of eugenics http://www.pbs.org/race/000_About/002-03_igodeeper.htm (accessed October 15, 2006).

32. Elof Carlson, "Scientific Origins of Eugenics" http:www.eugenicsarchive.org/html/eugenics/essay_2_fs.html (accessed December 10, 2006) and Steve Seldon, "Eugenics Popularization," Image Archive on the American Eugenics Movement, 2004, http//:www.eugenicsarchive.org/html/eugenics/essay_6_fs.html (accessed December 10, 2006); Pascoe, "Miscegenation Law," 169.

33. Lay, "Sexual Racism," 171.

34. Seldon, "Eugenics Popularization." The American Eugenics Society was founded as the American Eugenics Committee in 1921 and renamed in 1925 (ibid.).

Chapter 8

1. This analysis is based on David Schneider's germinal work on kinship in *American Kinship: A Cultural Account*, 2nd ed. (Chicago: University of Chicago Press, 1980). Most Americans are unaware of the rules and symbols of their kinship system or do not recognize that there is an American kinship system. Although anthropologists no longer claim universality for the kinship mechanisms I describe here, among them David Schneider himself, their historical effects on American kinship remain significant. See David Schneider (1984), *A Critique of the Study of Kinship* (Ann Arbor: University of Michigan Press); and Judith Butler (2002), "Is Kinship Always Already Heterosexual?" *differences* 13, no. 1:14–44.

2. Debates about homosexual marriage or sex in religious, moral, or medical terms could well camouflage this subconscious dread of mis-spent blood.

3. See Sally L. Kitch (1989), *Chaste Liberation: Celibacy and Female Cultural Status* (Urbana, IL: University of Illinois Press): 26–27, 34–35; and Naomi Zack (1995), "Mixed Black and White Race and Public Policy," *Hypatia* 10 (Winter): 122. Gender symbolism is neither identical to real world conditions nor consistent across racial groups. Still, gender symbolism typically restricts women in all racial and ethnic groups.

4. See Ian F. Haney López (1996), *White by Law: The Legal Construction of Race* (New York: New York University Press).

5. Quoted in Moten, "Racial Integrity or 'Race Suicide,'" 4. The Anglo Saxon Clubs of America approved of the KKK's goals but not its violent methods. Their founder was John Powell, pianist and author of White America (Dorr, "Arm in Arm," 152).

6. Zackodnik, "The Mulatto, Southern Courts, and Racial Identity," 440, n. 21. The word "mulatto" appeared in Virginia law as early as 1666 to indicate that mixed-race status did not exempt a person from slavery, according to Winthrop Jordan, *White Over Black*, 168.

7. Getman, "Sexual Control in the Slaveholding South," 130.

8. Lay, "Sexual Racism," 167.

9. Gary B. Nash (1995), "The Hidden History of Mestizo America," *The Journal of American History* 82, no. 3:10–11.

10. Malcomson, *One Drop of Blood*, 62–63; Richard Godbeer (1999), "Eroticizing the Middle Ground: Anglo-Indian Sexual Relations Along the Eighteenth-Century Frontier," in *Sex, Love, Race: Crossing Boundaries in North American History*, ed. Martha Hodes (New York: New York University Press), 94. In 1803, when he completed the Louisiana Purchase, Jefferson expressed his hope that Indians and whites would "meet and blend together, . . . intermix, and become one people,' thereby consolidating the country into 'one nation only." In 1808, he told an Indian delegation, "you will mix with us by marriage, your blood will run in our veins, and will spread with us over this great continent." William G. McLoughlin (1981), *Cherokee Renascence in the*

New Republic (Princeton, NJ: Princeton University Press), 34–37. Quoted in Malcomson, *One Drop of Blood*, 62–63.

11. Malcomson, *One Drop of Blood*, 159.

12. Ibid., 61–64.

13. Ibid., 83.

14. Reginald Horsman (1975), "Scientific Racism and the American Indian in the Mid-Nineteenth Century," *American Quarterly* 27, no. 2 (May): 158–59.

15. The proposal was delivered to the Superintendent of Indian Affairs, Colonel A. Cumming, via Indian Agent Jonathan W. Whitfield between August and October of 1854. It was included in the 1854-1855 Report of the Secretary of the Interior. U.S. House. Report of the Secretary of the Interior. *Executive Documents*. 33rd cong., 2nd Session, 1854-55, Volume 5: 302.

16. Horsman, "Scientific Racism and the American Indian," 159–160, 166.

17. Zackodnik, "The Mulatto, Southern Courts, and Racial Identity," 443.

18. Hodes, *White Women, Black Men*, 98–99.

19. Zackodnik, "The Mulatto, Southern Courts, and Racial Identity," 435. Zackodnik's analysis contradicts critical race theory, which holds that the "one-drop rule" solidified the denial of white privilege—especially the property value of whiteness—more rigidly than the scrutiny of bodies had done.

20. Quoted in Getman, *Sexual Control in the Slaveholding South*, 150.

21. Zackodnik, "The Mulatto, Southern Courts, and Racial Identity," 443.

22. Higginbotham and Kopytoff, "Racial Purity and Interracial Sex," 16–17.

23. Williams, "Introduction," 17–18.

24. For a particular case in which this occurred, see Hodes, *White Women, Black Men*, 115. For the history of *vis imaginativa*, see Londa Schiebinger, *Nature's Body*, 163. Peter Bardaglio explains that some judges also resisted divorce suits in cases of black babies born to white women. In two cases in 1832, North Carolina Chief Justice Thomas Ruffin told two men, who admitted to premarital intercourse with their fiancées, that any husband who marries a "wanton woman" deserves a black baby. Bardaglio, " 'Shamefull Matches,' " 120–21.

25. See Hodes, *White Women, Black Men*, 119.

26. Zackodnik, "The Mulatto, Southern Courts, and Racial Identity," 440.

27. Moran, *Interracial Intimacy*, 56–57.

28. Ibid., 55. Japanese women married to white men were more likely to be considered white, to avoid internment, and to receive permission to move to the West Coast than were Japanese men married to white women.

29. Zackodnik, "The Mulatto, Southern Courts, and Racial Identity," 440.

30. Hodes, "The Sexualization of Reconstruction Politics," 67.

31. Hickman, "The Devil and the One Drop Rule," 15–16.
32. Beth Day (1972), *Sexual Life between Blacks and Whites: The Roots of Racism* (New York: World Publishing), 50–51.
33. Somerville, *Queering the Color Line*, 84.
34. Day, *Sexual Life between Blacks and Whites*, 62.

Chapter 9

1. Hodes, *White Women, Black Men*, 144.
2. Paul Lombardo (2004), "Eugenics Sterilization Laws," Image Archive on the American Eugenics Movement, http//:www.eugenicsarchive.org/html/eugenics/essay_8_fs.html (accessed December 11, 2006).
3. Unlike race, intelligence, moral turpitude, or mental illness, sexually transmitted diseases can actually be measured in the blood. See Pascoe (2000), 169–70.
4. Of the thirty states whose anti-miscegenation laws stayed on the books until the civil rights movement, sixteen waited to remove them until (or well after) the Supreme Court nullified such laws in 1967: Alabama, Arkansas, Delaware, Florida, Georgia, Kentucky, Louisiana, Mississippi, Missouri, North Carolina, Oklahoma, South Carolina, Tennessee, Texas, Virginia and West Virginia. Fourteen states had anti-miscegenation laws but repealed them in the 1940s or 1950s: Arizona, California, Colorado, Idaho, Indiana, Maryland, Montana, Nebraska, Nevada, North Dakota, Oregon, South Dakota, Utah and Wyoming. Chapter 7: "The Laws against Race." http://www.eugenics-watch.com/roots/chap07.html (accessed December 15, 2006). Alabama was the last state to repeal its ant-miscegenation law because it was part of its state constitution. (In the required statewide vote in November 2000, 40 percent of the electorate voted to keep the ban.) South Carolina repealed its law in 1998. "Miscegenation - Anti-miscegenation laws." http://www.experiencefestival.com/a/Miscegenation_-_Anti-miscegenation_laws/id/1770956 (accessed January 16, 2007); and "Alabama Removes Ban on Interracial Marriage," *USA Today*, 7 November 2000, http://www.usatoday.com/news/vote2000/al/main03.htm (accessed January 16, 2007).
5. Hodes, "The Sexualization of Reconstruction Politics," 164, 176; R. Smith, *Civic Ideals*.
6. Getman, "Sexual Control in the Slaveholding South," 122–23; Weierman, " 'For the Better Government of Servants and Slaves,' " 11. Seventeenth-century Dutch Lutherans condoned interracial marriages and allowed Negroes into their church. See Graham Russell Hodges, "The Pastor and the Prostitute: Sexual Power among African Americans and Germans in Colonial New York," in Hodes, "The Sexualization of Reconstruction Politics," 61.
7. Brown, *Good Wives, Nasty Wenches, and Anxious Patriarchs*, 131.
8. Quoted in Jonathan L. Alpert (1970), "The Origin of Slavery in the United States—the Maryland Precedent," *American Journal of Legal History* 189:194–95.

9. Quoted in Alpert, "The Origin of Slavery in the United States," 209–11. Ten thousand pounds of tobacco was a huge fine.

10. Martinot, "Motherhood and the Invention of Race," 88.

11. Ibid. The scholars who agree that anti-miscegenation legislation had a female focus, despite gender-neutral or inclusive language, include Higginbotham and Krytoff, *Racial Purity and Interracial Sex*; López, *White By Law*; Lay, "Sexual Racism"; Hodes, *White Women, Black Men*; and Weierman, " 'For the Better Good of Servants and Slaves.' " Maryland's 1692 law also condemned to lifetime slavery all Negro men married to English women, according to Alpert (1970), 210. Such provisions certainly discouraged inter-racial marriage.

12. Weierman, " 'For the Better Government of Servants and Slaves,' " 7.

13. Higginbotham and Kopytoff, "Racial Purity and Interracial Sex," 15–16.

14. Ibid.

15. Lay, "Sexual Racism," 167–68.

16. Weierman, " 'For the Better Government of Servants and Slaves,' " 5. The 1723 law also prohibited all meetings between slaves and free blacks or whites and reduced the possibility of manumission for slaves (ibid.).

17. Ibid., 7–8. When English law replaced Louisiana's 1724 Code Noir in 1808, conflicts arose as white fathers tried to emancipate and leave property to their mixed-race children.

18. Bardaglio, " 'Shamefull Matches,' " 119.

19. Weierman, " 'For the Better Government of Servants and Slaves,' " 10.

20. Ibid.

21. Bardaglio, " 'Shamefull Matches,' " 117.

22. By the end of slavery, mulattoes born to white women and black men comprised only thirteen percent of all Negroes in the U.S. See Laurence Glasco (1988), "Miscegenation," in *Dictionary of Afro-American Slavery*, ed. Randall M. Miller and John David Smith (Westport, CT: Greenwood Press), 476.

23. Weierman, " 'For the Better Government of Servants and Slaves,' " 10. Rhode Island passed its law in 1881, Maine and Michigan followed in 1883 and Ohio in 1887.

24. Bardaglio, " 'Shamefull Matches,' " 122. Prison terms ranged from six months in Georgia to ten years in Florida, Mississippi, and North Carolina.

25. The following states were among those targeting Malays, Mongolians, and/or Chinese and Japanese in their anti-miscegenation statutes after the Civil War: Arizona; California; Idaho; Mississippi; Missouri; Montana; Nebraska; Nevada; Oregon; Utah; and Wyoming. The only jurisdictions that never had anti–miscegenation laws of any kind were Connecticut, the District of Columbia, Minnesota, New Hampshire, New Jersey, Vermont, and Wisconsin. David H. Fowler, "Northern Attitudes Towards Interracial Marriage: A Study of Legislation and Public Opinion in the Middle Atlantic States and the States of the Old Northwest," PhD diss., Yale University, 1968.

26. López, "Chance, Context, and Choice in the Social Construction of Race," 9–16.
27. Moran, *Interracial Intimacy*, 17.
28. Ibid., 31–32. The California criminal legislation was proposed in 1901 but not actually passed until 1905 because of procedural irregularities.
29. Ibid., 32. Moran quotes Assemblyman Johnson in the 1909 California legislative session.
30. Glenn, *Unequal Freedom*, 191.

Chapter 10

1. Higginbotham and Kopytoff, "Racial Purity and Interracial Sex," 22.
2. R. Smith, *Civic Ideals*, 69.
3. Hodes, *White Women, Black Men*, 197, 204, 206.
4. Ibid., 153, 155.
5. Harriet Jacobs's slave narrative contained stories of white women forcing slaves into sex, sometimes for revenge against their husbands or fathers (by choosing a mean slave to father a man's first grandchild, for example). Harriet A. Jacobs (1988), *Incidents in the Life of a Slave Girl*, Schomburg library of nineteenth-century black women writers (New York: Oxford University Press).
6. Hodes, *White Women, Black Men*, 176–79, 190–92, 196.
7. Hale, *Making Whiteness*, 235–36, 285–86.
8. Pfeifer, *Rough Justice*, 85–87.
9. Moran, *Interracial Intimacy*, 37–40.
10. Ibid., 200–01.
11. Higginbotham and Kopytoff, "Racial Purity and Interracial Sex," 21.
12. Dorothy Roberts (1997), *Killing the Black Body: Race, Reproduction, and the Meaning of Liberty* (New York: Pantheon), 43–44; Morgan, *Laboring Women*, 182–83.
13. Roberts, *Killing the Black Body*, 51–52.
14. Ibid., 14–15.
15. Williams, "Introduction," 15.
16. M. Smith, *American Archives*, 140–43. By their vote, the DAR ironically valorized the male-dominated political structures that had denied women access to the public sphere in which Revolutionary patriotism could be achieved.
17. Ibid., 150, 152–53. Cooper was also responding to patriarchy in the black community. She was addressing black men as well as the white community when she wrote, "Only the Black Woman can say 'when and where I enter, in the quiet, undisputed dignity of my womanhood . . . then and there the whole *Negro race enters with me.*' "
18. Ibid., 122, 125–27. In the family album formats marketed during the 1880s and 1890s, racial blood was monitored over the generations (à la

Galton) and historical influences were subordinated to individuals' prosperity and happiness.

19. Dorr, "Arm in Arm," 146–48.

20. According to Supreme Court Justice Oliver Wendell Holmes, in *Buck v. Bell* in 1927, preventing "feeble minded" women from reproducing would keep states from being "swamped with incompetence." Quoted in Moran, *Interracial Intimacy*, 83.

21. Dorr, "Arm in Arm," 149–50.

22. Ibid., 153.

23. Ibid., 156, 157, 159.

24. Richard B. Sherman (1988), " 'The Last Stand': The Fight for Racial Integrity in Virginia in the 1920s," *The Journal of Southern History* 54, no. 1 (February): 74–76; Dorr, "Arm in Arm," 151–52.

25. Ibid., 158. The internal quotation comes from a letter to the *Richmond Times-Dispatch* of February 28, 1926, by Donald C. Wingo.

PART III: CONCLUSION

1. Lyde Cullen Sizer (1999), "Still Waiting: Intermarriage in White Women's Civil War Novels," in *Sex, Love, Race*, ed. Hodes, 255–64.

PART IV: CITIZENSHIP

Part IV: Introduction

1. Alice Kessler-Harris (2001), *In Pursuit of Equity: Women, Men, and the Quest for Economic Citizenship in 20th Century America* (New York: Oxford University Press), 10.

2. Eileen Boris (2005), "On the Importance of Naming: Gender, Race, and the Writing of Policy History," *The Journal of Policy History* 17, no. 1:82–83.

3. Eileen Boris (1995), "The Racialized Gendered State: Constructions of Citizenship in the United States," *Social Politics* 2:162–63.

4. Glenn, *Unequal Freedom*, 53.

5. Ruth Lister (2003), *Citizenship: Feminist Perspectives*, 2nd ed. (New York: New York University Press), 14–15.

6. Aihwa Ong (1999), "Cultural Citizenship as Subject Making: Immigrants Negotiate Racial and Cultural Boundaries in the United States," in *Race, Identity, and Citizenship: A Reader*, ed. Rodolfo D. Torres, Louis F. Miron, and Jonathan Xavier Inda (New York: Blackwell), 263–264.

7. Some women were able to vote in school board elections in the nineteenth century. By 1900, twenty-four states allowed women to vote in such elections. See M. Margaret Conway et al. (2005), *Women and Political Participation: Cultural Change in the Political Arena* (Washington, DC: Congressional Quarterly Press), 7–8.

8. Martha Gardner, *The Qualities of a Citizen: Women, Immigration, and Citizenship, 1870-1965* (Princeton, NJ: Princeton University Press), 157.

9. Isenberg, *Sex and Citizenship in Antebellum America*, 21–26.

10. The Federalists' Naturalization, Alien Friends, Alien Enemies, and Sedition Acts of 1798 increased residency requirement for naturalized citizens to 14 years. Congress supported Thomas Jefferson's desire to liberalize such nativist measures in 1802, by reducing the residency requirement to five years in the U.S. and one year in the state in which the candidate for naturalization applied. A declaration of intent had to be filed three years before an application for citizenship. R. Smith, *Civic Ideals*, 162–68.

11. Nancy F. Cott (1998), "Marriage and Women's Citizenship in the United States, 1830–1934," *American Historical Review* 103, no. 5 (December): 1457.

12. Glenn, *Unequal Freedom*, 243.

Chapter 11

1. Carol Pateman (1988), *The Sexual Contract* (Stanford, CA: Stanford University Press), 8.

2. Charles W. Mills (1997), *The Racial Contract* (Ithaca, NY: Cornell University Press), 6.

3. Ibid., 14, 27, 32–33.

4. Ian F. Haney López, *White by Law*, 123.

5. Andrew Parker, Mary Russo, Doris Sommer, and Patricia Yaeger (1992), "Introduction," in *Nationalisms and Sexualities*, ed. Andrew Parker et al. (New York: Routledge), 5.

6. Brackette F. Williams, "Introduction," 6, 15, 9–10.

7. Brown, *Good Wives, Nasty Wenches, and Anxious Patriarchs*, 281.

8. Parker et al., "Introduction," 6, 11. Ghandi used such a trope to staunch national crises in India.

9. Anne McClintock (1991), " 'No Longer in a Future Heaven': Woman and Nationalism in South Africa," *Transition* 50:105.

10. Teresa de Lauretis (1988), "Sexual Indifference and Lesbian Representation," in Parker et al., *Nationalisms and Sexualities*, 7.

11. Parker et al., "Introduction," 6.

12. Williams, "Introduction," 9–10.

13. Ibid., 21, 22.

14. Ong, "Cultural Citizenship as Subject Making," 266.

15. Williams, "Introduction," 9.

16. Ong, "Cultural Citizenship as Subject Making," 263–65.

Chapter 12

1. Pauline Schloesser (2002), *The Fair Sex: White Women and Racial Patriarchy in the Early American Republic* (New York: New York University Press), 41–42; Albert Bushnell Hart (1905), "The Realities of Negro Suffrage,"

Proceedings of the American Political Science Association (2nd Annual Meeting) 2:150.

2. Cott, "Marriage and Women's Citizenship," 1457.

3. Ibid., 1451.

4. R. Smith, *Civic Ideals*, 390; Cott, "Marriage and Women's Citizenship," 1452.

5. Ann Marie Nicolosi (2001), " 'We Do Not Want Our Girls to Marry Foreigners': Gender, Race and American Citizenship," *NWSA Journal* 13, no. 3:1–21.

6. Cott, "Marriage and Women's Citizenship," 1455.

7. Joan Hoff-Wilson (1991), *Law, Gender, and Injustice: A Legal History of U. S. Women* (New York: New York University Press), 128.

8. Isenberg, *Sex and Citizenship in Antebellum America*, 196–97; 144–45.

9. Candice Lewis Bredbenner (1998), *A Nationality of Her Own: Women, Marriage, and the Law of Citizenship* (Berkeley: University of California Press), 58.

10. Isenberg, *Sex and Citizenship in Antebellum America*, 192–94. If strength is the qualification for citizenship, some women argued, why not rank men according to their strength? (ibid., 145).

11. Ibid., 195–203.

12. Ibid., 171, 173–74.

13. Cott, "Marriage and Women's Citizenship," 1453. Independence was such a norm of white manhood suffrage that state constitutions sometimes excluded paupers from the franchise, even after 1850, when most states eliminated property ownership as a voting qualification.

14. Isenberg, *Sex and Citizenship in Antebellum America*, 171, 107. A petition sent to the 1853 Massachusetts state constitutional convention argued that the law *could* have enabled the "incapacitated" to function and protect themselves instead of punishing them for their incapacity.

15. Ibid., 174.

16. R. Smith, *Civic Ideals*, 390.

17. Isenberg, *Sex and Citizenship in Antebellum America*, 108–09, 111.

18. Ibid., 202.

19. Ibid., 111–113, 202.

20. Ibid., 112.

21. The Fourteenth Amendment declared all persons born within the United States to be U.S. citizens, but Congress also amended naturalization requirements in 1870 and extended naturalization eligibility to "aliens being free white persons, and to aliens of African nativity and to persons of African descent." *An Act to amend the Naturalization Laws and to punish Crimes against the same, and for other Purposes, Statutes at Large of the United States of America, 1789–1873* 16 (1871): 254–256. That revision of §2169, U.S. Revised Statutes, actually paved the way for future confusion, since it appeared to apply a color test but did so by reference to geography.

22. Isenberg, *Sex and Citizenship in Antebellum America*, 147.
23. Gardner, *The Qualities of a Citizen*, 124, 15; Cott, "Marriage and Women's Citizenship," 1458.
24. Cott, "Marriage and Women's Citizenship," 1460.
25. Ibid., 1461.
26. Emphasis mine. Ibid., 1465; Bredbenner, *A Nationality of Her Own*, 9, 134–35.
27. Susan M. Sterett (1999), "Review: On Citizenship," *Law & Society Review* 33, no. 3:8.
28. Cott, "Marriage and Women's Citizenship," 1465.
29. Gardner, *The Qualities of a Citizen*, 124.
30. Xiaojian Zhao (2002), *Remaking Chinese America: Immigration, Family, and Community, 1940-1965* (New Brunswick, NJ: Rutgers University Press), 37–38.
31. Gardner, *The Qualities of a Citizen*, 121–25, 128.
32. Cott, "Marriage and Women's Citizenship," 1469.
33. Gardner, *The Qualities of a Citizen*, 156 n. 62, 174.
34. Ibid., 174; Sterett, "Review," 241; Zhao, *Remaking Chinese America*, 24.
35. Sterett, "Review," 243–44; Gardner, *The Qualities of a Citizen*, 231–32.
36. Cott, "Marriage and Women's Citizenship," 1473.
37. Isenberg, *Sex and Citizenship in Antebellum America*, 192–93.

Chapter 13

1. Bill Ong Hing (2004), *Defining America Through Immigration Policy* (Philadelphia: Temple University Press), 15; Hoff-Wilson, *Law, Gender, and Injustice* 175–76.
2. Judith Apter Klinghoffer and Lois Elkis (1992), " 'The Petticoat Electors': Women's Suffrage in New Jersey, 1776–1807," *Journal of the Early Republic* 12, no. 2:159–60, 167–69.
3. As the only state to enfranchise women, New Jersey was also the only state that debated the issue of female enfranchisement or disenfranchisement.
4. Klinghoffer and Elkis, " 'The Petticoat Electors,' " 184. The internal quote is from a legislator, originally quoted in Rev. John Pierpont's *Centinel of Freedom*, March. 16, 1802. Other related material can be found on pp.188–89 and 193.
5. Klinghoffer and Elkis, " 'The Petticoat Electors,' " 175, 187–90. Although aliens came under increased scrutiny as relations with Europe deteriorated in the early nineteenth century, exclusion from the franchise for most European male aliens was usually only temporary. White women who wanted to protest their own disenfranchisement recognized the futility of

doing so. Even though the state Supreme Court had ruled against that loss of rights in *Carpenter v. Cornish*, the New Jersey legislative council was the court of last resort.

6. Ibid., 190.

7. Isenberg, *Sex and Citizenship in Antebellum America*, 196–97.

8. Ong, "Cultural Citizenship as Subject Making," 266. White men were simultaneously jealous and resentful of black men's allegedly casual attitude toward industry.

9. Hart, "The Realities of Negro Suffrage," 151. Those colonies were Maryland, Pennsylvania, New York, New Jersey, New Hampshire, Virginia, Delaware, Rhode Island, North Carolina, South Carolina, and Georgia.

10. R. Smith, *Civic Ideals*, 170–71.

11. J. R. Pole (1958), "Representation and Authority in Virginia from the Revolution to Reform," *The Journal of Southern History* 24, no. 1 (February): 18. The religious exclusion was not dropped in Virginia until 1785.

12. Charles H. Wesley (1947), "Negro Suffrage in the Period of Constitution-Making, 1787-1865," *The Journal of Negro History* 32, no. 2:152–54.

13. Maryland restricted Negro suffrage in 1783 by statute and then again in 1801 and 1810 by a constitutional amendment that said suffrage was confined to every white freeman over the age of twenty-one. Wesley, "Negro Suffrage," 154.

14. Hart, "The Realities of Negro Suffrage," 150; Wesley, "Negro Suffrage," 160, 163.

15. As a territory, Wyoming had granted women the vote in 1869.

16. Wesley, "Negro Suffrage," 154; John Cimprich (1980), "The Beginning of the Black Suffrage Movement in Tennessee, 1864-65," *The Journal of Negro History* 65, no. 3:185; Wesley, "Negro Suffrage," 153, 156.

17. Alexander Keyssar (2000), *The Right to Vote: The Contested History of Democracy in the United States* (New York: Basic Books), 55.

18. Wesley, "Negro Suffrage," 159–60. Peter Augustus Jay was the son of Governor John Jay of New York, who was President of the Continental Congress and Chief Justice of the Supreme Court.

19. Wesley, "Negro Suffrage," 57.

20. Darlene Clark Hine and Earnestine Jenkins (1999), "Black Men's History: Toward a Gendered Perspective," in *A Question of Manhood: A Reader in U.S. Black Men's History and Masculinity*, ed. Darlene Clark Hine and Earnestine Jenkins (Bloomington: Indiana University Press), 15; Martin Summers (2004), *Manliness and Its Discontents: The Black Middle Class and the Transformation of Masculinity, 1900-1930* (Chapel Hill: University of North Carolina Press), 2.

21. James Oliver Horton and Lois E. Horton (1999), "Violence, Protest, and Identity: Black Manhood in Antebellum America," in *A Question of Manhood: A Reader in U.S. Black Men's History and Masculinty*, 382–83.

22. Leon F. Litwak (1958), "The Federal Government and the Free Negro, 1790–1860," *The Journal of Negro History* 43, no. 4 (October): 268.

23. Hine and Jenkins, "Black Men's History," 15.

24. Eric Foner (1965), "Politics and Prejudice: The Free Soil Party and the Negro, 1849-1852," *The Journal of Negro History* 50, no. 4:255.

25. Chase C. Mooney (1946), "The Question of Slavery and the Free Negro in the Tennessee Constitutional Convention of 1834," *The Journal of Southern History* 12, no. 4:493–94.

26. Ibid., 493–94.

27. Hart, "The Realities of Negro Suffrage," 150.

28. Grimké's references are to Haitian slaves, in his 1848 *Considerations Upon the Nature and Tendency of Free Institutions*. See John William Ward's edition of that work, published by The Belknap Press of Harvard University Press (Cambridge, 1968): 427. Grimké's sisters, Sarah and Angelina, were famous for their work in abolition and for confronting the sexism of Congregational ministers. Though a Justice on the Ohio Supreme Court (1836 until 1842), Frederick was more interested in writing. Six years after resigning from the Court, he published *The Nature and Tendency of Free Institutions*, in an attempt to define the "underlying principles of American democratic practice." Unlike his sisters, Frederick "accepted slavery on the basis of a belief in the racial inferiority of the Negro." He was also "skeptical about plans to reform the world and suspicious of the personal motivations of reformers themselves." Frederick died before he learned that his enslaved Negro nephews, fathered by his brother Henry, proved him wrong about race. Francis attended Princeton Theological Seminary and became pastor of the Fifteenth Street Presbyterian Church in Washington, D.C., and trustee of Howard University. Archibald Henry went to Harvard Law School, practiced law in Boston, and wrote biographies of William Lloyd Garrison and Charles Sumner. See Ward, ed., *Considerations Upon the Nature and Tendency of Free Institutions*, 2, 5–11.

29. Foner, "Politics and Prejudice," 250.

30. Litwak, "The Federal Government and the Free Negro," 274–75. Virginia declared that Negroes were not U.S. citizens in 1821.

31. Ibid, 270.

32. Ibid., 274–75. Taney went on to say that "Negroes were 'a separate and degraded people to whom the sovereignty of each state might accord or withhold such privileges as they deemed proper.'" Taney would later become Chief Justice of the Supreme Court and issue the majority opinion in the *Dred Scott* case in 1857 (ibid.).

33. Connecticut prohibited black male suffrage from 1814 until after the Civil War.

34. Litwak, "The Federal Government and the Free Negro," 273, 275.

35. Hart "The Realities of Negro Suffrage," 152, 158.

36. Ibid., 157–58.

37. Glenn, *Unequal Freedom*, 112. Glenn also argues that such extreme racism affected but did not consume African Americans, who became quite skillful at transforming segregation into congregation (127). The federal government was the first to violate the prohibition against denying the black vote. In 1874, Congress repealed the existing territorial government of the District

of Columbia and thereby ended the suffrage rights enjoyed there by black men since 1867. Ending home rule for the District prevented black majority rule. See Hart, "The Realities of Negro Suffrage," 158.

38. Horton and Horton, "Violence, Protest, and Identity," 385, 387.

39. Summers, *Manliness and Its Discontents*, 4.

40. *Two Centuries of Struggle* (2004), 8–9 available from http://www.crmvet.org/info/votehist.htm (accessed June 11, 2006).

41. Horton and Horton, "Violence, Protest, and Identity," 394–95; Jim Cullen (1999), " 'I's a Man Now': Gender and African American Men," in *A Question of Manhood: A Reader in U.S. Black Men's History and Masculinity*, ed. Darlene Clark Hine and Earnestine Jenkins (Bloomington: Indiana University Press), 493.

42. Yasuhide Kawashima (2003), *Strangers in Their Own Land: American Indian Citizenship in the United States*, 2, http://laboratoires.univ-reunion.fr/oracle/documents/406.html (accessed November 15, 2003).

43. Ibid., 1–2.

44. Alexander Keyssar (2000), *The Right to Vote: The Contested History of Democracy in the United States* (New York: Basic Books), 60.

45. McWhorter, "Sex, Race, and Biopower," 53.

46. Moran, *Interracial Intimacy*, 72–73, 49; Kawsashima, *Strangers In Their Own Land*, 4.

47. Moran, *Interracial Intimacy*, 74.

48. According to Susan Hartmann women were not granted "permanent, regular status in the military establishment" until World War II, and even now, "the juxtaposition of women and military service profoundly disturb[s] the sexual order." Quoted in Linda Kerber (1998), *No Constitutional Right to Be Ladies: Women and the Obligations of Citizenship* (New York: Hill and Wang), 263, 264.

49. Many tribes considered World War I just a "shooting war" and not the equivalent of "counting coups as befitted a real warrior." See Kawashima, *Strangers In Their Own Land*, 4.

50. Ibid.

51. One chief who took advantage of this offer was elected to the Mississippi House in 1831 and re-elected in 1835. He also served for 3 years in the state Senate. His 15,000-acre plantation was worked by 400 slaves. See Kawashima, *Strangers In Their Own Land*, 2–3.

52. Ibid.

53. Ibid.

54. By 1887, only 3,072 Indians became U.S. citizens by becoming the individual, tax-paying owners of their land. Sixty thousand Indians became citizens via their separation from their tribes, but at least 150,000 did not, since their tribal lands were not yet allotted. See Kawashima, *Strangers In Their Own Land*, 4.

55. R. Smith, *Civic Ideals*, 461.

56. Sally Roesch Wagner (2001), *Sisters in Spirit: Haudenosaunee (Iroquois) Influence on Early American Feminists* (Summertown, TN: Native Voices), 64–65,

72–73, 91–93. The Iroquois (or Haudenosaunee) Six Nation Confederacy in particular provided a model for the Founders' vision of the U.S. government. Matilda Gage believed that "the science of government reached the highest form known to the world" in the Six Nations, in large part because of the participation of women. Quoted in Wagner, *Sisters in Spirit*, 94.

57. R. Smith, *Civic Ideals*, 462; Kawashima, *Strangers In Their Own Land*, 5. Not all tribes accepted the terms of the Reorganization Act, but it motivated even those who didn't support it to create better tribal governments and to clarify the interconnection of the three jurisdictions over their fishing rights, criminal prosecutions, welfare benefits, education, and elections. Although forced assimilation of tribal children ended officially in 1933, many boarding schools continued to operate with more openness to tribal culture. The schools were revived after World War II.

58. Moran, *Interracial Intimacy*, 28.

59. Iris Chang (2003), *The Chinese in America* (New York: Viking), 93, 98, 118, 101.

60. Ibid., 173–74. There are discrepancies in reported numbers of Chinese women immigrants to the U.S. from 1908 to 1924. Shehong Chen reports that 6,623 Chinese women and girls entered the U.S. during that time, even as the total Chinese population dropped from 89,863 in 1900 to 74,954 in 1930. In addition, the number of American citizens of Chinese ancestry more than tripled (from roughly 9,000 to 31,000), in part because of those illegal wives and their children born on U.S. soil (Shehong Chen (2002), *Being Chinese, Becoming Chinese American* (Urbana: University of Illinois Press), 68–69). It is possible that immigration officials let more women into the country than the law allowed to accommodate men's right to determine their wives' domiciles and enjoy patriarchal family life (Bredbenner, *A Nationality of Her Own*, 124). It is also possible that Chen's figures include such illegal entries. According to Ronald Takaki, the largest number of Chinese illegal immigrants slipped into the country between the passage and enforcement of the Chinese Exclusion Act of 1882, but only 136 of 39,579 Chinese immigrants during that period were women. Another possibility is that the San Francisco fire of 1906, which destroyed many immigration records, allowed Chinese men to claim they had been born in San Francisco and were entitled to bring their wives to the U.S. According to Takaki, women constituted 5 percent of the Chinese population before the earthquake, but after the earthquake and until 1924, their percentage rose to about 25 percent. Increased immigration explains part of that increase. Before 1906 12–145 immigrated annually; 219 arrived in 1910; 356 arrived in 1915. Ronald Takaki (1989), *Strangers from a Different Shore: A History of Asian Americans* (Boston: Little, Brown), 41, 209.

61. Chang, *The Chinese in America*, 123; Lucie Cheng Hirata (1979), "Free, Indentured, Enslaved: Chinese Prostitutes in Nineteenth-Century America," *Signs* 5, no. 1 (Autumn): 14–16, 18.

62. Hing, *Defining America*, 4.

63. Van Nuys, *Americanizing the West*, 19.

64. Chang, *The Chinese in America*, 76.

65. Gardner, *The Qualities of a Citizen*, 17, 135.
66. Cott, "Marriage and Women's Citizenship," 1469–71.
67. For a detailed discussion of this process in twentieth-century Chinese American literature, see Eng, *Racial Castration*.
68. Jonathan W. Warren and Frances Winddance Twine (1997), "White Americans, the New Minority? Non-Blacks and the Ever-Expanding Boundaries of Whiteness," *Journal of Black Studies* 28, no. 2:211.
69. Chen, *Being Chinese*, 171–75.
70. Moran, *Interracial Intimacy*, 28–29, 30.

Chapter 14

1. Andres Reséndez (2005), *Changing National Identities at the Frontier: Texas and New Mexico, 1800-1850* (Cambridge: Cambridge University Press), 208–09.
2. Rosa Linda Fregoso (2003), *Mexicana Encounters: The Making of Social Identities on the Borderlands* (Berkeley: University of California Press), 136–37.
3. Horsman, "Scientific Racism and the American Indian," 167.
4. Francesco Cordasco, ed. (1990), *Dictionary of American Immigration History* (Metuchen, NJ: The Scarecrow Press), 606. Declining manufacturing jobs and the high cost of urban life in the Northeast made Puerto Ricans the poorest U.S. Latino group.
5. For a discussion of Texan fears of the rule of the Catholic Church in "Mexico's far North," see Reséndez, *Changing National Identities*, 28–29.
6. Rodríguez, "Challenging Racial Hegemony," 132; Rodolfo F. Acuña (2007), *Occupied America: A History of Chicanos*, 6th ed. (New York: Pearson, Longman), 169. By 1980, the government gave up and allowed Latinos to choose their own racial category.
7. Rodolfo F. Acuña (1981), *Occupied America: A History of Chicanos*, 2nd ed. (New York: Harper and Row), 334. This determination was made in *Keyes v. School District No. 1, Denver, Colorado*, 413 U.S. 189 (1973) (http://supreme.justia.com/us/413/189/) and reiterated in *Valerie Kline v. Henry Cisneros*, 316 U.S. 183 (1996) (http://www.ll.georgetown.edu/federal/judicial/dc/opinions/94opinions/94-5147a.html).
8. The terms in this section's subheading were used to explain why Mexican children should be excluded from Anglo schools at the turn of the twentieth century. See Acuña, *Occupied America*, 2nd ed., 303.
9. Richard Griswold del Castillo, "War's End: Treaty of Guadalupe Hidalgo" http://www.pbs.org/kera/usmexicanwar/war/wars_end_guadalupe.html (accessed January 25, 2007).
10. Acuña, *Occupied America*, 2nd ed., 48–49.
11. "Treaty of Guadalupe-Hidalgo; February 2, 1848; Perfected Treaties," The Avalon Project at Yale Law School, http://www.yale.edu/lawweb/avalon/diplomacy/mexico/guadhida.htm (accessed May 2, 2007).

12. David Montejano (1987), *Anglos and Mexicans in the Making of Texas, 1836-1986* (Austin: University of Texas Press), 311.

13. Juan Gómez-Quiñones (1994), *Roots of Chicano Politics, 1600-1940* (Albuqerque: University of New Mexico Press), 222–25.

14. Acuña, *Occupied America*, 2nd ed., 325.

15. Kawashima, *Strangers In Their Own Land*, 3–4.

16. Because the analysis in this chapter begins with the annexation of Texas territory in 1848, it omits some colorful history, such as the brief existence of the Republic of Fredonia (the Republic of Texas and part of New Mexico, aka the "Republic of Red and White Peoples") which excluded Mexicans. It also omits the Texan Santa Fe Expedition of 1841, which was designed to market goods and help New Mexicans "shake off the tiresome yoke of their [Mexican] task-masters," which it turns out they didn't want to do, and the 1846 Invasion of New Mexico by the Army of the West, led by Colonel Stephen Kearny. It, too, was designed to free New Mexicans from Mexico and subject the territory to U.S. law. American volunteer troops quickly defeated that rebellion, and the fighters were hanged. For details, see Reséndez, *Changing National Identities*.

17. Fregoso, *Mexican Encounters*, 131.

18. Acuña, *Occupied America*, 2nd ed., 100.

19. Van Nuys, *Americanizing the West*, 15, 25, 27.

20. Ricardo Romo (1993), "Responses to Mexican Immigration, 1910-1930," in *Beyond 1848: Readings in the Modern Chicano Historical Experience*, ed. Michael R. Ornelas (Dubuque, IA: Kendall/Hunt), 116–20; Dennis Wepman (2002), *Immigration: From the Founding of Virginia to the Closing of Ellis Island* (New York: Facts on File, Inc.), 234–85; Acuña, *Occupied America*, 2nd ed., 217–18.

21. Romo, "Responses to Mexican Immigration," 121–22, 124–25, 129.

22. David R. Maciel (1990), "Mexico in Aztlán and Aztlán in Mexico: The Dialectics of Chicano-Mexicano Art," in *Chicano Art: Resistance and Affirmation, 1965-1985*, ed. Richard Griswold Del Castillo, Teresa McKenna and Yvonne Yarbro-Bejarano (Los Angeles: Wright Art Gallery, UCLA), 110.

23. Acuña, *Occupied America*, 2nd ed., 303.

24. Acuña, *Occupied America*, 6th ed., 167–68, 174, 173.

25. Ibid., 231; Glenn, *Unequal Freedom*, 159–60.

26. Fregoso, *Mexican Encounters*, 134–35.

27. Ibid., 138.

28. Acuña, *Occupied America*, 2nd ed., 136; Romo, "Responses to Mexican Immigration," 130.

29. Alan M. Kraut (1994), *Silent Travelers: Germs, Genes, and the "Immigrant Menace"* (New York: Harper Collins), 81.

30. Acuña, *Occupied America*, 2nd ed., 42, 103.

31. Montejano, *Anglos and Mexicans*, 314; Acuña, *Occupied America*, 2nd ed., 102.

32. Acuña, *Occupied America*, 2nd ed., 101, 104–05; Acuña, *Occupied America*, 6th ed., 49.

33. Ibid., 62.

34. Acuña, *Occupied America*, 2nd ed., 42–43, 48; Montejano, *Anglos and Mexicans*, 315–16.

35. Montejano, *Anglos and Mexicans*, 315–16.

36. Van Nuys, *Americanizing the West*, 26; Acuña, *Occupied America*, 2nd ed., 44–45, 136–37, 128, 130.

37. Treaty of Peace Between the United States and Spain, December 10, 1898 (aka "Treaty of Paris"), The Avalon Project at the Yale Law School; http://avalon.law.yale.edu/19th_century/sp1898.asp (accessed February 19, 2007). Article X also guaranteed freedom of religion in the former Spanish territories, which included Cuba, Puerto Rico and other Spanish islands in the West Indies, and Guam. That was a concession to Catholicism that the U.S. government might not have made on its own.

38. Popular reforms instituted by the U.S. government included sanitation brigades in larger cities, free public education, trial by jury, the right of habeas corpus, the eight-hour workday, exemptions of all workers from income tax, and a national normal school—the University of Puerto Rico—which opened in 1903. Unpopular moves included the restriction of suffrage to literate or tax-paying adult men and restrictions on eligibility to run for public office. In addition, rural Puerto Ricans were coerced into plantation labor and U.S. soldiers committed racist attacks against Afro-Puerto Ricans before 1900. U.S. generals also limited the freedom of the island's press. See Eileen J. Suárez Findlay (1999), *Imposing Decency: The Politics of Sexuality and Race in Puerto Rico, 1870-1920* (Durham, NC: Duke University Press), 117–18.

39. Ibid., 118–19, 16.

40. The Jones Act of March 2, 1917, declared "All citizens of Porto Rico [sic] ... who ... are not citizens of any foreign country ... citizens of the United States" provided they did not take an oath to the contrary. *The Statutes at Large of the United States of America from December 1915 to March 1917, Jones Act*, 64th Cong., 2d sess., 1917:953.

41. John A. Regis, Jr., View of Congress, the Courts, and the Federal Government, http://www.puertoricousa.com/english/english_menu_views.htm (accessed October 15, 2007); Findlay, *Imposing Decency*, 118; Guillermo Moscosco, "Facts Regarding Puerto Rican Citizenship," *The San Juan Star*, September 17, 1997, 58, http://www.puertorico-herald.org/issues/1997-98misc/moscoso-970917.html; Chris Mooney, "Left-Wing Advocates of Puerto Rican Statehood Come under Fire from All Sides," *Lingua Franca* (April 2001): 52.

42. Guillermo Moscosco, "Debunking Some Often-Repeated Myths," *The San Juan Star*, August 25, 1997, 82 (http://www.puertorico-herald.org/issues/1997-98misc/moscoso-970825.html); Mooney, "Left Wing Advocates," 52. As a commonwealth, Puerto Rico is an *estado libre asociado*, which qualifies for a degree of self-government but remains part of the U.S. Despite a commonwealth's lack of voting representation in Congress and exclusion from voting in Presidential elections, its citizens are subject to the military draft. See Cordasco, *Dictionary of American Immigration History*, 606.

43. Although a few Puerto Ricans immigrated to the U.S. mainland starting in 1917, large numbers did not arrive until the trip became easier

and more affordable. Ninety thousand of the 1.6 million Puerto Ricans over sixteen on the mainland in 1966 migrated after 1955. By 1980, there were 2.5 million Puerto Ricans on the mainland (as compared with 3.1 million on the island), 100,000 of whom had migrated after 1975. By 1990, there were 2.7 million Puerto Ricans on the mainland (as compared with 3.5 million on the island). There were 3.8 million Puerto Ricans on the mainland by 1998. Puerto Ricans increasingly compete in segments of the labor market where wages have been stagnant or in decline and live in parts of cities suffering from political neglect. James Ciment, ed. (2001), *Encyclopedia of American Immigration*, Vol. 3 (Armonk, NY: Sharpe Reference), 1145, 1149.

44. Rodríguez, "Challenging Racial Hegemony," 131, 133.
45. Findlay, *Imposing Decency*, 119.
46. Ibid., 7–10, 16.
47. Ibid., 111–12, 122, 133, 205–06. Even American officials' support for the right to divorce, which became part of the revised Civil and Penal Codes drafted by the Legislative Assembly in 1902, was designed to make marriage more attractive.
48. Mooney, "Left Wing Advocates," 52.
49. Section 262 of the Revenue Act of 1921 granted a tax exclusion on income generated by businesses located in a U.S. possession that were incorporated under United States law. Deborah S. DiPiero (1997), "Puerto Rico's Need for Corporate Incentives Following the 1996 Amendment to Section 936," *Boston University International Law Journal* 15:549; Ediberto Roman (1997), "Empire Forgotten: The United States' Colonization of Puerto Rico," *Villanova Law Review* 42:1190, 1196.
50. Though Puerto Rico has never technically been a U.S. colony, the government's half-hearted denouncement of colonialism cannot hide the fact that the U.S. "participates in and benefits from [the] privileges" of colonialism. The Jones Act's stipulation that "all laws enacted by the Legislature of Porto [sic] Rico shall be reported to the Congress of the United States . . . which hereby reserves the power and authority to annul the same," supported a colonial relationship to the island. See Roman, "Empire Forgotten," 1147.
51. Michael Gonzalez-Cruz (1998), "The U.S. Invasion of Puerto Rico: Occupation and Resistance to the Colonial State, 1898 to the Present," *Latin American Perspectives* 25, no. 5:12. By 1910, 60 percent of arable land in Puerto Rico was given over to sugar cane.
52. Maria del Carmen Baerga-Santini (1996), "Exclusion and Resistance: Household, Gender, and Work in the Needlework Industry in Puerto Rico, 1914-1940," PhD diss., State University of New York.
53. Helen I. Safa (1995), *The Myth of the Male Breadwinner: Women and Industrialization in the Caribbean* (Boulder, CO: Westview Press), 174; Baerga-Santini, "Exclusion and Resistance," 148; Luz del Alba Acevado (1992), "Industrialization and Employment: Postwar Changes in the Patterns of Women's Work in Puerto Rico," in *Expanding the Boundaries of Women's History: Essays on Women in the Third World*, ed. Cheryl Johnson-Odim and Margaret Strobel (Bloomington: Indiana University Press), 228–30.

54. Alice E Colón-Warren and Idsa Algría-Ortega (1998), "Shattering the Illusion of Development: The Changing Status of Women and Challenges for the Feminist Movement in Puerto Rico," *Feminist Review* 59:105; Altagracia Ortiz (1998), "Puerto Rican Women Workers in the Twentieth Century: A Historical Appraisal of the Literature," in *Puerto Rican Women's History: New Perspectives*, ed. Linda C. Delgado and Felix V. Matos (Armonk, NY: M.E. Sharpe), 39.

55. Carmen Teresa Whalen (1998), "Labor Migrants or Submissive Wives: Competing Narratives of Puerto Rican Women in the Post-World War II Era," in *Puerto Rican Women's History: New Perspectives*, ed. Linda C. Delgado and Felix V. Matos, 219–21.

56. Baerga-Santini, "Exclusion and Resistance," 148, 202, 215. From 1914 to 1919, Puerto Rico went from nineteen needlework factories to 136 sewing factories and ten embroidery and drawn work workshops. The island was the principal supplier of handkerchiefs to the world between 1922 and 1929. By 1929, there were 265 embroidery and drawnwork factories and 545 sub-agencies in Puerto Rico.

57. During the same period, twenty-three percent of women workers were in domestic service and eight percent were in tobacco manufacturing. Men entered the needlework industry when it became mechanized in the 1930s. By 1933, machine mechanic and machine cutter jobs were designated as male occupations. Not coincidentally, the first needleworkers' union was founded in 1931. Baerga-Santini, "Exclusion and Resistance," 148, 202, 215, 140.

58. Whalen, "Labor Migrants or Submissive Wives," 214.

59. Profits from these tax-free companies were supposed to be reinvested in Puerto Rico, but most U.S. possession corporations "found other tax loopholes to repatriate their profits without paying taxes or investing in the territory." Roman, "Empire Forgotten," 1195.

60. Ivette Romero-Casareo (1994), "Whose Legacy?: Voicing Women's Rights from the 1870s to the 1930s," *Callaloo* 17, no. 3:770–89.

61. Vanessa Bauzá, "Puerto Rico: The Covert Campaign to Sterilize Women." *Ms.*, Sept./Oct., 1994:14.

62. Panos Institute Report (1994), "We Speak for Ourselves: Population and Development," Washington, DC, Panos Institute: 19.

63. Whalen, "Labor Migrants or Submissive Wives," 215–17. The contracts for domestic service provided a minimum of $25.00 per week with an increase of $2.50 every three months and a minimum salary of $35.00 per week if the employment continued at the end of the contract year. Women were limited to only (!) 10 hours of work per day and 48 hours per week.

64. Ralph J. Sierra, Jr. (1988), "A New Incentives Law for Puerto Rico," *The International Lawyer* 22:1037.

65. A maternity leave policy, which gave two months leave with half pay, was instituted in 1942. Services for women helped to reduce women's dependence on individual men by the 1950s. However, even as the number of women college graduates increased to 15 percent in 1990 (and became the majority by the 1980s), less educated men and women lost employment opportunities as labor-intensive manufacturing was replaced by a high-tech,

financial service economy. See Colón-Warren and Alegria-Ortega, "Shattering the Illusion of Development," 102–03.
66. Ortiz, "Puerto Rican Women Workers," 40–41.

Part IV: Conclusion

1. Siobhan B. Somerville (2005), "Notes toward a Queer History of Naturalization," *American Quarterly* 57, no. 3:660–62.
2. Siobhan B. Somerville (2005), "Sexual Aliens and the Racialized State: A Queer Reading of the 1952 U.S. Immigration and Nationality Act," in *Queer Migrations: Sexuality, U.S. Citizenship, and Border Crossings*, ed. Eithne Luibhéid and Lionel Cantú, Jr. (Minneapolis: University of Minnesota Press), 77–78.
3. Surgeon General of the U.S. (1918), *Manual of the Mental Examination of Aliens* (Washington, DC: Government Printing Office), 62–65.
4. Kraut, *Plato's Republic*, 275–76; Teresa Bright, Fred Rosenberg, Arthur Simon, and Arthur G. White, contr., (1985), "Chapter 7: Immigration," in *Sexual Orientation and the Law*, ed. Roberta Achtenberg (New York: Clark Boardman Co., Ltd.), 7-2-3, 7-21-22.
5. Morris B. Kaplan (1997), Sexual Justice: Democratic Citizenship and the Politics of Desire (New York: Routledge), 47; Bright et al., "Chapter 7: Immigration," 7-2.
6. Margot Canaday (2003), " 'Who Is a Homosexual?': The Consolidation of Sexual Identities in Mid-Twentieth-Century American Immigration Law," *Law and Social Inquiry* 38, no. 2:352–54.

PART V: IMPLICATIONS

Part V: Introduction

1. Laura Briggs (2000), "The Race of Hysteria: 'Overcivilization' and the 'Savage' in Late Nineteenth-Century Obstetrics and Gynecology," *American Quarterly* 52, no. 2:246–73.
2. Cynthia Neverdon-Morton (1989), *Afro-American Women of the South and the Advancement of the Race, 1895-1925* (Knoxville: University of Tennessee Press), 205, 235, 185.
3. Anita Shafer Goodstein (1998), "A Rare Alliance: African American and White Women in the Tennessee Elections of 1919 and 1920," *Journal of Southern History* 64, no. 2:219–20.
4. Becky Thompson (2002), "Multiracial Feminism: Recasting the Chronology of Second Wave Feminism," *Feminist Studies* 28, no. 2:337, 341, 344.
5. Goodstein, "A Rare Alliance," 246. Goodstein notes that Dr. Mattie E. Coleman (1870-1942), the African American leader who probably initiated the biracial alliance, later denied that any suffrage work was done by blacks

in Tennessee. Goodstein wonders whether that denial was irony or despair, since even in 1942, when she was interviewed, so little had really changed.

6. Susan M. Hartmann (1998), *The Other Feminists: Activists in the Liberal Establishment* (New Haven, CT: Yale University Press), 198, 188.

7. Winifred R. Poster (1995), "The Challenges and Promises of Class and Racial Diversity in the Women's Movement: A Study of Two Women's Organizations," *Gender and Society* 9, no. 6:673.

8. Andrea G. Hunter and Sherrill L. Sellers (1998), "Feminist Attitudes among African American Women and Men," *Gender and Society* 12, no. 1:81–82, 84, 97.

9. See Walker's 1995 anthology, *To Be Real: Telling the Truth and Changing the Face of Feminism* (New York: Anchor Books), and Jennifer Baumgardner and Amy Richards (2000) *Manifesta: Young Women, Feminism, and the Future* (New York: Farrar, Straus and Giroux).

10. Winifred Breines (2006), *The Trouble between Us: An Uneasy History of White and Black Women in the Feminist Movement* (New York: Oxford University Press), 108–09.

11. Thompson, "Multiracial Feminism," 349.

Chapter 15

1. Stephen P. Knadler (2003),"Traumatized Racial Performativity: Passing in Nineteenth-Century African-American Testimonies," *Cultural Critique* 55:63–100. Quoting Samira Kawash.

2. Gilroy, *Against Race*, 20.

3. Judith Butler (1990), *Gender Trouble: Feminism and the Subversion of Identity* (New York: Routledge).

4. Adrienne Cecile Rich (1976), *Of Woman Born: Motherhood as Experience and Institution* (New York: Norton); Gloria I. Joseph and Jill Lewis (1981), *Common Differences: Conflicts in Black and White Feminist Perspectives* (Garden City, NY: Anchor Press/Doubleday); Jean Renvoizé (1985), *Going Solo: Single Mothers by Choice* (Boston: Routledge); Jane Price Knowles and Ellen Cole ed. (1990), *Motherhood: A Feminist Perspective* (New York: Harrington Park Press); and Ellen Lewin (1993), *Lesbian Mothers: Accounts of Gender in American Culture* (Ithaca, NY: Cornell University Press).

5. Rosemarie Garland-Thomson (2002), "Integrating Disability, Transforming Feminist Theory," *NWSA Journal* 14, no. 3:1.

6. Amy Sueyoshi (2004), "Mindful Masquerades: Que(E)Rying Japanese Immigrant Dress in Turn-of-the-Century San Francisco," *Frontiers: A Journal of Women Studies* 25, no. 3:67-100.

7. For one cogent analysis of this phenomenon, see Leila J. Rupp and Verta A. Taylor (2003), *Drag Queens at the 801 Cabaret* (Chicago: University of Chicago Press).

8. Dorinne K. Kondo (2000), "(Re)Visions of Race: Contemporary Race Theory and the Cultural Politics of Racial Crossover in Documentary Theatre," *Theatre Journal* 52, no. 1:81–107.

9. Karin Aguilar-San Juan (1997), "Foreward: Breathing Fire, Confronting Power, and Other Necessary Acts of Resistance," in *Dragon Ladies: Asian American Feminists Breathe Fire*, ed. Sonia Shah (Boston: South End Press), x–xi.

10. Howard Winant (1994), "Where Culture Meets Structure: Race in the 1990's," in *Racial Conditions: Politics, Theory, Comparison* (Minneapolis: University of Minnesota Press), 36; Howard Winant (1994b), "The Theoretical Status of the Concept of Race," in *Racial Conditions*, 20.

11. Renya Ramirez (2007), "Race, Tribal Nation, and Gender: A Native Feminist Approach to Belonging," *Meridians: feminism, race, transnationalism* 7, no. 2:31.

12. Iris Marion Young (1994), "Gender as Seriality: Thinking About Women as a Social Collective," *Signs* 19, no. 3:729.

13. Ibid., 726–29. For Spivak's discussion of "strategic essentialism," see Gayatri Chakravorty Spivak and Donna Landry (1996), *The Spivak Reader: Selected Works of Gayatri Chakravorty Spivak* (New York: Routledge), 204–05, 214.

14. Maya J. Goldenberg (2007), "The Problem of Exclusion in Feminist Theory and Politics: A Metaphysical Investigation into Constructing a Category of 'Woman,'" *Journal of Gender Studies* 16, no. 2:150.

15. Grace Elizabeth Hale (1998), *Making Whiteness: The Culture of Segregation in the South, 1890-1940* (New York: Pantheon), 296.

Chapter 16

1. Winthrop Jordan, *White Over Black*; Michael Omi and Howard Winant (1986), *Racial Formation in the United States: From the 1960's to the 1980's* (New York: Routledge); Tomás Almaguer (1994), *Racial Fault Lines: The Historical Origins of White Supremacy in California* (Berkeley, CA: University of California Press); Richard Delgado and Jean Stefancic, ed. (1997), *Critical White Studies: Looking Behind the Mirror* (Philadelphia: Temple University Press); and Martin Bulmer and John Solomos (2004), *Researching Race and Racism* (London: Routledge).

2. Martha Menchaca (2001), *Recovering History, Constructing Race: The Indian, Black, and White Roots of Mexican Americans* (Austin, TX: University of Texas Press).

3. See Toni Morrison (1989), "Unspeakable Things Unspoken: The Afro-American Presence in American Literature," *Michigan Quarterly Review* 28, no. 1:1–34; and Toni Morrison (1992), *Playing in the Dark: Whiteness and the Literary Imagination* (New York: Vintage Books), 9.

4. Johnnetta Betsch Cole and Beverly Guy-Sheftall (2003), *Gender Talk: The Struggle for Women's Equality in African American Communities* (New York: Ballantine Books), 114–15, 146–47, 155.

5. Elaine H. Kim (1990), "'Such Opposite Creatures': Men and Women in Asian American Literature," *Michigan Quarterly Review* 29, no. 1:75–76.

6. Leslie Bow (2001), *Betrayal and Other Acts of Subversion: Feminism, Sexual Politics, Asian American Women's Literature* (Princeton, NJ: Princeton University Press), 7.

7. Eng, *Racial Castration*, 136, 94, 195.

8. Rafael L. Ramírez (1999), *What It Means to Be a Man: Reflections on Puerto Rican Masculinity*, trans. Rosa E. Casper (New Brunswick, NJ: Rutgers University Press), 15, 63–65.

9. See Martha C. Nussbaum (2007), *The Clash Within: Democracy, Religious Violence, and India's Future* (Cambridge, MA: Harvard University Press), especially 208–10. Other works by feminists expressing concern over gender oppression within communities of color during the 1970s, 80s, and 90s (and often targeting the equation of racial or ethnic progress or pride with oppressive forms of masculinity) include: Michelle Wallace (1975; rpt. 1995), "Anger in Isolation: A Black Feminist's Search for Sisterhood," *Words of Fire: An Anthology of African-American Feminist Thought*, ed. Beverly Guy-Sheftall (New York: The New Press), 220–27; Jacquelyn Grant (1979; rpt. 1995), "Black Theology and the Black Woman," in *Words of Fire*, 320–36; Yamila Azize-Vargas (1994), "The Emergence of Feminism in Puerto Rico, 1870-1930," in *Unequal Sisters*, ed. V. L. Ruiz and E. C. DuBois, 260–67; Patricia Williams (1991), *The Alchemy of Race and Rights* (Cambridge, MA: Harvard University Press); Margarita Mergal (1993), "Puerto Rican Feminism at a Crossroad: Challenges at the Turn of the Century," in *Colonial Dilemma: Critical Perspectives on Contemporary Puerto Rico*, ed. Edwin Meléndez and Edgardo Meléndez (Boston: South End Press), 131–41.

10. María de los Angeles Torres (2003), "Transnational Political and Cultural Identities: Crossing Theoretical Borders," in *Latino/a Thought: Culture, Politics, and Society*, ed. Francisco H. Vázquez and Rodolfo D. Torres (Lanham, MD: Rowman & Littlefield), 377–79.

11. Monica L. Miller (2003), "W.E.B. Du Bois and the Dandy as Diasporic Race Man," *Callaloo* 26, no. 3:740–46.

12. Ibid., 757–61.

Part V: Conclusion

1. McWhorter, "Sex, Race, and Biopower," 47, 40.

2. Ann Laura Stoler (1995), *Race and the Education of Desire: Foucault's History of Sexuality and the Colonial Order of Things* (Durham, NC: Duke University Press), 22, 55–56, 96.

Index

abolitionists, 51, 93, 96, 142, 186, 189, 287n28
African Americans, 6, 10, 229, 245, 248–249
  bodies, 61, 64, 74–76, 109
  and citizenship, 8, 161, 175, 179–180, 183–190
  lynching of, 7, 96, 98
  and manliness, 189–190, 248
  and motherhood, 227
  and racial blood, 119, 151
  and racial formation, 244
  and sexual projection, 90
  stereotypes of, 1
  voting rights, 190
  women, status of, 152, 175
  See also blacks; Negroes
Africans, 7, 18, 28, 203
  bodies, 32–33, 38, 44, 64, 74, 78, 92
  and British, 30, 54, 66–67
  and citizenship, 42, 175
  in the colonies, 65, 67, 71–72, 72–73, 74–76, 166
  European perceptions of, 31–33, 50
  gender and, 71, 82–83, 86–87
  men, 74–76, 92
  and naturalization, 119, 162, 175, 188, 195
  race and, 25, 27, 29, 30, 35, 37, 41–44, 86, 115
  and religion, 43
  and slavery, 33, 39, 41–42, 47, 49–52, 71–72, 77–79, 82, 87, 115, 127

Soemmerring, Samuel Thomas von on, 41
  women, 7, 33, 37, 72–74, 81, 92
  See also African Americans; blacks; Hottentots; Negroes
Aguilar-San Juan, Karin, 237
Alabama, 97, 116, 131, 133, 142, 143, 186, 189, 275n11, 279n4
Algonquian culture, 69
Almaguer, Tomás, 243
alterity, 166
American Eugenics Society (AES), 120–121
American Freedman's Inquiry Commission, 93, 148
American Indians. *See* Indians, American
Amerindians, 27, 31–32. *See also* Indians, American
Anderson, Benedict, 167
Anglo-Saxon Clubs of America, 125, 153–154, 277n5
Anthony, Susan B., 181, 188
anthropologists, 7, 28, 34, 38–41, 92, 191, 253, 260n34, 277n1
anti-miscegenation, 128, 134, 137, 143–145, 150. *See also* miscegenation
anti-miscegenation laws, 8, 121, 125, 126, 144, 150, 155, 189, 279n4, 280n11
  and Chinese men, 99, 143, 196, 280n25
  courts and, 137–138, 143
  and Filipino men, 149

299

anti-miscegenation laws *(continued)*
  and gender, 111, 139, 145
  and marriage, 137, 139–141, 143
  in Maryland, 81, 139–140
  as protection of white women, 147, 153
  and racial blood, 135, 144, 156
  and slavery, 139–143
  in Virginia, 81, 138, 140–141, 153
antisubordination politics, 9, 231, 238, 242
Anzaldúa, Gloria, 248
Aristotle, 19, 20, 23, 48, 50, 262n4
Arizona, 98, 203, 204, 206, 209, 211, 279n4, 280n25
Arkansas, 116, 143, 186, 279n4
Asian Americans, 6, 248
  citizenship, 195, 245
  and gender, 245–246
  literature, 102, 245
  men, 245
  women, 177, 237
  See also Asians; Chinese; Japanese Americans
Asians, 42, 219–220, 241
  bodies, 37, 61, 100
  in California, 144
  and citizenship, 177, 181, 190, 195, 198, 199–200, 221, 245
  masculinity and, 102–103, 236, 245
  and race, 27, 28, 29, 110, 118, 199, 204, 248
  and racial blood, 153
  sexuality and, 144, 149
  stereotypes of, 1, 100, 102, 245
  and voting rights, 190
  women, 93, 238, 245, 251
  See also Chinese; Japanese Americans

Baartmann, Saartje (Sarah Bartmann), 91
Baldwin, James, 114
Baumgardner, Jennifer, 231
beards, as racial markers, 37–38, 57
Bederman, Gail, 101

Bernier, Francois, 35–36, 37
biological race. *See* race, biological
Black Codes, 175
blacks, 10
  and Chinese men, 199
  and citizenship, 67, 175, 176
  feminization of male, 43
  free female, lynching of, 175
  free male, 8, 66, 96, 110, 116
  and inter-racial sex, 86
  miscegenation, 137–138, 140–141, 142
  and "one-drop rule," 117
  and phrenologists, 43
  and Racial Contract, 18
  racial inferiority of, 42, 119, 171
  and rape allegations, 147
  in the Renaissance, 30–31
  restrictions on free, 66, 75, 110, 116
  stereotypes of, 1
  and suffrage, 8, 161, 171, 183–185, 190
  term misapplied to Chinese, 45, 143
  See also African Americans; Africans; Negroes
blood
  as core category of racial formation, 6, 7–8, 45, 105
  familial, 123–125
  illegal, 134–135
  and race, 113–115
  See also racial blood
Blumenbach, Johann, 36–38
bodies, 42, 61–64, 71
  African, 32–33, 38, 44, 64, 74, 78, 92
  African American, 61, 64, 74–76, 109
  Asian, 37, 61, 100
  as core category of racial formation, 6–7, 31–33
  cultural, 81, 62–64, 67, 76, 81, 83, 87–88, 94, 95, 98, 100, 103, 105, 161

female, 31–34, 61, 72–74, 79–81,
    90, 92, 94, 95, 167, 173
male, 62, 74–76, 87, 95, 144
gendered, 62–64
Indian, 68, 71
racialized, 63, 102
stereotypes about, 61
borderland identities, 243, 247–250
Boris, Eileen, 3, 160
Bradley, Richard, 36–37
Bradwell v. Illinois, 174
breasts, 28, 31, 32–34, 38, 42, 259n17
Breines, Winifred, 231
Brewer, Lawrence Russell, 89, 95
Briggs, Laura, 227
Brown, Kathleen, 83, 167, 267
Brown v. Board of Education, 202
Bryan v. Walton, 134, 274n7
Buck v. Bell, 282n20
Bulmer, Martin, 243
Burke Act, 71, 194
Butler, Judith, 62, 235–236

Cable Act, 177–178, 198
Caldwell, Charles, 40, 117. *See also* phrenologists
California, 98, 144, 149, 195–196, 198, 203, 204, 206, 208, 209, 279n4, 280n25, 281n28, 281n29
Carpenter v. Cornish, 285–286n5
Child, Lydia Maria, 155, 268–269n15
Chin, Frank, 102, 245
Chinese, 6, 99–101
    and anti-miscegenation laws, 143
    and citizenship, 8, 162, 163, 171, 176, 177, 179, 195–200, 219–220
    immigration and naturalization of, 119, 162–163, 171, 176, 179, 195–200, 219–220, 289n60
    lynching of, men, 7, 98–101
    masculinity, 162, 199
    men and rape, 149
    and race, 45, 100, 110, 227
    and prostitution, 93, 195–197, 219
    and sexual projection, 90, 99, 101
    stereotypes of, 1, 4, 102, 199

women, 93, 176, 195–199, 289n60
    See also Asian Americans; Asians
citizenship, 8, 57–58, 156, 159–160, 165–166, 168–169
    African American, 8, 10, 161, 163, 175, 176, 179–180, 183–190
    and Africans, 42, 175
    American, 132, 159, 161, 171–172
    Asian American, 195, 245
    and Asians, 177, 181, 190, 195, 198, 199–200, 221, 245
    birthright, 160, 161, 174, 193, 195
    and Cable Act, 177–178, 198
    and Chinese, 8, 162, 163, 171, 176, 177, 179, 195–200, 219–220
    colonial, 66–67
    as core category of racial formation, 6, 8, 55, 57
    and the courts, 171–172, 173, 174, 176–177, 178, 181, 187
    derivative, 162, 172, 175–178, 195, 219
    and Filipinos, 149
    and free black women, 175
    gender and, 55, 111, 160–161, 162, 166, 171–173, 178–179, 183
    and Indians, American, 66, 68, 163, 171, 181, 190–195
    and Manifest Destiny, 173–174
    and Mexicans, 10, 132, 163, 171, 202–208
    naturalized, 160
    and privileges, 66–67, 132
    and Puerto Ricans, 163, 201, 211, 213–215
    and race, 111, 156, 162, 166, 175–178, 178–179, 179–180
    and racism, 179–180
    rights of, 159
    and slavery, 174–175
    statutes, 175–179, 195–199
    and women, 5, 55, 161, 162, 169, 171, 172–173, 174, 175–179
classification, as phase of racial ideology formation, 7, 15, 28, 34–40

climate, and complexion, 30, 34–36
clothing, as measure of "otherness," 32
coalitions. *See* social justice, coalitions for
Code Noir, 142, 280n17
Cole, Johnetta, 244–245
Collins, Patricia Hill, 2
Colorado, 98, 203, 279n4, 290n7
complexion, 15, 28, 41, 50, 67, 74
    and citizenship, 183
    and civilization, 32
    and climate, 30, 34–36
    colonists view of, 65
    and race, 65–66
    social, 213
Connecticut, 77, 183, 186, 188, 280n25, 287n33
Cooper, Anna Julia, 151
Cooper, James Fenimore, 128–129
Cott, Nancy, 178, 179
coverture, 56, 70–71, 181
    American views of, 70, 172–178, 180, 181, 183, 266n16
    and citizenship, 172, 173, 176, 177, 179–180
    English view of, 56, 70, 172–173, 174, 266n16
    and Indians, 70–71, 190, 193
    and race, 176
Cox, Earnest Sevier, 125–126
Crenshaw, Kimberlé, 2, 234
Creoles, 131
cultural bodies. *See* bodies, cultural
Culture Clash, 237

Daileader, Celia, 45, 262
Darwin, Charles, 39, 44–45, 118, 120
Darwin, Erasmus, 39
Daughters of the American Revolution (DAR), 151, 281n16
Davis, Rebecca Harding, 155
Dawes Act, 192, 194
Day, Beth, 88, 134
Delaware, 65, 116, 142–43, 184, 279n4, 286n9

Delgado, Richard, 243
de-masculation, 11, 64, 97
    of black men, 74–76, 85, 94
    of Indian men, 68
    of Mexican men, 208–209, 210
    of Puerto Rican men, 211, 214, 246
    and slavery, 49, 85
    of white men, 97
Democratic Party, 94, 149
Democrats, 137, 189
Dickinson, Anna, 155
Dill, Bonnie Thornton, 2, 234
dimorphism, 34, 38–42, 55
DNA, 114, 123
Dorr, Lisa, 152
Douglass, Frederick, 148, 151
Downes v. Bidwell, 211
Dred Scott v. Sanford, 116, 187, 191, 287n32
Du Bois, W. E. B., 89, 109, 190, 248–249, 276n31

Elkins, Lois, 182
Ellis, Havelock, 101
Eng, David, 102, 245
environmentalism, eighteenth-century, 37, 40
Equal Nationality Act (1934), 178, 179
ethnology, 117. *See also* phrenologists
eugenics, 109, 120–121, 137, 147, 216, 276n31
    and Asians, 144
    laws and, 150, 152–153
    and Mexicans, 207, 217
    and Puerto Ricans, 217
    sexology and, 90, 101
Euripides, 17–19
European American whites, 6, 42, 52, 65, 68, 71, 159, 162, 165, 169, 210
Expatriation Acts, 119, 176–177

familial blood. *See* blood, familial
Faust, Drew Gilpin, 85, 96–97, 101
Federalists, 182, 283n10
feme sole, 161, 172, 194

femininity, 29, 56, 62, 69, 105, 169, 175, 199, 236, 249
feminism, 229, 231, 233–234
feminists, 2, 19, 68, 159–160, 229, 230, 231, 233, 234, 238
feminist theory, 5, 9, 235–238, 238–242
Fernandes, Leela, 2, 234
Fields, Barbara, 63
Fifteenth Amendment, 119, 175, 179–180, 181, 183, 188, 189, 193
Filipinos, 149
Florida, 86, 95, 102, 116, 143, 186, 279n4, 280n24
Foucault, Michel, 3, 62, 66, 252–253
Fourteenth Amendment, 119, 138, 161, 179–180, 188, 193, 284n21
Fregoso, Rosa Linda, 201, 207
Fugitive Slave Law, 174

Gage, Matilda Joslyn, 194, 265n8, 288–289n56
Galton, Francis, 120, 152
Gardner, Martha, 178, 179
Garland-Thomson, Rosemarie, 236
gender, 2–3, 4, 27
    citizenship and, 165–169
    defined, 9–10
    dimorphism, 38–42, 55, 168, 169
    entitlement, 21
    familial blood and, 123–125
    Indians and, 127–129
    mulattoes and, 125–127
    nation-states and, 52–56
    and race, 9, 58, 165–169, 233, 236, 237, 247, 251
    and racial blood, 130–133
    racialized, 2, 29, 139, 242, 251
    and reputation, 133–134
    role complementarity, 38
    and slavery, 47–49, 51–52, 82–83, 85–87
gender ideology, 4–5, 6, 7, 9, 15, 57–58, 63, 64, 72, 233, 236, 253
    and citizenship, 166
    and marriage, 23
    and racial formation, 244
    roots of, 3, 17–24, 25, 29, 48, 52
    and slavery, 79–80
gendered cultural bodies, 62–64, 105
gendered race, 2, 5, 34–40, 71–76, 105, 163, 195, 219, 234. *See also* race; racialized gender
gendered racial formation, 4–7, 9, 21–23, 27–28, 63, 65–68, 105, 228, 233, 238, 240, 253
    African, 71–76
    Indian, 68–71
gendered racial ideology, 6, 7, 15–16, 21–23, 28, 79, 160
gendering, 10
Genesis, Book of, 18–21, 24, 35, 42–43
genitalia, 31, 38, 89, 91–92, 95, 236, 246, 259n31
gens, 3, 52–54, 66
Georgia, 97, 109, 110, 116, 141, 143, 148, 189, 269n25, 274n7, 275n11, 279n4, 280n24, 286n9
Getman, Karen, 82, 84, 86
Gillman, Laura, 3, 91, 234
Gilroy, Paul, 235, 249
Glenn, Evelyn Nakano, 2–3, 160, 234
Goldberg, Jonathan, 168
Goldenberg, Maya, 241
Gooch, William, 67
Goodstein, Anita Shafer, 229
Grant, Jacquelyn, 2, 234
Grant, Madison, 120, 137
Greek roots of gender ideology, 3, 17–19, 35, 36, 48
Grimké, Angelina and Sarah, 19, 287n28
Grimké, Frederick, 187, 287n28
Guadalupe Hidalgo, Treaty of, 201, 203, 208
guns, as male prerogative, 74–76, 167
Guy-Sheftall, Beverly, 244–245

Hale, Grace Elizabeth, 94–95
Hall, Kim, 30

Harris, Trudier, 95, 270n37
Hartmann, Susan, 230, 288n48
Hawai'i, 144, 197
Hesiod (*Theogony*), 18–19
Hodes, Martha, 83, 86, 132, 133
homosexual projection, 94–98, 98–99
homosexuality, 8, 90, 100, 101–103, 123–124, 155, 227
　and citizenship, 163, 168, 219–221
　and lynching, 94–96, 98–99
　and McCarran-Walter Act, 220–221
　and race, 220–221
Hoover, Herbert, 206
Hopkins, Pauline, 102, 155
Horsman, Reginald, 66
Hottentots, 33, 38, 40, 91–92
humors, theory of, 30, 34–38, 259n28, 260n34
Hunter, Andrea, 230
hypodescent, 117, 129, 137, 147, 201, 253

Idaho, 279n4, 280n25
Illinois, 174, 184
Immigration Acts, 162, 198, 205, 219
immigration and naturalization, 159–160
　Africans and, 119, 162, 175, 188
　Asians and, 195, 199–200
　and Chinese, 119, 162–163, 171, 176, 179, 195–200, 219–220, 289n60
　gender and, 162
　homosexuals and, 8, 219–220
　Indians and, 191
　laws, 119, 152, 162, 176, 179, 197–198
　men and, 168, 179
　Mexicans and, 205–206, 210
　policy, 162, 284n21
　race and, 159, 162
　restrictions on, 154, 162, 176, 207
　women and, 176, 179, 220
　See also Immigration Acts; Naturalization Acts

Indian Citizenship Act (1924), 195
Indian Removal Act (1830), 71
Indian Reorganization Act (1934), 195
Indiana, 120, 143, 184, 186, 279n4
Indians, American, 7, 10, 25
　British views of, 66–68
　citizenship, 66, 68, 163, 171, 181, 190–195, 200
　coverture and, 70, 191
　de-masculation of male, 68, 194
　English views of, 68–69, 128
　gendered racial formation of, 68–71, 192–194
　and intermarriage, 128–129, 140, 142, 191
　Jacksonian politics, 129
　male suffrage, 73, 184, 190
　as "middle-bloods," 127–129
　paternalism toward, 119, 190–195
　and race, 35, 37, 65–67, 110, 127, 201–202
　and racial blood, 115, 117, 127, 129, 153
　racialization of, 71, 129
　and religion, 71
　and reservations, 117, 191, 194
　and slavery, 77
　women, 73, 192–194, 239
　See also Amerindians
Indians, Pueblo and Mexican, 204, 209
interpretation, as phase of racial ideology formation, 7, 15, 28–34
interracial marriage. *See* marriage, interracial
inter-racial political collusion, 82, 138
inter-racial progeny, 81, 93, 116, 125–126, 137–140, 143. *See also* mulattoes
inter-racial rape. *See* rape, interracial
inter-racial relationships, 75–76, 93, 126, 155, 180

inter-racial sexual relations, 86, 88, 93–94, 102, 118, 125, 126, 140, 142, 149, 150
intersectionality, 2–4, 6, 9, 225, 227, 231–232, 233–234, 238, 251–252

Jacks, James W., 93, 271n13
Jacksonian policies, 71, 117, 127, 129, 276n17
Jacobs, Harriett, 80, 268–269n15
Japanese Americans, 133, 144, 199, 200, 278n28
Jefferson, Thomas, 79–80, 83, 84, 128, 141, 191, 276n17, 277n10
Jim Crow
 laws, 130, 181, 189
 policies, 92–93, 172, 175, 202
Jones-Shafroth Act (Federal Relations Act), 211
Jordan, Winthrop, 63, 79–80, 243
jus sanguinis, 161, 176
jus soli, 161, 176

Kant, Immanuel, 24–25
Kentucky, 116, 143, 184, 279n4
Kessler-Harris, Alice, 159
Keyes v. School District No. 1, Denver, Colorado, 290n7
Kim, Elaine, 245
Kline, Valerie v. Henry Cisneros, 290n7
Klinghoffer, Judith, 182
Knadler, Stephen, 234
Kondo, Dorinne, 237
Krafft-Ebing, Richard von, 101
Ku Klux Klan (KKK), 94, 148, 154, 189, 209, 277n5

Latinas, 1, 4, 32, 238
 See also *Mexicanas*
Latinos, 1, 6, 10, 61, 102, 110, 118, 144, 190, 200–202, 217–218
 See also Mexicans; Mexicanos; Mexican-Americans; Puerto Ricans
Lavater, Johann Kaspar, 40

Legare, Hugh, 188
Lerner, Gerda, 48, 256n2, 263n5
Linnaeus, Carl, 36, 38, 39, 259n31
Lister, Ruth, 160
Loomba, Ania, 27, 30
Lords Commissioners (British), 67
Louisiana, 130, 131, 133, 142, 143, 186, 189, 277n10, 279n4
Loving v. Virginia, 138
lynching, 86, 89, 90, 92, 101, 149, 227, 245
 of African Americans, 7, 87, 94–95, 96, 148, 175, 189
 of Chinese, 7, 98–101
 heterosexual rationale for, 90–94
 homosexual projection and, 94–97, 99
 lust and, 64, 96, 105
 of Mexicans, 7, 98–101
 and race, 96, 99
 rape, 94–95, 96, 99, 101, 148–49, 246
 women and, 149, 175, 245, 262n73

Maine, 142, 184, 280n23, 124–125
Malays, 111, 149, 280n25
Malcomson, Scott, 50, 128
male bonding, 167–168
male dominance, 34, 226, 238
 biblical justification for, 51
 and citizenship, 169
 as cultural marker, 43, 53
 and family, 124–125
 feminism and, 160
 gender and, 38–42, 244, 248
 male bonding and, 167
 race and, 57, 248
 slavery and, 79, 87
male superiority, 30, 34, 37, 40, 92
Manifest Destiny, 128, 171, 173–174, 201
manliness. See masculinity
Manly, Alexander, 149
Mansfield, Edward, 174
Marble, Mary, 236–237

marriage
  Anglo Mexican inter-, 208–209
  anti-miscegenation laws and, 135, 137–143
  Cable Act and, 177–178
  and citizenship, 172, 175–177, 178–179, 219
  as control (of women), 23, 55, 124, 169, 174, 213
  and coverture, 70
  eugenics and, 152
  and gender ideology, 23
  and Indians, 127–128, 129, 191–192, 265n8, 277n10
  interracial, 75–76, 81, 137–143, 144, 155, 191, 280n11
  and men, 176–178
  and mulattas, 134
  and Puerto Ricans, 216, 217
  and race, 138–139
  regulation of, 81, 138–139, 141, 238
  religion and, 21, 51–52, 219, 263n10
  significance of, 143
  and slavery, 49, 85, 139–140, 174
  and women, 55, 133, 174, 176–179, 219
Married Women's Independent Nationality Act. *See* Cable Act
Married Women's Property Acts, 70, 172, 266n16
Marshall, John (Chief Justice), 190, 191, 193
Maryland
  anti-miscegenation laws, 81, 139–140, 141, 143, 279n4, 286n9
  free black male suffrage in, 184
  interracial marriage in, 75, 286n9
  and racial blood, 115, 126
  status-of-the-mother laws, 81
masculine prerogatives, 11, 54, 63, 68, 74–75, 85, 90, 111, 189, 209, 218, 241
masculinity, 168–169, 226, 236
  and black men, 185–186, 189, 190, 248, 249
  and Chinese men, 162, 199
  and citizenship, 171
  European views of, 29, 56, 69
  and homosexuality, 96
  Indian views of, 69, 192
  and lynching, 95–97, 101
  norms of, 62, 186
  and power, 105, 208
  and Puerto Rican men, 214, 246
  white ideas about, 68–69, 84–87, 92, 100, 101–103, 159, 185–187, 192
Massachusetts, 77–78, 81, 142, 173, 175, 183, 184, 188, 269n19, 284n14
  Bond of Liberties, 78
Matsuda, Mari, 231
McCarran-Walter Act, 220–221
Meigs, Charles, 151
Menchaca, Martha, 243
mestizos, 132–133, 144, 204, 206, 209
Mexican Americans, 203, 204–210, 248
Mexicanas, 99, 207
Mexicanos, 10, 203, 205–210, 214
Mexicans, 6, 118
  and Anglo marriage for land scheme, 208–209
  and *bracero* program, 205
  and "Chicano Movement," 209
  and citizenship, 8, 10, 132, 163, 171, 202–207
  de-masculation of male, 64, 90, 103, 207, 208, 210
  discrimination against, 206
  in films, 207
  Indians, 204, 209
  and intermarriage, 144, 209
  lynching of men, 7, 98–101
  and marriage-for-land scheme, 208–209
  and "mongrelism," 201, 207, 217
  rape allegations directed at, 149
  and segregation, 209
  and sexual projection, 90, 101–103
  women, 93, 206, 208

See also Latinas; Latinos; *Mexicanas*; *Mexicanos*
Michigan, 120, 280n23
"middle bloods," 127–129
Miller, Monica, 248–249
Mills, Charles, 165
Minnesota, 280n25
Minor, Virginia, 172, 181
miscegenation, 45, 155–156
  defined, 118, 137
  and eugenics, 120
  laws, 138, 140, 142
  and Mexicans, 207
  and mulattas, 134, 142–143
  and white men, 154
  and white women, 140, 147, 153, 154
  See also anti-miscegenation
misogyny, 15, 18, 21, 55, 226, 235, 239, 246
Mississippi, 100, 116, 133, 142, 143, 184, 186, 269n25, 279n4, 280nn24–25, 288n51
Mississippi River, 71, 266n19
Missouri, 93, 116, 142, 143, 186, 279n4, 280n25
Mongolians, 111, 143, 280n25
mongrelism, 201, 202, 212, 217
monogenesis, 35–36, 40–42
Montana, 98, 279n4, 280n25
Moran, Rachel, 192
Morgan, Jennifer, 30, 33
Morgan, Louis Henry, 191
Morrison, Toni, 85, 90, 155, 244
Morton, Samuel George, 41, 118, 129
Mosse, George, 167
motherhood, 8, 75, 111, 145, 156, 226, 227, 228
  and anti-miscegenation laws, 147
  lesbian, 236
  and racial blood, 150–154
Mott, Lucretia, 194
mulattas, 133–134, 142, 151
mulattoes, 10, 131, 137, 201
  and anti-miscegenation laws, 139–141, 142, 144

  and gender, 125–127
  literary depictions of, 102, 134
  progeny, 93, 118, 137, 139, 150
  and racial blood, 115–116, 127, 130
  restrictions on, 66–67, 73
  and slavery, 82, 126
  suffrage, 184
  See also inter-racial relationships

nation-states, development of, 16, 52–56, 166–170, 237
National Immigration Restriction Act (1924), 152
Native Americans, 10, 239. *See also* Indians, American
naturalists, 7, 28, 34–36, 37, 38, 39, 91
naturalization. *See* immigration and naturalization
Naturalization Acts, 119, 219, 283n10
Nature, 2, 21, 23, 24, 28, 36, 37, 39, 43, 56, 113, 123–124
Nebraska, 116, 279n4, 280n25
Negroes, 10
  bodies, 44, 79, 83, 109
  in California, 144
  citizenship for, 163, 181, 187–188
  de-masculation of male, 92, 186–187
  European views of, 39–41
  female, 83–84, 140, 151–152
  and intermarriage, 81, 137, 139–141, 143–144, 152
  lynching of, 96
  male, 86
  and male suffrage, 66, 73, 182–185, 186
  and race, 45, 85, 100, 152, 154, 187
  and racial blood, 115–118, 126, 128, 130–131, 153, 201
  and religion, 43
  restrictions on, 67
  and slavery, 82–84, 110
  See also African Americans; Africans; blacks

Nevada, 203, 279n4, 280n25
Neverdon-Morton, Cynthia, 228
New Hampshire, 184, 280n25, 286n9
New Jersey, 116, 161, 175, 186, 196, 280n25, 285n3, 285–286n5, 286n9
　Compromise, 181–184
New Mexico, 98, 203–204, 206, 208, 291n16
New York, 65, 99, 120, 153, 171, 173–174, 184–185, 216, 286n18
Nicolosi, Anne Marie, 172
Nineteenth Amendment, 178, 179
North Carolina, 150
　and anti-miscegenation laws, 141, 143, 279n4
　and black male suffrage, 184, 186, 189, 286n9
　court cases, 110, 132, 133, 278n24
　and intermarriage, 75, 128
　and "one-drop rule," 130
　and racial blood, 115, 130, 141, 149
North Dakota, 116, 279n4
Norton, Mary Beth, 87
Nott, Josiah, 41, 117–118, 129
Nussbaum, Felicity, 33

Ohio, 116, 119, 175, 186, 276n25, 280n23, 287n28
Oklahoma, 116, 203, 279n4
Omi, Michael, 243
"one drop rule," 116–117, 118, 130–131, 153, 278n19
Ong, Aihwa, 169
oppression, 2, 4, 6, 48, 71, 165, 211, 227, 229, 230, 239, 298n9
Oregon, 98, 116, 279n4, 280n25
Ovington, John, 38, 40, 91–92

partus sequitur patrem, 161
partus sequitur ventrum, 80, 161. *See also* "status-of-the-mother" laws
Pascoe, Peggy, 137–138
"passing," 126, 132, 134, 235, 237
Pateman, Carole, 165

paternalism, 70, 119, 211–212
patriarchy, 54, 165, 225, 238, 239
　and Anglo Saxon Clubs, 154
　Asian American men and, 245
　and citizenship, 161
　and control, 69, 75, 83, 85, 87, 124
　Daughters of the American Revolution (DAR) and, 151
　Du Bois, W. E. B. on, 190
　entitlements of, 62
　and families, 55, 124–125, 148, 191, 192, 289n60
　Indians and, 191–192
　and plantation system, 96
　race and, 105
　roots of, 18, 29, 53, 256n2, 263n5
　slavery and, 85, 87, 263n5
　state formation and, 55
　white supremacy and, 242
　women and, 48, 53, 55, 131, 148, 151, 154, 190, 236
Pennsylvania, 119, 142, 154, 184, 186, 286n9
Petersson, Olaf, 160
phrenologists, 40–43, 92, 117–118
Pinar, William, 89, 95, 96, 101
Pisan, Christine de, 55
Plessey v. Ferguson, 116
Pocahontas exception, 116–117, 128
political play, 235–238
polygenesis, 38, 41–43, 117–118, 120
Posnock, Ross, 249
Poster, Winifred, 230
Powell, John, 153, 277n5
Powhatan, 69
practico-inert realities, 240–242
Preservation of Racial Integrity Act (RIA), 116, 153–154
Proclamation Act (1763), 70–71
prostitutes, 86, 92, 93, 97, 99, 162, 213, 241
prostitution, Chinese, 195–197, 219
proto-racialism, 27, 27–29, 31, 34, 36, 66, 76
　Anglo Saxon, 66, 71, 154, 187
　definition of, 10

distinctions in, 64, 72
in religion, 27–29
Puerto Ricans, 201–202
citizenship and, 163, 201, 210–211, 213–215, 216
de-masculation of male, 211, 214, 215, 218, 246
and *Downes v. Bidwell*, 211
and the Foraker Act, 211
gender and, 213, 215
and Jones-Shafroth Act, 211
"mongrelism"of, 212
and needlework industry, 215
Operation Bootstrap, 217
and race, 212
racial formation of, 210–217
and reproduction, 216–217, 228
and U.S. occupation, 211–214
women, 214, 215, 216–217

querelles des femmes, 55

race, 2–3, 62–63, 74
Bernier, Francois and, 35–36, 37
biological, 15, 17–18, 24, 27, 34, 48, 49, 53, 65
and blood, 111, 113–115
Blumenbach, Johann and, 36
Bradley, Richard and, 36, 37
classification of, 5, 15, 34–40, 119–120, 131, 133, 138, 260–261n57
Darwin, Erasmus and, 39
definition of, 9–10, 63
and gender, 233
gendered. *See* gendered race
as *gens*, 3, 52–53
history of term, 27, 53, 65
and homosexuality, 102, 220–221
Linneaus, Carl and, 36
and lynching, 96, 99
and marriage, 138–139
and nation-states, 53–56
ranking of, 40–45, 117
scientific, 36
and sexual projection, 89–90
and skin color, 30–31, 34, 41–42, 63, 65–66, 102, 116
and slavery, 71–76, 79–84
Sommering, Samuel Thomas von and, 41
Vaillant, Sebastien and, 39
racial blood, 7–8, 44–45, 109–111
American, 115–117
and anti-miscegenation laws, 135, 141, 144, 156
black, 130–133
and the courts, 110, 130
defined, 113
and eugenics, 121
and gender, 119, 121 (chap 8)
Indian, 127–129, 130
measuring, 115–117
and men, 131–132, 154
as metaphor, 113–114, 124
mulatto, 125–127, 130
ranking, 117–121, 130
and reputation, 130, 131, 132
and skin color, 109
and slavery, 115
and violence, 114
white, 45, 111, 121, 123, 126, 144, 147–150, 150–154, 183, 192
women, as transmitters of white, 45, 127, 133, 147, 150
See also blood
Racial Contract, 18, 165–166, 168
racial formation, 1, 4–6, 72, 105, 247
of Asians (Chinese), 93, 98–101, 101–103, 143–145, 177, 195–200
of black female, 72–74, 77–79, 79–81, 83–84, 87–88, 90–92, 125–127, 133–134, 142–143, 174–175
of black male, 74–76, 77–79, 83–84, 84–87, 90–92, 93–94, 94–98, 125–127, 130–133, 143–145, 147–150, 183–190
black-white paradigm of, 10, 47, 63, 97, 100, 110, 118, 159, 201, 238, 248
Blumenbach, Johann and, 36

racial formation *(continued)*
  gender and, 233, 240, 243, 244–247
  and homosexual citizenship, 219–221
  of Indian, American, 68–71, 127–129, 190–195
  principles of gendered, 21–23, 23–25
  and racial blood, 113–121
  roots of, 27–28, 61–64, 65–67
  of white American female, 62–63, 65–67, 72–74, 74–76, 82–83, 83–84, 85, 87–88, 93–94, 125–127, 133–134, 143–145, 147–150, 150–154, 172–174, 174–175, 175–180
  of white American male, 82–83, 93–94, 94–98, 101–103, 125–127, 179–180
  of Latinos (Puerto Rican and Mexican), 98–101, 101–103, 202–210, 210–217
racial ideology, 4–6
  and citizenship, 166, 206
  development stages of, 28, 34, 94
  gendered. *See* gendered racial ideology
  nation-states and, 47, 52–56
  principles promoting, 21–23
  sexual undercurrents of, 90–92, 92–94, 94–98, 98–101, 101–103
  slavery and, 47–52, 79–84, 84–87, 87–88
racial violence, 89, 98, 114, 208, 227
racialism, 10, 30, 72. *See also* proto-racialism
racialist thinking, 18, 57, 64, 66, 72, 138, 185
racialized gender. *See* gender, racialized
racism, 4, 11, 30, 48, 98, 226, 231
  blacks, directed at, 50, 71, 148
  Chinese, directed at, 100
  and citizenship, 179–180
  and coverture, 179
  Du Bois, W. E. B. on, 89
  and feminism, 229
  Foucault, Michel and, 252
  gender and, 90
  legal system and, 234
  Mexicans, directed at, 100
  and racial blood, 156
  scientific, 36–37, 44–45, 117–118, 119–120, 129, 201
  and slavery, 71, 117
  See also racialism
Radical Hour, 119–120, 155, 162, 189
Ramírez, Rafael, 246
Ramirez, Renya, 239
ranking, as phase of racial ideology formation, 7, 15, 28, 40–45, 117
rape, 246–247
  accusations of, 8, 111, 144–145, 147–150, 156
  of black women, 80, 95, 125, 126, 148, 150, 175, 245
  courts and, 97–98
  Filipino men and, 149
  lynching and, 94–96, 101, 148, 149
  and politics, 148–149
  race and, 126
  racial blood, 125
  and Scottsboro cases, 97
  slavery and, 80, 82, 83–84, 86, 126, 148, 150, 227
  white women and, 87, 94, 97, 99, 132, 147–149, 251
Reconstruction, 93, 113, 119–120, 126, 131, 188–189
religion, 28–29
  gender ideology and, 18–19, 20–21, 35
  gendered racial ideology and, 28, 42–43
  Indians and, 68–69
  and marriage, 51–52
  and "otherness," 28–29, 32
  and skin color, 29
  and slavery, 51–52
Republican Party, 119, 162, 182, 189, 213, 276n27
Republicans, 137, 143, 148, 182, 186
Rhode Island, 142, 184, 280n23, 286n9

Richards, Amy, 231
Roberts, Dorothy, 150
Roosevelt, Theodore, 151
roots
    of American citizenship, 171–172
    of colonial community, 166
    of gender ideology, 3, 17–19, 18–21, 23–24, 35, 36, 48
    of nation-states, 52–54
    of patriarchy, 18, 29, 53, 256n2, 263n5
    of slavery, 47–52
    of term "race," 27, 53
Rousseau, Jean Jacques, 24–25

Schiebinger, Londa, 42, 257n14, 278n24
scientific racism. *See* racism, scientific
Scottsboro cases, 97
Sellers, Sherrill, 230
seriality, 240–241
Seuyoshi, Amy, 236–237
sex, 2, 4, 9–10
sexism, 4, 9, 209, 229, 230, 234, 239, 240, 287n28
sexology, 90, 101–102
Sexual Contract, 165–166, 168
sexual inversion, 90, 101–102
sexual projection, 6, 63–64, 89–90, 144
    and deviance, 92
    heterosexual, 90–92, 92–94
    homosexual, 94–98
    and lynching, 94–98, 101–103
    and rape, 94–95
    and women, 93–94, 95
Shanks v. Dupont, 172
skin color, 77, 100, 114
    and anti-miscegenation laws, 138
    Blumenbach, Johann on, 36
    British views of, 30, 50, 66
    and citizenship, 200
    and gender, 30, 47
    and Greeks, 35
    historical representations of, 30
    and humors, 30, 34, 35

    Latinos and, 202
    mestizos and, 132
    mulattoes and, 126, 130
    and polygenesis, 42
    Puerto Ricans and, 213
    and race, 30–31, 34, 41, 63, 65–66, 102, 105, 115–116
    and religion, 29–30, 42
    and slavery, 42, 47, 49–51, 67, 77, 78, 109, 115
    value of white, 36, 41
    See also complexion
slavery, 16, 45, 57, 67, 110, 117
    of Africans, 33, 39, 41–42, 47, 49–52, 71–72, 77–80, 82, 87, 115, 127, 150
    and anti-miscegenation laws, 139–143
    and baptism, 78–79
    British view of, 78
    colonial, 71–72, 74–75, 77–79
    court cases, 174
    coverture and, 174–175
    and gender, 47–49, 51–52, 82–83, 85–87
    Indian, 77
    and mulattoes, 82, 126
    and progeny, 126, 138
    quasi-, of Chinese, 195–199
    and race, 71–76, 79–84
    and racial blood, 115
    racial ideology and, 47–52, 79–84, 84–87, 87–88
    and rape, 80, 82, 83–84, 86, 126, 148, 150, 227
    religion and, 51–52
    and sexual exploitation, 49, 80–81, 88
    and sexual relationships, 138–143
    and skin color, 42, 47, 49–51, 67, 77, 78, 109, 115. *See also* complexion
    and slave trade, 30, 33, 42, 47, 49–50, 78
    and "status-of-the-mother" laws, 80–81, 126, 139
    and unrest, 82–83

slavery *(continued)*
    in Virginia, 67, 74, 77, 78, 79, 81
        82, 86, 268n2, 274n7, 277n1
    and voting rights, 185
    of women, 79–81, 82–85, 87–88, 93
    white women and, 85, 87–88
Smith, Anna Deavere, 237
Smith, Charles Hamilton, 37
Smith, Rogers, 70, 78, 119, 174
Smith, Samuel Stanhope, 41
social justice, 9, 225, 228, 230–231,
    237, 238
    coalitions for, 5, 9, 225–231, 234,
        238, 240, 242
Soemmerring, Samuel Thomas von,
    41
Sojourner Truth, 233, 237
Solomos, John, 243
Somerset v. Stewart, 78
Somerville, Siobhan, 102
South Carolina, 52, 81, 116, 131, 143,
    189, 279n4, 286n9
South Dakota, 279n4
Spencer, Herbert, 44–45
Spivak, Gayatri, 240–241
Stanton, Elizabeth Cady, 19, 265n8
State v. Jones, 269n25
"status-of-the-mother" laws, 80–81,
    126, 139
Stefancic, Jean, 243
stereotypes, 1, 4, 61–62, 249
    gender, 49, 102, 162
    gendered racial, 199, 238
    racial, 155, 185–186, 210, 213
Stewart, Maria, 189
Story v. State, 97
suffrage, 67, 161, 180
    African American, 8, 73, 183–187,
        188–190, 193, 229
    Asian, 190
    and gender, 8, 172, 181–182, 184
    Indian, 73, 190, 193
    Latino, 190
    male, universal, 183
    for mulattoes, 73
    in New Jersey, 181–183, 184
    in New York, 171
    and politics, 182, 189
    Puerto Rican, 212, 292n42
    and race, 172, 181–182, 184–185,
        185–187, 190
    requirements for, 183, 190, 284n13
    women, 70, 180, 184, 193, 229, 233

Taney, Roger, 187, 188, 287n32
Tennessee, 94, 143, 184, 186, 229,
    279n4, 295–96n5
Terrell, Mary Church, 148
Texas, 89, 103, 133, 143, 186, 201–
    206, 209–210, 275n11, 279n4,
    291n16
Theogony (Hesiod), 18–19
Thirteenth Amendment, 119
Thompson, Becky, 229, 231
tithe (tax), 72–73, 75–76, 140
Toomer, Jean, 102
torture, 85, 86, 89, 94, 95, 166,
    270n37
travel narratives, 29–30, 31–33, 40, 91
Tuana, Nancy, 53

United States v. Thind, 200
Utah, 116, 203, 279n4, 280n25

Vermont, 184, 280n25
Virginia, 55, 79 84, 86, 142, 152
    Anglo-Saxon Clubs in, 153–154
    anti-miscegenation laws, 140–141,
        153, 279n4
    and British, 67–68
    Indians, 68, 128
    and inter-racial marriage, 75–76,
        128, 138, 142, 153
    labor laws, 72, 268n2
    Loving v. Virginia, 138
    miscegenation in, 140–141
    "one-drop rule," 116–117, 153
    Preservation of Racial Integrity
        Act (RIA), 116, 153, 154
    property laws, 74–75
    and racial blood, 81, 115–116, 128,
        153, 277n1

racialism in, 66–67, 72
slavery, 67, 74, 77, 78, 79, 81 82, 86, 268n2, 274n7, 277n1
"status-of-the-mother" laws, 81, 126, 139
tithing laws, 72–73, 75
voting rights, 66, 184, 189, 286n9, 287n30
women, 72–73, 81, 140–141, 142, 152, 153
vis imaginativa, 131–32, 150, 278n24
Vogt, Carl, 43
voting rights. *See* suffrage
Voting Rights Act (1965), 190

Walker, Rebecca, 231
Ware, Jourdan, 148
Wells, Ida B., 96, 148, 151, 271n13, 272n29
wench, 73–74, 83
West, Richard, 67
West Virginia, 143, 279n4
Wheeler, Roxann, 30, 32
White, Deborah Gray, 84
white racial supremacy, doctrine of, 3, 4, 7, 21, 68, 87, 89, 90, 123, 165, 227, 229, 238–240, 253
  Anglo Saxon clubs and, 154, 277n5
  and black-white racial paradigm, 10, 47, 63, 97, 100, 110, 118, 159, 201, 238, 248

Blumenbach, Johann and, 36
and Chinese threat, 100
feminists and, 160
and gendered racial ideologies, 7, 123
Ku Klux Klan (KKK) and, 154, 209
Loving v. Virginia, 138
and mulattoes, 126
patriarchy and, 242
and racial blood, 111, 115, 144–145, 150–151, 153–154
and racial minorities, 44–45
and racism, 90
sexual projection and, 93–95
Spencer, Herbert and, 44
women and, 44–45, 86, 127, 145, 147, 150–151, 153–154, 156
Whites, LeeAnn, 101
Wiegman, Robyn, 43, 63, 92, 264n1
Wiggam, Albert Edward, 152
Williams, Brackette, 56, 132, 168
Winant, Howard, 238–239, 243
Wisconsin, 98, 280n25
Wyoming, 98, 184, 279n4, 280n25, 286n15

Young, Iris Marion, 240

Zackodnik, Teresa, 131–132
Zinn, Maxine Baca, 2
Zohar, 42–43